MW01273298

TEACHING WRITING

TEACHING WRITING
Landmarks and Horizons

Edited by
Christina Russell McDonald
and
Robert L. McDonald

With a Foreword by Gary Tate
With a Postscript by Steve North

Southern Illinois University Press
Carbondale and Edwardsville

Copyright © 2002 by the Board of Trustees,
Southern Illinois University
Chapter 14 copyright © 2002 by Kurt Schick
All rights reserved
Printed in the United States of America
05 04 03 02   4 3 2 1

Publication partially supported by a grant from the Faculty Development Committee at Virginia Military Institute.

Library of Congress Cataloging-in-Publication Data

Teaching writing : landmarks and horizons / edited by Christina R.
McDonald and Robert L. McDonald ; foreword by Gary Tate.
    p. cm.
   Includes bibliographical references and index.
     1. English language—Rhetoric—Study and teaching. 2. Report
writing—Study and teaching (Higher). I. McDonald, Christina R.,
1966– II. McDonald, Robert L., 1964–

PE1404.T3995 2002
808'.042'0711—dc21
ISBN 0-8093-2454-7 (pbk.: alk. paper)   2002018779

Printed on recycled paper. ♻

The paper used in this publication meets the minimum requirements of American National Standard for Information Sciences—Permanence of Paper for Printed Library Materials, ANSI Z39.48-1992. ∞

Contents

Part Two. Horizons: New Essays in Composition Pedagogy

Foreword

Gary Tate

Two related thematic undercurrents run through this book just as they have run through composition studies since its disciplinary beginnings in the 1950s and 1960s: the dichotomy between theory and practice and the search for a usable past.

Although generally undocumented in the field's literature and denied by those who argue that this dichotomy is a false one, the tension between those who have theorized in print and those who have taught writing has been very real. Ironically, of course, the theorists have often been writing teachers themselves, but that has not saved them from the complaints of other teachers that their articles and books seldom move beyond theory, that they provide little help with how their theories should influence what happens "in my class on Monday morning." These complaints seldom get into print—they are not the stuff of journal articles—but anyone who talks to the people who do most of the teaching of writing in our colleges has heard such mutterings.

On the other hand, the scholars who struggle with theoretical issues in their writing are often critical of the demands for "practical teaching tips." Their impatience is directed at teachers who will not do the necessary intellectual work of discovering the practical pedagogical implications of theoretical discussions. Again, these feelings are more often expressed in private or indirectly in public forums—as in a conference speaker's quick dismissal of questions about classroom application. It should also be noted that the favorite mode of publication in composition studies—the journal article—does not, because of typical length restrictions, lend itself to the working out of the pedagogical implications of the ideas expressed in the article.

Fortunately, there are signs that the tensions between theory and practice are not as severe as they once were. As recent graduate students and part-time teachers who have been graduate students shoulder more and more of the composition teaching load, we have for the first time in this country a cadre of writing teachers unafraid of theory. Educated at a time when theory in one form or another has dominated English departments, these teachers are often expert in not only understanding theoretical issues but also in using theoretical insights in their teaching. Thus, as better-educated teachers enter the college writing classrooms in this country, the gap that has troubled the discipline for so many years is gradually narrowing.

The search for a usable past, this book's other major theme, has occupied distinguished composition scholars for many years, although its relationship to the theory/practice dichotomy has gone largely unnoticed. Academic disciplines, much like individual human beings, create the past they need. In the case of composition studies, a past was needed that would highlight the growing professionalism and intellectual vigor of the new work that was being done in the 1960s and 1970s. Looking back on the teaching of writing in the first half of the twentieth century, influential writers saw only misguided, untheorized attempts to tinker with the surface features of student prose. Failing to notice more enlightened teaching during these years—the occasional use of workshops or an emphasis on peer critiques and revisions, for example—the discipline created a useful label with which to damn the entire enterprise: current-traditional rhetoric. Thus the teaching of these early years was reduced to a three-word phrase. It could now be dismissed without further study. At about the same time, the rebirth of interest in classical rhetoric provided a theoretically rich tradition to contrast with the shallowness of current-traditional rhetoric. In a short time, the discipline had created a noble past for itself in ancient Greece while dismissing with contempt the work of several generations of more recent scholars and teachers.

We should not undervalue the immense and beneficial influence that classical rhetoric has had on composition studies. At the same time, we should acknowledge that much teaching in the past was based on ideas and techniques that needed to be rejected. However, our recent past might repay further attention and study. Our discipline is surely old enough and secure enough as it enters the new millennium that it need no longer slay its immediate ancestors in order to be free to pursue its own paths of inquiry. In addition, it is time to reject what has grown out of this attitude toward our past: a strong tendency to reject or ignore the work of ten or twenty years ago. Such an habitual response leads to a training of new teachers and scholars in which the work of the 1960s, 1970s, and 1980s is largely ignored in classes and seminars in which only the most current thinking is studied. And yet it has been my experience that when graduate students who have been immersed in current thought are sent back, for example, to the journal issues of these earlier years, they invariably return excited about at least some of what they have found and puzzled about why no one is talking about these issues today.

Finally, a word about the relationship between the two themes I have been discussing. In their attempts to create a usable past for the endeavor—attempts that were probably necessary for the health of the new discipline—historians chose to vilify the teaching of college writing in the early years of the twentieth century. In doing so, they played a role in helping to create the theory/practice dichotomy. This happened, in part at least, because current-traditional rhetoric was still very much alive in college classrooms, and so the many criticisms of the practice of earlier teaching could easily be read as criticism of current teaching practices. And so overworked teachers who had little time to read theory were now being told that they needed to change their teaching in fundamental ways. "Tell us how," they cried. But that, at least from their point of view, seldom happened. Thus what began as a reevaluation of the past was often read unfortunately as an attack on present practices that alienated many teachers.

By its arrangement and its contents, this collection of essays performs at least two important functions for teachers of writing: it demonstrates that the work of our recent past is still valuable, and it contributes to the efforts of recent years to bridge the gap between theory and practice. Such a new vision of our history and a new level of understanding between practitioners and theorists could provide the foundation for a more productive, enlightened disciplinary future.

Preface

In a recent review essay, Pat Belanoff observes that "Too much of the theory in [composition studies] has not been tested by or even linked to practice. After reading theory-dominated works, I confess that I am moved to respond, 'So what?' or 'What do I do in the classroom if I agree with you?'" (401). This is not an uncommon sentiment among teachers of writing. The abstractions of theory can seem quite remote indeed, an intellectual indulgence simply unavailable to the ordinary teacher guiding ninety or so students through a required course each semester. We of course realize, as Charles I. Schuster wrote some years ago in detailing the "theory/practice dichotomy" in the discipline, that "theory is not opposed to practice" but is instead its "inseparable" companion: that really "every move made in the classroom is grounded in theory" (42). But like Belanoff, we wish that our scholarship, however theoretical its focus, would more regularly suggest how the *practical* forms the heart of composition studies—that "our connection to the classroom is our strength and ultimately our rationale for being a discipline at all" (401). Emphasizing this connection in an historical context is the primary purpose of this book.

In part one, "Landmarks: Classic Essays on the Teaching of Writing," eight distinguished scholars—many of whom have played major roles in shaping the discipline of rhetoric and composition studies—present essays that they believe discuss momentous topics in the history of composition pedagogy. We invited these scholars to write a brief preface outlining what seemed important about the essay when it was first published and what relevance it continues to have for teachers of writing. We were delighted and in some instances pleasantly surprised by the essays chosen for this section. The reader will find that some familiar pieces are included, such as those true "landmarks" that are famous for having caused teachers to rethink pedagogy in vital terms: Janet Emig's "Writing as a Mode of Learning" (1977), which gave us an early, clear argument for the cognitive applications of writing instruction; David Bartholomae's "The Study of Error" (1980), which so well articulated a challenge to rethink our notions of the problems confronting students we call "basic" writers; Nancy Sommers's "Responding to Student Writing" (1982), which illustrated the necessity of teachers' reflection on the actual messages being communicated in their evaluation of students' prose; and Peter Elbow's "Reflections on Academic Discourse" (1991), which fueled a renewed debate not only over the purpose of the college writing course but also over the role of the composition teacher in the postmodern academy.

But a few of the contributors to this section took us up on the invitation to select an essay that perhaps deserves more attention than it has received— excellent pieces that somehow mark distinct moments in our thinking about composition pedagogy but that have gone underacknowledged in the profession. These "landmarks-waiting-to-be-discovered," perhaps, emerge as some of the highlights of this collection: D. Gordon Rohman's "Pre-Writing: The Stages of Discovery in the Writing Process," which in 1965 provided one of the very first scholarly articulations of a process-oriented pedagogy; Richard M. Coe's "Rhetoric 2001," which, with its futuristic title, charged teachers in 1974 to recognize "a revolution in consciousness" within the culture at large that made older, mechanistic forms of thinking and writing obsolete; and finally Janice M. Lauer's 1993 essay "Rhetoric and Composition Studies: A Multimodal Discipline," which explicates some discipline-enriching virtues of rejecting the old split between "composition" and "rhetoric" in favor of research and experimental pedagogies that are "interanimated" by a variety of interdisciplinary modes of inquiry and practice.

The only selections in part one that we as editors imposed are the two pieces from Erika Lindemann and Gary Tate's 1993 *College English* exchange on the use of literature in composition. This pair of essays caused such a stir that we felt they warranted a place in the collection, and we were pleased that Wendy Bishop agreed to provide the introduction and context explaining the amazing, continuing currency of an issue that has been with us practically since the formulation of composition studies as a field.

Often echoing topics and arguments raised in part one, the second half of the book, "Horizons: New Essays in Composition Pedagogy," presents a set of original essays that we hope will encourage dialogue and debate among teachers of writing. The section opens with two explorations of the very concept of pedagogy—what it means to be a teacher, particularly a composition teacher, in the contemporary classroom. In "The Slave of Pedagogy: Composition Studies and the Art of Teaching," Nancy Myers provides a stimulating historical perspective on this topic, analyzing the disciplinary challenges inherent in the etymology of *pedagogy,* which poses a metaphorical link between "the art of teaching" and the Greek *paedagogus,* a slave who was assigned to be the guardian of a school-aged boy. In "Imagining Our Teaching Selves," Christina Russell McDonald explores the professional and personal effects of the tension between the public persona and the private self whenever we situate ourselves as *teacher* for a group of composition students.

The next several essays in this section take up a range of controversies as they invite us to link our pedagogical choices with deliberate contemplation of our goals for the courses we are teaching. In "Imaginative Literature: Creating Opportunities for Multicultural Conversations in the Composition Classroom," Linda Woodson adds her voice to the perennial deliberations on the place of literature in the composition classroom, explaining experiences that have led her to conclude that literature *can* function vitally in the teaching of writing, particularly when used to stimulate critical responses to concepts such as class and culture. Similarly, as the topic of academic discourse and the legitimacy of the personal experience narrative continues to simmer, in "Irrigation: The Political Economy of Personal Experience" Carol Reeves and Alan W. France report on an experimental collaborative pedagogy that demonstrates how a carefully conceived assignment of this type functions within "the traditional self-reflective, self-revelatory purposes of a liberal arts education." And responding to a dearth of serious explorations into teaching students the various possibilities of self-representation in writing, in "What Are Styles and Why Are We Saying Such Terrific Things about Them?" Rebecca Moore Howard and several participants in a graduate seminar on stylistics at Texas Christian University mount a persuasive case and offer some helpful advice for teachers trying to develop "a valid, vibrant pedagogy of style."

The final three essays in part two take iconoclastic looks at quite urgent topics in the profession. In "Valuating Academic Writing," Kurt Schick challenges teachers to address what he perceives as a broad-scale disciplinary unwillingness to confront the necessity of evaluating writing by reconceiving that process in more positive terms, what he calls the "reconstructive social action" of *"valuation."* David Chapman, in "Brave New (Cyber)-World: From Reader to Navigator," provides a skeptical (and uncompromising) review of the ease with which teachers and administrators have allowed the writing classroom to become the site of a literacy too tied to the use of computer technology. Paul Heilker appropriately concludes this section with "Learning to Walk the Walk: Mentors, Theory, and Practice in Composition Pedagogy," a series of studied reflections on how the relationships beginning teachers form with their mentors can influence the development of their thinking about a variety of pedagogical "truths" in teaching writing.

Finally, we would like to dedicate this volume to our own mentor and friend, Gary Tate. In "The One Who Attends," the essay that we have included here as a postscript, Steve North examines Tate's career to demonstrate how an exemplary professional life might evolve in unconventional terms. As composition studies has grown in sophistication and achieved disciplinary legitimacy, North writes, we have permitted ourselves to adopt the common academic ideal for identifying excellence: "expertise that is, in its turn, understood to be embodied in properly anointed experts: major players, big names, voices to be reckoned with. The Ones Who Hold Forth." By contrast, those who "attend"—those who devote their scholarly energies to absorbing, synthesizing, and representing the primary trends of scholarship, whether as editors, teachers, or teachers of teachers—are frequently discounted in "our disciplinary mythology." As North's essay demonstrates, Gary Tate's distinguished contributions to composition studies have appeared primarily as the fruits of his "attending" to the questions and concerns of a developing field. For over thirty-five years, he has assumed the role of auditor or mentor for an entire profession, taking the time to listen, to ask questions, and to shape and to represent the currents of our thinking about the work of teaching writing. As he and Edward P. J. Corbett wrote in the preface to the first edition of *The Writing Teacher's Sourcebook,* they wanted to assemble a volume that would indicate and foster the emerging "professionalism" among teachers:

> We hope that this collection will prompt other teachers to share the fruits of their experience, their thinking, their research. But above all, we hope that this collection will encourage all of us to become more knowledgeable and more effective teachers of writing. (ix)

May this book, in its theoretical dimension and its invitations to practice, be approached in the same spirit.

Works Cited

Belanoff, Pat. "A Plethora of Practice: A Dollop of Theory." *College English* 42 (2000): 394–402.

Schuster, Charles I. "Theory and Practice." *An Introduction to Composition Studies.* Ed. Erika Lindemann and Gary Tate. New York: Oxford UP, 1991. 33–48.

Tate, Gary, and Edward P. J. Corbett, eds. *The Writing Teacher's Sourcebook.* New York: Oxford UP, 1981.

Acknowledgments

The editors would like to acknowledge foremost the persistence and patience of the contributors to this collection, who stayed with the project through its long initial planning stages and first publisher's bankruptcy. Then, they willingly revised their work again when Karl Kageff and the good people at Southern Illinois University Press adopted us and offered such perceptive suggestions for improvements to the manuscript. Words, as they say, are not enough to express our gratitude for your good will—all of you.

Unfortunately, in the time since we began working on the collection, two of our contributors have met untimely, sad deaths. Robert J. Connors died in a motorcycle accident just a few months after he completed the final draft of his introduction to D. Gordon Rohman's "Pre-Writing." His approach in this piece is vintage Bob Connors, and we admit that we are more saddened than we are pleased to be including it as, perhaps, his last published work. The week before the final revised manuscript was due to SIUP, another contributor, Alan W. France, died following a tough battle with cancer. Al presented an early draft of the essay he and Carol Reeves were writing for this collection in a special session at the 2000 meeting of the Conference on College Composition and Communication in Minneapolis. We will remember him fondly for his passion and his humor in that session, where he spoke eloquently about the capacities of teaching writing to change people's lives.

We would like to thank Charles F. Brower IV, Dean of the Faculty; Emily Miller, head of the Department of English and Fine Arts; and the Faculty Development Committee, all at Virginia Military Institute, for supporting our work on this project. And we thank as well Vergie Moore and Donna Potter for their very efficient secretarial assistance in transcribing the reprinted essays in part one.

Finally, great love and thanks to our daughter, Grace Elizabeth, who tolerated the tag-team parenting required for us to collaborate on a project other than her remarkable little self.

PART ONE
Landmarks: Classic Essays on the Teaching of Writing

I

Introduction to D. Gordon Rohman's "Pre-Writing: The Stage of Discovery in the Writing Process"

Robert J. Connors

Historical study is, for those of a certain cast of mind, ultimately a humbling endeavor, for it presents constant reminders of the transitory nature of almost all achievement and the finally unpredictable outcomes of our struggles. Our work and reputations will all rest in the hands of others; we are all finally given over, as Auden said of Yeats, to unfamiliar affections. To few people in the "modern" version of our field has this happened more overtly than to the varied band of teachers and writers who thought of themselves as the writing-process movement.[1] From 1964, when the first works were published proposing that the field of teaching composition needed to turn from concern with the written product to concern with the process of writing, up through 1987, when nearly all of the movement's several strands came under powerful theoretical fire, the writing-process movement was a potent force in the creation of the field of composition studies. The following article, D. Gordon Rohman's "Pre-Writing" (1965), is one of the first and one of the most clearly articulated of the essays published defining the beliefs and goals of that movement.

For those who have not read Rohman for a long time or for those who have perhaps met him only in quick cites or secondary or bibliographic mentions of "prewriting," the clarity, depth, and epistemological seriousness of the essay may be a surprise. We are used to attacks on the position Rohman here represents that call it naive, alogical, or self-indulgent. Returning to the source and reading Rohman in the context of his time allows us to gain a fresh vision of the revolution in teaching writing that he and other process-movement writers sought. It also reveals a complexity and an awareness of social and logical necessities that are too often elided when contemporary commentators discuss the writing-process movement and its ideas.

D. Gordon Rohman and his colleague Albert O. Wlecke began their work together in 1963 as part of Project English, a government-supported series of research studies into the most effective ways to teach language. The result of the study was their long report, "Construction and Application of Models for Concept Formation in Writing," published in 1964. The article "Pre-Writing," written by Rohman alone for *College Composition and Communication,* was their general report to the field. Rohman was not the first to propose that writing be studied as a process or even the first in our field's literature.[2] But it was the first important statement of many of the themes that would be heard during the next decade from writers as diverse as James Moffett, Donald Murray, Peter Elbow, Janet Emig, James Britton, Donald Stewart, and Roger Garrison.

Along with Moffett's "I, You, and It," in *CCC* later in 1965, Rohman's work defined many of the intellectual tasks the writing-process movement set itself. How is writing related to thinking? What is the relation of the individual to the subject? What patterns of meaning are sharable? How might heuristic processes be used instead of rigid rules in teaching? How can we learn from expert writers in ways more useful than dissecting their finished products?

These were not, of course, absolutely new questions; some of them go back to Hatfield's National Council of Teachers of English *Experience Curriculum* of 1935, with its emphases on structure, order, and cumulation in learning. But Rohman is asking them here with real urgency; they were alive in a new way for him in 1964. Looking again at "Pre-Writing" reminds us of how important and lasting a contribution the writing-process movement has made to our field because it so clearly calls up for us the field as these teachers found it. It was a world of composition in which students were assigned to read classic essays that were analyzed in class for their beauties, then assigned to write essays as good on the basis of the analyses. It was a world in which most teacher commentary on papers was formal. It was a world in which students were given one shot, one draft, which was expected to be perfect, and then asked to move on to the next paper. It was a world, as Rohman says in a trenchant line, in which all teachers did for students was "to give them standards to judge the goodness or badness of their finished effort. *We haven't really taught them how to make that effort.*" For all our talk of a postprocess world of composition studies, there are many elements of the preprocess world that no one would wish to return to, and we need to learn to appreciate how much of the fruitful ground we take for granted today was laboriously cleared and planted by teachers such as Rohman.

Another useful reminder we get from rereading Rohman is how thoroughly the writing-process movement of the 1960s was involved with other efforts at educational and epistemological reform going on at the same time. Sputnik brought about serious governmental support for the ferment of interest in how learning actually takes place going on in the late 1950s, and it is no accident that serious educational research in a number of fields dates from that time. (Those who remember the new math of that period can see the clear resemblances.) The various Project English studies did not take place in a vacuum. Most obvious in Rohman's thinking is the influence of Jerome Bruner, whose ideas on process-based learning had immense popularity in the early 1960s. Rohman's easy references to Dorothy Sayers, Denis de Rougemont, Erich Fromm, and William James demonstrate that this movement was never anti-intellectual, as has sometimes been claimed. It may in some sense have been anti-academic—though we see little of this in Rohman—and that may be one reason why it came under such sustained fire as academics with advanced degrees took over the field.

It is not hard to see the elements in this essay that have been disproved or superseded. It is, after all, thirty-five years old. But many of these elements were superseded by further research into the writing process itself. Rohman's clear division between thinking and writing was interrogated by Britton and Emig; his simple three-part stage model of the writing process was complicated by Flower's and Perl's cognitive research; his heuristics were replaced by more naturalistic methods. But the questions that motivated Rohman have never been answered completely or satisfactorily. We are still seeking the best heuristics to use to let students integrate their subject contexts with their personal contexts. We are still trying to balance self-actualization with the demands of the world as we teach young people to communicate in writing. We still wrestle with Rohman's hard question: "To what end do we teach writing?" And his then-revolutionary position that good writing must involve "the discovery by a responsible person of his uniqueness within his subject," that learning to write must involve a teacher's helping students convert events into experiences by expressing them first to self, then to others, is *not* naively expressivist; it is, in fact, an idea we take for granted now.

"The past isn't dead," said Faulkner, "it isn't even past." We must refuse simplistic characterizations of our own past because too simple a story, though it may be comforting, does not help us adequately understand the complexities of our own time. We owe an attentive reading not only to Rohman but also to ourselves.

Notes

1. On the general and defensible principle that groups of people should be accorded the right to name themselves, I will use this term throughout. I am aware that I differ here from several powerful movements determined to use the terms "expressivism" or "vitalism" or "romanticism" to discuss these figures. But just as a democratic socialist would not wish to be referred to as a "communist," or a Christian would probably object to being called a "fundamentalist," process-writing movement figures feel that such ex post facto terms for them are inaccurate and reductive. I would suggest that we as a field should defer to people we describe and eschew naming them in terms that may be insulting.

2. The first major mention of teaching writing as a process that I can find in the literature is Barriss Mills, "Writing as Process," in 1953. But that article generally fell on stony ground; Mills was making an intellectual rather than a passionate argument, and the world was not prepared for major educational change in 1953.

Works Cited

Hatfield, W. Wilbur, ed. *An Experience Curriculum in English.* New York: Appleton-Century, 1935.

Mills, Barriss. "Writing as Process." *College English* 15 (1953): 21–26.

Moffett, James. "I, You, and It." *College Composition and Communication* 16 (1965): 243–48.

Rohman, D. Gordon, and Albert O. Wlecke. *Construction and Application of Models for Concept Formation in Writing.* (U.S.O.E. Cooperative Research Project No. 2174) East Lansing: Michigan State University Cooperative Reprints, 1964.

Pre-Writing: The Stage of Discovery in the Writing Process (1965)

D. Gordon Rohman

I. The Principle

Writing is usefully described as a process, something which shows continuous change in time like growth in organic nature. Different things happen at different stages in the process of putting thoughts into words and words onto paper. In our Project English experiment,[1] we divided the process at the point where the "writing idea" is ready for the words and the page: everything before that we call "Pre-Writing," everything after "Writing" and "Re-Writing." We concerned ourselves mainly with Pre-Writing for two reasons: It is crucial to the success of any writing that occurs later, and it is seldom given the attention it consequently deserves.

Pre-Writing we defined as the stage of discovery in the writing process when a person assimilates his "subject" to himself. In our Project, we sought (1) to isolate and describe the principle of this assimilation and (2) to devise a course that would allow students to imitate its dynamics.

To find answers to the first problem, the principle of Pre-Writing, we asked the question: what sort of "thinking" precedes writing? By "thinking," we refer to that activity of mind which *brings forth* and develops ideas, plans, designs, not merely the entrance of an idea into one's mind; an active, not a passive enlistment in the "cause" of an idea; conceiving, which includes consecutive logical thinking but much more besides; essentially the imposition of pattern upon experience.[2] Several important assumptions underlie our question:

a. Thinking must be distinguished from writing.
b. In terms of cause and effect, thinking precedes writing.
c. Good thinking can produce good writing; and, conversely, without good thinking, good writing is impossible.
d. Good thinking does not always lead to good writing; but bad thinking can never lead to good writing.

This essay first appeared in *College Composition and Communication* 16 (1965): 106–12. Copyright © 1965 by the National Council of Teachers of English. Reprinted with permission.

e. A failure to make a proper distinction between "thinking" and writing has led to a fundamental misconception which undermines so many of our best efforts in teaching writing: if we train students how to recognize an example of good prose ("the rhetoric of the finished word"), we have given them a basis on which to build their own writing abilities. All we have done, in fact, is to give them standards to judge the goodness or badness of their finished effort. *We haven't really taught them how to make that effort.*

f. A knowledge of standards is not enough to produce good writing; in practice such critical principles usually have a *negative* value: students are enabled to recognize more vividly their own inadequacies.

g. From a creative point of view, the standards established by the rhetoric of the finished word are too remote, too abstract. It is not enough to know *about* goodness; we must know it from experience. Whereas the classical practice of imitation held up the finished masterpiece for the example, we sought ways for students to imitate the creative principle itself which produces finished works. Unless we can somehow introduce students to the dynamics of creation, we too often simply discourage their hopes of ever writing well at all. As Jerome Bruner writes in *The Process of Education,* the way to make schooling "count" is to give students an understanding of the fundamental structure of whatever subjects they take.[3]

In writing, this fundamental structure is *not* one of content but of method. Students must learn the structure of thinking that leads to writing since there is no other "content" to writing apart from the dynamic of conceptualizing. "You can't write writing," as one critic once wrote. But can you isolate the principle that underlies all writing? And can you then practice that principle in whatever "subjects" you may choose?

Because this stage we call Pre-Writing is within the mind and consequently hidden, it must necessarily be what John Ciardi calls a "groping." Ciardi describes the process introspectively as without end, "but in time the good writer will acquire not only a sense of *groping for* but a sense of having *groped to:* he begins to know when he has finally reached whatever he was reaching for."[4] The paradox gives us an important clue, we believe, to the principle of Pre-Writing: writers set out in apparent ignorance of what they are groping for; yet they recognize it when they find it. In a sense they knew all along, but it took sort of heuristic process to bring it out. When it is "out," they have discovered their subject; all that's left is the writing of it.

Pre-Writing, then, is that stage which concerns itself with "discovery." But we must attempt to state the principle objectively to throw as much light as possible upon Ciardi's term "groping." Discovery of what? Not of *something* at all, but of a pattern of somethings. Bruner, again, says in his essay "The Act of Discovery," that "Discovery, whether by a schoolboy going it on his own or by a scientist cultivating the growing edge of his field, is in its essence a matter of rearranging or transforming evidence in such a way that one is enabled to go beyond the evidence so reassembled to new insights."[5] It is more useful to think of writing not as made up of words but of *combinations* of words. The meaning of writing is the meaning of the combination, the pattern that the meanings of the many words make when fused by a writer's consciousness in the moment of "discovery." What the writer is groping for (in Ciardi's term) is that combination that "clicks" for him; an arrangement that will fit his subject to him and him to his subject.

So far we have attempted to describe the formative stages of any writing; we must add now that we believe "good writing" is that discovered combination of words which allows a person the integrity to dominate his subject with a pattern both fresh and original. "Bad writing," then, is an echo of someone else's combination which we have merely taken over for the occasion of our writing. "Bad writing" is the "Letters for All Occasions" sort of book: writing problems identified and solved in advance of any person's encountering them, a specific collection of models of "good form" (i.e. manners) ready-cast. But we contend that "good writing" must be the discovery by a responsible person of his uniqueness within his subject.

By "person" we mean one who stands at the center of his own thoughts and feelings with the sense that they begin in him. He is concerned to make things happen and not simply to allow things to happen to him; he seeks to dominate his circumstances with words or actions.

Another way of putting it would be to say that every writing occasion presents the writer with two contexts to discover: one we might call the "subject context," that is, some *things* about a "subject" that may be learned in an encyclopedia. But obviously reading an encyclopedia does not enable one to write essays. The writer has a second, more crucial, context to discover, what we might call the "personal context": that special *combination* of words which makes an essay his and not yours or mine. We submit that "good writing" is that which has involved a writer responsible enough to discover his personal context within the "subject context," and "bad writing" is that which has not. (In neither case is "correctness" an issue. "Bad writing" can be, often is, flawlessly "correct.")

The late Dorothy Sayers described as "conversion" what she thought happened within persons in the formative stages of their writing.[6] An "event" was converted into an "experience." An event she distinguished as something that happens to one—but one does not necessarily experience it (like the "subject context"). He only experiences a thing when he can express it to his own mind (the "personal context"). A writer, she goes on, is a man who not only suffers the impact of external events, but experiences them. He puts the experience into words in his own mind, and in so doing recognizes the experience for what it is [for him, we might add]. To the extent that we can do that, we are all writers. A writer is simply a man like ourselves with an exceptional power of revealing his experience by expressing it, first to himself [Pre-Writing], and then to others [Communicating] so that we recognize the experience as our own too. When an "event" is so recognized, it is converted from something happening *to* us into something happening *in* us. And something to which we happen. The writer gropes for those words which will trigger this transformation.

A good deal of behavioral research, in writing as well as in other things, has attempted to ignore the reality of the conscious, responsible, willing person. We cannot commit this fundamental error as researchers of the writing process. Without a person at the center, the process is meaningless; prose without a person *in*forming it could better be written by a computer programmed with all the stereotyped responses of our culture. A fundamental question faces those in English and those in the government who support its research: to what end do we teach writing? If it is to "program" students to produce "Letters and Reports for All Occasions," it is not only ignoble but impossible. The imp of the perverse in students will simply thwart any attempts to reduce them to regimented sentences. However, if it is to enlighten them concerning the powers of creative discovery within them, then it is both a liberal discipline and a possible writing program. We must recognize and use as the psychologists do in therapy, a person's desire to actualize himself. Such a desire makes mental healing possible; such a desire makes writing possible since writing is one important form of self-actualization. What we must do is place the principle of actualizing in the minds of students and the methods of imitating it in their hands.

II. Imitation

Our practical problem was to devise ways that students might imitate the principle of Pre-Writing. We employed three means chiefly: (1) the keeping of a journal, (2) the practice of some principles derived from the religious Meditation, and (3) the use of the analogy.

Because we assumed that the process of transformation was nothing if not personal, we began our course by asking students to "collect themselves" in a journal. We demanded daily performance of some sort, although we did not specify length. We mimeographed a long list of questions that we hoped would provoke our students to some discovery of what they believed, what they felt, what they knew. In the process of introspection, formalized by the daily writing in the journal, we hoped to mobilize the consciousness of every student writer. If writing is a groping process for what it is in us that "tallies" with a subject, then the more familiar we are with ourselves, the better the chances of our "groping to" some discoveries in writing. To guide our students somewhat, we reprinted for them several entries from Henry Thoreau's journal which concerned the art of keeping a journal; such entries illustrated as well as described the process of self-discovery.

The great majority of students came to value their journal above anything else in the course. Perhaps for many it was the first time they had ever been encouraged to get themselves stated. As one student wrote, "I established a discovery of myself *for myself,* a feeling for language in my journal entries. . . . I learned through the use of perspective to see the subject as it appears from a personal sense of what is real." Another wrote, "I wrote in my journal for several weeks before I realized that I was doing so for more than just a course. It began to mean something to me. It became more than just a proving ground for my themes. . . . It became a vital part in my whole life." We are convinced that the journal *works* as a "method"; more important, we are convinced that good writers are persons with a *real involvement* in their subjects and in themselves. Is not one of the basic curses of typical writing courses their pervasive sense of "phony involvement," not only of the student with the set topics of his themes, but of the teacher with an approach wholly outside and tangential to the problem? The journal was one way we sought to make the course *real* to students; it also made it real to teachers because the writing in the journal was, more often than not, worth reading.

The second technique was to use some principles taken from the religious discipline of the Meditation. Our assumption, you will recall, is that writing is a personally transformed experience of an event. Bruner quotes from the English philosopher Weldon: "We solve a problem or make a discovery when we impose a puzzle form on a difficulty to convert it into a problem that can be solved in such a way that it gets us where we want to be. This is, we recast the difficulty into a form that we know how to work with—then we work it. Much of what we speak of as discovery consists of knowing how to impose a workable kind of form on various kinds of difficulties."[7]

We were attracted to the Meditation because it seemed to provide us with a model or "*puzzle* form" that might give students an inner knowledge transforming their "events" into "experiences." Our use of a method as rigid in outline as the Meditation to provoke spontaneity and originality may seem paradoxical. The solution of the apparent paradox lies in the word "original": We sought not "novelty" but "reaction from the origins." The personal, patterned response that characterizes Pre-Writing issues from the same sort of dynamic interplay of self and world that the Meditation depends upon. The Meditation, like a puzzle, asks its questions in such a way that they can be solved by us. As Erich Fromm writes in his essay "The Creative Attitude," to be original does not primarily mean to discover something new, but to *experience* in such a way that the experience originates in me. The Meditation was precisely designed to achieve this effect: to experience religious doctrine in such a way that the experience no longer merely happens *to* you but *in* you. The Meditation involves the willful employment of the mind in progression of stages on a process of transformation of religious "subjects" into personal experiences. Its whole intention is to make personally real what Whitehead would call the "inert" ideas of religious doctrine. The typical Meditation begins by assuming that the most obvious entry into a person's consciousness is through his senses. And in the "Composition of Place," the person meditating must seek to bind his subject to some definite picture which illustrates it. He must give to airy nothing a local habitation; must find the "objective correlative" of dogma; must imagine himself present and aware in scenes that embody principles. Whereas, before, he has an "outsider's" disengaged knowledge, he now seeks that "insider's" knowledge which binds him in heart and soul to the subject being meditated, so as to set the will on fire with the love of God. Not the specific skills of this or that school of meditation, but the principle of "discovery" that lies within all the schools of meditation attracted us to this ancient art. The Meditation was designed to be a heuristic model, something which served to unlock discovery. We adapted the discipline to our use to give students both a sense of direction to their groping, and an actual "puzzle" to impose on their writing problems. First, we said, compose a "place" for your subject, one where you can "live." Keep composing until you reach the point that your understanding of your "subject" is experienced within, until, in other words, the "event" of your subject happening *to* you becomes an "experience" happening *within* you. With such a discovery, the urge to "get it down" usually increases to the point that the will directs the actual writing of words to begin.

We assume, in using the Meditation, that knowledge must become personal and that one effective way of achieving this is by insisting that knowledge become concrete, since persons react more to the concrete than they do to the abstract. In addition, by returning our students to the concrete world of the five senses, we encourage them to "earn" their abstractions. We insist that they escape from the thought clichés which pass for "writing" and "thinking" in our culture by a return to the thing freshly experienced. Within this real encounter lies hope for creative surprise and new insight "to set the will on fire" to write.

Student comments indicate that the process of Meditation can give them the *experience* of insight. "Once I started to 'see' the concrete details within my subjects," wrote one student of the "Composition of Place," "the writing process became easier for me, for I could 'respond' more fully to the subject." Another wrote, "This course also taught me to look at things as if it were the first time and I had never seen them before." Another concluded, "I now think of subjects in relation to my experiences."

The third major approach we used to allow students to imitate the dynamics of "Pre-Writing" is the analogy. The journal encouraged students to discover themselves; the meditation put into their hands a "puzzle form" of discovery. The analogy, we hoped, would illustrate the "bisociation" of all experience. That is, as human beings, we are enabled to know anything in our present simply because we have known similar things in our past to which we compare the present. Each act of present "knowing" associates the present with the past as another instance. That is why we say that a writer is one who recognizes present events as special cases of transformed "experience" known before. Writers are people who *recognize* things, and their life is full of the "shocks of recognition" when what they are "groping for" becomes finally something "groped to." Miss Sayers observes that "the perception of likenesses, the relating of like things to form a new unity, and the words 'as if'" pretty well describe the creative process of writing.[8]

The analogy also gave us another "puzzle form," a "converting mechanism" to allow students to imitate the dynamics of transformation that we believe are at the heart of Pre-Writing. Analogy illustrates easily and to almost everyone how an "event" can become an "experience" through the adoption of what Miss Sayers called an "as if" attitude. That is, by arbitrarily looking at an event in several different ways, "as if" it were this *sort* of thing, or that *sort* of thing, a student can actually experience transformation from the inside. We ask students to choose an analogical "vehicle" which has already been an "experience" for them, that is, something already converted from "outside" to "inside." Then we ask them to apply this "vehicle" to the as yet undiscovered possibilities of their subject. The analogy functions both as a focus and a catalyst for "conversion" of event into experience. It also provides, in some instances, not merely the heuristic for discovery but the actual pattern for the entire essay that follows. The creative mind, as we have assumed throughout this paper, works not primarily by analysis or measurement of observables as machines work, but by building images of unity out of what William James called the blooming, buzzing confusion of events. "Creation," as Denis de Rougemont writes, is not "something from nothing" as with the Deity, but rather is better comprehended as a different arrangement of elements already known according to laws known or knowable. Therefore it is better understood as composition. Art, that is, represents reality. And the analogy reproduces the "re-presentation" process in miniature. By rearranging and reassembling the focus of our experience of things, analogy puts into our hands a ready-made model of prewriting discovery. In addition, analogy also provides practice with the concrete world of the five senses, and, by enlisting the student writer in a personally-experienced encounter with his subject freshly seen from the perspective of a new analogy, we have provided him with the "motor" to make his subject "go" for him.

As one student wrote of the analogy, "When one approaches a topic, he needs an 'angle' or a concept for approach. If he looks into his more familiar and concrete world, he can find a number of things he knows well. If he sets these up alongside of the broader topic, relationships will evolve. His thoughts will be directed; his language will be freshened. . . . Analogy is an exploratory device; it can be a structuring and unifying device." Another wrote, "The analogy approach stresses organization and growth— perhaps the most important part of thought—rather than layout." Another confessed, "To my surprise, the analogical approach worked, and I've gained new insights. . . ." Another wrote of the analogy, "It is a technique that seems to bring an abstract subject closer to the reader, and the writer too, for that matter. . . . For not only did the subject seem clearer to me, but through an interesting perspective, writing actually was fun. I learned to 'play' with ideas, to let myself go, to gain new insight. . . ." Another concluded that analogies "help to achieve new and significant thought, lead you through some kind of structured thought, giving you a unity of order in the paper, and provide you with a language to work with."

III.

To conclude: in our brief project research, we sought to isolate the structuring principle of all Pre-Writing activity and then to devise exercises to allow students to imitate that principle in their own "Pre-Writing." Ours did not pretend to be a complete course in writing: the rhetoric of effective communication needs to follow any discovery of a structuring concept. But without the rhetoric of the mind, it seemed to us, no course in the rhetoric of the word could make up for the fact that the writer has discovered essentially nothing to say. In fact, to continue to teach rhetoric without attention to discovery reinforces that indifference to meaning that characterizes the modern world of politics and advertising. We have sought, in other words, not only to identify and practice a principle, but to insist that the principle is valuable only when alive and used within the consciousness of an aware, responsible person.

The kind of wiring that our project produced was that which immediately follows the discovery of fresh insight; it was not necessarily a kind of writing suitable to all possible occasions for written discourse. We believe, however, that writing grounded in the principle of personal transformation ought to be the *basic* writing experience for all students at all levels, the propaedeutic to all subsequent and more specialized forms of writing. The evidence of our testing programs clearly shows that writing produced under these conditions is first, good in itself. Our essays showed a statistically significant superiority to essays produced in control sections. But more important to our way of thinking are the indirect effects of this approach which introduces students to the dynamics of creative response itself:

a. It can lead students to produce writing good in itself.
b. It can train students to creative discovery in other fields, since the psychology of creative surprise is not restricted to writing.
c. It makes writing of a worthwhile kind *possible* to more students than traditional modes, especially those based upon imitation of the finished product ever could. And by making writing possible to average students, we also make it more desirable. Our students more often than not ended up our course liking to write; perhaps for the first time they felt within themselves, along their pulses, that sense of power, of self-fulfillment, which the psychologists call "self-actualization."

As one student wrote, "I felt compelled to write, but not because it meant a grade, rather because I did not want to disappoint the professor or myself." As another put it, "I was made to feel that I was capable of creating something new. I was brought to an awareness of the world about me that I had just taken for granted. I really began to 'see.'" These must ultimately be the major reasons we teach persons to write: the renewed sense of self, the renewed vision of things.

Notes

1. "Construction and Application of Models for Concept Formation in Writing," U.S. Office of Education Cooperative Research Project Number 2174.
2. We shall be talking about two different and distinct kinds of structure: that which

Jerome Bruner refers to as the fundamental organization of a subject such as mathematics or biology; and that pattern of meanings which a writer gives to a subject. To keep the two separate, we shall use "structure" to refer to the characteristic combinatorial principle of Pre-Writing; and we shall use "pattern" to refer to the individual organization that every writer imposes upon his work.

3. (Cambridge, 1962), p. 11.

4. *Saturday Review,* XLV (Dec. 15, 1962), 10.

5. *On Knowing: Essays for the Left Hand* (Cambridge, 1962), pp. 82–83.

6. Dorothy Sayers, "Towards a Christian Aesthetic," *The New Orpheus: Essays Towards a Christian Poetic,* ed. Nathan A. Scott (New York, 1964), pp. 14–15.

7. *On Knowing,* pp. 93–94.

8. "Creative Mind," *Unpopular Opinions* (New York, 1947), p. 57.

2

Introduction to Richard M. Coe's "Rhetoric 2001"

Erika Lindemann

Richard M. Coe's "Rhetoric 2001" first appeared in *Freshman English News* in spring 1974. In the judgment of Edward P. J. Corbett, Peter Elbow, and Mina Shaughnessy, Coe's essay merited first place in that year's *Freshman English News* essay contest. The essay takes its title from Stanley Kubrick's *2001: A Space Odyssey* (1968), one of the most important science-fiction films of the twentieth century. Produced, directed, and coauthored by Kubrick, the film speculates about the role of technology in human evolution and about the possibility of contact with extraterrestrial intelligence, represented in the film by huge, black monoliths that appear as catalysts for human creativity and progress. Divided into four sections or episodes, the film premiered in New York on April 3, 1968, eight months before Apollo 8 carried American astronauts into lunar orbit for the first time and over a year before Neil Armstrong and Edwin Aldrin walked on the moon (Geduld 27–28).

Some critics have characterized *2001: A Space Odyssey* as a "mythology of intelligence" (Geduld 29, Kagan 162). It charts the odyssey of human intelligence, beginning with the first bone-wielding hominid of four million years ago, continuing with the space explorers of the twenty-first century, and ending with Kubrick's Star-Child, who returns "home" to Earth as an extraordinary intelligence whose characteristics continue to generate debate among those who see the film. These transformations in intelligence coincide with changes in technology and are inspired by responses to the monoliths. The ultimate reputation of Kubrick's film rests with its special effects, the juxtaposition of visual elements and musical themes, and the nonlinear strategies Kubrick uses to tell his story.

One of the striking features of *2001: A Space Odyssey* is that it uses few words. The first episode contains no dialogue, and other sections omit narration or expository scenes that traditionally help audiences make sense of characters and plot. Confronted with what are in effect ellipses, viewers must fill in the gaps by means of visual associations acting on the subconscious. Kubrick's aesthetic creates "a conflict between the causal logic of linear conventions (where the world is organized into straight lines and rationalized forms) and the associative logic of a creative interiority (where the world is assembled into parallel planes and imaginative shapes)" (Nelson 102).

What has all of this to do with teaching writing? What has Kubrick to do with comp? Kubrick illustrates what Coe defines in "Rhetoric 2001" as "a revolution in consciousness." Just as Kubrick requires audiences to develop new ways of seeing his film by expressing his "mythology of intelligence" through nonlinear forms and unconventional visual and auditory associations, so too twentieth-century changes in consciousness require students and their teachers to learn new ways of thinking. Writing teachers have always taught thinking, which cannot be separated entirely from expression, but our ways of thinking have changed. The transition from the Machine Age to the Computer Age has brought with it a shift from linear, mechanistic thinking to what Coe calls cybernetic thinking.

Though this shift has had a greater impact in the natural and social sciences than in the humanities, writing teachers must generally understand these changes if they are to help their students effectively employ new ways of thinking. "Rhetoric 2001" illustrates this shift with two examples. The first illustration, especially evident in computer and information sciences, represents a relatively new way of thinking about cause and effect. Coe explains, "we teach this mode of development simply by asking 'WHY?' and demanding a 'logical' explanation." Simple cause and effect suited nineteenth-century science but has limitations today, offering appropriate explanations only for some phenomena. A cybernetic alternative to simple causality is "overdetermination," which asks, "WHY NOT?" Overdetermination "assumes first that anything is possible (governed only by the laws of probability) and then asks what factors prevented all the things which did not happen." According to Coe, teachers can continue to teach cause and effect but should teach overdetermination as well, recognizing in *reductio ad absurdum,* carrying an argument to its extreme, a thought-pattern essential to Darwin's explanation of evolutionary processes and to our students' understanding of biological systems.

A second thought-pattern, analysis, similarly needs realigning. The principle that the whole is equal to the sum of its parts (summativity) works well if we want to understand how a gasoline engine operates: take the engine apart, analyze each of the parts, then arrange them in a "logical" way. But if our subject "is not in reality fragmented, divisible, or serial," if in fact its qualities are interrelated or exist simultaneously, then mechanistic analysis becomes a liability to understanding what we are investigating. Sometimes the whole is other than the sum of its parts, a principle Coe calls "nonsummativity." Ecological systems, works of art and literature, families and other social structures are best understood by examining the interrelationships of components, not the characteristics of individual parts. Nonsummativity also explains why we cannot successfully isolate the "parts" of good writing, effective teaching, or student learning: human communication is so dynamic, its components or variables so interconnected, that isolating them obscures the complexities of the interacting whole.

In the final section of "Rhetoric 2001," Coe urges us to build better models for our work with students. Traditional composition courses, he claims, are based on a mechanistic model, which once may have served students well but which can yield "error-producing mechanisms" in a world that has changed. A rhetoric of the Computer Age, on the other hand, respects the interrelatedness of writing and thinking skills, emphasizes communicative relationships, contextualizes ideas, and helps people "understand, cope with, and control the social and technological changes of our times."

I chose Coe's essay for inclusion in this volume in part because it appeared in *Freshman English News* (now *Composition Studies*), a journal whose impact on a generation of composition teachers remains underappreciated. Begun by Gary Tate in 1972, *Freshman English News* provided an important scholarly forum exclusively devoted to the first-year writing course. Its articles were practical, student oriented, and like Coe's "Rhetoric 2001," sometimes challenging. The periodical also offered young composition specialists a forum for publishing their work, and for those of us whose Ph.D.'s ill-prepared us for teaching writing and directing writing programs, *Freshman English News* served as an essential resource for our professional growth.

Like many of the articles appearing in *Freshman English News* during the 1970s, Coe's "Rhetoric 2001" calls for rethinking the purpose of the first-year composition course. It is a difficult essay to read and requires thoughtful rereading. Coe wrote it at a time when the model for most composition courses was itself mechanistic. Students first engaged the parts of speech, then revised sentences, then constructed paragraphs exhibiting various "modes of development," and eventually, late in the course, wrote one or two essays. This building-block approach was summative. It assumed that students become good writers by practicing the "parts" before tackling whole discourse. In the 1970s, even the writing-as-process model, a relatively new way of thinking about writing instruction, risked becoming mechanistic. Some teachers encouraged students to prewrite, write, and rewrite their assignments as if following mechanistic instructions for building a gasoline engine. Multiple-choice tests asking students to label, rather than use, various prewriting strategies were not unheard of. Regarding composing as a lockstep series of sequential activities is no better than assuming that good writing results from manipulating successively larger units of written language. Neither view produces meaningful communication. Instead, Coe reminds us, thought and its expression must remain the focus of any composition course. Writing courses grounded in rhetoric relate thinking and writing and make explicit the processes by which human beings communicate. They teach "human-ness" by helping students develop those skills of thinking and language that enable them better to "comprehend, order, evaluate and control their experience."

To reach these goals, however, Coe encourages writing teachers to become more knowledgeable about the "ecosystem of ideas" that students encounter on entering college. Though he supports teaching writing as process, even traditional modes of development, he wants us to know more about the ways of thinking and communicating characteristic not only of the humanities but of the sciences and social sciences as well. We do not need all of the technical details, he assures us, but we need a generalized understanding of thought-patterns in other disciplines to help students manage the interdisciplinary contexts in which they work, and more important, to avoid teaching modes of thought that have become obsolete, even dangerous. A rhetoric for the new age must be holistic and integrative.

In arguing that the focus of first-year composition courses should be rhetoric-across-the-disciplines, Coe's essay is as relevant today as it was when it appeared over twenty-five years ago. It provokes questions about the kinds of thinking and writing students must engage. It challenges us, not to abandon what we know and do as writing teachers, but rather to talk more often with colleagues in other disciplines so that we can develop new, integrative perspectives on our students' work. And it cautions us against hubris, against regarding the humanities as somehow more humane than those disciplines that have transformed our culture. The message of "Rhetoric 2001" is that our place in the academy is fragile, like that of any organism threatened with ecological change. Standing above and apart from our environment becomes a liability. Cooperating with our changed times represents intelligent adaptive behavior. Teaching our students how to think and communicate effectively in 2001 and beyond not only contributes to their success but also to the vitality of the entire academic ecosystem.

Works Cited

Geduld, Carolyn. *Filmguide to* 2001: A Space Odyssey. Bloomington: Indiana UP, 1973.
Kagan, Norman. *The Cinema of Stanley Kubrick.* New York: Holt, 1972.
Nelson, Thomas Allen. *Kubrick: Inside a Film Artist's Maze.* Bloomington: Indiana UP, 1982.

Rhetoric 2001 (1974)

Richard M. Coe

Amazingly, the assertion that we live in a century of major technological and social transformation is already a cliché. Even the assertion that the proportions and velocity of this transformation are unrivaled in the history of our species begins to grow trite. We in English, like our colleagues throughout the humanities, associate this widely-recognized revolution with atomic reactors, computers and television circuits. We conceive of it as essentially scientific and have allowed ourselves to be intimidated by its complex mathematics and technical jargon.

In doing so we have sold ourselves short. Like all major changes in human culture, however material their bases, this is also a revolution in consciousness. Our most basic thought-patterns, those we have come to think of as "natural," are being called into question. And human consciousness—thinking—is precisely our area of expertise. What we traditionally call "culture" is collective consciousness; what we call communications skills are the techniques by which consciousness is expressed, exchanged, and changed.

Simply, the ecological crisis may be traced to three determining factors: (a) technological progress, (b) population increase, and (c) certain outmoded attitudes and thought-patterns.[1] Together these three determinants form a vicious circle of growth. Given our present consciousness, technological progress allows and leads to increased population which causes shortages and other problems which we solve with more technological progress which leads to increased population, etc. This vicious circle can be broken by a technological breakdown (pollution or depletion of raw materials), a population decrease (famine), or a change in consciousness. In other words, only a change in certain outmoded attitudes and thought-patterns can prevent disaster.

These attitudes and thought-patterns are outmoded not only because their practical consequence is an environmental crisis; they have also been found theoretically inadequate by scientists in diverse fields. Exceptional scientists—notably Wiener (cybernetics), Bertalanffy (biology), Boulding (economics), Bateson (anthropology), and Buckley (sociology)—have de-

This essay first appeared in *Freshman English News* 3.1 (Spring 1974): 1–3, 9–13. Copyright © 1974 by *Freshman English News*, now *Composition Studies*. Reprinted with permission.

tected a common direction which unites the most advanced trends in modern science, in Bertalanffy's phrase, a correspondence "of laws and conceptual schemes in different fields."[2] It is this generalized direction, more than the particular discoveries of any particular discipline, which has implications for the future of the humanities in particular and human consciousness in general. It is because of this generalized shift that we who teach communications skills have an exceptionally significant service to offer.

At the 1971 NCTE convention, the popular futurist, Alvin Toffler, asserted the special potential of certain aspects of "English" for helping people understand, cope with and even control the technological and social changes of our times. Even before our ecological problems, it was "clear" to the noted philosopher of science, Herbert Feigl, that "nothing is more urgent for education today than a social philosophy that will be appropriate and workable in an age of science."[3] The Club of Rome[4] executive committee lists first among the implications of its study of the limits to growth the need to initiate "new forms of thinking that will lead to a fundamental revision of human behaviour."[5] Various scientists have the data necessary for evolving these new forms of thinking; various humanists possess the necessary communicational and epistemological problem-solving skills. The trick will be to combine our resources by transcending traditional disciplinary boundaries.

The primary educational function of the humanities has always transcended content: no one studies *Hamlet* or the history of the Roman Empire because of the factual content has direct utility. The task of the humanities is to teach human-ness; the students' reward is not information so much as it is the raising or expansion of their consciousness such that they can better comprehend, order, evaluate and control their experience. The importance of learning to think and feel is central to the humanistic creed: in Anglo-American tradition it dates back to Sir Philip Sidney's argument that poetry is an educator and mental nourisher because it enlarges the human mind and character. Even the "lowly" freshman composition course, in addition to transmitting certain specific writing skills, has traditionally embodied this generalized humanistic function. In fact, composition has always been especially important because it teaches communications skills. Rhetoric includes invention and logic because perception and thinking cannot be totally separated from expression. That is why prewriting and logic are included in composition handbooks. By example, by indirection, and sometimes even intentionally, composition teachers have always taught thinking.

Of all humanities, therefore, those of whose subjects center on communications skills (speaking, writing, teaching and media) are in the best position to provide what Toffler, Feigl, and Club of Rome request. Precisely because our subjects have the least formal content and greatest emphasis on process, precisely because our usual backgrounds in art and literature make us (in McLuhan's words) less insensitive to the "diverse and discontinuous life of forms" and less "shut off from Blake's awareness or that of the Psalmist that we become what we behold,"[6] precisely because we have not been too thoroughly indoctrinated in linear mechanistic thinking, it is in our power to make a contribution which may be crucial to the future of our species. Some of our innovative methods already begin to provide parts of the new integrative perspective; what we must do is to expand and order that contribution.

First we must facilitate communication by "translating" the various technical jargons into a commensurable and comprehensible language. This is a task for those of us with some scientific and mathematical ability working with scientific advisors, linguists and communications experts. Second we must learn which thought-patterns are not only practical (i.e., ecological), but correct. Third we must integrate the newly-accessible forms into the consciousness of our culture.

The preliminary work has been already sufficiently advanced by exceptional scientists and communications theorists that we can define the latter part of the project; we can even delineate broadly the content and methods of a composition course which would enable students to begin to comprehend the coming consciousness of the 21st century. It is important to note first that these changes are not dictated solely by science. A social awareness of the inadequacies of the old mode underlay the absurdist and existential literature of the 50's as surely as it had earlier been manifest in cubism and surrealism. The same awareness led American beat writers to seek outside our culture for alternate thought patterns. In the 60's hippies and the new left (in their very different ways) sought alternate social, ethical, and cognitive structures. Even materialistic corporations have restructured their channels of internal communications with the guidance of information and communication theorists. Although often undifferentiated, describable only vaguely as a generalized anxiety, this same awareness that certain traditional patterns are outmoded has filtered down to the general populace. The commensurable element throughout is the realization that basic thought- and behavior-patterns which have served the Occident well at least since the renaissance/reformation are becoming obsolete; when we confront our most complicated, pressing, and confusing problems, these patterns no longer work with sufficient reliability. Certain "common sense" values no longer work, or work only within carefully limited contexts; "common sense" is implicit in the logic of composition methods; to create the composition course of the future we will have to make explicit and reevaluate the values implicit in the traditional composition course.

Within academia, the coming of a new mode is foreshadowed by the increasing necessity to violate the old classifications and compartmentalizations of knowledge. The biologist has had to learn chemistry, physics, and cybernetic information theory to understand the simple cell. The psychologist has had to learn sociology, anthropology, neurology, and sometimes even Buddhism to understand schizophrenia. Likewise we in the humanities will have to acquire an overview of the natural and social sciences in order to serve our function in this scientific century, a function which might well include a role as counterweight. Fortunately we will not need all the technical details: a generalized understanding together with a careful study of the conclusions will be more than adequate, especially since we can be assured of a plethora scientists more than willing to criticize whenever we overreach ourselves. Our prejudices toward the diversion and classification of knowledge—prejudices not unrelated to our teaching of division and classification as standard modes of development—will be a much more serious obstacle.

Every major scientific advance has implied a shift of human consciousness. Scientific discoveries are accepted only after a shift in consciousness has begun to make them relevant, and their acceptance leads to further shifts. The Copernican revolution was much more than a recalculation of the movements of planets, even though its original goal had been merely the computation of a more accurate calendar; Copernicus' thesis had been argued as early as Ancient Greece. The Mendelian genetics we learned in high school was categorically rejected when Mendel proposed it. General relativity is more than an explanation of the three anomalies which were puzzling Einstein and his colleagues; certainly it has been interpolated well beyond the bounds of physics. Cybernetics likewise has implications far beyond computers.

The exceptional significance of the current shift is indicated by its parallel development in many diverse disciplines. The breadth of its manifestations, however, makes it much more difficult to comprehend: there are as many jargons as there are disciplines. The same breadth of its manifestations, on the other hand, make it that much more exciting and world-shaking: once comprehended it can be applied everywhere. One could adopt the language of quantum physics, gestalt psychology, dialectics, cybernetics, general system theory, or half a dozen other disciplines. One could describe a shift of emphasis from stasis to process, entity to relationship, atom to gestalt, scaler to tensor, component to system, analytics to dialectics, causality to constraint, bioenergetics to communication, or at least a dozen other parallel shifts. This shift (and it is *one* shift despite all the varied jargon) reflects the transition from the Machine Age to the Computer Age, the transition from an age characterized by an energy explosion to an age characterized by an information explosion. For the non-specialist, therefore, it is easiest to comprehend as a movement from mechanistic to cybernetic thinking. This movement is clear in both the "hard" and the social science. It has had little impact in the humanities, although parallel tendencies are occasionally observable. It has had virtually no impact on common sense—yet.

Common sense includes the laws of arithmetic: e.g., summativity (the whole is equal to the sum of its parts, 1+1=2). In 1881 a physicist named Michelson did an experiment which seemed to demonstrate that light did not obey the law of simple addition. For several decades the physicists, who like everybody else believed in arithmetic, tried to find his mistake. Much like undergraduates in the laboratory who get the "wrong" results, they repeated his experiment, trying to get different results or to find alternate inductions. Finally Einstein assumed that Michelson's experiment was accurate and that the laws of arithmetic needed revision. (In order to do so, he adopted a non-Euclidean geometry which postulates that *no* line can be drawn parallel to a given line—another assumption which contradicts common sense and experience.) The result was atomic power—and the knowledge that ordinary arithmetic and geometry are accurate only below certain speeds and within certain relatively small spaces.

This example from physics is appropriate because what is here is called mechanistic thinking operates according to a set of energy analogies derived from the 19th century physics, sometimes characterized as the billiard ball model of the universe. Despite what most of us don't know about Newtonian physics, mechanistic conceptions underlie much of our ordinary thinking. Even those of us who have never heard of the law of conservation of energy apply it regularly far beyond the bounds of physics. It is true that once a billiard ball of a certain weight has obtained a certain speed, it has a measurable momentum which must be expended. By analogy we think of psychological energy as behaving similarly. We assume that a psychological drive has momentum and that if it is diverted it will find an outlet elsewhere: if you stop smoking cigarettes, you will start biting your nails; if you stop biting your nails you had best start chewing gum or you will expend that repressed energy by beating your children. The analogy is so pervasive, because it is only partially untrue, that we seem to see it confirmed every where. And yet we all know people who (perhaps after an initial "cold turkey" period) have stopped smoking without either chewing gum or becoming aggressive monsters. Upon reflection we must admit that psychological energies are not quantifiable in such a way as to either prove or disprove a law of the conservation of psychic energy and that sometimes psychic energy seems to just disappear.

(To assume that it has then always been repressed is tautological.) The great danger of common sense is that it is usually not subject to reflection.

Here the system theorist can help us. System theory postulates two sets: in one (closed systems) physical energy analogies do work, effects equal causes, summativity applies; in the other (open systems) information dominates and an entirely new group of analogies explains the behavior much more accurately. This distinction can be made clear, even to those who know nothing about system theory, by the following example.

If you kick a stone its reaction is predictable. A careful measurement of the force and direction of your kick, of the weight and shape of the stone, and of the obstacles in its path will enable you to perfectly predict its motion. Effect equals cause. If, however, you kick a dog instead of a stone, the situation is more complicated. When you kick a dog you are conveying not energy, but information. Certainly it takes some energy to carry that information, but measurements of that energy explain very little. As in many other cases, a small amount of energy can convey a great deal of information. The dog may cringe, run away, attack, whine or react in any number of other ways. In any event, it takes the energy for its response from its own energy system. It evaluates the information received from the kick in terms of its own consciousness and has a certain freedom from deterministic causality in choosing its response. To predict that response you need to know not about the dog's energy system, but about its information system: what memories does it have of you? of kicks? of previous attacks on human beings? does it regard the ground upon which you stand as part of its territory?

Clearly, information systems are more complicated than energy systems. What is being asserted here, however, is something more than that: information systems operate on an entirely different logical order than energy systems and by a distinct set of rules. If this is true, it follows that applying (conscious or unconscious) energy analogies to an information dominated situation is a type of logical fallacy. Like any other logical fallacy it may lead to either true or false conclusions. What then are the alternatives?

Computer specialists, in order to solve concrete problems, have worked out laws for their information-oriented computers. These laws have demonstrably broader applications;[7] the thought-patterns implicit in these laws are commensurable with the general direction of modern science. They have implications even for that very common information-oriented system, expository writing. And, most interestingly, they are much more commensurable with traditional humanistic principles than were the laws of 19th century empirical science.[8] Although there are a few crucial concepts which defy easy translation and force us to learn a few new words, most of the cybernetic laws can be expressed in ordinary language. Some of them will turn out to be familiar; after all, we do live in this world and are far from impervious to it. Most of us believe that, except in certain relatively simple learning situations, human behavior is more complicated than stimulus-response (i.e., cause-effect).

What then is the alternative to causality? And what does it have to do with freshman composition? The second question is easier to answer. One way or another, most of us teach causal modes of development. The text which was assigned to me together with my first composition courses actually had a section on cause-to-effect development. More commonly, we teach this mode of development simply by asking "WHY?" and demanding a "logical" explanation. It is good that we do so. A causal explanation is one step beyond an analogical explanation and two steps beyond an illogical explanation or non-explanation. In teaching this mode, or any other, however, we should make clear its limitations and alternatives. Most of us (I for one) have not been precisely aware of the limitations and alternatives to causality. How else does one answer the question, "WHY?"

The key word for understanding the cybernetic alternative to causality is overdetermination, a word invented by Freud to explain dream symbol formation. Overdetermination implies an overabundance of causes, a superfluity of reason. Overdetermination is how, in fact, biological systems most commonly operate—and with good reason: a human being's urge to eat, for example, is regulated by appetite, habit, social convention and various other factor; if low blood sugar were the only motivation, any disturbance in this single line of control could result in death. Thus an excess of motivating factors has survival value. Evolutionary processes have, therefore, constrained all life forms toward overdetermination.

To seek a cause in such a situation is an oversimplification, a logical fallacy which may lead to false conclusions. If I see a person eating a hot dog the determinants may include low blood sugar, coincidental convenience, cultural eating habits, ignorance of the ingredients, being in a hurry, and perhaps even complicated oedipal symbolisms. There is no way to "add up" this diverse set of determinants into anything resembling a "cause."

Instead of asking "WHY?" cybernetic explanation therefore asks "WHY NOT?" Cybernetic explanation assumes first that anything is possible (governed only by the laws of probability) and then asks what factors prevented all the things which did not happen. That person ate that hot dog because low blood sugar and habit prevented non-eating, cultural eating patterns prevented teriyaki, being in a hurry prevented glazed duck, lack of money prevented steak, etc. This type of cybernetic logic is equivalent to *reductio ad absurdum*. It is the same mode Darwin used for his theory of evolution.

Darwin began by assuming that, everything else being equal, only probability would explain the fauna and flora. Since many existing species seemed non-probable, he asked what was not equal, what factors prevented the alternatives from surviving. His answer was that environmental determinants made the potential alternatives less viable than the species which survived. The slogan "survival of the fittest" is not Darwin's, nor that of any other biologist; it was invented by social philosopher Herbert Spencer. Darwinian natural selection means merely the extinction of the unfit: "In nature we find . . . everything which is not *so* inexpedient as to endanger the existence of the species."[9] This is how the Argus pheasant survives his cumbersome tail feathers. The grossly unfit mutants die, but, because natural selection does not operate according to linear causality, the survivors embody a great deal of genetic variation. And since it is precisely the variants who survive when the environment changes, evolution would not work were it not an overdetermined process.

Simple causality is the appropriate explanation for physical systems, like kicking the stone. Overdetermination is the appropriate explanation for information systems, like kicking the dog. Freshman composition teachers should not stop teaching cause-to-effect development; but they should start teaching overdetermination (or *reductio ad absurdum*) as well—and explaining which mode is appropriate for which type of situation.

Linear causality forms part of the general pattern of perception of anyone raised in our future. Experimental evidence indicates that it is much easier for students to learn material which fits into that pattern than material which challenges it. Consequently, I proceed very carefully. I begin with demonstration and discussion, move on to collection of further examples by the students, then ask for utilization and development of those examples in explanation, and only finally do I assign application in argument.

Virtually any content involving human motivation or social behavior can be used for the initial demonstration. I have even begun with the material which forced Freud to invent the word *overdetermination:* dream analysis. I use dreams from Freud's texts, my own dreams, and dreams the students have been collecting in their journals. I do not mention overdetermination until after the students understand how dream symbols work; then I use what they have come to understand about dreams as a means to introduce the concept of overdetermination. Examples from film and literature could equally well be used as a basis since (as Freud recognized) they utilize similar types of symbols. A short like "Frank Film" (Pyramid) is especially good because both its thesis and its techniques deal with the complexity of human behavior.

It would also be possible to begin with problem-examples, such as the following:

> A student is studying late on the last night of finals week because he has three examinations on the last day. He runs out of cigarettes. Tired and groggy, he goes downstairs to buy some more. He cuts across an alley to an all-night store. A car with one headlight and bad brakes comes down the alley. The driver, who had taken her last final that day and had been celebrating, tries to stop, but cannot. The police form which must be filled out asks, "What was the cause of the accident?"

Remove almost any single element from the story and the accident does not occur, for example if the student did not smoke or if the finals schedule had been rationalized so that no one had more than one final on any given day. At the very least, an analysis of this problem must consider multiple causality. If it is extended to include questions like "what motivates so many of us to smoke despite clear evidence that tobacco fumes are detrimental to our health?" or "why do we drink and drive?" then the analysis must consider overdetermined social behavior and motivation. It must involve discussion of any levels of reality. On one level the determinants of smoking, for example, are psychological: parental example, peer pressure, need for oral stimulation in tense situations, etc. That level alone is overdetermined. If we add to it explanations of why students are tense during finals, why tobacco is legal and available in our society, and so on, we add another set of overdetermined levels. One could continue *ad infinitum*. In the classroom, I stop when it is clearly impossible to isolate a single cause or even a single level of causality.

Since overdetermination is a quality of all human motivation, it is possible to move easily from posed examples to more real examples. One could raise, for example, the question of why each student (or the teacher) has come to class. The combination of economic (money), social (status), and psychological (identify) reasons is bound to be overdetermined.

Having explained the concept of overdetermination and how it is distinct from simple causality, I then send the students out to collect examples. Essentially I am using the collection technique I learned from Ken Macrorie; the only difference is that the students are collecting examples of overdetermination instead of "fabulous realities" or bits of interesting dialog.

Collection leads into writing. An example of overdetermination usually takes a paragraph just to present. The next step, just as with any other collected material, is to ask for a longer piece of writing based on or utilizing what was collected. And overdetermined explanations flow naturally into argument, if only because there is usually an implicit assertion that the overdetermined explanation is more accurate than oversimplified alternatives. A final assignment might begin with the statement that it is a logical fallacy to seek simple causal explanations for overdetermined situations and proceed by comparison/contrast and examples to substantiate that thesis. If the examples come from within one general subject (e.g., ecology, education, or parent-child relations), this assignment can produce a very tight argumentative essay. One of its virtues is that it includes both causal and overdetermined explanation and a statement about the circumstances under which each is appropriate. Thus the students' ability to produce explanation is both improved and expanded.

The modes of analysis we teach should be similarly revamped. One rule of ordinary Western thought asserts that a whole is equal to the sum of its parts. (People who read and teach poems have always doubted this one.) A methodological corollary has been that one takes apart what one would understand, analyzes each of the parts (or variables) separately, and then arranges the analyzed parts in a logical series. This procedure is an example of mechanical thinking; it is very effective if you want to understand how a gasoline engine produces power. It does not work as well when you are trying to understand a person or a poem. Although this mode can be traced to ancient Greece and elsewhere, it obtained dominance in 17th Century Europe. Descartes, one of the fathers of this approach, determined to "divide each of the difficulties . . . into as many parts as possible" and to "think in an orderly fashion, beginning with the things which were simplest and easiest to understand and gradually and by degrees reaching toward more complex knowledge, *even treating as though ordered materials were not necessarily so.*"[10] As McLuhan notes, "rational" has for the West long meant uniform and sequential; consequently "mechanization is achieved by fragmentation of any process and by putting the fragmented parts in a series."[11]

If, however, what you would understand is not in reality fragmented, divisible, or serial, if in fact its characteristic qualities are based on the simultaneous existence and interrelation of its parts, then a falsification follows from mechanical analysis. Mechanical analysis can then be retained only if its reductive falsification is compensated for within a larger methodological schema. Failure to do so is one of the reasons for the ecological crisis. Western culture especially has a pathological tendency to look only at the parts, to not see the forest for the trees. We tend to think it is the individual (or individual corporation, or individual nation) that matters; we think in terms of "us" against "them," "us" against the environment. Actually the unit of evolutionary survival is organism-plus-environment: that organism which "wins against" its environment becomes extinct. Until recently there was a seemingly infinite frontier because we did not have the power to defeat the whole ecosystem; until recently therefore these thinking patterns were not so very destructive to the survival of the human race. Now these same patterns have become a liability.

I would be ridiculous, of course, to blame freshman composition for the forms of thinking which pervade the communication of our society. Such modes of development as classification, division, mechanical analysis, definition by genus + differentia, and either/or deduction merely reinforce the socially dominant forms. These modes are, moreover, useful, and we should continue to teach them; but we should do so in the context of heavily-emphasized integrative modes for which we will have to develop pedagogies. As the Club of Rome study points out, "it is through knowledge of wholes that we gain understanding of components, and not vice versa. . . ."[12] Even with the gasoline engine, where mechanical analysis is appropriate, we cannot understand the function of the components without knowing the structure and purpose of the whole. When what we must repair is not an engine, but an ecosystem, a holistic approach is that much more vital.

Boulding asserts that "at the present stage of human knowledge our theoretical constructs are fairly adequate at the lower levels (of complexity and organization), but become increasingly inadequate as we proceed to higher levels."[13] The system theorist will confirm this statement: our ordinary modes are adequate for closed systems, but become increasingly inadequate for systems which are increasingly "open" to their "environments." Nonsummativity—the whole being other than the sum of its parts—is one of the first principles of open system analysis. As a system increases in complexity, its behavior is determined more by its entire pattern of interrelationships and less by the "nature" of its components.

For centuries western science concentrated on systems in which this principle is not important. As Warren Weaver noted in 1948, classical science was concerned with either linear causality or unorganized complexity.[14] Linear causality can be handled by the Cartesian principle of independent variables: the scientist varies the causal factors one at a time while holding the rest of the system constant; in effect he deals with one part at a time as Descartes advocated. Unorganized complexity is handled by statistical methods which effectively reduce the problem to probable causality.

In the 1920's, however, science began to run into systems so dynamic and interconnected that varying one factor at a time was impossible. Over the intervening decades, methods based on independent variables have been increasingly less useful. Attempts to discover which genes control which hereditary traits, for example, are being abandoned in face of evidence that the configuration of entire chromosomes is in most cases more significant than the "nature" of any individual gene.[15] This type of finding parallels the gestalt psychologists' assertion that perception is determined not by the individual stimulus, but by the overall pattern of stimulation. The parallel extends to all fields dealing with organized complexity.

Attempts to deal with only one part of an organized complexity are sometimes harmless, but they can also be disastrous. For several decades DDT did increase agricultural yields and save people from malaria; it is now exterminating the animals which eat the affected insects. It has been found in the flesh of arctic polar bears and other fish-eating mammals. DDT is now approaching danger levels at the top of the food chain (us). A similarly interrelated system has been found in family therapy. Psychiatrists treating schizophrenic children often find that a child cured in the hospital relapses shortly after returning home. Analyzing the family as a system, they find that maintenance of the family's *status quo* often requires one member to be "crazy." To use an oversimplified example, the children might be growing up and the parents, to maintain their accustomed roles, might "need" one child to remain dependent. Often it is the behavior of some person other than the one manifesting symptoms which must be changed to allow a permanent cure. Parallels in the behavior of larger groups are such that Buckley uses system theory as a model for sociology.[16]

The non-summativity of open systems has implications not only for the teaching of composition, but for research in composition and composition pedagogy as well. Empirical research has begun to be extremely useful in our field. It has, however, failed to isolate the independent variables which define good writing or those which define good pedagogy. As we all know, moreover, there is a contradiction between our sense that we sometimes succeed in teaching people to write better and research findings.

Human communication is a highly open system. It is therefore extremely overdetermined and characterized by great nonsummativity. Consequently one should not expect to be able to fully isolate independent variables. Empirical approaches, moreover, must delete from consideration anything which cannot be quantified or regularized. It is precisely what cannot be quantified or regularized which is most important in developing those sensitivities which make for good writing. I do not think it is necessary to defend the value of empirical research in our field; its accomplishments and potential are evident. On the other hand, we must recognize that no amount of empirical research will ever totally succeed in isolating the "parts" of good writing or the "causes" of student improvement.

As this discussion indicates, non-summativity and overdetermination are closely related concepts: both are characteristics of the same type of systems. They can be taught similarly, with some students perhaps even simultaneously. That both contradict the students' socialized "common sense" can be partially overcome by showing how they support such values as individual diversity and free will, values which do form part of most students' systems of belief. My basic teaching methods remain demonstration and discussion, collection of examples, utilization and development of those examples in explanation, and then application in argument.

Visual approaches can also be extremely useful. Escher drawings and other visual illusions demonstrate graphically that the students' own perceptions are both conventional and characterized by immediate perception of whole images, not construction from parts. I also use collages. My assumption is that the process of composing bits of information into a whole statement is essentially similar whether those bits are pictures or phrases. Because collage-making is a more unusual process than sentence building, students can often recognize principles of organization more easily while creating collage compositions. The potential for visual illustration of generalizations about composition and communication is by itself a subject for an essay.[17] The point to be made here is that because the images of a collage are not arranged in linear order like the words in a sentence, they exemplify quite obviously a complexly-interacting whole.

Various other concepts from cybernetic communication theory have implication for composition and other communication skills courses. Other philosophical and scientific advances also have important implications. The preceding discussion of overdetermination and non-summativity was intended to be exemplary. Other concepts could have been used and the full import of any one concept will probably not be totally clear except in the context of the entire set of interrelated theories. The more important point has to do with models and model-building.

The concept of model-building is a commonplace among scientists, but is not well-known among composition teachers. Implicit in contemporary scientific method is the recognition that models underlie all of our perceptions, thoughts, and communications. This paper, for example, is an argument that a mechanical model underlies the traditional freshman composition rhetoric. A model then is a gestalt, a paradigm, a set of metaphors or analogies. It is impossible to perceive, think or communicate without using models;[18] consciously or unconsciously we make our choices about which models to use. Just as one may apply various metaphors to the same object, one may use various models—in both cases to very different effect.

One of the categorical syllogisms of traditional logic is sometimes presented in rhetorics as the alternative syllogism. A is B, B is not equal to C, A therefore is not C; an elephant is an animal, an animal cannot be a flower, an elephant therefore is not a flower. Within bounds that is a very excellent syllogism. Outside those bounds there are two sets of cases in which its application would be detrimental. The narrower set is illustrated by the behavior of light. The syllogism and common sense both indicate that if light is a particle it cannot be a wave and if light is a wave it cannot be a particle. And yet, as any undergraduate physics major will testify, light must be thought of as both wave and particle. From some perspectives light behaves like a particle, from others like a wave; for some purposes one must use one model, for some the other. Although the physicists (who also have common sense) would very much like to overturn them, such paradoxes have become part of even the most conservative science. In this set of cases, however, there is always the hope that some brilliant mind will discover a third model which avoids the contradiction.

In the broader set there is no such hope. One can avoid contradiction only by differentiating distinct logical levels or by applying some kind of psychological relativity. If I am trying to figure out why my car won't start, I should think of a gasoline engine mechanically and test each component independently. If, however, I am trying to design a new engine for that same car, I must think of a gasoline engine as an interrelated system. If I am trying to understand a schizophrenic's family, I should think of it as an interrelated system. If I am providing therapy for one member of that family perhaps I should hold that person individually responsible for his or her actions. If I am trying to maximize the profits of the corporation for which I work, I should think in an "us" vs. "them" dichotomy. If I am trying to avoid ecological disaster, I should think of an interrelated world system. In all these cases the models are obviously just that—models. One chooses the model which is most appropriate to his purpose, just as scientists choose the experimental model which will best answer their questions and just as a computer programmer chooses the model which will allow the computer to perform the relevant computations.

When we teach writing we inevitably teach various kinds of models. When we teach narration and description the models and their implications are relatively simple. In these forms, as in any kind of reportage, the writer's main problem is selectivity. No matter what is being narrated or described, completeness is impossible. So the writer must make a set of decisions about what is relevant and what is irrelevant and what less important. To make these decisions the writer clearly must have a sense of purpose, and, of course, different purposes will yield different selections.

When, however, we get beyond reportage we are inevitably teaching our students to think; that is, we are inevitably presenting models of logic.

We are teaching them how to move from the particular to the general and from the general to the particular. We are teaching them how to connect bits of information. And inevitably we are teaching them that certain connections are permissible while other connections are not. In short, we are one significant influence supplying them with the models by which they will do their future thinking.

In ordinary times all this might not be very important. But these are extraordinary times. The world is changing, and human consciousness is changing with it. This revolution in consciousness includes significant alternatives to our ordinary modes of thought. Some of our traditional modes, moreover, are inappropriate when applied to certain aspects of our changed environment. Since such a situation exists, its investigation is properly a part of rhetorical study. And the fruits of that investigation belong in every communications skill course.

In periods when the environment is stable, it is useful for organisms to rely on instincts, habits, and other unconscious modes of decision-making. Every decision which can be made unconsciously frees the consciousness for other tasks. Unconscious decision-making is quicker, more efficient and more reliable. Touch typing by conditioned reflex, for example, is in these ways better than hunt-and-peck; it also leaves consciousness free to think about the content of the message being typed.

If, on the other hand, the environment is changing, all these unconscious patterns lose their reliability. Where they had allowed for more flexibility, they now provide only for more error. Because the world we live in is changing so quickly, many of the unconscious models by which we think have become error-producing mechanisms. The solution is to make the patterns conscious so that we may use them critically instead of habitually. One place in which some of this consciousness should be created is the composition classroom.

Restated as a rhetorical principle, the main point of the preceding paragraphs is that a symbol may have different meanings in different contexts and, conversely, that the meaning of a symbol cannot be determined out of context. Words (and certain other types of symbols) have definite denotations. In certain situations we try to be more concerned with these "objective" denotations than with broader meanings; often this is what we mean by objectivity in the classroom and in professional communication. But the vast bulk of human communication (and the totality of animal communication) is primarily concerned with more subjective, relational meaning.[19] That meaning varies with context. In the context of one relationship, saying "I'm sorry" may mean "I don't love you anymore." In another it may mean, "I love you"; and in a third it may literally mean "I'm sorry."

The survival of *Homo sapiens* has always been based on superior adaptability, on the ability to distinguish different contexts and choose the appropriate behavior.

Having no fur, we can choose the clothing appropriate to various contexts; thus we can live everywhere from the tropics to the arctic. There are absolutes on more abstract logical levels (e.g., the high value attached to survival), but those absolutes take various forms relative to various contexts or environments. For an inland Eskimo survival means a diet which is at least 25% fat; that same diet would mean heart attack to a professor in California.

The principle applies equally to the biological ecosystem and to the ecosystem of ideas. The Boy Scout who twenty years ago memorized the rule that one should always bury cans and other non-burnable garbage has had the environmental context shift out from under him. Most backpacking areas are so crowded these days that the people would be burying cans faster than the earth could decompose them. Although the higher-level value of preserving for other hikers an undamaged natural environment still applies, the specific rule has been totally inverted—now a good Boy Scout carries out his unburnable garbage. What this example illustrates is the tendency to memorize low-level rules instead of understanding higher-level principles. This tendency leads to inappropriate behavior when the context shifts. (Students will enjoy collecting illustrations of this pattern.)

In logic and rhetoric the absolute value is to use a system which best represents reality and which consequently allows us to best function in reality. Descartes' method was the form that absolute value took on the lower logical level; relative to the historical period which renaissance/reformation was a transition into (and which the 20th century seems to be a transition out of), Cartesian logic was a progressive development. In that context it meant "I will not be prejudiced by a religious dogma when I seek scientific knowledge": thus it produced an approach which was more functional than the approaches which had preceded it. In the latter half of the 20th century, however, Cartesian logic means "I refuse to recognize the complex interrelatedness of reality"; thus it contradicts our desire to use the approach which best represents reality.

Likewise the (essentially Cartesian) rhetoric which was appropriate and was quite properly used as the basis for our composition courses in the past needs to be modified for the composition courses of the future. The higher level principle remains the same: we wish to teach our students to communicate with maximum effectiveness. Because the world is changing, however, the means to that maximum effectiveness are not quite the same as they were in the past.

The first axiom of the new rhetoric should be that writing skills and thinking skills are interrelated; the pedagogical consequence is that they should therefore be taught simultaneously. We see the validity of this axiom quite literally when we correct student papers. The style which uses ambiguous antecedents for demonstrative pronouns correlates highly with overgeneralized thinking; similarly, disorganized paragraphs can often be cured by helping the student to think more clearly. We see it when we write ourselves: nascent ideas become manifest and developed through the process of communicating them; similarly, unnoticed contradictions become apparent and are resolved. We see it in our pedagogy; premature formal and grammatical demands sometimes inhibit free thinking and creativity; similarly, instruction in prewriting and logic improves student drafts.

The focus of freshman composition must, of course, be on writing skills. But any communication skills course must embody a rhetoric and must utilize some content. At present that content may be personal experience, expository essays, literature, linguistics, or various other possibilities. Since a writer must begin with what he or she knows, personal experience will presumably continue to be the starting point. When students are ready to move beyond the personal, however, when we have helped them to develop an informed rather than a merely personal experience, then the content of freshman composition may as well be the human communications process itself. Freshman composition could then explicitly help to develop the consciousness called for above. It could supply whatever data and theory students need to understand the communications relationships in which they inevitably participate and to avoid the logical fallacies which are most prevalent and dangerous in our time.

The emphasis should be on communicative relationships, internal (perception-cognition-expression) as well as external (sender-message-receiver)—not on the isolated message. One uses standard spelling, for example, not because it is virtuous, but because nonstandard spelling usually produces undesired reactions in the reader.

Sometimes we may use literature, e.g., for models of non-Cartesian, holistic modes. Sometimes we may use media study, e.g., to build awareness of audience or to explicate the differences between mass and individual modes. Sometimes we may use linguistics, e.g., to explain the effects of cultural relativity on certain communication processes or to explain why a certain sentence pattern sounds "awkward." Undoubtedly we shall have to cull material from diverse disciplines and diverse aspects of reality. But always the real content should be the communications process and always the student should be gaining a clearer consciousness of that process.

More important than the content, however, is the rhetoric. On the freshman level, rhetorics are often not discussed explicitly, but there is always a rhetoric implicit in the skills being taught. The rhetoric embodied in our freshman courses should be appropriate for the world in which we are and will be living. It should be a rhetoric of the Computer Age, not of the Machine Age. It should be a rhetoric for an age approaching the limits to material growth. It should not hinder, but help people to understand, cope with, and control the social and technological changes of our times. It should, moreover, be sufficiently holistic and integrative for a world on the brink of ecological disaster.

This paper is tentative in all but its general theme. Its goal is to define a task and to set off a discussion. From that discussion we should emerge with an appropriate rhetoric. The very process of discussion will force us to discover the content which best matches that rhetoric and to devise the concrete modes which embody its principles. We will also need to develop (largely I suspect from innovative techniques we are already using) a pedagogy appropriate to that rhetoric.

When we have the rhetoric, that content, those concrete modes, and that pedagogy, we will be ready to teach our students cognitive and communication skills appropriate to contemporary reality and to the reality of the foreseeable future. We will have composition programs which lead rather than follow the consciousness of their time. We shall also be able to provide a significant service to our colleagues in other disciplines who are striving to convey similar systemic concepts and skills. And perhaps, in a small way, we shall help improve the survival chances of humanity.

May it be so.

Notes

1. Gregory Bateson, *Steps to an Ecology of Mind* (New York; Ballantine, 1972), pp. 490 ff. Bateson's model is useful because of its extreme simplicity. When using it, however, one should be aware that it reifies each of the three factors. Thus they seem to be independent forces rather than interactive processes and the crucial question of who controls them never arises.

2. Ludwig von Bertalanffy, *General System Theory* (New York: George Braziller, 1968), p. 87.

3. Herbert Feigl, "The Scientific Outlook: Naturalism and Humanism," rpt. In Feigl and Broderick, eds., *Readings in the Philosophy of Science* (New York: Appleton-Century-Crofts, 1953), p. 9.

4. The Club of Rome, founded in 1966, is a think tank and research center whose members include scientists, economists, business people, and high-level civil servants. It examines how human beings manage the world, seeks to address global imbalances caused by differing population and economic growth, and urges greater understanding of the interdependence among human beings and between the human and natural worlds.—E. L.

5. Donella H. Meadows, et. al., *The Limits to Growth* (New York: Signet, 1972), p. 194.

6. Marshall McLuhan, *The Medium Is the Message* (New York: Bantam, 1967), p. 45. *Understanding Media* (New York: Signet, 1964), p. 33.

7. See Norbert Wiener, *The Human Use of Human Beings* (New York: Avon, 1967); Bateson and Ruesch, *Communication* (New York: Norton, 1967); Kenneth Boulding, *The Image* (Ann Arbor: University of Michigan Press, 1956); Walter Buckley, *Sociology and Modern Systems Theory* (Englewood Cliffs, N. J.: Prentice-Hall, 1967).

8. See, for example, Bertalanffy on free will, pp. 114–16, 221; Bateson on teleology, pp. 426–39.

9. Konrad Lorenz, *On Aggression* (New York: Bantam, 1967), p. 148.

10. Rene Descartes, *Discourse on Method,* trans. L. J. Lafleur (New York: Liberal Arts, 1956), p. 12 (italics added).

11. *Understanding Media,* pp. 30 and 27.

12. Meadows, *et al.,* p. 192.

13. Boulding, p. 29.

14. "Science and Complexity," *American Scientist,* 36 (1948).

15. See Theodosius Dobzhansky, *Genetic Diversity and Human Equality* (New York: Basic Books, 1973), esp. p. 35. In this non-technical book, Dobzhansky, the world's most renowned living geneticist, dismantles the basis upon which Arthur R. Jensen built his theory of the significance of racial differences in IQ scores.

16. Buckley, *op. cit.*

17. Isabella Halsted and Patricia Lawrence are working on one such essay, foreshadowed by their demonstration, "Perception and Writing: A Media Approach for Open Admissions Students," at the 1974 CCCC meeting. A former graduate assistant, Jerry Baker, introduced me to the technique of collage self-portraits which can be used to show students the connections between self-image and communications to and from the "self." They are also useful when discussing the differences between verbal and non-verbal communication and for illustrating virtually any principle of organization.

18. See N. R. Hanson, *Patterns of Discovery* (Cambridge: Cambridge University Press, 1958), esp. chapter I; P. K. Feyerabend, "Problems of Empiricism" in R. G. Colodny, ed.,

Beyond the Edge of Certainty (Englewood Cliffs, N.J.: Prentice-Hall, 1965); and T. S. Kuhn, *The Structure of Scientific Revolutions,* 2nd ed. (Chicago: University of Chicago Press, 1970). Kuhn's otherwise valuable book must be qualified in just the same manner as Bateson's model of ecological crisis (see note one, above).

19. Bateson, pp. 366–67.

3

Introduction to Janet Emig's "Writing as a Mode of Learning"

Lisa Ede and Andrea Abernethy Lunsford

We can easily remember the first time we read Emig's groundbreaking 1977 essay, "Writing as a Mode of Learning." Looking back over the last twenty-five years and rereading her work today, we see that what drew us to her essay in 1977 is what draws us to it today: her passionate engagement with the processes of writing, thinking, and learning; her attention to the nature and significance of the material, embodied practices of real writers (often, though not always, student writers); her theoretical and method-ological pluralism; and her strong commitment to social justice. At the time, major figures in the field often worked (and worked productively) within a well-established tradition, as Edward P. J. Corbett did within the classi-cal rhetorical tradition. Others, such as James Kinneavy, James Moffett, and Frank D'Angelo, wrestled with master narratives. In "Writing as a Mode of Learning," Emig focused specifically on an oft-repeated but largely un-substantiated claim that writing enables thinking. Drawing on an eclectic range of theories and traditions, including cognitive psychology, the his-tory of education and educational research, experimental studies of brain research, and creative writing, Emig provides such substantiation, demon-strating that writing is not a "veil" or "dress" of thought but is, rather, in-extricably related to thought and thus to learning. As readers will discover, Emig's argument is driven by a sense of pedagogical urgency: in the con-clusion of "Writing as a Mode of Learning," she calls for her essay to "start a crucial line of inquiry: for unless the losses to learners of not writing are compellingly described and substantiated by experimental and speculative research, writing itself as a central academic process may not long endure."

Rereading Janet Emig's work is important to us for additional reasons. Although Emig has only recently taken an explicitly feminist stance as a scholar—in 1995 she and Louise Wetherbee Phelps coedited *Feminine Principles and Women's Experience in American Composition and Rhetoric*—Emig has, we believe, consistently enacted a feminist ethics, rhetoric, and politics. She has done so most often against strong odds: as Jerry Nelms has demonstrated, in her early career Emig struggled long and hard to find even meager institutional support for her work. Her struggle is in many ways emblematic of the struggle of rhetoric and composition for a metaphoric room of its own in the academy, and her perseverance and eventual success have inspired many.

So when Robert and Christina McDonald asked us to select an essay we see as having played a critical role in the development of composition studies during the last thirty years, we thought quickly of Janet Emig and her work. Choosing one specific essay, however, proved a bit more difficult. Indeed, it might seem most natural to include a part of Emig's 1971 landmark volume *The Composing Processes of Twelfth Graders,* the book that in many respects launched the writing process movement and inspired decades of productive scholarship. Yet as we continued to think about Emig's body of work, we kept circling back to this essay, which, from our present-day perspective, represents an important milestone for several scholarly and pedagogical projects in our field.

The most obvious milestone involves the writing process movement. By the time Emig's essay appeared in *College Composition and Communication* in 1977, the movement was gaining real momentum. News of James Britton and Nancy Martin's massive 1966–71 study of student writing in British schools was circulating in conferences and journal articles (the report of the study appeared in 1975); D. Gordon Rohman's 1965 *CCC* essay on prewriting and Janice M. Lauer's 1970 "Heuristics and Composition" motivated further research on the role of invention in composing; James Moffett's 1968 *Teaching the Universe of Discourse* called attention to the helpfulness of a developmental perspective on writing; and the Bay Area Writing Project (which spawned the powerful National Writing Project) began to hail a national audience soon after its inception in 1974. As case-study research and cognitive-based studies of the writing process began to appear, Emig recognized the need to stand back momentarily from an immersion in the details related to specific processes of writing in order to think more generally—and critically—about the nature of writing, thinking, and learning.

Her "Writing as a Mode of Learning" represents a powerful example of such analysis, for this essay incisively challenges the separation of thinking and writing inscribed in the rhetorical (and compositional) tradition since at least the time of Ramus. This turn to theorizing is characteristic of the dialogic relationship animating all of Emig's work: her intensely practical and particular studies are almost always embedded in a larger search for theories that will account for the processes and practices she analyzes.

Like Emig's other work from the 1970s, "Writing as a Mode of Learning" is important for the role that it played in catalyzing—and furthering—research and pedagogy on the writing process. In addition, her essay played a critical role in helping to authorize another major project of composition: the writing across the curriculum (WAC) movement. For as David Russell observes in *Writing in the Academic Disciplines, 1980–1990,* Emig's essay provided strong "intellectual moorings" for WAC (278). Rereading Emig's essay decades after it was published, we still find her revisioning of the relationship between writing and learning persuasive. In this relatively brief, straightforward, and accessible essay, Emig articulates a transforming vision of what it means to learn and to write.

In working on this introduction, we have recognized yet another connection between Emig's "Writing as Mode of Learning" and the ongoing work of composition studies. For though some scholars associated with composition's turn to social construction have identified Emig's work with the writing process movement and cognitive research methods, and thus have implicitly or explicitly devalued it, we believe that the claims Emig makes in her essay played a central role in enabling later arguments that stretch beyond those associated with the writing process and writing across the curriculum to social construction itself. True: in her essay Emig portrays writing and thinking primarily as solitary activities, and she sets up a fairly rigid binary between writing and speaking. Indeed, as Emig herself has recognized, she undervalues the role that collaborative inquiry and writing can play in the learning process (Nelms 116) and overemphasizes the distinctions between writing and speaking (Web 122). But in her essay she also acknowledges and articulates the powerful role that writing and learning can play in constructing one's world, asserting, for instance, that "successful learning is . . . engaged, committed, personal learning. Indeed, impersonal learning may be an anomalous concept, like the very notion of objectivism itself." Such a statement recognizes that, as Marilyn Cooper argues in her 1986 essay "The Ecology of Writing" (an early argument for writing as a social process), writing "is not simply a way of thinking but more fundamentally a way of acting," a way of engaging with the world

(375). In important and instrumental ways, it seems to us, Emig's work helped make Cooper's argument—and many others that take a social construction perspective—viable.

Since retirement from her teaching position at Rutgers University, Emig has continued to study the complex, dynamic process of writing, thinking, and learning. As a result, we can look forward to continuing to learn from her and her work for many years to come. In the meantime, however, we invite readers of this volume to enjoy a rereading of a key text in composition studies, Janet Emig's "Writing as a Mode of Learning."

Works Cited

Bay Area Writing Project. <http://sorcier.soe.berkeley.edu/outreach.bawp/whatis.html>.

Britton, James, Tony Burgess, Nancy Miller, Alex McLeod, and Harold Rosen. *The Development of Writing Abilities (11–18)*. London: Macmillan Education, 1975.

Cooper, Marilyn. "The Ecology of Writing." *College English* 48.4 (1986): 364–75.

Corbett, Edward P. J. *Classical Rhetoric for the Modern Student*. New York: Oxford, 1965.

D'Angelo, Frank. *A Conceptual Theory of Rhetoric*. Cambridge: Winthrop, 1975.

Emig, Janet. *The Composing Processes of Twelfth Graders*. Urbana, IL: NCTE, 1971.

———. *The Web of Meaning*. Upper Montclair, NJ: Boynton, 1983.

———. "Writing as a Mode of Learning." *College Composition and Communication* 18 (1977): 122–28.

Kinneavy, James. *A Theory of Discourse*. Englewood Cliffs, NJ: Prentice-Hall, 1971.

Lauer, Janice. "Heuristics and Composition." *College Composition and Communication* 21 (1970): 396–404.

Moffett, James. *Teaching the Universe of Discourse*. Boston: Houghton, 1968.

Nelms, Gerald. "Reassessing Janet Emig's *The Composing Processes of Twelfth Graders:* An Historical Perspective." *Rhetoric Review* 13 (1994): 108–30.

Phelps, Louise, and Janet Emig, eds. *Feminine Principles and Women's Experience in American Composition and Rhetoric*. Pittsburgh: U of Pittsburgh P, 1995.

Rohman, D. Gordon. "Pre-Writing: The Stage of Discovery in the Writing Process." *College Composition and Communication* 16 (1965): 106–12.

Russell, David. *Writing in the Academic Disciplines, 1870–1990: A Curricular History*. Carbondale: Southern Illinois UP, 1991.

Writing as a Mode of Learning (1977)

Janet Emig

Writing represents a unique mode of learning—not merely valuable, not merely special, but unique. That will be my contention in this paper. The thesis is straightforward. Writing serves learning uniquely because writing as process-and-product possesses a cluster of attributes that correspond uniquely to certain powerful learning strategies.

Although the notion is clearly debatable, it is scarcely a private belief. Some of the most distinguished contemporary psychologists have at least implied such a role for writing as heuristic. Lev Vygotsky, A. R. Luria, and Jerome Bruner, for example, have all pointed out that higher cognitive functions, such as analysis and synthesis, seem to develop most fully only with the support system of verbal language—particularly, it seems, of written language.[1] Some of their arguments and evidence will be incorporated here.

Here I have a prior purpose: to describe as tellingly as possible *how* writing uniquely corresponds to certain powerful learning strategies. Making such a case for the uniqueness of writing should logically and theoretically involve establishing many contrasts, distinctions between (1) writing and all other verbal languaging processes—listening, reading and especially talking; (2) writing and all other forms of composing, such as composing a painting, a symphony, a dance, a film, a building; and (3) composing in words and composing in the two other major graphic symbol systems of mathematical equations and scientific formulae. For the purposes of this paper, the task is simpler, since most students are not permitted by most curricula to discover the values of composing, say, in dance, or even in film; and most students are not sophisticated enough to create, to originate formulations, using the highly abstruse symbol system of equations and formulae. Verbal language represents the most *available* medium for composing; in fact, the significance of sheer availability in its selection as a mode for learning can probably not be overstressed. But the uniqueness of writing among the verbal languaging processes does need to be established and supported if only because so many curricula and courses in English still consist almost exclusively of reading and listening.

This essay first appeared in *College Composition and Communication* 28 (1977): 122–28. Copyright © 1977 by the National Council of Teachers of English. Reprinted with permission.

Writing as a Unique Languaging Process

Traditionally, the four languaging processes of listening, talking, reading, and writing are paired in either of two ways. The more informative seems to be the division many linguists make between first-order and second-order processes with talking and listening characterized as first-order processes; reading and writing, as second-order. First-order processes are acquired without formal or systematic instruction; the second-order processes of reading and writing tend be learned initially only with the aid of formal and systematic instruction.

The less useful distinction is that between listening and reading as receptive functions and talking and writing as productive functions. Critics of these terms like Louise Rosenblatt rightfully point out that the connotation of passivity too often accompanies the notion of receptivity when reading, like listening, is a vital, construing act.

An additional distinction, so simple it may have been previously overlooked, resides in two criteria: the matters of origination and of graphic recording. Writing is originating and creating a unique verbal construct that is graphically recorded. Reading is creating or re-creating *but not* originating a verbal construct that is graphically recorded. Listening is creating or re-creating but not originating a verbal construct that is not graphically recorded. Talking is creating *and* originating a verbal construct that is not graphically recorded (except for the circuitous routing of a transcribed tape). Note that a distinction is being made between creating and originating, separable processes.

For talking, the nearest languaging process, additional distinctions should probably be made. (What follows is not a denigration of talk as a valuable mode of learning.) A silent classroom or one filled only with the teacher's voice is anathema to learning. For evidence of the cognitive value of talk, one can look to some of the persuasive monographs coming from the London Schools Council project on writing: *From Information to Understanding* by Nancy Martin or *From Talking to Writing* by Peter Medway.[2] We also know that for some of us, talking is a valuable, even necessary, form of pre-writing. In his curriculum, James Moffett makes the value of such talk quite explicit.

But to say that talking is a valuable form of pre-writing is not to say that writing is talk recorded, an inaccuracy appearing in far too many composition texts. Rather, a number of contemporary trans-disciplinary sources suggest that talking and writing may emanate from different organic sources and represent quiet different, possibly distinct, language functions. In *Thought and Language,* Vygotsky notes that "written speech is a separate linguistic function, differing from oral speech in both structure and mode of functioning."[3] The sociolinguist Dell Hymes, in a valuable issue of *Daedalus,* "Language as Human Problem," makes a comparable point: "That speech and writing are not simply interchangeable, and have developed historically in ways at least partly autonomous, is obvious."[4] At the first session of the Buffalo Conference on Researching Composition (4–5 October 1975), the first point of unanimity among the participant-speakers with interest in developmental psychology, media, dreams and aphasia was that talking and writing were markedly different functions.[5] Some of us who work rather steadily with writing research agree. We also believe that there are hazards, conceptually and pedagogically, in creating too complete an analogy between talking and writing, in blurring the very real differences between the two.

WHAT ARE THESE DIFFERENCES?

1. Writing is learned behavior; talking is natural, even irrepressible, behavior.
2. Writing then is an artificial process; talking is not.
3. Writing is a technological device—not the wheel, but early enough to qualify as primary technology; talking is organic, natural, earlier.
4. Most writing is slower than most talking.
5. Writing is stark, barren, even naked as a medium; talking is rich, luxuriant, inherently redundant.
6. Talk leans on the environment; writing must provide its own context.
7. With writing, the audience is usually absent; with talking, the listener is usually present.
8. Writing usually results in a visible graphic product; talking usually does not.
9. Perhaps because there is a product involved, writing tends to be a more responsible and committed act than talking.
10. It can even be said that throughout history, an aura, an ambience, a mystique has usually encircled the written word; the spoken word has for the most part proved ephemeral and treated mundanely (ignore, please, our recent national history).
11. Because writing is often our representation of the world made visible, embodying both process and product, writing is more readily a form and source of learning than talking.

Unique Correspondences Between Learning and Writing

What then are some *unique* correspondences between learning and writing? To begin with some definitions: Learning can be defined in many ways, according to one's predilections and training, with all statements about learning of course hypothetical. Definitions range from the chemo-physiological ("Learning is changed patterns of protein synthesis in relevant portions of the cortex")[6] to transactive views drawn from both philosophy and psychology (John Dewey, Jean Piaget) that learning is the re-organization or confirmation of a cognitive scheme in light of an experience.[7] What the speculations seem to share is consensus about certain features and strategies that characterize successful learning. These include the importance of the classic attributes of re-inforcement and feedback. In most hypotheses, successful learning is also connective and selective. Additionally, it makes use of propositions, hypotheses, and other elegant summarizers. Finally, it is active, engaged, personal—more specifically self-rhythmed—in nature.

Jerome Bruner, like Jean Piaget, through a comparable set of categories, posits three major ways in which we represent and deal with actuality: (1) enactive—we learn "by doing"; (2) iconic—we learn "by depiction in an image" and (3) representational or symbolic— we learn "by restatement in words."[8] To overstate the matter, in enactive learning, the hand predominates; in iconic, the eye; and in symbolic, the brain.

What is striking about writing as a process is that, by its very nature, all three ways of dealing with actuality are simultaneously or almost simultaneously deployed. That is, the symbolic transformation of experience of verbal language is shaped into an icon (the graphic product) by the enactive hand. If the most efficacious learning occurs when learning is re-inforced, then writing through its inherent re-inforcing cycle involving hand, eye, and brain marks a uniquely powerful multi-representational mode for learning.

Writing is also integrative in perhaps the most basic possible sense: the organic, the functional. Writing involves the fullest possible functioning of the brain, which entails the active participation in the process of both the left and the right hemispheres. Writing is markedly bispheral, although in some popular accounts, writing is inaccurately presented as a chiefly left-hemisphere activity, perhaps because the linear written product is somehow regarded as analogue for the process that created it; and the left hemisphere seems to process material linearly.

The right hemisphere, however, seems to make at least three, perhaps four, major contributions to the writing process—probably, to the creative process generically. First, several researchers, such as Geschwind and Snyder of Harvard and Zaidal of Cal Tech, through markedly different experiments, have very tentatively suggested that the right hemisphere is the sphere, even the *seat,* of emotions.[9] Second—or perhaps as an illustration of the first—Howard Gardner, in his important study of the brain-damaged, notes that our sense of emotional appropriateness in discourse may reside in the right sphere:

> Emotional appropriateness, in sum—being related not only to *what* is said, but to how it is said and to what is *not* said, as well—is crucially dependent on right hemisphere intactness.[10]

Third, the right hemisphere seems to be the sources of intuition, of sudden gestalts, of flashes of images, of abstractions occurring as visual or spatial wholes, as the initiating metaphors in the creative process. A familiar example: William Faulkner noted in his *Paris Review* interview that *The Sound and the Fury* began as the image of a little girl's muddy drawers as she sat in a tree watching her grandmother's funeral.[11]

Also, a unique form of feedback, as well as reinforcement, exists with writing, because information from the *process* is immediately and visibly available as that portion of the *product* already written. The importance for learning of a product in a familiar and available medium for immediate, literal (that is, visual) re-scanning and review cannot perhaps be overstated. In his remarkable study of purportedly blind sculptors, Geza Revesz found that without sight, persons cannot move beyond a literal transcription of elements into any manner of symbolic transformation—by definition, the central requirement of re-formulation and re-interpretation, i.e., revision, that most aptly named process.[12]

As noted in the second paragraph, Vygotsky and Luria, like Bruner, have written importantly about the connections between learning and writing. In his essay "The Psychobiology of Psychology," Bruner lists as one of six axioms regarding learning: "We are connective."[13] Another correspondence then between learning and writing: in *Thought and Language,* Vygotsky notes that writing makes a unique demand in that the writer must engage in "deliberate semantics"—in Vygotsky's elegant phrase, "deliberate structuring of the web of meaning."[14] Such structuring is required because, for Vygotsky, writing centrally represents an expansion of inner speech, that mode whereby we talk to ourselves, which is "maximally compact" and "almost entirely predicative"; written speech is a mode which is "maximally detailed" and which requires explicitly supplied subjects and topics. The medium then of written verbal language requires the establishment of systematic connections and relationships. Clear writing by definition is that writing which signals without ambiguity the nature of conceptual relationships, whether they be coordinate, subordinate, superordinate, causal, or something other.

Successful learning is also engaged, committed, personal learning. Indeed, impersonal learning may be an anomalous concept, like the very notion of objectivism itself. As Michael Polanyi states simply at the beginning of *Personal Knowledge:* "the ideal of strict objectivism is absurd." (How many courses and curricula in English, science, and all else does that one sentence reduce to rubble?) Indeed, the theme of *Personal Knowledge* is that

> into every act of knowing there enters a passionate contribution of the person knowing what is being known, . . . this coefficient is no mere imperfection but a vital component of his knowledge.[15]

In *Zen and the Art of Motorcycle Maintenance,* Robert Pirsig states a comparable theme:

> The Quality which creates the world emerges as a *relationship* between man and his experience. He is a *participant* in the creation of all things.[16]

Finally, the psychologist George Kelly has as the central notion in his subtle and compelling theory of personal constructs man as a scientist steadily and actively engaged in making and re-making his hypotheses about the nature of the universe.[17]

We are acquiring as well some empirical confirmation about the importance of engagement in, as well as self-selection of, a subject for the student learning to write and writing to learn. The recent Sanders and Littlefield study, reported in *Research in the Teaching of English,* is persuasive evidence on this point, as well as being a model for a certain type of research.[18]

As Luria implies in the quotation above, writing is self-rhythmed. One writes best as one learns best, at one's own pace. Or to connect the two processes, writing can sponsor learning because it can match its pace. Support for the importance of self-pacing to learning can be found in Benjamin Bloom's important study "Time and Learning."[19] Evidence for the significance of self-pacing to writing can be found in the reason Jean-Paul Sartre gave last summer for not using the tape-recorder when he announced that blindness in his second eye had forced him to give up writing:

> I think there is an enormous difference between speaking and writing. One rereads what one rewrites. But one can read slowly or quickly: in other words, you do not know how long you will have to take deliberating over a sentence. . . . If I listen to a tape recorder the listening speed is determined by the speed at which the tape turns and not by my own needs. Therefore I will always be either lagging behind or running ahead of the machine.[20]

Writing is connective as a process in a more subtle and perhaps more significant way, as Luria points out in what may be the most powerful paragraph of rationale ever supplied for writing as heuristic:

> Written speech is bound up with the inhibition of immediate synpractical connections. It assumes a much slower, repeated mediating process of analysis and synthesis, which makes it possible not only to develop the required thought, but even to revert to its earlier stages, thus transforming the sequential chain of connections in a simultaneous, self-reviewing structure. Written speech thus represents a new and powerful instrument of thought.[21]

But first to explicate: writing inhibits "immediate synpractical connections." Luria defines *synpraxis* as "concrete-active" situations in which language does not exist independently but as a "fragment" of an ongoing action "outside of which it is incomprehensible."[22] In *Language and Learning,* James Britton describes it succinctly as "speech-cum-action."[23] Writing, unlike talking, restrains dependence upon the actual situation. Writing as a mode is inherently more self-reliant than speaking. Moreover, as Bruner states in explicating Vygotsky, "Writing virtually forces a remoteness of reference on the language user."[24]

Luria notes what has already been noted above: that writing, typically, is a "much slower" process than talking. But then he points out the relation of this slower pace to learning: this slower pace allows for—indeed, encourages—the shuttling among past, present, and future. Writing, in other words, connects the three major tenses of our experience to make meaning. And the two major modes by which these three aspects are united are the processes of analysis and synthesis: analysis, the breaking of entities into their constituent parts; and synthesis, combining or fusing these, often into fresh arrangements or amalgams.

Finally, writing is epigenetic, with the complex evolutionary development of thought steadily and graphically visible and available throughout as a record of the journey, from jottings and notes to full discursive formulations.

For a summary of the correspondences stressed here between certain learning strategies and certain attributes of writing, see table 1.

This essay represents a first effort to make a certain kind of case for writing—specifically, to show its unique value for learning. It is at once over-elaborate and under specific. Too much of the formulation is in the off-putting jargon of the learning theorist, when my own predilection would have been to emulate George Kelly and to avoid terms like *reinforcement* and *feedback* since their use implies that I have inside a certain paradigm about learning I don't truly inhabit. Yet I hope that the essay will start a crucial line of inquiry; for unless the losses to learners of not writing are compellingly described and substantiated by experimental and speculative research, writing itself as a central academic process may not long endure.

Table 1. Unique Cluster of Correspondences Between Certain Learning Strategies and Certain Attributes of Writing

Selected Characteristics of Successful Learning Strategies	Selected Attributes of Writing, Process and Product
(1) Profits from multi-representational and integrative re-inforcement	(1) Represents process uniquely multi-representational and integrative
(2) Seeks self-provided feedback: (a) immediate (b) long-term	(2) Represents powerful instance of self-provided feedback: (a) provides product uniquely available for *immediate* feedback (review and re-evaluation) (b) provides record of evolution of thought since writing is epigenetic as process-and-product
(3) Is connective: (a) makes generative conceptual groupings, synthetic and analytic (b) proceeds from propositions, hypotheses, and other elegant summarizers	(3) Provides connections: (a) establishes explicit and systematic conceptual groupings through lexical, syntactic, and rhetorical devices (b) represents most available means (verbal language) for economic recording of abstract formulations
(4) Is active, engaged, personal— notably self-rhythmed	(4) Is active, engaged, personal—notably self-rhythmed

---

Notes

1. Lev S. Vygotsky, *Thought and Language,* trans. Eugenia Hanfmann and Gertrude Vakar (Cambridge: The M.I.T. Press, 1962); A. R. Luria and F. Ia. Yudovich, *Speech and the Development of Mental Processes in the Child,* ed. Joan Simon (Baltimore: Penguin, 1971); Jerome S. Bruner, *The Relevance of Education* (New York: W. W. Norton and Co., 1971).

2. Nancy Martin, *From Information to Understanding* (London: Schools Council Project Writing Across the Curriculum, 11–13, 1973): Peter Medway, *From Talking to Writing* (London: Schools Council Project Writing Across the Curriculum, 11–13, 1973).

3. Vygotsky, p. 98.

4. Dell Hymes, "On the Origins and Foundations of Inequality Among Speakers," *Daedalus,* 102 (Summer, 1973), 69

5. Participant-speakers were Loren Barrett, University of Michigan; Gerald O'Grady, SUNY/Buffalo; Hollis Frampton, SUNY/Buffalo; and Janet Emig, Rutgers.

6. George Steiner, *After Babel: Aspects of Language and Translation* (New York: Oxford University Press, 1975), p. 287.

7. John Dewey, *Experience and Education* (New York: Macmillan, 1938); Jean Piaget, *Biology and Knowledge: An Essay on the Relations between Organic Regulations and Collective Processes* (Chicago: University of Chicago Press, 1971).

8. Bruner, pp. 7–8.

9. Boyce Rensberger, "Language Ability Found in Right Side of Brain," *New York Times,* 1 August 1975, p. 14.

10. Howard Gardner, *The Shattered Mind: The Person after Brain Damage* (New York: Alfred A. Knopf, 1975), p. 372.

11. William Faulkner, *Writers at Work:* The Paris Review Interviews, ed. Malcolm Cowley (New York: The Viking Press, 1959), p. 130.

12. Geza Revesz, *Psychology and Art of the Blind,* trans. H. A. Wolff (London: Longmans-Green, 1950).

13. Bruner, p. 126

14. Vygotsky, p. 100.

15. Michael Polanyi, *Personal Knowledge: Toward a Post-Critical Philosophy* (Chicago: University of Chicago Press, 1958), p. viii.

16. Robert Pirsig, *Zen and the Art of Motorcycle Maintenance* (New York: William Morrow and Co. Inc., 1974), p. 212.

17. George Kelly, *A Theory of Personality: The Psychology of Personal Constructs* (New York W. W. Norton and Co., 1963).

18. Sara E. Sanders and John H. Little, "Perhaps Test Essays Can Reflect Significant Improvement in Freshman Composition: Report on Successful Attempt," *RTE,* 9 (Fall 1975), p. 145–53.

19. Benjamin Bloom, "Time and Learning," *American Psychologist,* 29 (September 1974) p. 682–88.

20. Jean-Paul Sartre, "Sartre at Seventy: An Interview," with Michel Contat, *New York Review of Books,* 7 August 1975.

21. Luria, p. 118.

22. Luria, p. 50.

23. James Britton, *Language and Learning* (Baltimore: Penguin, 1971), pp. 10–11.

24. Bruner, p. 47.

4

Introduction to David Bartholomae's "The Study of Error"

John Trimbur

David Bartholomae's "The Study of Error" is one of those articles that everyone knows, whether they have read it or not. Now, when I say "knows," I don't just mean knows about it, say, as the 1980 Richard Braddock Award Winner and subsequently acknowledged, along with Mina Shaughnessy's "Diving In" and *Errors and Expectations,* as a founding statement of what we understand basic writing to signify for composition studies. I mean knows it bone-deep, at a nearly visceral level, not so much as a scholarly contribution as an inescapable sentiment—a matter of social allegiance to the struggles, in composition classrooms, of ordinary writers. At any rate, this was my experience reading "The Study of Error" to prepare this introduction: I could not be sure I had actually read it, and yet I knew it—or perhaps I should say recognized it—both as a source of utter generosity and solidarity with student writers and as an argument so persuasive I could not imagine I had ever thought otherwise.

To read "The Study of Error" twenty years (a full generation) after it was published is to encounter a way of reading student writing that answers those who would doubt the maturity and linguistic resourcefulness of basic writers and deny them a place in higher learning. (I can't help thinking of New York mayor Rudy Giuliani, his educational ideologue Heather MacDonald, and all the other educators and policymakers currently intent on curtailing the access of "underprepared" and "nontraditional" students to a college education.) In Bartholomae's view, basic writing is not what you find in the simplified writing tasks and workbook exercises that make up a basic skills curriculum. Instead, basic writing must be understood in terms of what "students *do* or *produce*." Accordingly, the "errors" in basic writing—the idiosyncratic, incoherent, and unconventional features of the prose—amount first of all to "evidence of intention," as basic writers seek to approximate and control the codes of print literacy. Moreover, as Bartholomae notes, given the fact that readers in English studies have developed elaborate and sympathetic ways to understand how and why literary texts depart from expected conventions, there is no reason why we can't shift these learned habits of close reading from the elevated modes of writing we call literature to the verbal expressions of basic writing students.

As I say, reading (or rereading, as the case may be) "The Study of Error" provided the pleasure of returning to a ground of belief that for me—and I know for many writing teachers—now seems unassailable. Still, like returning home or to any familiar place twenty years later, there is a sobering effect mixed in the nostalgia. I do not mean simply what the passage of time does to our perspective, though surely aspects of "The Study of Error" appear in retrospect to be very much of their moment, such as Bartholomae's particular use of linguistics and his implied trust in research programs, developmental schemes, and accumulative results. There is also, and to my mind more tellingly, the way that "The Study of Error" entered, at the level of lived experience, into the collective biography of a generation of writing teachers, expressing the best hopes of those of us teaching at the time, often in deplorable conditions, in basic writing, open admission, and equal opportunity programs.

My intent here, I hope to make clear, is not to romanticize that moment "around 1980" but to come to accounts with it.[1] I'm aware in this regard of the narcissism of my own generation of baby boomers and the self-congratulatory tendency to tell you how great it was and how, like Woodstock or the March on the Pentagon, you should have been there and what you missed. I want to resist this cheap (and now thoroughly commodified) nostalgia. And yet I'm also acutely aware that the smell of pot and tear gas was still lingering in the air in 1980, even as the Reagan era began. So let me put it this way: here I am, now deep in my middle age, writing about a moment twenty years ago in the hopes of interesting the rising generation of writing teachers and theorists in what "The Study of Error" could possibly mean for all of us. Here are two possibilities.

First, "The Study of Error" figures as an anticipatory sign of what you can do, as a writing teacher, with the kind of close reading developed in literary studies—once, as Bartholomae urges, you shift this habit of attention from the aesthetically valued text to ordinary writing. Glancing backwards anyway, it looks virtually inevitable that from "The Study of Error" would come Bartholomae's subsequent work, such as "Inventing the University," *Facts, Artifacts, and Counterfacts,* and *Ways of Reading,* and his debates with Peter Elbow, marked as they are by the influence of poststructuralism and composition's turn to textualist theories. My point, however, is that to fix "The Study of Error" in its moment is to denote a time before we knew all that much about Derrida, Barthes, and Foucault, when a generation of writing teachers raised on the New Criticism (and largely without the advantages of graduate education in rhetoric or composition) mobilized the only resources available to them—to use close reading and the tenets of practical criticism not as a technical facility with literary analysis (as postwar literature textbooks make the New Criticism out to be) but, in the spirit of F. R. Leavis and the *Scrutiny* project, as a matter of accountability and a means of discriminating judgment and the criticism of life.[2] What "The Study of Error" presses on us is the possibility of becoming a new kind of reader, to see student texts—in particular those of basic writers—not in terms of cultural and linguistic deficits but as expressions of ordinary people struggling to acquire the power of literacy. Whether Bartholomae highjacked the New Criticism to do this or simply joined its natural sympathies to the popular forces seeking open access to higher education is a question that might be answered a number of ways, depending, no doubt, on your view of the mission of English studies and the relationship between composition and literature.

My second point is more dire. While it's reasonable, I believe, to see "The Study of Error" as an important instance of writing teachers in the 1970s and early 1980s using their literary training to rerepresent literacy and illiteracy, correctness and error, standard English and subordinate vernaculars, we have nonetheless failed to institutionalize these incontestable intellectual gains in a system of popular higher education. If anything, as I've already suggested, conservative politicians are currently speaking in a discourse of "standards" to undermine the belief we find so powerfully articulated in "The Study of Error" that basic writers are in fact legitimate and educable students. At CUNY, in the California state system, and throughout the nation, the term "literacy" is being mobilized once again to explain the success and failure of students in class society, to withhold academic credit for basic writing courses, or to farm them out to entrepreneurs in the private sector as "precollege" remediation.

The final footnote in "The Study of Error" provides a sense of what it will take to reverse these trends. Bartholomae says, "The research for this study was funded by a research grant from the National Council of Teachers of English." In what might otherwise be seen simply as the normal academic courtesy of acknowledgement, Bartholomae helps us see that the project of basic writing depends in critical ways on the allocation of resources. In this regard, it is useful to recall that the basic writing program at the University of Pittsburgh, in its heyday at least, deployed team teaching (a notoriously non–cost effective arrangement), and the collection *Facts, Artifacts, and Counterfacts* stands as a telling indication of what can be done when you've got enough money to do it. To my mind, there is an inescapable bottom line to "The Study of Error"—not to mention the hopes of a generation of writing teachers to open American colleges and universities to ordinary people—and that is, to put it bluntly, a matter of political economy and the political will to secure support for a literate democracy.

Notes

1. "Around 1980" is the title of Bartholomae's afterword to Victor J. Vitanza's collection *Pre/Text: The First Decade* (U of Pittsburgh P, 1993)—and in turn is borrowed from the title of Jane Gallop's book of feminist criticism *Around 1981: Academic Feminist Literary Theory* (Routledge, 1991).

2. It's worth noting that Leavis was concerned crucially with influencing pedagogy as well as literary standards and that Leavisites trained in the 1930s and 1940s at Cambridge were instrumental in establishing the National Association of Teachers of English and the adult education movement in the postwar period.

Works Cited

Bartholomae, David. "Inventing the University." *When a Writer Can't Write: Studies in Writer's Block and Other Composing Process Problems.* Ed. Mike Rose. New York: Guilford, 1985. 134–65.

———. "The Study of Error." *College Composition and Communication* 31 (1980): 253–69.

———. "Writing with Teachers: A Conversation with Peter Elbow." *College Composition and Communication* 46 (1995): 62–71.

Bartholomae, David, and Anthony R. Petrosky. *Facts, Artifacts, and Counterfacts.* Upper Montclair, NJ: Boynton, 1986.

Shaughnessy, Mina. "Diving In: An Introduction to Basic Writing." *College Composition and Communication* 27 (1976): 234–39.

———. *Errors and Expectations: A Guide for the Teacher of Basic Writing.* New York: Oxford UP, 1977.

The Study of Error (1980)

David Bartholomae

It is curious, I think, that with all the current interest in "Basic Writing,"
little attention has been paid to the most basic question: What is it? What
is "basic writing," that is, if the term is to refer to a phenomenon, an activity, something a writer does or has done, rather than to a course of instruction? We know that across the country students take tests of one sort or
another and are placed in courses that bear the title, "Basic Writing." But
all we know is that there are students taking courses. We know little about
their performance as writers, beyond the bald fact that they fail to do what
other, conventionally successful, writers do. We don't, then, have an adequate description of the variety of writing we call "basic."

On the other hand, we have considerable knowledge of what Basic Writing courses are like around the country, the texts that are used, the approaches taken. For some time now, "specialists" have been devising and
refining the technology of basic or developmental instruction. But these
technicians are tinkering with pedagogies based on what? At best on models of how successful writers write. At worst, on old text-book models that
disregard what writers actually do or how they could be said to learn, and
break writing conveniently into constituent skills like "word power," "sentence power," and "paragraph power." Neither pedagogy is built on the
results of any systematic inquiry into what basic writers do when they write
or into the way writing skills develop for beginning adult writers. Such basic
research has barely begun. Mina Shaughnessy argued the case this way:

> Those pedagogies that served the profession for years seem no longer
> appropriate to large numbers of students, and their inappropriateness
> lies largely in the fact that many of our students . . . are adult begin-
> ners and depend as students did not depend in the past upon the class-
> room and the teacher for the acquisition of the skill of writing.

If the profession is going to accept responsibility for teaching this kind
student, she concludes, "We are committed to research of a very ambitious
sort."[1]

This essay first appeared in *College Composition and Communication* 31 (1980): 253–60. Copyright © 1980 by the National Council of Teachers of English. Reprinted with permission.

Where might such research begin, and how might it proceed? We must begin by studying basic writing itself—the phenomenon, not the course of instruction. If we begin here, we will recognize at once that "basic" does not mean simple or childlike. These are beginning writers, to be sure, but they are not writers who need to learn to use language. They are writers who need to learn to command a particular variety of language—the language of a written, academic discourse—and a particular variety of language use—writing itself. The writing of a basic writer can be shown to be an approximation of conventional written discourse; it is a peculiar and idiosyncratic version of a highly conventional type, but the relation between the approximate and the conventional forms is not the same as the relation between the writing, say, of a 7th grader and the writing of a college freshman.

Basic writing, I want to argue, is a variety of writing, not writing with fewer parts or more rudimentary constituents. It is not evidence of arrested cognitive development, arrested language development, or unruly or unpredictable language use. The writer of this sentence, for example, could not be said to be writing an "immature" sentence in any sense of the term, if we grant her credit for the sentence she intended to write:

> The time of my life when I learned something, and which resulted in a change in which I look upon life things. This would be the period of my life when I graduated from Elementary school to High school.

When we have used conventional T-unit analysis, and included in our tabulations figures on words/clause, words/T-unit and clauses/T-unit that were drawn from "intended T-units" as well as actual T-units, we have found that basic writers do not, in general, write "immature" sentences. They are not, that is, 13th graders writing 7th grade sentences. In fact, they often attempt syntax whose surface is more complex than that of more successful freshman writers. They get into trouble by getting in over their heads, not only attempting to do more than they can, but imagining as their target a syntax that is *more* complex than convention requires. The failed sentences, then, could be taken as stages of learning rather than the failure to learn, but also as evidence that these writers are using writing as an occasion to learn.

It is possible to extend the concept of "intentional structures" to the analysis of complete essays in order to determine the "grammar" that governs the idiosyncratic discourse of writers imagining the language and conventions of academic discourse in unconventional ways. This method of analysis is certainly available to English teachers, since it requires a form of close reading, paying attention to the language of a text in order to determine not only what a writer says, but how he locates and articulates meaning. When a basic writer violates our expectations, however, there is a tendency to dismiss the text as non-writing, as meaningless or imperfect writing. We have not read as we have been trained to read, with a particular interest in the way an individual style confronts and violates convention. We have read, rather, as policemen, examiners, gate-keepers. The teacher who is unable to make sense out of a seemingly bizarre piece of student writing is often the same teacher who can give an elaborate explanation of the "meaning" of a story by Donald Barthelme or a poem by e. e. cummings. If we learn to treat the language of basic writing *as* language and assume, as we do when writers violate our expectations in more conventional ways, that the unconventional features in the writing are evidence of intention and that they are, therefore, meaningful, then we can chart systematic choices, individual strategies, and characteristic processes of thought. One can read Mina Shaughnessy's *Errors and Expectations* as the record of just such a close reading.[2]

There is a style, then, to the apparently bizarre and incoherent writing of a basic writer because it is, finally, evidence of an individual using language to make and transcribe meaning. This is one of the axioms of error analysis, whether it be applied to reading (as in "miscue analysis"), writing, or second-language learning. An error (and I would include errors beyond those in the decoding or encoding of sentences) can only be understood as evidence of intention. They are the only evidence we have of an individual's idiosyncratic way of using the language and articulating meaning, of imposing a style on common material. A writer's activity is linguistic and rhetorical activity; it can be different but never random. The task for both teacher and researcher, then, is to discover the grammar of *that* coherence, of the "idiosyncratic dialect" that belongs to a particular writer at a particular moment in the history of his attempts to imagine and reproduce the standard idiom of academic discourse.[3]

All writing, of course, could be said to only approximate conventional discourse; our writing is never either completely predictable or completely idiosyncratic. We speak our own language as well as the language of the tribe and, in doing so, make concessions to both ourselves and our culture. The distance between text and conventional expectation may be a sign of failure and it may be a sign of genius, depending on the level of control and intent we are willing to assign to the writer, and depending on the insight we acquire from seeing convention so transformed. For a basic writer the distance between text and convention is greater than it is for the run-of-the-mill freshmen writer. It may be, however, that the more talented the freshman writer becomes, the more able she is to increase again the distance between text and convention.

We are drawn to conclude that basic writers lack control, although it may be more precise to say that they lack choice and option, the power to make decisions about the idiosyncrasy of their writing. Their writing is not, however, truly uncontrolled. About the actual distance from text to convention for the basic writer, we know very little. We know that it will take a long time to traverse—generally the greater the distance the greater the time and energy required to close the gap. We know almost nothing about the actual sequence of development—the natural sequence of learning—that moves a writer from basic writing to competent writing to good writing. The point, however, is that "basic writing" is something our students *do* or *produce;* it is not a kind of writing we teach to backward or unprepared students. We should not spend our time imagining simple or "basic" writing tasks, but studying the errors that emerge when beginning writers are faced with complex tasks.

The mode of analysis that seems most promising for the research we need on the writer's sequence of learning is error analysis. Error analysis provides the basic writing teacher with both a technique for analyzing errors in the production of discourse, a technique developed by linguists to study second language learning, and a theory of error, or, perhaps more properly, a perspective on error, where errors are seen as (1) necessary stages of individual development and (2) data that provide insight into the idiosyncratic strategies of a particular language user at a particular point in his acquisition of a target language. Enough has been written lately about error analysis that I'll only give a brief summary of its perspective on second language or second dialect acquisition.[4] I want to go on to look closely at error analysis as a method, in order to point out its strengths and limits as a procedure for textual analysis.

George Steiner has argued that all acts of interpretation are acts of translation and are, therefore, subject to the constraints governing the passage from one language to another.[5] All our utterances are approximations, attempts to use the language of, say, Frank Kermode or the language, perhaps of our other, smarter, wittier self. In this sense, the analogy that links developmental composition instruction with second language learning can be a useful one—useful that is, if the mode of learning (whatever the "second" language) is writing rather than speaking. (This distinction, I might add, is not generally made in the literature on error analysis, where writing and speech are taken as equivalent phenomena.) Error analysis begins with the recognition that errors, or the points where the actual text varies from a hypothetical "standard" text, will be either random or systematic. If they are systematic in the writing of an individual writer, then they are evidence of some idiosyncratic rule system—an idiosyncratic grammar or rhetoric, and "interlanguage" or "approximative system."[6] If the errors are systematic across all basic writers, then they would be evidence of generalized stages in the acquisition of fluent writing for beginning adult writers. This distinction between individual and general systems is an important one for both teaching and research. It is not one that Shaughnessy makes. We don't know whether the categories of error in *Errors and Expectations* hold across a group, and, if so, with what frequency and across a group of what size.

Shaughnessy did not find, however, predictable patterns in the errors in the essays she studied. She demonstrated that even the most apparently incoherent writing, if we are sensitive to its intentional structure, is evidence of systematic, coherent, rule-governed behavior. Basic writers, she demonstrated, are not performing mechanically or randomly but making choices and forming strategies as they struggle to deal with the varied demands of a task, a language, and a rhetoric. The "systems" such writing exhibits provide evidence that basic writers *are* competent, mature language users. Their attempts at producing written language are not hit and miss, nor are they evidence of simple translation of speech into print. The approximate systems they produce are evidence that they can conceive of and manipulate written language as a structured, systematic code. They are "intermediate" systems in that they mark stages on route to mastery (or, more properly, on route to conventional fluency) of written, academic discourse.

This also, however, requires some qualification. They *may* be evidence of some transitional stage. They may also, to use Selinker's term, be evidence of "stabilized variability," where a writer is stuck or searching rather than moving on toward more complete approximation of the target language.[7] A writer will stick with some intermediate system if he is convinced that the language he uses "works," or if he is unable to see errors *as* errors and form alternate hypotheses in response.

Error analysis begins with a theory of writing, a theory of language production and language development, that allows us to see errors as evidence of choice or strategy among a range of possible choices or strategies. They provide evidence of an individual style of using the language and making it work; they are not a simple record of what a writer failed to do because of incompetence or indifference. Errors, then, are stylistic features, information about *this* writer and *this* language; they are not necessarily "noise" in the system, accidents of composing, or malfunctions in the language process. Consequently, we cannot identify errors without identifying them in context, and the context is not the text, but the activity of composing that presented the erroneous form as a possible solution to the problem of making a meaningful statement. Shaughnessy's taxonomy of error, for example, identifies errors according to their source, not their type. A single type of error could be attributed to a variety of causes. Donald Freeman's research, for example, has shown that, "subject-verb agreement . . . is a host of errors, not one." One of his students analyzed a "large sample of real world sentences and concluded that there are at least eight different kinds, most of which have very little to do with one another."[8]

Error analysis allows us to place error in the context of composing and to interpret and classify systematic errors. The key concept is the concept of an "interlanguage" or an "intermediate system," an idiosyncratic grammar and rhetoric that is a writer's approximation of the standard idiom. Errors, while they can be given more precise classification, fall into three main categories: errors that are evidence of an intermediate system; errors that could truly be said to be accidents, or slips of the pen as writer's mind rushes ahead faster than his hand; and, finally, errors of language transfer, or, more commonly, dialect interference, where in the attempt to produce the target language, the writer intrudes forms from the "first" or "native" language rather than inventing some intermediate form. For writers, this intrusion most often comes from a spoken dialect. The error analyst is primarily concerned, however, with errors that are evidence of some intermediate system. This kind of error occurs because the writer *is* an active, competent language user who uses his knowledge that language is rule-governed, and who uses his ability to predict and form analogies, to construct hypotheses that can make an irregular or unfamiliar language more manageable. The problem comes when the rule is incorrect or, more properly, when it is idiosyncratic, belonging only to the language of this writer. There is evidence of an idiosyncratic system, for example, when a student adds inflectional endings to infinitives, as in this sentence, "There was plenty the boy had to *learned* about birds." It also seems to be evident in a sentence like this: "This assignment calls on *choosing* one of my papers and making a last draft out of it." These errors can be further sub-divided into those that are in flux and mark a fully transitional stage, and those that, for one reason or another, become frozen and recur across time.

Kroll and Schafer, in a recent *CCC* article, argue that the value of error analysis for the composition teacher is the perspective it offers on the learner, since it allows us to see errors "as clues to inner processes, as windows into the mind."[9] If we investigate the pattern of error in the performance of an individual writer, we can better understand the nature of those errors and the way they "fit" in an individual writer's program for writing. As a consequence, rather than impose an inappropriate or even misleading syllabus on a learner, we can plan instruction to assist a writer's internal syllabus. If, for example, a writer puts standard inflections on irregular verbs or on verbs that are used in verbals (as in "I used to runned"), drill on verb endings will only reinforce the rule that, because the writer is overgeneralizing, is the source of the error in the first place. By charting and analyzing a writer's errors, we can begin in our instruction with what a writer *does* rather than with what he fails to do. It makes no sense, for example, to impose lessons on the sentence on a student whose problems with syntax can be understood in more precise terms. It makes no sense to teach spelling to an individual who has trouble principally with words that contain vowel clusters. Error analysis, then, is a method of diagnosis.

Error analysis can assist instruction at another level. By having students share in the process of investigating and interpreting the patterns of error in their writing, we can help them begin to see those errors as evidence of hypotheses or strategies they have formed and, as a consequence, put them in a position to change, experiment, imagine other strategies. Studying their own writing puts students in a position to see themselves as language users, rather than as victims of a language that uses them.

This, then, is the perspective and the technique of error analysis. To interpret a student paper without this frame of reference is to misread, as for example when a teacher sees an incorrect verb form and concludes that the student doesn't understand the rules for indicating tense or number. I want, now, to examine error analysis as a procedure for the study of errors in written composition. It presents two problems. The first can be traced to the fact that error analysis was developed for studying errors in spoken performance.[10] It can be transferred to writing only to the degree that writing is like speech, and there are significant points of difference. It is generally acknowledged, for example, that written discourse is not just speech written down on paper. Adult written discourse has a grammar and rhetoric that is different from speech. And clearly the activity of producing language is different for a writer than it is for a speaker.

The "second language" a basic writer must learn to master is formal, written discourse, a discourse whose lexicon, grammar and rhetoric are learned not through speaking and listening but through reading and writing. The process of acquisition is visual not aural. Furthermore, basic writers do not necessarily produce writing by translating speech into print (the way children learning to write would); that is, they must draw on a memory for graphemes rather than phonemes. This is a different order of memory and production from that used in speech and gives rise to errors unique to writing.

Writing also, however, presents "interference" of a type never found in speech. Errors in writing may be caused by interference from the act of writing itself, from the difficulty of moving a pen across the page quickly enough to keep up with the words in the writer's mind, or from the difficulty of recalling and producing the connections that are necessary for producing print rather than speech, conventions of spelling, orthography, punctuation, capitalization and so on. This is not, however, just a way of saying that writers make spelling errors and speakers do not. As Shaughnessy pointed out, errors of syntax can be traced to the gyrations of a writer trying to avoid a word that her sentence has led her to, but that she knows she cannot spell.

The second problem in applying error analysis to the composition classroom arises from special properties in the taxonomy of errors we chart in student writing. Listing varieties of errors is not like listing varieties of rocks or butterflies. What a reader finds depends to a large degree on her assumptions about the writer's intention. Any systematic attempt to chart a learner's errors is clouded by the difficulty of assigning intention through textual analysis. The analyst begins, then, by interpreting a text, not by describing features on a page. And interpretation is less than a precise science.

Let me turn to an example. This is part of a paper that a student, John, wrote in response to an assignment that asked him to go back to some papers he had written on significant moments in his life in order to write a paper that considered the general question of the way people change.

> This assignment call on chosing one of my incident making a last draft out of it. I found this very differcult because I like them all but you said I had to pick one so the Second incident was decide. Because this one had the most important insight to my life that I indeed learn from. This insight explain why adulthood mean that much as it dose to me because I think it alway influence me to change and my outlook on certain thing like my point-of-view I have one day and it might change the next week on the same issue. So in these frew words I going to write about the incident now. My experience took place in my high school and the reason was out side of school but I will show you the connection. The situation took place cause of the type of school I went too. Let me tell you about the situation first of all what happen was that I got suspense from school. For thing that I fell was out of my control sometime, but it taught me alot about respondability of a growing man. The school suspense me for being late ten time. I had

accummate ten dementic and had to bring my mother to school to talk to a conselor and Prinpicable of the school what when on at the meet took me out mentally period.

One could imagine a variety of responses to this. The first would be to form the wholesale conclusion that John can't write and to send him off to a workbook. Once he had learned how to write correct sentences, then he could go on the business of actually writing. Let me call this the "old-style" response to error. A second response, which I'll call the "investigative approach," would be to chart the patterns of error in this particular text. Of the approximately 40 errors in the first 200 words, the majority fall under four fairly specific categories: verb endings, noun plurals, syntax, and spelling. The value to pedagogy is obvious. One is no longer teaching a student to "write" but to deal with a limited number of very specific kinds of errors, each of which would suggest its own appropriate response. Furthermore, it is possible to refine the categories and to speculate on and organize them according to cause. The verb errors almost all involve "s" or "ed" endings, which could indicate dialect interference or a failure to learn the rules for indicating tense and number. It is possible to be even more precise. The passage contains 41 verbs; only 17 of them are used incorrectly. With the exception of four spelling errors, the errors are all errors of inflection and, furthermore, these errors come only with regular verbs. There are no errors with irregular verbs. This would suggest, then, that when John draws on memory for a verb form, he gets it right; but when John applies a rule to determine the ending, he gets it wrong.

The errors of syntax could be divided into those that might be called punctuation errors (or errors that indicate a difficulty perceiving the boundaries of the sentence), such as

> Let me tell you about the situation first of all what happen was that I got suspense from school. For thing that I fell was out of my control sometime, but it taught me a lot about respondability of a growing man.

and errors of syntax that would fall under Shaughnessy's category of consolidation errors,

> This insight explain why adulthood mean that much as it dose to me because I think it always influence me to change and my outlook on certain thing like my point-of-view I have one day and it might change the next week on the same issue.

One would also want to note the difference between consistent errors, the substitution of "situation" for "situation" or "suspense" for "suspended," and unstable ones, as for example, when John writes "cause" in one place and "because" in another. In one case John could be said to have fixed on a rule; in the other he is searching for one. One would also want to distinguish between what might seem to be "accidental" errors, like substituting "frew" for "few" or "when" for "went," errors that might best be addressed by teaching a student to edit, and those whose causes are deeper and require time and experience, or some specific instructional strategy.

I'm not sure, however, that this analysis provides an accurate representation of John's writing. Consider what happens when John reads this paper out loud. I've been taping students reading their own papers, and I've developed a system of notation, like that used in miscue analysis,[11] that will allow me to record the points of variation between the writing that is on the page and the writing that is spoken, or, to use the terminology of miscue analysis, between the expected response (ER) and the observed response (OR). What I've found is that students will often, or in predictable instances, substitute correct forms for the incorrect forms on the page, even though they are generally unaware that such a substitution was made. This observation suggests the limits of conventional error analysis for the study of error in written composition.

I asked John to read his paper out loud, and to stop and correct or note any mistakes he found. Let me try to reproduce the transcript of that reading. I will underline any substitution or correction and offer some comments in parentheses. The reader might first go back and review the original. Here is what John read:

> This assignment calls on <u>choosing</u> one of my incident making a last draft out of it. I found this very dif<u>f</u>icult because I like them all but you said I <u>had</u> to pick one so the Second incident was decided <u>on.</u> Because (John goes back and rereads, connecting up the subordinate clause.) So the second incident was decided on because this one had the most important insight to my life that I indeed learn<u>ed</u> from. This insight explains why adulthood <u>meant</u> that much as it dose to me because I think it alway<u>s</u> influence<u>s</u> me to change and my outlook on certain thing<u>s</u> like my point-of-view I have one day and it might change the next week on the same issue. (John goes back and rereads, beginning with "like my point of view," and he is puzzled but makes no additional changes.) So in these <u>few</u> words <u>I'm</u> going to write about the incident now. My exp<u>e</u>rience took place <u>be</u>cause of the type of school I went to (John had written "too.") Let me tell you about the situation (John comes to a full stop.) first of all what happen<u>ed</u> was that I got <u>suspended</u> from school (no full stop) for thing<u>s</u> that I <u>felt</u>

was out of my control sometime, but it taught me a lot about <u>respon-sibility</u> of a growing man. The school <u>suspended</u> me for being late ten times. I had <u>accumulated</u> (for "accumate") ten <u>demerits</u> (for "de-mentic") and had to bring my mother to school to talk to a counse-lor and <u>the Principal</u> of the school (full stop) what <u>went</u> on at the meet<u>ing</u> took me out mentally (full stop) period (with brio).

I have chosen an extreme case to make my point, but what one sees here is the writer correcting almost every error as he reads the paper, even though he is not able to recognize that there *are* errors or that he has corrected them. The only errors John spotted (where he stopped, noted an error and cor-rected it) were the misspellings of "situation" and "Principal," and the sub-stitution "chosing" for "choosing." Even when he was asked to reread sen-tences to see if he could notice any difference between what he was saying and the words on the page, he could not. He could not, for example, see the error in "frew" or "dementic" or any of the other verb errors, and yet he spoke the correct form of every verb (with the exception of "was" after he had changed "thing" to "things" in "for thing*s* that I *felt* was out of my control") and he corrected every plural. His phrasing as he read produced correct syntax, except in the case of the consolidation error, which he puzzled over but did not correct. It's important to note, however, that John did not read that confused syntax as if no confusion were there. He sensed the dif-ference between the phrasing called for by the meaning of the sentence and that which existed on the page. He did not read as though meaning didn't matter or as though the "meaning" coded on the page was complete. His problem cannot be simply a syntax problem, since the jumble is bound up with his struggle to articulate this particular meaning. And it is not simply a "thinking" problem—John doesn't write this way because he thinks this way—since he perceives that the statement as it is written is other than that which he intended.

When I asked John why the paper (which went on for two more pages) was written all as one paragraph, he replied, "It was all one idea. I didn't want to have to start all over again. I had a good idea and I didn't want to give it up." John doesn't need to be "taught" the paragraph, at least not as the paragraph is traditionally taught. His prose is orderly and proceeds through blocks of discourse. He tells the story of his experience at the school and concludes that through his experience he realized that he must accept responsibility for his tardiness, even though the tardiness was not his fault but the fault of the Philadelphia subway system. He concludes that with this realization he learned "the responsibility of a growing man." Further-more John knows that the print code carries certain conventions for ordering and presenting discourse. His translation of the notion that "a paragraph develops a single idea" is peculiar but not illogical.

It could also be argued that John does not need to be "taught" to produce correct verb forms, or, again, at least not as such things are conventionally taught. Fifteen weeks of drill on verb endings might raise his test scores but they would not change the way he writes. He *knows* how to produce correct endings. He demonstrated that when he read, since he was reading in terms of his grammatical competence. His problem is a problem of performance, or fluency, not of competence. There is certainly no evidence that the verb errors are due to interference from his spoken language. And if the errors could be traced to some intermediate system, the system exists only in John's performance as a writer. It does not operate when he reads or, for that matter, when he speaks, if his oral reconstruction of his own text can be taken as a record of John "speaking" the idiom of academic discourse.[12]

John's case also highlights the tremendous difficulty such a student has with editing, where a failure to correct a paper is not evidence of laziness or inattention or a failure to know correct forms, but evidence of the tremendous difficulty such a student has objectifying language and seeing it as black and white marks on the page, where things can be wrong even though the meaning seems right.[13] One of the hardest errors for John to spot, after all my coaching, was the substitution of "frew" for "few," certainly not an error that calls into question John's competence as a writer. I can call this a "performance" error, but that term doesn't suggest the constraints on performance in writing. This is an important area for further study. Surely one constraint is the difficulty of moving the hand fast enough to translate meaning into print. The burden imposed on their patience and short term memory by the slow, awkward handwriting of many inexperienced writers is a very real one. But I think the constraints extend beyond the difficulty of forming words quickly with pen or pencil.

One of the most interesting results of the comparison of the spoken and written versions of John's text is his inability to *see* the difference between "frew" and "few" or "dementic" and "demerit." What this suggests is that John reads and writes from the "top down" rather than the "bottom up," to use a distinction made by cognitive psychologists in their study of reading.[14] John is not operating through the lower level process of translating orthographic information into sounds and sounds into meaning when he reads. And conversely, he is not working from meaning to sound to word when he is writing. He is, rather, retrieving lexical items directly, through a "higher level" process that by-passes the "lower level" operation of phonetic translation. When I put *frew* and *few* on the blackboard, John read them both as "few." The lexical item "few" is represented for John by either orthographic array. He is not, then, reading or writing phonetically, which is a sign, from one perspective, of a high level of fluency, since the activity is automatic and not mediated by the more primitive operation of translating speech into print or print into speech. When John was writing, he did not produce "frew" or "dementic" by searching for sound/letter correspondences. He drew directly upon his memory for the look and shape of those words; he was working from the top down rather than the bottom up. He went to stored print forms and did not take the slower route of translating speech into writing.

John, then, has reached a stage of fluency in writing where he directly and consistently retrieves print forms, like "dementic," that are meaningful to him, even though they are idiosyncratic. I'm not sure what all the implications of this might be, but we surely must see John's problem in a new light, since his problem can, in a sense, be attributed to his skill. To ask John to slow down his writing and sound out words would be disastrous. Perhaps the most we can do is to teach John the slowed down form of reading he will need in order to edit.

John's paper also calls into question our ability to identify accidental errors. I suspect that when John substitutes a word like "when" for "went," this is an accidental error, a slip of the pen. Since John spoke "went" when he read, I cannot conclude that he substituted "when" for "went" because he pronounces both as "wen." This, then, is not an error of dialect interference but an accidental error, the same order of error as the omission of "the" before "Principal." Both were errors John corrected while reading (even though he didn't identify them as errors).

What is surprising is that, with all the difficulty John had identifying errors, he immediately saw that he had written "chosing" rather than "choosing." While textual analysis would have led to the conclusion that he was applying a tense rule to a participial construction, or over-generalizing from a known rule, the ease with which it was identified would lead one to conclude that it was, in fact, a mistake, and not evidence of an approximate system. What would have been diagnosed as a deep error now appears to be only an accidental error, a "mistake" (or perhaps a spelling error).

In summary, this analysis of John's reading produces a healthy respect for the tremendous complexity of transcription, for the process of recording meaning in print as opposed to the process of generating meaning. It also points out the difficulty of charting a learner's "interlanguage" or "intermediate system," since we are working not only with a writer moving between a first and a second language, but a writer whose performance is subject to the interference of transcription, of producing meaning through the print code. We need, in general, to refine our understanding of performance-based errors, and we need to refine our teaching to take into account the high percentage of error in written composition that is rooted in the difficulty of performance rather than in problems of general linguistic competence.

Let me pause for a moment to put what I've said in the context of work error analysis. Such analysis is textual analysis. It requires the reader to make assumptions about intention on the basis of information in the text. The writer's errors provide the most important information since they provide insight into the idiosyncratic systems the writer has developed. The regular but unconventional features in the writing will reveal the rules and strategy operating for the basic writer.

The basic procedure for such analysis could be outlined this way. First the reader must identify the idiosyncratic construction; he must determine what is an error. This is often difficult, as in the case of fragments, which are conventionally used for effect. Here is an example of a sentence whose syntax could clearly be said to be idiosyncratic:

> In high school you learn alot for example Kindergarten which I took in high school.[15]

The reader, then, must reconstruct that sentence based upon the most reasonable interpretation of the intention in the original, and this must be done *before* the error can be classified, since it will be classified according to its cause.[16] Here is Shaughnessy's reconstruction of the example given above: "In high school you learn a lot. For example, I took up the study of Kindergarten in high school." For any idiosyncratic sentence, however, there are often a variety of possible reconstructions, depending on the reader's sense of the larger meaning of which this individual sentence is only a part, but also depending upon the reader's ability to predict how this writer puts sentences together, that is, on an understanding of this individual style. The text is being interpreted, not described. I've had graduate students who have reconstructed the following sentence, for example, in a variety of ways:

> Why do we have womens liberation and their fighting for Equal Rights ect. to be recognized not as a lady but as an Individual.

It could be read, "Why do we have women's liberation and why are they fighting for Equal Rights? In order that women may be recognized not as ladies but as individuals." And, "Why do we have women's liberation and their fight for equal rights, to be recognized not as a lady but as an individual?" There is an extensive literature on the question of interpretation and intention in prose, too extensive for the easy assumption that all a reader has to do is identify what the writer would have written if he wanted to "get it right the first time." The great genius of Shaughnessy's study, in fact, is the remarkable wisdom and sympathy of her interpretations of student texts.

Error analysis, then, involves more than just making lists of the errors in a student essay and looking for patterns to emerge. It begins with the double perspective of text and reconstructed text and seeks to explain the difference between the two on the basis of whatever can be inferred about the meaning of the text and the process of creating it. The reader/researcher brings to bear his general knowledge of how basic writers write, but also whatever is known about the linguistic and rhetorical constraints that govern an individual act of writing. In Shaughnessy's analysis of the "kindergarten" sentence, this discussion is contained in the section on "consolidation errors" in the chapter on "Syntax."[17] The key point, however, is that any such analysis must draw upon extra-textual information as well as close stylistic analysis.

This paper has illustrated two methods for gathering information about how a text was created. A teacher can interview the student and ask him to explain his error. John wrote this sentence in another paper for my course:

I would to write about my experience helping 1600 childrens have a happy christmas.

The missing word (I would *like* to write about . . .) he supplied when reading the sentence aloud. It is an accidental error and can be addressed by teaching editing. It is the same kind of error as his earlier substitution of "when" for "went." John used the phrase, "1600 childrens," throughout his paper, however. The conventional interpretation would have it that this is evidence of dialect interference. And yet, when John read the paper out loud, he consistently read "1600 children," even though he had said he did not see any difference between the word he spoke and the word that was on the page. When I asked him to explain why he put an "s" on the end of "children," he replied, "Because there were 1600 of them." John had a rule for forming plurals that he used when he wrote but not when he spoke. Writing, as he rightly recognized, has its own peculiar rules and constraints. It is different from speech. The error is not due to interference from his spoken language but to his conception of the "code" of written discourse.

The other method for gathering information is having students read aloud their own writing, and having them provide an oral reconstruction of their written text. What I've presented in my analysis of John's essay is a method for recording the discrepancies between the written and spoken versions of a single text. The record of a writer reading provides a version of the "intended" text that can supplement the teacher's or researcher's own reconstruction and aid in the interpretation of errors, whether they be accidental, interlingual, or due to dialect interference. I had to read John's paper very differently once I had heard him read it.

More importantly, however, this method of analysis can provide access to an additional type of error. This is the error that can be attributed to the physical and conceptual demands of writing rather than speaking; it can be traced to the requirements of manipulating a pen and the requirements of manipulating the print code.[18]

In general, when writers read, and read in order to spot and correct errors, their responses will fall among the following categories:

1. overt corrections—errors a reader sees, acknowledges, and corrects;
2. spoken corrections—errors the writer does not acknowledge but corrects in reading;
3. no recognition—errors that are read as written;
4. overcorrection—correct forms made incorrect, or incorrect forms substituted for incorrect forms;
5. acknowledged error—errors a reader senses but cannot correct;
6. reader miscue—a conventional miscue, not linked to error in the text;
7. nonsense—In this case, the reader reads a non-sentence or a nonsense sentence as though it were correct and meaningful. No error or confusion is acknowledged. This applies to errors of syntax only.

Corrections, whether acknowledged or unacknowledged, would indicate performance-based errors. The other responses (with the exception of "reader miscues") would indicate deeper errors, errors that, when charted, would provide evidence of some idiosyncratic grammar or rhetoric.

John "miscues" by completing or correcting the text that he has written. When reading researchers have readers read out loud, they have them read someone else's writing, of course, and they are primarily concerned with the "quality" of the miscues.[19] All fluent readers will miscue; that is, they will not repeat verbatim the words on the page. Since fluent readers are reading for meaning, they are actively predicting what will come and processing large chunks of graphic information at a time. They do not read individual words, and they miscue because they speak what they expect to see rather than what is actually on the page. One indication of a reader's proficiency, then, is that the miscues don't destroy the "sense" of the passage. Poor readers will produce miscues that jumble the meaning of a passage, as in

Text: Her wings were folded quietly at her sides.
Reader: Her wings were floated quickly at her sides.

or they will correct miscues that do not affect meaning in any significant way.[20]

The situation is different when a reader reads his own text, since this reader already knows what the passage means and attention is drawn, then, to the representation of that meaning. Reading also frees a writer from the constraints of transcription, which for many basic writers is an awkward, laborious process, putting excessive demands on both patience and short-term memory. John, like any reader, read what he expected to see, but with a low percentage of meaning-related miscues, since the meaning, for him, was set, and with a high percentage of code-related miscues, where a correct form was substituted for an incorrect form.

The value of studying students' oral reconstruction of their written texts is threefold. The first is a diagnostic tool. I've illustrated in my analysis of John's paper how such a diagnosis might take place.

It is also a means of instruction. By having John read aloud and, at the same time, look for discrepancies between what he spoke and what was on the page, I was teaching him a form of reading. The most dramatic change in John's performance over the term was in the number of errors he could spot and correct while re-reading. This far exceeded the number of errors he was able to eliminate from his first drafts. I could teach John an editing procedure better than I could teach him to be correct at the point of transcription.

The third consequence of this form of analysis, or of conventional error analysis, has yet to be demonstrated, but the suggestions for research are clear. It seems evident that we can chart stages of growth in individual basic writers. The pressing question is whether we can chart a sequence of "natural" development for the class of writers we call basic writers. If all non-fluent adult writers proceed through a "natural" learning sequence, and if we can identify that sequence through some large, longitudinal study, then we will begin to understand what a basic writing course or text or syllabus might look like. There are studies of adult second language learners that suggest that there is a general, natural sequence of acquisition for adults learning a second language, one that is determined by the psychology of language production and language acquisition.[21] Before we can adapt these methods to a study of basic writers, however, we need to better understand the additional constraints of learning to transcribe and manipulate the "code" of written discourse. John's case illustrates where we might begin and what we must know.[22]

Notes

1. Mina Shaughnessy, "Some Needed Research on Writing," *CCC,* 28 (December, 1977), 317, 388.

2. Mina Shaughnessy, *Errors and Expectations: A Guide for the Teacher of Basic Writing* (New York: Oxford University Press, 1977).

3. The term "idiosyncratic dialect" is taken from S. P. Corder, "Idiosyncratic Dialects and Error Analysis," in Jack C. Richards, ed., *Error Analysis: Perspectives on Second Language Acquisition* (London: Longman, 1974), pp. 158–71.

4. Barry M. Kroll and John C. Schafer, "Errors Analysis and the Teaching of Composition," *CCC,* 29 (October, 1978), 243–48. See also my review of *Errors and Expectations* in Donald McQuade, ed., *Linguistics, Stylistics and the Teaching of Composition* (Akron, Ohio: L & S Books, 1979), pp. 209–20.

5. George Steiner, *After Babel: Aspects of Language and Translation* (New York: Oxford University Press, 1975).

6. For the term "interlanguage," see L. Selinker, "Interlanguage," in Richards, ed., *Error Analysis,* pp. 31–55. For "approximate system," see William Nemser, "Approximate Systems of Foreign Language Learners," in Richards, ed., *Error Analysis,* pp. 55–64. These are more appropriate terms than "idiosyncratic dialect" for the study of error in written composition.

7. The term "stabilized variability" is quoted in Andrew D. Cohen and Margaret Robbins, "Toward Assessing Interlanguage Performance: The Relationship Between Selected Errors, Learner's Characteristics and Learner's Explanations," *Language Learning,* 26 (June, 1976), p. 59. Selinker uses the term "fossilization" to refer to single errors than recur across time, so that the interlanguage form is not evidence of a transitional stage. (See Selinker, "Interlanguage.") M. P. Jain distinguishes between "systematic," "asystematic" and "nonsystematic" errors. (See "Error Analysis: Source, Cause and Significance" in Richards, ed., *Error Analysis,* pp. 189–215.) Unsystematic errors are mistakes, "slips of the tongue." Systematic errors "seem to establish that in certain areas of language use the learner possesses construction rules." Asystematic errors lead one to the "inescapable conclusion" that "the learner's capacity to generalize must improve, for progress in learning a language is made by adopting generalizations and stretching them to match the facts of the language."

8. Donald C. Freeman, "Linguistics and Error Analysis: On Agency," in Donald McQuade, ed., *Linguistics, Stylistics and the Teaching of Composition* (Akron, Ohio: L & S Books, 1979) pp. 143–44.

9. Kroll and Schafer, "Error Analysis and the Teaching of Composition."

10. In the late 60's and early 70's, linguists began to study second language acquisition by systematically studying the actual performance of individual learners. What they studied, however, was the language a learner would speak. In the literature of error analysis, the reception and production of language is generally defined as the learner's ability to hear, learn, imitate, and independently produce *sounds.* Errors, then, are phonological substitutions, alterations, additions, and subtractions. Similarly, errors diagnosed as rooted in the mode of production (rather than, for example, in an idiosyncratic grammar or interference from the first language) are errors caused by the difficulty a learner has hearing or making foreign sounds. When we are studying written composition, we are studying a different mode of production, where a learner must see, remember, and produce marks on a page. There may be some similarity between the grammar-based errors in the two modes, speech and writing (it would be interesting to know to what degree this is true), but there should be marked differences in the nature and frequency of performance-based errors.

11. See Y. M. Goodman and C. L. Burke, *Reading Miscue Inventory: Procedure for Diagnosis and Evaluation* (New York: Macmillan, 1972).

12. Bruder and Hayden noticed a similar phenomenon. They assigned a group of students exercises in writing formal and informal dialogues. One student's informal dialogue contained the following:

What going on:
It been a long time . . .
I about through . . .
I be glad . . .

When the student read the dialogue aloud, however, these were spoken as

What's going on?
It's been a long time . . .
I'm about through . . .
I'll be glad . . .

See Mary Newton Bruder and Luddy Hayden, "Teaching Composition: A Report on a Bidialectal Approach," *Language Learning,* 23 (June, 1973), 1–15.

13. See Patricia Laurence, "Error's Endless Train: Why Students Don't Perceive Errors," *Journal of Basic Writing,* 1 (Spring, 1975), 23–43, for a different explanation of this phenomenon.

14. See, for example, J. R. Fredericksen, "Component Skills in Reading" in R. R. Snow, P. A. Federico, and W. E. Montague, eds., *Aptitude, Learning, and Instruction* (Hillsdale, N.J.: Erlbaum, 1979); D. E. Rumelhart, "Toward an Interactive Model of Reading," in S. Dornic, ed., *Attention and Performance VI* (Hillsdale, N.J.: Erlbaum, 1977); and Joseph H. Denks and Gregory O. Hill, "Interactive Models of Lexical Assessment During Oral Reading," paper presented at Conference on Interactive Processes in Reading, Learning Research and Development Center, University of Pittsburgh, September 1979.

Patrick Hartwell argued that "apparent dialect interference in writing reveals partial or imperfect mastery of a neural coding system that underlies both reading and writing" in a paper, "'Dialect Interference' in Writing: A Critical View," presented at CCCC, April 1979. This paper is available through ERIC. He predicts, in this paper, that "basic writing students, when asked to read their writing in a formal situation, . . . will make fewer errors in their reading than in their writing." I read Professor Hartwell's paper after this essay was completed, so I was unable to acknowledge his study as completely as I would have desired.

15. This example is taken from Shaughnessy, *Errors and Expectations,* p. 52.

16. Corder refers to "reconstructed sentences" in "Idiosyncratic Dialects and Error Analysis."

17. Shaughnessy, *Errors and Expectations,* pp. 51–72.

18. For a discussion of the role of the "print code" in writer's errors, see Patrick Hartwell, "Dialect Interference in Writing: A Critical View."

19. See Kenneth S. Goodman, "Miscues: Windows on the Reading Process," in Kenneth S. Goodman, ed., *Miscue Analysis: Applications to Reading Instruction* (Urbana, Illinois: ERIC, 1977), pp. 3–14.

20. This example was taken from Yetta M. Goodman, "Miscue Analysis for In-Service Reading Teachers," in K. S. Goodman, ed., *Miscue Analysis,* p. 55.

21. Nathalie Bailey, Carolyn Madden, and Stephen D. Krashen, "Is There a 'Natural Sequence' in Adult Second Language Learning?" *Language Learning*, 24 (June, 1974), 235–43.

22. This paper was originally presented at CCCC, April 1979. The research for this study was funded by a research grant from the National Council of Teachers of English.

5

Introduction to Nancy Sommers's "Responding to Student Writing"

Edward M. White

Nancy Sommers's short and unpretentious 1982 article is a genuine classic. It seems as fresh today as when I read it for the first time almost two decades ago. Responding to writing has for a century and a half taken up a substantial part of every writing teacher's work week, so much a part of the academic scene that hardly anyone thought to question just how it was going on or why. It was, to extend Pat Belanoff's comment on grading, "the dirty little thing we do in our closets" (ix). Sommers's article shone a light inside that closet and the light has not gone out since. She not only presented genuinely useful quasiexperimental research, including one of the first uses of computers in composition studies, but also made us see our most familiar activity in a new way, thus opening a new field of study. Furthermore, her writing has a grace and irony seldom seen in scholarship in that day, or, indeed, in any day.

The essay struck home and continues to reverberate because every writing teacher has at some point written the useless or destructive or contradictory comments that Sommers has isolated. When she points to the confusion of commenting on editing errors even as we are asking students to rethink or even delete the material to be edited—our general failure to distinguish process from product commentary—she strikes a blow to the teacher lore hiding in every red pen; those of us who conduct workshops for writing teachers know how deeply embedded the urge to correct is in the profession. And correct we do, even if we know from experience that our corrections usually do not lead to better writing. There is an undercurrent of insecurity in many writing teachers that expresses itself in endless overmarking of everything, lest the student or someone else (another teacher? a parent? a grammar policeman?) suspect the teacher to be ignorant of the finer points of prose. And there is even a less generous hostility in some teachers to students who do not demonstrate whatever the teacher takes to be basic skill (which should, of course, have been mastered in previous classes), expressed in such common metaphors for grading as "bleeding all over the page." One English teacher I hardly knew sent me a friendly note concluding with a teacherly, complimentary close: not "cordially" or "sincerely" but rather "keep the red ink flowing." Thus does the teacher agenda replace the student agenda for writing, the ideal text in the teacher's head replace the real text the student produced, and the search for error replace the more difficult quest to help students improve. Terrible pedagogy, to be sure, but which of us has never been guilty of it?

Sommers's caustic ironies punctuate the essay's sharp attack on responding as usual, in memorable sentences: "the remarkable contradiction of developing a paragraph after editing the sentences in it represents the confusion we encountered in our teachers' commenting styles"; "one could easily remove all the comments from this paragraph and rubber stamp them on another student text, and they would make as much or as little sense on the second text as they do here"; "the teacher holds a license for vagueness while the student is commanded to be specific." Who can forget the stern injunction from one of the responders telling the student to "think more about what you are thinking about"? One hardly knows whether to laugh or to cry at such reminders of what goes wrong with our practice.

We can see the influence of this article in a series of books and articles, all of which take Sommers's research as their starting point. Most obvious is the work done by Richard Straub and Ronald Lunsford, first in their *Twelve Readers Reading: Responding to College Student Writing* (1995) and then in Straub's *Responding to Student Writing* (1999). Straub and Lunsford adopt Sommers's research strategy of collecting teacher responses to specific student essays and seeking to find patterns in these responses. Books by Sarah Freedman, Chris Anson, and others listed in the selected bibliography in Straub have followed her lead, though from different perspectives. Chapters on responding in two of my own books are profoundly indebted to her insights. Workshops and courses for writing teachers, writing across the curriculum workshops, and teaching assistant orientations have in part been shaped by the new awareness of ways of responding illuminated by Sommers's piercing perceptions.

To be sure, the article has flaws that are more noticeable today than they were in the early 1980s. We must take the research as summarized by the author, without the charts and evidence that we might now expect to see. We get only a glimpse of the three student texts on which the research sample commented and no context whatever for the writing or commenting. The validity of the conclusions depends on the writer's ethos and our common experience. For instance, we are asked to accept the contrast between "the calm, reasonable language of the computer" and "the hostility and mean-spiritedness of most of the teachers' comments" without seeing either. Further, Sommers's assumptions about the purpose of responding to student writing are presented as givens, without theoretical or historical justification: "Instead of finding errors or showing students how to patch up parts of their texts, we need to sabotage our students' conviction that the drafts they have written are complete and coherent." True enough, we may say, but where does this particular "need" come from, and is there really only one right way to conceive of responding to every student, in whatever circumstance? The force of this article does not arise from its compelling data or its attention to the dimensions of its issue. What readers react to is its rhetorical power, based on our common experience as teachers and, I suspect, our common guilt about our failures to react with sufficient sensitivity and professionalism to too many students in too many classes.

We still know too little about effective ways to respond to student writing. We need much more knowledge about how and why teachers do what they do. Sometimes it seems as if responding to student writing is close to parenting, in its peculiar intimacy, in its irreducible one-on-one relationship, in its replication of bad as well as good practice from generation to generation. We often seem to do to our students what our teachers did to us, not unnaturally, since without such interventions as Sommers provides that is all we have to model ourselves on. If this is one secret cause of child abuse in parenting, we might suppose it to be an analogous cause of student abuse in responding. And we need to know more about the various ways students learn or do not learn from teacher comments, a matter about which very little research has been done. We need to hear student voices on this subject as well as those of teachers and researchers. The door Sommers opened into our dark closet could be opened much wider and the light could be much brighter.

But Sommers's essay is the landmark, the essential beginning of this quest. Its terse and witty summary of what has gone wrong with what "consumes the largest proportion of our time" still has the power to stimulate and embarrass us. It has changed the pedagogy of all who have read it and forced us to consider what we are doing when we write intimate notes to our students on their texts. Finally, its focus on "helping our students become more effective writers" sets a model for pedagogical writing research, which too often has ignored this fundamental purpose. Whatever else we may do as teachers, we must communicate clearly with our students about their writing, or nothing else we may do will much matter.

Works Cited

Anson, Chris, ed. *Writing and Response: Theory, Practice, Research.* Urbana, IL: NCTE, 1989.

Belanoff, Pat. Foreword. *The Theory and Practice of Grading Writing: Problems and Possibilities.* Ed. Frances Zak and Christopher Weaver. Albany, NY: State U of New York P, 1998.

Freedman, Sarah Warshauer. *Response to Student Writing.* Urbana, IL: NCTE, 1987.

Straub, Richard. *A Sourcebook for Responding to Student Writing.* Cresskill, NJ: Hampton, 1999.

Straub, Richard, and Ronald F. Lunsford. *Twelve Readers Reading: Responding to College Student Writing.* Cresskill, NJ: Hampton, 1995.

White, Edward M. "Responding to and Grading Student Writing." *Assigning, Responding, Evaluating: A Writing Teacher's Guide.* 3rd ed. New York: St. Martin's, 1999. 142–48.

———. "Responding to Student Writing." *Teaching and Assessing Writing: Recent Advances in Understanding, Evaluating, and Improving Student Performance.* 2nd ed. San Francisco: Jossey-Bass, 1994. 103–18.

Responding to Student Writing (1982)

Nancy Sommers

More than any other enterprise in the teaching of writing, responding to and commenting on student writing consumes the largest proportion of our time. Most teachers estimate that it takes them at least 20 to 40 minutes to comment on an individual student paper, and those 20 to 40 minutes times 20 students per class, times 8 papers, more or less, during the course of a semester add up to an enormous amount of time. With so much time and energy directed to a single activity, it is important for us to understand the nature of the enterprise. For it seems, paradoxically enough, that although commenting on student writing is the most widely used method for responding to student writing, it is the least understood. We do not know in any definitive way what constitutes thoughtful commentary or what effect, if any, our comments have on helping our students become more effective writers.

Theoretically, at least, we know that we comment on our students' writing for the same reasons professional editors comment on the work of professional writers or for the same reasons we ask our colleagues to read and respond to our own writing. As writers we need and want thoughtful commentary to show us when we have communicated our ideas and when not, raising questions from a reader's point of view that may not have occurred to us as writers. We want to know if our writing has communicated our intended meaning and, if not, what questions or discrepancies our reader sees that we, as writers, are blind to.

In commenting on our students' writing, however, we have an additional pedagogical purpose. As teachers, we know that most students find it difficult to imagine a reader's response in advance, and to use such responses as a guide in composing. Thus, we comment on student writing to dramatize the presence of a reader, to help our students to become that questioning reader themselves, because, ultimately, we believe that becoming such a reader will help them to evaluate what they have written and develop control over their writing.[1]

Even more specifically, however, we comment on student writing because we believe that it is necessary for us to offer assistance to student writers

This essay first appeared in *College Composition and Communication* 32 (1982): 148–56. Copyright © 1982 by the National Council of Teachers of English. Reprinted with permission.

when they are in the process of composing a text, rather than after the text has been completed. Comments create the motive for doing something different in the next draft; thoughtful comments create the motive for revising. Without comments from their teachers or from their peers, student writers will revise in a consistently narrow and predictable way. Without comments from readers, students assume that their writing has communicated their meaning and perceive no need for revising the substance of their text.[2]

Yet as much as we as informed professionals believe in the soundness of this approach to responding to student writing, we also realize that we don't know how our theory squares with teachers' actual practice—do teachers comment and students revise as the theory predicts they should? For the past year my colleagues, Lil Brannon, Cyril Knoblauch, and I have been researching this problem, attempting to discover not only what messages teachers give their students through their comments, but also what determines which of these comments the students choose to use or to ignore when revising. Our research has been entirely focused on comments teachers write to motivate revisions. We have studied the commenting styles of thirty-five teachers at New York University and the University of Oklahoma, studying the comments these teachers wrote on first and second drafts, and interviewing a representative number of these teachers and their students. All teachers also commented on the same set of three student essays. As an additional reference point, one of the student essays was typed into the computer that had been programmed with the "Writer's Workbench," a package of twenty-three programs developed by Bell Laboratories to help computers and writers work together to improve a text rapidly. Within a few minutes, the computer delivered editorial comments on the student's text, identifying all spelling and punctuation errors, and suggesting alternatives, offering a stylistic analysis of sentence types, sentence beginnings, and sentence lengths, and finally, giving our freshman essay a Kincaid readability score of 8th grade which, as the computer program informed us, "is a low score for this type of document." The sharp contrast between the teachers' comments and those of the computer highlighted how arbitrary and idiosyncratic most of our teachers' comments are. Besides, the calm, reasonable language of the computer provided quite a contrast to the hostility and mean-spiritedness of most of the teachers' comments.

The first finding from our research on styles of commenting is that *teachers' comments can take students' attention away from their own purposes in writing a particular text and focus that attention on the teachers' purpose in commenting.* The teacher appropriates the text from the student by confusing the student's purpose in writing the text with her own purpose in commenting. Students make the changes the teacher wants rather than those that the student perceives are necessary, since the teachers' concerns imposed on the text create the reasons for the subsequent changes. We have all heard our perplexed students say to us when confused by our comments: "I don't understand how you want me to change this" or "Tell me what you want me to do." In the beginning of the process there was the writer, her words, and her desire to communicate her ideas. But after the comments of the teacher are imposed on the first or second draft, the student's attention dramatically shifts from "This is what I want to say," to "This is what you the teacher are asking me to do."

This appropriation of the text by the teacher happens particularly when teachers identify errors in usage, diction, and style in a first draft and ask students to correct these errors when they revise; such comments give the student an impression of the importance of these errors that is all out of proportion to how they should view these errors at this point in the process. The comments create the concern that these "accidents of discourse" need to be attended to before the meaning of the text is attended to.

It would not be so bad if students were only commanded to correct errors, but, more often than not, students are given contradictory messages; they are commanded to edit a sentence to avoid an error or to condense a sentence to achieve greater brevity of style, and then told in the margins that the particular paragraph needs to be more specific or to be developed more. An example of this problem can be seen in the following student paragraph (see fig. 1).

In commenting on this draft, the teacher has shown the student how to edit the sentences, but then commands the student to expand the paragraph in order to make it more interesting to a reader. The interlinear comments and the marginal comments represent two separate tasks for this student; the interlinear comments encourage the student to see the text as a fixed piece, frozen in time, that just needs some editing. The marginal comments, however, suggest that the meaning of the text is not fixed, but rather that the student still needs to develop the meaning by doing some more research. Students are commanded to edit and develop at the same time; the remarkable contradiction of developing a paragraph after editing the sentences in it represents the confusion we encountered in our teachers' commenting styles. These different signals given to students, to edit and develop, to condense and elaborate, represent also the failure of teachers' comments to direct genuine revision of the text as a whole.

Moreover, the comments are worded in such a way that it is difficult for students to know what is the most important problem in the text and what

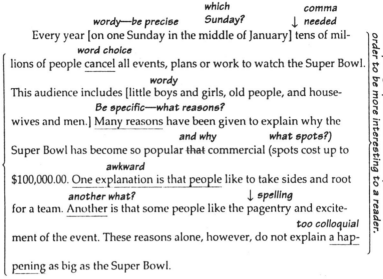

Fig. 1

problems are of lesser importance. No scale of concerns is offered to a student, with the result that a comment about spelling or a comment about an awkward sentence is given weight equal to a comment about organization or logic. The comment that seemed to represent this problem best was one teacher's command to his student: "Check your commas and semicolons and think more about what you are thinking about." The language of the comments makes it difficult for a student to sort out and decide what is most important and what is least important.

When the teacher appropriates the text for the student in this way, students are encouraged to see their writing as a series of parts—words, sentences, paragraphs—and not as a whole discourse. The comments encourage students to believe that their first drafts are finished drafts, not invention drafts, and that all they need to do is patch and polish their writing. That is, teachers' comments do not provide their students with an inherent reason for revising the structure and meaning of their texts, since the comments suggest to students that the meaning of their text is already there, finished, produced, and all that is necessary is a better word or phrase. The processes of revising, editing, and proofreading are collapsed and reduced to a single trivial activity, and the students' misunderstanding of the revision process as a rewording activity is reinforced by their teachers' comments.

It is possible, and it quite often happens, that students follow every comment and fix their texts appropriately as requested, but their texts are not improved substantially, or, even worse, their revised drafts are inferior to their previous drafts. Since the teachers' comments take the students' attention away from their own original purposes, students concentrate more, as I have noted, on what the teachers commanded them to do than on what they are trying to say. Sometimes students do not understand the purpose behind their teachers' comments and take these comments very literally. At other times students understand the comments, but the teacher has misread the text and the comments, unfortunately, are not applicable. For instance, we repeatedly saw comments in which teachers commanded students to reduce and condense what was written, when in fact what the text really needed at this stage was to be expanded in conception and scope.

The process of revising always involves a risk. But, too often revision becomes a balancing act for students in which they make the changes that are requested but do not take the risk of changing anything that was not commented on, even if the students sense that other changes are needed. A more effective text does not often evolve from such changes alone, yet the student does not want to take the chance of reducing a finished, albeit inadequate, paragraph to chaos—to fragments—in order to rebuild it, if such changes have not been requested by the teacher.

The second finding from our study is that *most teachers' comments are not text-specific and could be interchanged, rubber-stamped, from text to text.* The comments are not anchored in the particulars of the students' texts, but rather are a series of vague directives that are not text-specific. Students are commanded to "Think more about [their] audience, avoid colloquial language, avoid the passive, avoid prepositions at the end of sentences or conjunctions at the beginning of sentences, be clear, be specific, be precise, but above all, think more about what [they] are thinking about." The comments on the following student paragraph illustrate this problem (see fig. 2).

One could easily remove all the comments from this paragraph and rubber-stamp them on another student text, and they would make as much or as little sense on the second text as they do here.

We have observed an overwhelming similarity in the generalities and abstract commands given to students. There seems to be among teachers an accepted, albeit unwritten canon for commenting on student texts. This uniform code of commands, requests, and pleadings demonstrates that the teacher holds a license for vagueness while the student is commanded to be specific. The students we interviewed admitted to having great difficulty with these vague directives. The students stated that when a teacher writes in the margins or as an end comment, "choose precise language," or "think more about your audience," revising becomes a guessing game. In effect,

↓ *Begin by telling your reader*
  what you are going to write about.
In the sixties it was drugs, in the seventies it was rock and roll.

avoid—"one of the"
Now in the eighties, <u>one of the</u> most controversial subjects is nuclear

elaborate
power. The United States is <u>in great need of its own</u> source of power.

Because of environmentalists, coal is not an acceptable source of energy.

be specific
[Solar and wind power have not yet received the technology necessary

avoid — "it seems"
to use them.] It <u>seems</u> that nuclear power is the only feasible means

right now for obtaining self-sufficient power. However, too large a per-

centage of the population are against nuclear power claiming it is un-

be precise
safe. <u>With as many problems</u> as the United States is having concerning

energy, it seems a shame that the public is so quick to "can" a very fea-

sible means of power. Nuclear energy should not be given up on, but

rather, more nuclear plants should be built.

Think more about your reader.

Thesis sentence needed

Fig. 2

the teacher is saying to the student, "Somewhere in this paper is imprecise language or lack of awareness of an audience and you must find it." The problem presented by these vague commands is compounded for the students when they are not offered any strategies for carrying out these commands. Students are told that they have done something wrong and that there is something in their text that needs to be fixed before the text is acceptable. But to tell students that they have done something wrong is not to tell them what to do about it. In order to offer a useful revision strategy to a student, the teacher must anchor that strategy in the specifics of the student's text. For instance, to tell our student, the author of the above paragraph, "to be specific," or "to elaborate," does not show our student what questions the reader has about the meaning of the text, or what breaks in logic exist, that could be resolved if the writer supplied specific information; nor is the student shown how to achieve the desired specificity.

Instead of offering strategies, the teachers offer what is interpreted by students as rules for composing; the comments suggest to students that writing is just a matter of following the rules. Indeed, the teachers seem to impose a series of abstract rules about written products even when some of them are not appropriate for the specific text the student is creating.[3] For instance, the student author of our sample paragraph presented above is commanded to follow the conventional rules for writing a five-paragraph essay—to begin the introductory paragraph by telling his reader what he is going to say and to end the paragraph with a thesis sentence. Somehow these abstract rules about what five-paragraph products should look like do not seem applicable to the problems this student must confront when revising, nor are the rules specific strategies he could use when revising. There are many inchoate ideas ready to be exploited in this paragraph, but the rules do not help the student to take stock of his (or her) ideas and use the opportunity he has, during revision, to develop those ideas.

The problem here is a confusion of process and product; what one has to say about the process is different from what one has to say about the product. Teachers who use this method of commenting are formulating their comments as if these drafts were finished drafts and were not going to be revised. Their commenting vocabularies have not been adapted to revision and they comment on first drafts as if they were justifying a grade or as if the first draft were the final draft.

Our summary finding, therefore, from this research on styles of commenting is that the news from the classroom is not good. For the most part, teachers do not respond to student writing with the kind of thoughtful commentary which will help students to engage with the issues they are writing about or which will help them think about their purposes and goals in writing a specific text. In defense of our teachers, however, they told us that responding to student writing was rarely stressed in their teacher-training or in writing workshops; they had been trained in various prewriting techniques, in constructing assignments, and in evaluating papers for grades, but rarely in the process of reading a student text for meaning or in offering commentary to motivate revision. The problem is that most of us as teachers of writing have been trained to read and interpret literary texts for meaning, but, unfortunately, we have not been trained to act upon the same set of assumptions in reading student texts as we follow in reading literary texts.[4] Thus, we read student texts with biases about what the writer should have said or about what he or she should have written, and our biases determine how we will comprehend the text. We read with our preconceptions and preoccupations, expecting to find errors, and the result is that we find errors and misread our students' texts.[5] We find what we look for; instead of reading and responding to the meaning of a text, we correct our students' writing. We need to reverse this approach. Instead of finding errors or showing students how to patch up parts of their texts, we need to sabotage our students' conviction that the drafts they have written are complete and coherent. Out comments need to offer students revision tasks of a different order of complexity and sophistication from the ones that they themselves identify, by forcing students back into the chaos, back to the point where they are shaping and restructuring their meaning.[6]

For if the content of a student text is lacking in substance and meaning, if the order of the parts must be rearranged significantly in the next draft, if paragraphs must be restructured for logic and clarity, then many sentences are likely to be changed or deleted anyway. There seems to be no point in having students correct usage errors or condense sentences that are likely to disappear before the next draft is completed. In fact, to identify such problems in a text at this early first draft stage, when such problems are likely to abound, can give a student a disproportionate sense of their importance at this stage in the writing process.[7] In responding to our students' writing, we should be guided by the recognition that it is not spelling or usage problems that we as writers first worry about when drafting and revising our texts.

We need to develop an appropriate level of response for commenting on a first draft, and to differentiate that from the level suitable to a second or third draft. Our comments need to be suited to the draft we are reading. In a first or second draft, we need to respond as any reader would, registering questions, reflecting befuddlement, and noting places where we are puzzled about the meaning of the text. Comments should point to breaks in logic, disruptions in meaning, or missing information. Out goal in commenting on early drafts should be to engage students with the issues they are considering and help them clarify their purposes and reasons in writing their specific text.

For instance, the major rhetorical problem of the essay written by the student who wrote the second paragraph (the paragraph on nuclear power) quoted above was that the student had two principal arguments running through his text, each of which brought the other into question. On the one hand, he argued that we must use nuclear power, unpleasant as it is, because we have nothing else to use; though nuclear energy is a problematic source of energy, it is the best of a bad lot. On the other hand, he also argued that nuclear energy is really quite safe and therefore should be our primary resource. Comments on this student's first draft need to point out this break in logic and show the student that if we accept his first argument, then his second argument sounds fishy. But if we accept his second argument, his first argument sound contradictory. The teacher's comments need to engage this student writer with this basic rhetorical and conceptual problem in his first draft rather than impose a series of abstract commands and rules upon his text.

Written comments need to be viewed not as an end in themselves—a way for teachers to satisfy themselves that they have done their jobs—but rather as a means for helping students to become more effective writers. As a means for helping students, they have limitations; they are, in fact, disembodied remarks—one absent writer responding to another absent writer. The key to successful commenting is to have what is said in the comments and what is done in the classroom mutually reinforce and enrich each other. Commenting on papers assists the writing course in achieving its purpose; classroom activities and the comments we write to our students need to be connected. Written comments need to be an extension of the teacher's voice—an extension of the teacher as reader. Exercises in such activities as revising a whole text or individual paragraphs together in class, noting how the sense of the whole dictates the small changes, looking at options, evaluating actual choices, and then discussing the effect of these changes on revised drafts—such exercises need to be designed to take students through the cycles of revising and to help them overcome the anxiety we all feel at reducing what looks like a finished draft into fragments and chaos.

The challenge we face as teachers is to develop comments which will provide an inherent reason for students to revise; it is a sense of revision as discovery, as a repeated process of beginning again, as starting out new, that our students have not learned. We need to show our students how to seek, in the possibility of revision, the dissonances of discovery—show them through our comments why new choices would positively change their texts, and thus to show them the potential for development implicit in their own writing.

Notes

1. C. H. Knoblauch and Lil Brannon, "Teacher Commentary on Student Writing: The State of the Art," *Freshman English News,* 10 (Fall, 1981), 1–3.

2. For an extended discussion of revision strategies of student writers, see Nancy Sommers, "Revision Strategies of Student Writers and Experienced Adult Writers," *College Composition and Communication,* 31 (December, 1980), 378–88.

3. Nancy Sommers and Ronald Schleifer, "Means and Ends: Some Assumptions of Student Writers," *Composition and Teaching,* 2 (December, 1980), 69–76.

4. Janet Emig and Robert P. Parker, Jr., "Responding to Student Writing: Building a Theory of the Evaluating Process," unpublished papers, Rutgers University.

5. For an extended discussion of this problem see Joseph Williams, "The Phenomenology of Error," *College Composition and Communication,* 32 (May, 1981), 152–68.

6. Ann Berthoff, *The Making of Meaning* (Montclair, NJ: Boynton/Cook Publishers, 1981).

7. W. U. McDonald, "The Revising Process and the Marking of Student Papers," *College Composition and Communication,* 24 (May, 1978), 167–70.

6

Introduction to Peter Elbow's "Reflections on Academic Discourse: How It Relates to Freshmen and Colleagues"

Lynn Z. Bloom

I love what's in Peter Elbow's "Reflections on Academic Discourse: How It Relates to Freshmen and Colleagues" (1991). I love its learning, intelligence, sophistication—even mere facts and naked summaries of articles and books; I love Elbow's reasoning, inference, and evidence; I love his theory and am captivated by his style. But, like Elbow, I hate academic discourse. I refuse to write in a language I don't talk or teach in. I won't assign reading in dense, esoteric language unless there's no equivalent alternative. Although my students can get away with *discourse, dialogic* (my astute spellcheck would substitute *diabolic*), and even the routine substitution of *text* for *work at hand* or other longer synonyms, I urge them to eschew academic polysyllabicism. And I rebut their lamentations, "How can I abandon a style I've spent four years cultivating in graduate school?" with "Well if that's what we've spent four years teaching you, we've have failed our jobs." For, like Elbow, I'm convinced that it's possible to sound smart and, well, pretty academic without concealing one's point and one's persona in a thicket of impenetrable language.

For these reasons I teach "Reflections on Academic Discourse" in every course every semester—either overtly, to graduate students, or covertly, to undergrads. Elbow's philosophy undergirds the faculty workshops I give as part of our writing across the curriculum program, my collaborative work in teaching agriculture faculty to teach writing, and much of my own writing. The view that writing should be clear, precise, and to the point, that it should be understandable and accessible—dare I say, *resonates*—with colleagues in other departments across the university. "We don't want our students to write in the *flowery*"—yes, they always say *flowery*—"language you teach in the English department. Our engineering (or business, or agriculture, or pharmacy) students need to communicate clearly with industry, with clients—or the bridge will fall down."

Here—to spell them out—are the reasons why I think "Reflections on Academic Discourse" is a key piece for all writing teachers, all teachers of anything, and all students. It's groundbreaking. By the time it was published, in 1991, the polysyllabic purveyors of academic discourse had for more than two decades—since the advent of deconstructionism and its attendant delights—been escalating demands that students and faculty alike should write in increasingly abstruse and jargon-laden language. Someone smart had to speak up to oppose this hegemonic takeover, and Elbow came to the rescue in the clarion voice of real-world reason. "Reflections" made it clear that, as with many other subjects (the round earth; the solar system; the circulation of blood throughout the body; the writing process), what now seems obvious—that students can enjoy writing and will write by choice if it is meaningful and manageable—wasn't necessarily obvious to those needing to hear these simple sane words over and over and over again. Elbow's "larger view of human discourse" gives him an accurate understanding of the transience of academic work: "life is long and college is short. Very few of our students will ever have to write academic discourse after college." Thus Elbow's informed and practical pedagogy makes it clear that students should be writing for their very lives in language that will last them a lifetime; they should not be trained to ventriloquize language they don't understand and won't use when released from linguistic captivity into the wilds of the workplace. (Here I resist a Foucauldian analysis.)

"Reflections on Academic Discourse" is sensible, intelligent, and insightful about language. Elbow, following Linda Flower, observes "there is no Platonic entity called 'academic discourse' which one can define and master"; consequently, "we can't teach academic discourse because there's no such thing to teach." Not only are English teachers "not qualified" to teach students how to write (and hence think) "like a historian or biologist," there are so many varieties of academic discourse even within English that there is no consensus on what sort to use—the Germanic "bulldozer tradition"; the "genial slightly talky British tradition"; poststructuralist, Marxist, psychoanalytic, and other "allusive, gamesome" versions of language.

"Reflections on Academic Discourse" is written in a human voice spoken by a real person, not an academic abstraction. Elbow's voice (not his actual person—how much do we really know about the private, or even the public life, of this genial, slightly talky author?) is consistently manifested in the vertical pronoun and in accessible language. His work puts his philosophy right up front, never trying to "peel away from messages the evidence of how those messages are situated as the center of personal, political, or cultural interest"; he never uses academic jargon to mask with fake objectivity the fact that he as an author and teacher brings to his subject "personal interests, concerns, and uncertainties" comparable to those that other teachers and students feel. But then, as an "established insider," Elbow can take "certain liberties, risks, tones, and stances"—in his style and his substance that, he admits, are "not usually taken by the unannealed."

Discourse is indeed power, as Elbow observes. But in "Reflections on Academic Discourse," as in *Writing Without Teachers* and *Writing with Power,* his deliberately democratic stance, respectful of both students and teachers, is calculated to give power to all the people—those in his mind (the teachers), and those in his heart and soul—the students, always and especially the students. Thus I particularly love (besides the beginning and the middle), the ending to "Reflections." There Elbow makes specific suggestions for writing assignments and classroom practices that get away from playing the "game of right and wrong," where "all authority is with the teacher (as the only representative of the academic discourse community in the room); and the student's whole task is finding right answers of which the teacher is sole arbiter." It is heartening to find Elbow's conclusion embedded in the classroom, the source and context of the ideal discourse community, if not of academic discourse. There, we can encourage our students "to discover and even savor the range of large and small rewards which attend their own writing and thinking," at the same time that we can rediscover for ourselves what Elbow reminds us, that "the activity of writing becomes self-rewarding though never effortless," on the best days, as Robert Frost says, "the sweetest dream that labor knows."

Works Cited

Elbow, Peter. *Writing Without Teachers.* New York: Oxford UP, 1971.
———. *Writing with Power: Techniques for Mastering the Writing Process.* New York: Oxford UP, 1981.
Frost, Robert. "Mowing." *Selected Poems of Robert Frost.* Ed. Robert Graves. New York: Holt, 1963.

Reflections on Academic Discourse: How It Relates to Freshmen and Colleagues (1991)

Peter Elbow

I love what's in academic discourse: learning, intelligence, sophistication—even mere facts and naked summaries of articles and books; I love reasoning, inference, and evidence; I love theory. But I hate academic discourse. What follows is my attempt to work my way out of this dilemma. In doing so I will assume an ostensive definition of academic discourse: it is the discourse that academics use when they publish for other academics. And what characterizes that discourse? This is the question I will pursue here.

As a teacher of freshman writing courses, my problem is this. It is obvious why I should heed the common call to teach my students academic discourse. They will need it for the papers and reports and exams they'll have to write in their various courses throughout their college career. Many or even most of their teachers will expect them to write in the language of the academy. If we don't prepare them for these tasks we'll be shortchanging them—and disappointing our colleagues in other departments. It's no good just saying, "Learn to write what's comfy for you, kiddies," if that puts them behind the eight-ball in their college careers. Discourse carries power. This is especially important for weak or poorly prepared students—particularly students from poorer classes or those who are first in their families to come to college. Not to help them with academic discourse is simply to leave a power vacuum and thereby reward privileged students who have already learned academic discourse at home or in school—or at least learned the roots or propensity for academic discourse. (Shirley Brice Heath shows how middle class urban families instinctively give home training in the skills that teachers want: labeling and defining and so forth. Children from other classes and backgrounds get plenty of language training, but their skills are mistaken by teachers for no skill.) Still, I remain troubled.

This essay first appeared in *College English* 53 (Feb. 1991): 135–55. Copyright © 1991 by the National Council of Teachers of English. Reprinted with permission.

It also included a note directing readers to consult the growing body of empirical research on representative academic texts of different disciplines and on what happens as actual students engage in learning to use academic discourse discussed in the work of Bazerman, Herrington, McCarthy, and Myers.

The Need for Nonacademic Writing in Freshman Writing Courses

I am troubled, first, by the most extreme position—the idea of giving over the freshman writing course entirely to academic discourse. Here are three brief arguments for teaching nonacademic discourse in freshman writing courses. These are not arguments against academic discourse; only for teaching something else in addition.

First, life is long and college is short. Very few of our students will ever have to write academic discourse after college. The writing that most students will need to do for most of their lives will be for their jobs—and that writing is usually very different from academic discourse. When employers complain that students can't write, they often mean that students have to *unlearn* the academic writing they were rewarded for in college. "[E]ach different 'world of work' constitutes its own discourse community with its own purposes, audiences, and genres. The FDA, for example, produces documents vastly different from those of the Air Force; lawyers write in genres different from those of accountants" (Matalene vi).

But to put the argument in terms of writing that people have to do is to give in to a deeply unwriterly and pessimistic assumption—held by many students and not a few colleagues, namely that no one would ever write except under compulsion. Why should people assume without discussion that we cannot get students to write by choice? In my view, the best test of a writing course is whether it makes students more likely to use writing in their lives: perhaps to write notes and letters to friends or loved ones; perhaps to write in a diary or to make sense of what's happening in their lives; perhaps to write in a learning journal to figure out a difficult subject they are studying; perhaps to write stories or poems for themselves or for informal circulation or even for serious publication; perhaps to write in the public realm such as letters to the newspaper or broadsides on dormitory walls. I don't rule out the writing of academic discourse by choice, but if we teach only academic discourse we will surely fail at this most important goal of helping students use writing by choice in their lives. I don't succeed with all my students at this goal, but I work at it and I make progress with many. It is not an unreasonable goal.

In a workshop with teachers not long ago I was struck with how angry many teachers got at a piece of student writing. It was not particularly good (it was about falling asleep while writing an assigned essay and waking up on a Greek island with "topless maidens"), but what infuriated these teachers was not really the mediocre quality but that the writer said in a piece of process writing that the piece was easy and fun to write and that he didn't revise it much because most people in his group liked it. I sensed resentment against the most basic impulses that are involved in being a writer: to have fun telling a story and to give pleasure to others. We need to get students to write by choice because no one can learn to write well except by writing a great deal—far more than we can assign and read.

Second, I want to argue for one *kind* of nonacademic discourse that is particularly important to teach. I mean discourse that tries to render experience rather than explain it. To render experience is to convey what I see when I look out the window, what it feels like to walk down the street or fall down—to tell what it's like to be me or to live my life. I'm particularly concerned that we help students learn to write language that conveys to others a sense of their experience—or indeed, that mirrors back to themselves a sense of their own experience from a little distance, once it's out there on paper. I'm thinking about autobiographical stories, moments, sketches—perhaps even a piece of fiction or poetry now and again.

I am really arguing that we take a larger view of human discourse. As writing teachers our job is to try to pass on the great human accomplishment of written language. Discourse that explains is part of that accomplishment, but discourse that renders is equally great—equally one of the preeminent gifts of human kind. When students leave the university unable to find words to render their experience, they are radically impoverished. We recognize the value of rendering experience when we teach reading. That is, most of the texts we teach in English courses are literary pieces that render experience. Yet we hesitate to teach students to write discourse that renders. And if we don't do it, no one else will. For virtually all the other disciplines ask students to use language only to explain, not to render. It's important to note, by the way, that rendering is not just an "affective" matter—what something "feels" like. Discourse that renders often yields important new "cognitive" insights such as helping us see an exception or contradiction to some principle we thought we believed. (For example, a rendering of an evening's struggle with writing might well force us to adjust some dearly loved theoretical principle about the writing process.)

Third, we need nonacademic discourse even for the sake of helping students produce good academic discourse—academic language that reflects sound understanding of what they are studying in disciplinary courses. That is, many students can repeat and explain a principle in say physics or economics in the academic discourse of the textbook but cannot simply tell a story of what is going on in the room or country around them on account of that principle—or what the room or country would look like if that principle were different. The use of academic discourse often masks a lack of genuine understanding. When students write about something only in the language of the textbook or the discipline, they often distance or insulate themselves from experiencing or really internalizing the concepts they are allegedly learning. Often the best test of whether a student understands something is if she can translate it out of the discourse of the textbook and the discipline into everyday, experiential, anecdotal terms.

Thus, although we may be unsatisfied unless students can write about what they are learning in the professional discourse of the field—majors, anyway—we should be equally unsatisfied unless they can write about it *not* using the lingo of the discipline. (Vygotsky and Bakhtin make this same point: Vygotsky, when he describes the need for what he calls "scientific" or "formal" concepts to become intertwined in the child's mind with "everyday" or experienced concepts [82ff]; Bakhtin, when he explores the process by which people transform "the externally authoritative word" into the "internally persuasive word" [*Discourse and the Novel* 336ff].) I'm all for students being able to write academic discourse, but it bothers me when theorists argue that someone doesn't know a field unless she can talk about it in the discourse professionals use among themselves. There are plenty of instances of people who know a lot about engines or writing but don't know the professional discourse of engineering or composition. There's something self-serving about defining people as ignorant unless they are like us. (Besides, much of the talk about students learning academic discourse in their disciplinary courses seems to assume those students are majoring in that subject. But most students are not majors in most courses they take, for example, most students in English courses are non-majors who never take more than one or two English courses in their career. Do we really expect them to write the academic discourse of English? If so, we must mean something peculiar by "academic discourse.")

Let me repeat that I've made no negative arguments against teaching academic discourse, only positive arguments for teaching something else in addition. But the case for teaching academic discourse is usually an argument from practicality, and I insist that it's just as practical to teach other kinds of discourse—given the students' entire lives and even the needs of good academic discourse.

Trying to Make the Problem Go Away

The fact is that we can't teach academic discourse because there's no such thing to teach. Biologists don't write like historians. This is not news. Pat Bizzell and Joe Harris, among others, write thoughtfully about the differences among communities of discourse. Linda Flower writes: "there is no Platonic entity called 'academic discourse' which one can define and master" (3). So although some students may need to write like historians or biologists, few of us in English can teach them to do so. To write like a historian or biologist involves not just lingo but doing history or biology—which involves knowing history and biology in ways we do not. In short we are not qualified to teach most kinds of academic discourse.

But I want to push this further. Suppose we made an empirical study of the nature of discourse in English studies. Think of the differences we'd find—the different discourses in our field:

- The bulldozer tradition of high Germanic scholarship. Give no prominence to your own ideas. Emphasize the collecting and integrating of the ideas and conclusions of others. Or if you want to say something, avoid saying it until you have demonstrated that you have summarized and shown the shortcomings of previous works in the literature. Cite everything—sometimes even your own ideas under the guise of someone else's. (Not such an alien practice, after all: it is a commonplace among journalists that the only way to get your article to say what you want it to say is to quote someone saying it.)

- The genial slightly talky British tradition—which also connects with the rhetorical tradition (e.g., work by people like C. S. Lewis and Wayne Booth). This tradition gives us discourse that is fully scholarly and professional, but it is nevertheless likely to talk to the reader—sometimes even make anecdotal digressions or personal asides. Citations and references tend to be kept to a minimum. We can deride this as a tradition of privilege and authority ("Gentlemen don't cite everything. If you don't recognize the tacit footnotes you're not one of us"), but it is also the tradition of the amateur that welcomes the outsider. (Notice the structural implications that have gotten attached to these two traditions. Most of my teachers in college and graduate school wanted opening and closing paragraphs that provided readers a definite map of what my essay would be about and a definite summary of what it concluded: the voice of the German tradition says "Announce at the border what you have to declare." But I had other teachers who spoke for the British tradition and counted such signposting as a weakness in writing. I can still hear one of them: "Don't talk about what you're going to do, just do it. Just start with the point that belongs first and readers won't need an introduction." The same for transitions: "If you put your points in the right order, they won't need explanatory connections or transitions; they'll *follow*. Just think straight.")

- Poststructuralist, continental discourse: allusive, gamesome—dark and deconstructive. Again few footnotes, little help to those who haven't already read what they are alluding to.

- German Critical or Marxist discourse that is heavy on abstraction, special diction and terminology—and very consciously ideological. Practitioners would insist that anything less ideological is a cop-out.
- Psychoanalytic criticism uses its own linguistic and intellectual practices. When *College English* devoted two issues to psychoanalytic criticism in 1987, I heard colleagues complain, "These people write a completely separate language."
- The field of composition is particularly diverse. Some of its discourse is unashamedly quantitative and "social science." Imagine setting yourself the goal of publishing in *Research in the Teaching of English, College Composition and Communication,* and *Pre/Text:* you would need three different discourses. Steve North counts seven discourse communities in composition, involving not just different lingos but ways of knowing.
- I think of two Creoles: the Chicago Aristotelian dialect of R. S. Crane and fellows, and the New York intelligentsia dialect of Lionel Trilling and Irving Howe and fellows.
- Notice the subtle difference between the discourse of people who are established in the profession and those who are not—particularly those without tenure. Certain liberties, risks, tones, and stances are taken by established insiders that are not usually taken by the unannealed. Discourse is power.
- Notice finally the pedagogically crucial distinction between how academics write to each other and how they have come to expect students to write to them as teachers. We see here the ubiquitous authority dimension of discourse. Students must write "up" to teachers who have authority over them—often being assigned to write to experts about a subject they are just struggling to learn. In contrast, academics write "across" to fellow academics—usually explaining what they have worked out to readers who don't know it. (Sarah Freedman did an interesting piece of research in which she had teachers respond to essays by students—only some of the essays were actually written by teachers or professionals. One of her findings was that teachers were often bothered by the writing of the nonstudents—the "grown-ups" as it were—because it wasn't sufficiently deferential.)
- Suppose a student in a literature course asks me whether it's appropriate to bring in her feelings or some event from her personal life as part of the data for the interpretation of a text. There is no clear answer in English: it is appropriate in psychoanalytic and reader response criticism and certain kinds of feminist criticism—but not in many other literary discourses. What about data from the author's life and opinions? Again, for some English courses it's appropriate, for others not. Suppose a stu-

dent argues against a critic's position by bringing in that critic's class, gender, politics, or sexual affiliations—or professional training. Some English professors call this out of bounds, others do not.

Thus, I can't tell my students whether academic discourse in English means using lots of structural signposts or leaving them out, bringing in their feelings and personal reactions or leaving them out, giving evidence from the poet's life for interpretations or leaving that out, referring to the class, gender, and school of other interpreters or leaving that out—nor finally even what kind of footnotes to use. Even if I restrict myself to composition studies, I can't tell them whether academic discourse means quantitative or qualitative research or philosophical reflection. In short it's crazy to talk about academic discourse as one thing.

But It Won't Go Away

Not only can't I stop myself from talking about academic discourse in the singular, I can't help looking for an academic discourse I could teach in freshman writing courses. Couldn't there be some larger entity or category—academic writing in general—a generic Stop and Shop brand of academic discourse that lies beneath all those different trade names? (And I often buy generic.) A certain deep structure or freeze-dried essence of academic discourse that is larger than what we've looked for so far? A stance or a way of relating to our material that reaches across the differences between disciplines?

What would seem central to such a conception of academic discourse is the giving of reasons and evidence rather than just opinions, feelings, experiences: being clear about claims and assertions rather than just implying or insinuating; getting thinking to stand on its own two feet rather than leaning on the authority of who advances it or the fit with who hears it. In describing academic discourse in this general way, surely I am describing a major goal of literacy, broadly defined. Are we not engaged in schools and colleges in trying to teach students to produce reasons and evidence which hold up on their own rather than just in terms of the tastes or prejudices of readers or how attractively they are packaged?

Thus the conventions of academic discourse may seem difficult or ungainly, but they reflect the diligence needed to step outside one's own narrow vision—they are the conventions of a certain impersonality and detachment all working toward this large and important goal of separating feeling, personality, opinion, and fashion from what is essential: Clear positions, arguments, and evidence (see Bartholomae 155; Olson 110). And so this idea of a single general intellectual goal behind the variety of different academic discourses is attractive.

But the very appeal of academic discourse as I have just described it tends to rest on the assumption that we can separate the ideas and reasons and arguments from the person who holds them; that there are such things as unheld opinions—assertions that exist uninfluenced by who says them and who hears them—positions not influenced by one's feelings, class, race, gender, sexual orientation, historical position, etc.—thinking that "stands on its own two feet." In the end, behind this conception of academic discourse in general is a bias toward objectivity or foundationlism—a bias which many of us have come to resist on the basis of work by a host of thinkers from Polanyi to Fish.

Most academics, certainly in English and composition, are more sympathetic to the contrasting rhetorical bias—a preference for seeing language in terms of speech acts: discourse is always talking to someone—trying to have an impact on someone. Grammar books and logic books may be full of disembodied propositions that we can think of in terms of disinterested truth value—messages without senders and receivers—but *discourse* as used by human beings is always interested, always located in a person speaking and an audience listening. We've learned that many of our difficulties and disputes and confusions come from falling into assuming that discourse is detached, nonrhetorical, and not a speech act—learned, as Bizzell says, that "an absolute standard for the judgment of truth can never be found, precisely because the individual mind can never transcend personal emotions, social circumstances, and historical conditions" (40).

In short, the very thing that is attractive and appealing about academic discourse is inherently problematic and perplexing. It tries to peel away from messages the evidence of how those messages are situated as the center of personal, political, or cultural interest; its conventions tend toward the sound of reasonable, disinterested, perhaps even objective (shall I say it?) men.

Am I saying that people who write academic discourse pretend to be objective or assume that there are absolute standards for truth? Of course not. (Though some do—such as this professor of physics: "Scientific communication is faceless and passionless by design. Data and conclusions stand bare and unadorned, and can be evaluated for what they are without prejudice or emotion. This kind of impersonal communication has helped science achieve the status of public knowledge, a coinage of truth with international currency. It's like Sgt. Joe Friday used to say: 'The facts, Ma'am, just the facts'" [Raymo 26].) Yet when people use academic discourse they are using a medium whose conventions tend to imply disinterested impersonality and detachment—a medium that is thus out of sync with their intellectual stance—a bias toward messages without senders and receivers.

I wonder if this mismatch doesn't help explain why the discourse we see in academic journals is so often ungainly or uncomfortable and not infrequently tangled.

Let me illustrate these implications of detachment by looking at three violations of academic discourse that naïve students sometimes commit. First, they overuse the first person, for example, "I'm only saying what I think and feel—this is just my opinion." Second, naïve students are liable to use the second person too much and too pointedly, sometimes even speaking directly to us as particular reader ("As you stressed to us Tuesday in class, ..."). Third, they are apt to refer to Hemingway as "Ernest." What interests me is how these violations highlight what the conventions of academic discourse usually disguise: that discourse is coming from a subject with personal interest, concerns, and uncertainties (even professional academics sometimes feel uncertain); that discourse is directed to a reader who is also situated in her subjectivity; and that discourse is about an author who is also asserted to be a person like the writer. (Notice yet another divergence among academic discourses in English: academic biographers get to call Hemingway "Ernest.")

But of course if pure objectivity is discredited, it doesn't mean we must embrace pure subjectivity and bias: "Hooray! I've read Kuhn and Fish and there's only subjectivity. Everyone has a bias, so I don't have to try to interrogate my own." Good academic discourse doesn't pretend to pure objectivity, yet it also avoids mere subjectivity. It presents clear claims, reason, and evidence, but not in a pretense of pure, timeless, Platonic dialectic but in the context of arguments that have been or might be made in reply. Most academics reflect in their writing and teaching a belief that passionate commitment is permissible, perhaps even desirable—so long as it is balanced by awareness that it is a passionate position, what the stakes are, how others might argue otherwise. In short, as academics we don't pretend to write as God from an objective or universal spot of ground immune from history and feelings; nevertheless we feel it's possible to have a *bit* of detachment with our left eye as it were—a certain part of one's mind that flies up to the seventh sphere with Troilus and sees, "Ah yes, I'm really taking a strong position here—and I've got a big personal stake in this."

This intellectual stance transforms the dichotomy ("killer dichotomies" Ann Berthoff calls them) between subjective and objective. That is, the very act of acknowledging one's situatedness and personal stake invites, and is itself a movement toward, enlargement of view—not that it's a guarantee. Conversely, if someone pretends to be disinterested and objective, she invites smallness of view because she doesn't locate her interest in a larger picture: she tempts herself into believing that her view *is* the larger picture.

Here then, finally, is a definition of generic academic discourse that sounds right. It's essentially a rhetorical definition: giving reasons and evidence, yes, but doing so as a person speaking with acknowledged interests to others—whose interest and position one acknowledges and tries to understand. I'm for it. I try to teach it. I want my students to have it.

But there is a problem. Though this intellectual stance is characteristic of academic discourse at its best, it is also characteristic of much nonacademic discourse—such as that produced by writers like Montaigne, Woolf, Orwell, Paul Goodman, even William Gass or Joan Didion. If I get my students to achieve this admirable stance in their writing, they still might not be producing what most professors would call academic discourse or look for in assigned essays. Indeed have we not all sometimes sent and received letters that were written even in personal expressive discourse with this intellectual stance: in which we made claims, gave reasons and evidence, acknowledged our position—and just as effectively organized our discourse and set our arguments within the context of others who have written on the matter—without writing as we tend to write in our professional publications? (See *Pre/Text* 11.1 & 2 [1990] for a collection of personal or expressive writing engaged in the work of academic discourse.) In short, I think I've described a prominent feature of good writing—so of course it characterizes good academic writing—but it simply doesn't distinguish academic writing from nonacademic writing.

There are other attractive definitions of academic discourse which lead to the same dilemma. Flower writes: "The goals of self-directed critical inquiry, of using writing to think through genuine problems and issues, and of writing to an imagined community of peers with a personal rhetorical purpose—these distinguish academic writing. . ." (28). She further specifies two common "practices" which "stand as critical features of academic discourse which often limit entry and full participation in the academic community. . . . 1) integrating information from sources with one's own knowledge and 2) interpreting one's reading/adapting one's writing for a purpose" (3). Susan Peck MacDonald writes: "[I]t is problem-solving activity that generates all academic writing" (316). (It is interesting to see MacDonald rather than Flower focus on "problem solving," but a moment's thought explains the apparent paradox: Flower "uses up" problem solving by characterizing *all* writing as problem solving.) These too are characteristic features of good academic discourse, but they are no more useful than my earlier definition for distinguishing academic discourse from nonacademic discourse. In short, we must beware of talking as though the academy has a monopoly on a sound intellectual stance toward one's material and one's readers.

Maybe it's not, then, the intellectual stance or task that distinguishes academic discourse but certain stylistic or mechanical conventions—not the deep structure but certain surface features.

Mannerisms: Stylistic Conventions or Surface Features of Academic Discourse

Just as it was interesting to dig for some common or generic intellectual practices behind the variations in different discourses, let me now try to dig for some common or generic surface features of academic discourse. An example will help: a paragraph from James Berlin's essay, "Contemporary Composition: The Major Pedagogical Theories."

> My reasons for presenting this analysis are not altogether disinterested. I am convinced that the pedagogical approach of the New Rhetoricians is the most intelligent and most practical alternative available, serving in every way the best interests of our students. I am also concerned, however, that writing teachers become more aware of the full significance of their pedagogical strategies. Not doing so can have disastrous consequences, ranging from momentarily confusing students to sending them away with faulty and even harmful information. The dismay students display about writing is, I am convinced, at least occasionally the result of teachers unconsciously offering contradictory advice about composing—guidance grounded in assumptions that simply do not square with each other. More important, as I have already indicated and as I plan to explain in detail later on, in teaching writing we are tacitly teaching a version of reality and the student's place and mode of operation in it. Yet many teachers (and I suspect most) look upon their vocations as the imparting of a largely mechanical skill, important only because it serves students in getting them through school and in advancing them in their professions. This essay will argue that writing teachers are perforce given a responsibility that far exceeds this merely instrumental task. (766)

Berlin writes a clean, direct prose. That is, I could have chosen a sentence like this one from the currently fashionable theory laden tradition:

> Now, literary hypospace may be defined as the lexical space which, having been collapsed to exclude almost all referentiality but that generated by verbal echoes alone, glows like an isotope with a half-

life of meaning co-extensive with its power to turn its tropes into al-
lotropes or "transformational" (in the Chomskyan sense) nodes, capable of liberating the "deep structures" of metaphoricity from buried layers of intertextuality. (Rother 83)

Or this sentence from R. S. Crane and the venerable Chicago Aristotelian
tradition:

[A] poet does not write poetry but individual poems. And these are
inevitably, as finished wholes, instances of one or another poetic kind,
differentiated not by any necessities of the linguistic instrument of
poetry but primarily by the nature of the poet's conception, as finally
embodied in his poem, of a particular form to be achieved through
the representation, in speech used dramatically or otherwise, of some
distinctive state of feeling, or moral choice, or action, complete in itself
and productive of a certain emotion or complex of emotions in the
reader. (96)

It's because Berlin's prose is open and clear that I look to it for some
general or common features of the academic style. Berlin has just named
what he conceives as the four "dominant theories" or approaches to composition and announced his plans to explore each in detail in his essay. Thus
in this early paragraph he is "mapping" or "signposting" for the reader:
explaining what he is going to do and laying out the structure. Even though
there is a wide range of custom as to the degree of signposting in different
academic discourses, signposting is probably the most general or common
textual convention of academic discourse. Thus the last sentence of his
paragraph—introducing his thesis near the start of his essay—is particularly conventional.

It is the convention of explicitness. That is, only nonacademic discourse
is allowed to merely imply what it is saying. A nonacademic piece can
achieve marvelous thinking and yet not really work it out explicitly; indeed
the effectiveness of such a piece may derive from having the principal claim
lurk rather than announce itself. Fine. But in academic writing it is a convention always to say what you are saying. Thus there is a grain of truth in
the old perverse chestnut of advice: "First say what you're going to say, then
say it, then say what you've already said." Academic discourse is business,
not pleasure (and so business writing asks for even more explicit signposting
than most academic writing).

But there is also a convention of inexplicitness in academic discourse.
Look at the first sentence of Berlin's paragraph: "My reasons for presenting this analysis are not altogether disinterested." He is not using this mock-

elegant double negative to hide what he is saying, yet the conventions or voice of academic discourse have led him to use a double negative rather than come out and say positively what he is actually saying, namely, "I have a stake in this analysis." And those same academic conventions have led him to write a sentence about reasons with the verb "to be" rather than a sentence about a person with an active verb (my reasons not being disinterested rather than me having a stake). Perhaps some readers hear a tone of quiet irony in his phrase, "not altogether disinterested," but I don't hear him actually being ironic; he's just falling into a syntactic commonplace of academic discourse, the double negative combined with understatement. For after this sentence he virtually comes out and says (using a number of "I"s), that his analysis of composition into four theories is designed to show why his theory is best. Indeed the subtext of the whole article is a celebration of the idea that all discourse is interested or biased—by definition—and that an "altogether disinterested" position is impossible. Yet in an essay that never hides its "I" and in which Berlin takes full responsibility for his interested position, discourse has led him to conclude the paragraph with a sentence about the essay arguing rather than him arguing. It seems to me, then, that in the convention or voice of his academic discourse, there are locations left over from an intellectual stance of disinterested objectivity: the ideal of conclusions issuing "perforce" from reasons and arguments rather than from the play of interested positions. Somewhere in his new book, *Works and Lives,* Clifford Geertz makes a distinction between "author-saturated" and "author-evacuated" prose. The stylistic conventions of academic discourse are the conventions of author-evacuated prose.

Double negatives and irony are both ways of saying something without saying it. I'm not calling Berlin evasive here. Rather I'm trying to highlight the interesting fact that in an extremely non-evasive essay, his use of academic discourse led him into a locution that goes through the motions of being evasive—and a locution whose verbal conventions carry some wisps of former irony. This may sound like a paradox—conventions of both explicitness and inexplicitness—but it is not. Academic discourse tries to be direct about the "position"—the argument and reasons and claim. Yet it tends to be shy, indirect, or even evasive about the texture of feelings or attitude that lie behind that position.

Because Berlin's prose is not pretentious or obscure, it illustrates all the more clearly that academic discourse also leads to a somewhat formal language. I'm not talking about technical terms that are necessary for technical concepts; I'm talking about a tendency simply to avoid the everyday or common or popular in language. For example, academic discourse leads

Berlin in just one paragraph to say "full significance of their pedagogical strategies" rather than "implications of how they teach"; "mode of operation" rather than "how they act." It leads to words and phrases like "imparting of a largely mechanical skill," "the dismay students display," "perforce," "merely instrumental task," "far exceeds." This is not difficult or convoluted language by any means; merely language that avoids the ordinary more than he probably would do if he were writing the same thoughts in a memo to the same teachers he is addressing with this article—or in *Harpers* or *Hudson Review.*

Berlin uses a special term, "epistemic," as central to this essay. One might call it a technical term that is necessary to the content (you can't talk about penicillin without the word "penicillin"). But (and colleagues argue with me about this) I don't think "epistemic" really permits him to say anything he couldn't say just as well without it—using "knowledge" and other such words. Admittedly it is the mildest of jargon these days and its use can be validly translated as follows: "A bunch of us have been reading Foucault and talking to each other and we simply want to continue to use a word that has become central in our conversation." But through my experience of teaching this essay to classroom teachers (the very audience that Berlin says he wants to reach), I have seen another valid translations: "I'm not interested in talking to people who are not already part of this conversation."

Indeed, there is what I would call a certain rubber-gloved quality to the voice and register typical of most academic discourses—not just author-evacuated but also showing a kind of reluctance to touch one's meanings with one's naked fingers. Here, by way of personal illustration, are some examples of changes made by editors of academic journals working on manuscripts of mine that were already accepted for publication. The changes are interesting for being so trivial: that is, there is no reason for them except to add a touch of distance and avoid the taint of the ordinary:

> —*who has a strong sense of* changed to *who retains a deep conviction that*
> —*always comes with* changed to *is always accompanied by*
> —*when I dropped out of graduate school* changed to *when I interrupted my graduate education*
> —*I started out just writing to aid my memory* changed to *At first I wanted only to aid my memory*
> —[About a teacher I am interviewing and quoting] *he sometimes talks about students as though he doesn't give a damn about them* changed to . . . *as if they meant nothing to him*

I chose Berlin for my analysis because we can see academic discourse leading him into locutions of indirectness and detachment, even vestigial objectivity—when he is clearly taking the opposite intellectual stance. But I also chose Berlin because I want to piggy-back on his main point: "in teaching writing we are tacitly teaching a version of reality and the student's place and mode of operation in it." I agree, but I want to state an obvious corollary: in *using a discourse* we are also tacitly teaching a version of reality and student's place and mode of operation in it. In particular we are affirming a set of social and authority relations. Here are four things that I think are taught by the surface mannerisms or stylistic conventions of academic discourse:

1. A version of reality. The convention of explicitness and straightforward organization in academic discourse teaches that we can figure out what we really mean and get enough control over language to actually say it—directly and clearly. I confess I more or less believe this and think it's a good convention to teach. Of course I also acknowledge what has come to be called the deconstructive view of language and reality, namely that we can never get complete control over language and reality, that there will always be eddies of subversive meaning and wisps of contrary implication in anything we write, no matter how clear and direct we make it, so that a new critic or deconstructor can always find gaps *(aporiae)* in what looks straightforward. Indeed, as I insisted in my opening section, we should also try to teach the opposite convention of inexplicitness—teach people to relinquish control over language so that it leads where we never expected it to go, says things we didn't think we had in mind. I am talking about consciously trying to unleash the subversive forces of language (for example in freewriting) instead of trying to keep them in check. This subversive kind of writing is equally valuable and leads to an equally important view of reality. Nevertheless the convention of explicitness is something I affirm and want to teach.

2. Academic discourse also teaches a set of social and authority relations: to talk to each other as professionals in such a way as to exclude ordinary people. That is, in the academic convention of using more formal language and longer and more complex sentences with more subordinate clauses (for example, calling that kind of language "the deployment of hypotaxis rather than parataxis"), academics are professing that they are professionals who do not invite conversation with nonprofessionals or ordinary people. Many groups act this way. Doctors don't say "thumbbone," and the medical profession went out of its way to mistranslate Freud's *ich, ueber ich* and *es* into *ego, super ego,* and *id*—rather than

into the *I, over I,* and *it* that Freud clearly intended with his German (Betelheim 49–62). It may be common for groups to try to prove that they are professional by means of this kind of exclusionary language, but I wonder if we really want to teach this discourse-stance once we notice the messages it sends: "We don't want to talk to you or hear from you unless you use our language." (Ostensibly the goal is to exclude the hoi polloi, but the bigger threat may be from intellectual non-academics who may be more learned and thoughtful.) Howard Becker is a respected sociologist who argues that there is no need for jargon and exclusionary discourse even in that field. He describes a graduate seminar engaged in revising and untangling someone's essay, where a student suddenly blurts: "Gee . . . when you say it this way, it looks like something anybody could say." Becker's comment: "You bet" (7).

3. I often hear behind the stylistic and textual conventions of academic discourse a note of insecurity or anxiety. Students may deal with their insecurity by saying, "This is just my opinion. . . . Everyone is entitled to their own opinion" and so on. But having led many workshops for students and faculty members, I've noticed that faculty members are usually *more* anxious than students about sharing their writing with each other. Of course faculty members have greater reason for anxiety: the standards are higher, the stakes are higher, and they treat each other more badly than they treat students. But it turns out that the voice and stylistic conventions of academic discourse serve extremely well to cover this understandable anxiety. Think about how we talk when we're nervous: our voice tends to sound more flat, gravelly, monotone, and evacuated. We tend to "cover" ourselves by speaking with more passives, more formal language, more technical vocabulary. We often discover that we sound more pompous than we intended. Bakhtin ("Discourse in Life") explores how meaning is carried by intonation and how our speech tends to lose intonation and thus meaning when we feel unsafe. Even in Berlin's fairly direct language, I hear that characteristically flat tone with little intonation. Not, probably, that he was anxious, but that he availed himself of stylistic conventions that avoid intonation and take a somewhat guarded stance.

4. Finally, I sometimes see in the stylistic conventions of academic discourse an element of display. Despite the lack of intonation, there is often a slight effect of trying to impress or show off (though I don't see this in Berlin). That is, even though academics can write as peers and professionals to colleagues, it is helpful to notice how even grown up, full-fledged academics are sometimes so enmeshed in the rhetorical context

of school discourse that they keep on writing as though they are perform-ing for teachers with authority over them. Many academics have never written except to a teacher. We may be three thousand miles away, ten-ured, and middle-aged, but we are often still writing about the same field we wrote our dissertations on and writing to the very same teachers we had to impress in order to get tenure. Think about the stylistic strata-gems of bright, intellectually excited, upperclass majors who grow up to be professors: how do they deal with that school situation of having to write "up" to readers with more knowledge and more authority—and needing to distinguish themselves from their peers? I believe that the conventions of academic discourse—voice, register, tone, diction, syn-tax, and mannerism—often still carry vestigial traces of this authority transaction of trying to show off or impress those who have authority over us and to distinguish ourselves from our peers.

Really, of course, I'm talking about *ethos:* how do academics create au-thority and credibility when they write to each other? William Stafford thinks we get off easy on this score compared to poets:

> If you were a scientist, if you were an explorer who had been to the moon, if you were a knowing witness about the content being pre-sented—you could put a draft on your hearer's or reader's belief. Whatever you said would have the force of that accumulated back-ground of information; and any mumbles, mistakes, dithering, could be forgiven as not directly related to the authority you were offering. But a poet—whatever you are saying, and however you are saying it, the only authority you have builds from the immediate performance, or it does not build. The moon you are describing is the one you are creating. From the very beginning of your utterance you are creating your own authority. (62–63)

As academics, that is, we have various aids to authority. The most obvious one is to take a ride on the authority of others—and so (naming, finally, the most conspicuous stylistic convention in the genre) academics use foot-notes and quote important figures in our writing. What we write is not just a neat idea we had that we send out to be judged on its own merits; it builds on Aristotle and echoes Foucault. And our discourse conventions teach us to be learned not only in our quotations and citations but also in the other linguistic mannerisms we use. And so—though we may be modest, open, and democratic as persons—the price we pay for a voice of authority is a style that excludes ordinary readers and often makes us sound like an inse-cure or guarded person showing off.

Implications for Teaching Freshman Writing

I hope I am not too unkind in my reading of the stylistic conventions of academic discourse, but it helps me understand that I can happily devote a large proportion of my freshman writing activity to the admirable larger intellectual tasks like giving good reasons and evidence yet doing so in a rhetorical fashion which acknowledges an interested position and tries to acknowledge and understand the positions of others. (Also Flower's "self-directed critical inquiry . . . to an imagined community of peers" [28]; or MacDonald's "problem-solving.") These are the kinds of intellectual practices I want to teach—and in fact already do. But now I can continue to work on them and not feel guilty or defensive about neglecting academic discourse for merely "sensible" writing. Indeed my work on these goals should be slightly transformed by my knowledge that in pursuing them I *am* working on academic discourse—which is only one kind of discourse and that, as Berlin implies, it involves a particular reading of the world, and as Bizzell insists, there are "personal, social, and historical interests in academic discourse." And as I see better that these admittedly sensible intellectual tasks are only some among many, I feel more secure in my commitment to spend a significant portion of the course emphasizing nonacademic discourse with other intellectual tasks—discourse that renders rather than discourse that explains.

I want to emphasize here, however, that my reason for isolating the stylistic mannerisms and giving less attention to them is not just a matter of personal distaste. Serious pedagogical consequences are at stake. The intellectual tasks of academic discourse are significantly easier for students to learn when separated from its linguistic and stylistic conventions. That is, it is not alienating for almost any students to be asked to learn to engage in the demanding intellectual tasks of clarifying claims and giving reasons and so forth (however difficult they may be), but it is definitely alienating for many students to be asked to take on the voice, register, tone, and diction of most academic discourse. If we have to learn a new intellectual stance or take on difficult intellectual goals, we'll probably have better luck if we don't at the same time have to do it in a new language and style and voice. (Teachers of English as a second language have learned that students do better on difficult school tasks if they can use the language they find comfortable.)

And as for those students who are sophisticated enough to take on the voice of academic discourse without much trouble, many of them get seduced or preoccupied with that surface dimension and learn only to mimic it while still failing to engage fully the intellectual task. Putting it crassly, students can do academic work even in street language—and indeed using the vernacular helps show whether the student is doing real intellectual work or just using academic jive.

Besides, learning new intellectual practices is not just a matter of practicing them; it is also a matter of thinking and talking about one's practice. Or, speaking academically, students need metacognition and metadiscourse to help them understand just what these new intellectual practices are that they are being asked to learn. Toward this end, many teachers make heavy use of "process writing" in which students try to describe and analyze what they have written and how they went about writing it (see Elbow and Belanoff 12 and passim).

But everybody does better at metacognition and metadiscourse if he or she can use ordinary language. Flower provides intriguing evidence for this point. She starts with her finding that "students often demonstrated the underlying cognitive abilities to analyze, synthesize, or reconceptualize that would support these high potential strategies, . . . [yet] such strategies do not appear to be live options in their repertoire. Why?" (7). She goes on to note that "metacognition could play a large role in helping students to learn and engage in new types of discourse" (8). Her essay suggest that her research process itself is probably one of the best ways to produce this meta-awareness and task awareness in students. That is, she had the students produce speak-aloud protocols of their thinking and writing, then look at those protocols, and then discuss some of them in class. Here are a couple of examples of metadiscourse or process writing that students had a chance to discuss:

> So anyway, . . . so I wrote five or six pages on nothing, but included the words "African nationalism" in there once in a while. I thought, why this is just like high school, I can get away with doing this. I got the paper back, and it was a C minus or a C or something like that. It said "no content." And I was introduced to the world of college writing. (9)

> I started with "There are several theories as to the most efficient strategies concerning time management." Which is really bad—And I wrote like a page of this. I just stopped and I went: This is just so bad—and I just said, like—I have to take this totally from my own point of view. (PAUSE) *But first I have to get a point of view.* (12)

Flower doesn't make this point, but it seems to me that the students probably wouldn't think so clearly and frankly about their own thinking and discourse if they weren't using ordinary language. The vernacular helps them talk turkey.

The intellectual practices of academic discourse are not only more appealing to me than its stylistic conventions, they are also more useful. That is, even though there may be differences between what counts as evidence and valid reasoning in various disciplines and even subdisciplines, the larger intellectual activities we've focused on are useful in most academic disciplines—and of course in much nonacademic writing, too. The stylistic conventions, on the other hand, seem more local and variable—and in my view carry problematic intellectual and social implications. No one seems to defend the stylistic conventions themselves—merely the pragmatic need for them. I find many academics dislike them but feel guilty and furtive about it. Richard Rorty put it bluntly in a recent interview: "I think that America has made itself a bit ridiculous in the international academic world by developing distinctive disciplinary jargon. It's the last thing we want to inculcate in the freshmen" (7). Finally, I suspect students can learn the surface features of academic style better if they have first made good progress with the underlying intellectual practices. When students are really succeeding in doing a meaty academic task, then the surface stylistic features are more likely to be integral and organic rather than merely an empty game or mimicry.

What specific teaching practices does this analysis suggest? I've tried these:

- Ask students for a midprocess draft that summarizes something (for example, a piece of reading, a difficult principle from another course, the point of view of a classmate, or a discussion): pure summary, simply trying to get it right and clear—as it were for God. Then ask them for a major revision so that the material is not just summarized but rather interpreted and transformed and used in the process of creating a sustained piece of thinking of their own—and for a real human audience. And ask also for process writing with each piece and spend some class time afterwards discussing the differences between the two intellectual tasks.

- Ask students for a piece of writing that renders something from experience. The test of success is whether it makes readers experience what they're talking about. Then ask them for a different piece of writing that is built from that writing—an essay that figures out or explains some issue or solves a conceptual (rather than personal) problem. I don't ask them to suppress their own experience for this piece, but to keep it from being the focus: the focus should be the figuring out or the solving. The test of success for this piece is whether it does the conceptual job. Again, ask for process writing with each piece of writing and then discuss in class the differences between the two intellectual tasks.

- Ask students to write a midprocess draft of an essay, and then for the next week's assignment ask them to make two revisions of the same draft: one in which they try to be completely objective and detached, the other in which they acknowledge their point of view, interest, bias—and figure out how to handle that rhetorical problem. Again, process writing with each piece and class discussion afterwards emphasizing the differences between the two intellectual tasks. This system also speaks to another concern: how to get students to do substantive rather than perfunctory revising—how to insist that revisions be genuinely different, even if not necessarily better.

As for those problematic stylistic conventions of academic discourse: my analysis helps me feel a little better about neglecting them, but I will continue to spend a bit of time on them in my course. The obvious approach would be to describe these stylistic features formally or as a genre. But Sheryl Fontaine points out that there's an uncanny similarity between teaching academic discourse formally and teaching correctness. In both cases we are back to a game of right and wrong; all authority is with the teacher (as the only representative of the academic discourse community in the room); and the student's whole task is finding right answers of which the teacher is sole arbiter.

Besides, a form or genre is always an artificial construct that represents compromise among the actual practices of live writers. If our goal is to tell students what stylistic features are characteristic of the writing in a given discipline, no answer will fit all the particular teachers they will meet—and the answers will be even more out of whack if we are talking about the discourse teachers actually want from students on assignments, because those practices differ even more widely.

- To help students think about style and voice not as generic or formal matters but as audience matters, I use a variation on the process I just described: asking for two revisions of the same midprocess draft, perhaps one for me as teacher and the other for casual friends; or one for people who know a lot about the topic and the other for readers who don't; or one for adults and the other for children; or one for a school newspaper and the other for a teacher.
- Once in the semester I ask for a paper that explains or discusses something students are studying in another course—and again two revisions. One version is for us in this course, considered as amateurs; the other version is for students and the teacher in the other course, considered as professionals. I ask the students to try out both drafts on us and on some

students in the other course—and if possible on the teacher in the other course. A rhetorical and empirical approach dictates these procedures, a way of learning by interacting with readers and seeing how they react, rather than by studying forms and genres of discourse.

- I also like to get a teacher from another discipline to visit my class and distribute copies of a couple of essays that she has assigned and graded and to talk about them. I ask her to tell what kind of assignments and tasks she gives, what she is looking for, and especially to talk in some frank detail about how she reads and reacts to student writing. I try to get this colleague to give some movies of her mind as she reads—in effect an informal speak-aloud protocol of her reading. And there are two issues I bring up if she doesn't do so: how does she react when she finds a vernacular or nonacademic voice in student writing? And does she assign any nonacademic discourse in her course (for example journal writing or stories or letters or newspaper articles about what they are studying)? I want students to hear how this teacher from another discipline reacts to these issues. I also try to get her to speculate about what her colleagues would say on all these matters.

- In effect, I'm talking about doing a bit of informal ethnography—realizing that I am the most convenient ethnographic subject. That is, in recent years I have often found myself giving my reactions to students on their papers in a more reflective way: noticing myself as a member of the profession and as an individual and trying to help students interpret my reactions in a more anthropological way. I think more about multiple audiences and find myself making comments like these: "I am bothered here—I'll bet most teachers would be—but perhaps general readers wouldn't mind." Or "I liked this passage, but I suspect a lot of teachers would take it as an inappropriately personal digression—or as too informal or slangy."

The central principle here is this: I cannot teach students the particular conventions they will need for particular disciplines (not even for particular teachers within the same discipline), but I can teach students the principle of discourse variation—between individuals and between communities. I can't teach them the forms they'll need, but I can sensitize them to the notion of differences in form so that they will be more apt to look for cues and will pick them up faster when they encounter them. Or to put it somewhat negatively, I'm trying to protect myself and keep my students from saying to my colleagues in history or psychology, "But my freshman English teacher likes this kind of writing that you failed me for!" What I want my students to go away thinking is more like this: "My freshman

English teacher was good at telling us what went on in his mind as he read our papers—what he found strong and weak, what he like and didn't like. But he set things up so we were always seeing how different members of the class and even people outside the class had different perceptions and reactions and standards and followed different conventions—how other people in other communities read differently. He tried to get us to listen better and pick up quicker on conventions and reactions." (If only we could write our students' evaluations of our teaching!) This inductive and scattered approach is messy—frustrating to students who want neat answers. But it avoids giving them universal standards that don't hold up empirically. And more than that, it is lively, interesting, and writerly because it's rhetorical rather than formal.

A Final Note: "But at my Back . . ."

Don't forget to notice how fast academic discourse is changing—certainly in our discipline and probably in others. And these changes are really an old story. It wasn't so long ago, after all, that Latin was the only acceptable language for learned discourse. Gradually the other European dialects became acceptable—vernacular, vulgar, and of the people, more democratic, closer to the business of the everyday and to feelings. Yet it seems to me that many academics seem more nervous about changes in discourse—and especially incursions of the vernacular—than changes in ideas or content or doctrine. Many happily proclaim that there is no truth, no right interpretation; many say they want more voices in the academy, dialogue, heteroglossia! But they won't let themselves or their students write in language tainted with the ordinary or with the presence and feelings of the writer.

Yet despite this fear of change, change is what we are now seeing even in the deep structure or central intellectual practices of academic discourse:

- Deconstructionists make a frontal attack on straight, organized prose that purports to mean what it says. They have gotten a good hearing with their insistence that language always means something different from what it says, that seemingly plain and direct language is the most duplicitous discourse of all, and that fooling around is of the essence.
- Feminists attack the idea that good writing must follow linear or hierarchical or deductive models of structure, must persuade by trying to overpower, must be "masterful."
- Bruner and scholars of narrative attack the assumption that thinking is best when it is structured in terms of claims, reason, warrants, and evidence. Narrative is just as good a form for thinking.

- Academic discourse has usually focused outward: on issues or data. But now the focus of academic discourse is more and more often discourse and thinking itself. In effect, much academic discourse is metadiscourse.
- In a host of ways, genres are becoming blurred. It is worth quoting Geertz:

> [T]he present jumbling of varieties of discourse has grown to the point where it is becoming difficult either to label authors (What is Foucault—historian, philosopher, political theorist? What is Thomas Kuhn—historian, philosopher, sociologist or knowledge?) or to classify works. . . . It is a phenomenon general enough and distinctive enough to suggest that what we are seeing is not just another redrawing of the cultural map—the moving of a few disputed borders, the marking of some more picturesque mountain lakes—but an alternation of the principles of mapping. Something is happening to the way we think about the way we think. (19–20)

Arguments that any currently privileged set of stylistic conventions of academic discourse are inherently better—even that any currently privileged set of intellectual practices are better for scholarship or for thinking or for arguing or for rooting out self-deception—such arguments seem problematic now.

In the end, then, I conclude that I should indeed devote plenty of time in my freshman writing course to the intellectual practices of academic discourse; but also work on nonacademic practices and tasks, such as on discourse that renders rather than explains. (And our discussion about the difference between these two uses of languages will help both.) Similarly, I should devote a little bit of time to the stylistic conventions or voices of academic discourse; but only as part of a larger exploration of various voices and styles—an exploration centered not on forms but on relationships with various live audiences. Let me give Joe Harris the last word: "What I am arguing against, though, is the notion that our students should necessarily be working towards the mastery of some particular, well-defined sort of discourse. It seems to me that they might better be encouraged towards a kind of polyphony—an awareness of and pleasure in the various competing discourses that make up their own" (17).

Works Cited

Bakhtin, Mikhail. "Discourse and the Novel." *The Dialogic Imagination: Four Essays.* Ed. Michael Holquist. Trans. Caryl Emerson and Michael Holquist. Slavic Series 1. Austin: U of Texas P, 1981. 259–422.

———. "Discourse in Life and Discourse in Art (Concerning Sociological Poetics)." *Freud-*

ianism: A Marxist Critique. Trans. I. R. Titunik. Ed. Neal H. Bruss. New York: Academic, 1976. 93–116.

Bartholomae, David. "Inventing the University." *When A Writer Can't Write.* Ed. Mike Rose. New York: Guilford, 1985. 134–65.

Bazerman, Charles. *Shaping Written Knowledge: Genre and Activity of the Experimental Article in Science.* Madison: U of Wisconsin P, 1988.

Becker, Howard. *Writing for Social Scientists.* Chicago: U of Chicago P, 1986.

Berlin, James. "Contemporary Composition: The Major Pedagogical Theories." *College English* 44 (1982): 766–77.

Bettelheim, Bruno. *Freud and Man's Soul.* New York: Knopf, 1983.

Bizzell, Pat. "Foundationalism and Anti-Foundationalism in Composition Studies." *Pre/Text* 7.1–7.2 (1986): 37–56.

Crane, R. S. "The Critical Monism of Cleanth Brooks." *Critics and Criticism: Ancient and Modern.* Chicago: U of Chicago P, 1951. 83–107.

Elbow, Peter, and Pat Belanoff. *A Community of Writers: A Workshop Course in Writing.* New York: Random, 1989.

Flower, Linda. "Negotiating Academic Discourse." Reading-to-Write Report No. 10. Technical Report No. 29. Berkley, CA: Center for the Study of Writing at University of California, Berkeley, and Carnegie Mellon [May 1998].

Fontaine, Sheryl. "The Unfinished Story of the Interpretive Community." *Rhetoric Review* 7.1 (Fall 1988): 86–96.

Freedman, Sarah, C. Greenleaf, and M. Sperling. "Response to Student Writing." Research Report No. 23. Urbana, IL: NCTE, 1987.

Geertz, Clifford. "Blurred Genres: The Refiguration of Social Thought." *Local Knowledge: Further Essays in Interpretive Anthropology.* New York: Basic, 1983. 19–35.

———. *Works and Lives: The Anthropologist as Author.* Palo Alto: Stanford UP, 1988.

Harris, Joe. "The Idea of Community in the Study of Writing." *College Composition and Communication* 40.1 (February 1989): 11–22.

Heath, Shirley Brice. *Ways with Words: Language, Life, and Work in Communities and Classrooms.* New York: Cambridge UP 1983.

Herrington, Anne. "Composing One's Self in a Discourse: Students' and Teachers' Negotiations." *Constructing Rhetorical Education: From the Classroom to the Community.* Ed. D. Charey and M. Secor. Carbondale: Southern Illinois UP, [1992].

———. "Teaching, Writing, and Learning: A Naturalistic Study of Writing in an Undergraduate Literature Course." *Advances in Writing Research, Vol. 2: Writing in Academic Discourse.* Ed. D. Jolliffe. Norwood, NJ: ABLEX, 1988: 133–66.

Hirsch, E. D., Jr. *The Aims of Interpretation.* Chicago P, 1978.

MacDonald, Susan Peck. "Problem Definition in Academic Writing." *College English* 49 (1987): 315–30.

Matalene, Carolyn B. Introduction. *Worlds of Writing: Teaching and Learning in the Discourse Communities of Work.* Ed. Carolyn B. Matalene. New York: Random, 1989. v–xi.

McCarthy, Lucille. "A Stranger in Strange Lands: A College Student Writing Across the Curriculum." *Research in the Teaching of English* 21 (1987): 233–65.

Myers, Greg. *Writing Biology.* Madison: U of Wisconsin P, 1990.

North, Stephen. *The Making of Knowledge in Composition: Portrait of an Emerging Field.* Upper Montclair, NJ: Boynton, 1987.

Olson, David R. "Writing: The Divorce of the Author from the Text." *Exploring Speaking—Writing Relationships: Connections and Contrasts.* Ed. B. M. Kroll and R. J. Vann. Urbana, IL: NCTE, 1981. 99–110.

Raymo, Chet. "Just the Facts, Ma'am." *Boston Globe* 27 February 1989: 26.

Rorty, Richard. "Social Construction and Composition Theory: A Conversation with Richard Rorty." *The Journal of Advanced Composition* 9.1 and 9.2: 1–9.

Rother, James. "Face-Values on the Cutting Floor: Some Versions of the Newer Realism." *American Literary Realism* 21.2 (Winter 1989): 67–96.

Stafford, William. "Making a Poem/Starting a Car on Ice." *Writing the Australian Crawl: Views on the Writer's Vocation.* Ann Arbor: U of Michigan P, 1978. 61–75.

Vygotsky, Lev. *Thought and Language.* Trans. Eugenia Hanfman and Gertrude Vakar. Cambridge: MIT P, 1962.

7

Introduction to Janice M. Lauer's "Rhetoric and Composition Studies: A Multimodal Discipline"

Richard Leo Enos

On March 26, 1999, Janice M. Lauer gave her acceptance speech for the 1998 Conference on College Composition and Communication Exemplar Award. This award honors individuals for outstanding service to our discipline. During the address, Professor Lauer synthesized her perspective on composition. Her views, which are based on the experiences of a long and distinguished career, help us to understand our present and future status. More important for the purpose of this volume, her acceptance speech gives us insight to her 1993 essay "Rhetoric and Composition Studies: A Multimodal Discipline." Lauer's acceptance speech emphasizes how composition studies has evolved into a "new rhetoric." Although published less than a decade ago, this essay has already emerged as a landmark piece in capturing the direction of our discipline.

The principle reason for the positive reception of this essay is also the same reason why Lauer's observations are so appropriate for this collection. "Rhetoric and Composition Studies: A Multimodal Discipline" underscores the value of inclusive and collaborative approaches to both teaching and research. That is, research should be grounded in and focused on the improved teaching of writing. Composition as a new rhetoric, through Lauer's essay, establishes a fundamentally essential condition: writing, especially the teaching of writing, is a researchable topic. As a new rhetoric, writing can be studied and its principle heuristics generalized and applied. Lauer's essay makes it clear that we can do much more than observe student writers in our classrooms. We can nurture and direct student writing in order to stimulate creativity and sensitivity to structure. Empowering students with such skills is the essence of Lauer's essay.

One of the most important observations made in Janice Lauer's speech was her understanding of the nature of composition studies. The range of changes, methods, and approaches to the study of composition, she argued, are best understood when we see composition as a manifestation of one of the new rhetorics. We, in turn, might best understand Lauer's comments about how composition is best understood as a new rhetoric by providing an historical perspective to rhetoric. Our discipline was founded when we first sought to provide a system, or *techne,* that facilitated oral expression. As writing evolved from an aid to memory to a *techne* in its own right, some concepts—such as voice and tone—were appropriated for written composition. Some of the heuristics of oral composition transferred well. Other features of oral composition that did not make the "leap" to written expression—in true Darwinian fate—failed to survive in the literate domain. Even in these nascent efforts, the attempts to apply, to test, and to refine systems of literate expression through various resources was a forerunner to the approach and mentality that would serve our field well. Research in rhetoric and composition studies is a systematic way of seeking the most sensitive methods and theories of how we express our thoughts and sentiments in writing.

Lauer's observation, expressed in her brief acceptance speech, is explicated thoroughly in her essay "Rhetoric and Composition Studies: A Multimodal Discipline." What this essay says to teachers of composition can hardly be improved here: Lauer's argument is clear and direct. What can be underscored, however, is what this essay says to us indirectly. That is, there are several points that are not the focus of the essay but rather are the consequences of maintaining a multimodal focus. Lauer's essay reveals benefits that are valuable for the readers of this volume. While (as mentioned above) these come to us indirectly, they are no less important to our field in their insight and application.

The orientation of this essay is revealed in its title. In fact, the significance of the essay is disclosed in its indefinite article: rhetoric and composition is best understood as "a" multimodal discipline. How can rhetoric and composition be viewed as one discipline, and how can it be univocal while, at the same time, it is multimodal? For Lauer, composition studies as a new rhetoric is a discipline not defined by or wedded to a methodology but rather oriented toward solving problems of literacy. That is, the temperament of composition studies is best understood as a problem-solving activity. Understanding how writers express their thoughts and sentiments requires a grasp not only of complex cognitive processes but also of how those processes function in social interaction. The intricate web of social and cognitive action means that solving writing problems requires an interaction of methods.

Lauer's essay not only explains well our recent developments in refining methods, it also says as much about our mentality toward researching literacy. Lauer discusses three dominant modes of inquiry in composition: rhetorical, historical, and empirical. Each of these three research modes has been the basis for advancing theories that seek to explain writing processes. Yet, as Lauer illustrates, the interanimation of these three methods generates dynamic new heuristics that would not have existed if these three approaches had remained autonomous. The implications of this intertextuality of research methods is a major point of the essay. In fact, multimodality has prompted a new orientation for research. In the past, scholars tended to be identified by their methods, their modes of inquiry. Giving primacy to methodology, however, limited our choice and selection of research topics: "good problems" were only the ones that "fit" our methods. This mind-set is a great deal like being a carpenter who has a hammer—and only a hammer—and is looking only for nails, even if some of our tasks call for screwdrivers and saws. "Building" a theory calls for many of the tools in our tool chest.

Our discipline is a "new rhetoric" in yet another dimension. We now realize that research itself is an argument, that we must provide plausible explanations that warrant our interpretations to members of our academic community who assess the merits of our observations. As Lauer illustrates, issues of "reliability" and "validity" are evidentiary *topoi* that are intended to gain the adherence of readers. In this sense, multimodality is a way of building strong cases, a heteroglossia of supporting evidence that explains much by triangulating modes of inquiry for the purposes of advancing jurisprudentially strong interpretations that are offered as solutions to writing problems.

"Rhetoric and Composition Studies: A Multimodal Discipline" provides a rich explanation of the new rhetoric that we are experiencing in composition studies. The inclusive and open temperament that is an indirect benefit of this approach to composition takes more time, tolerance, and effort than our past habits of single-mode (and single-minded) inquiry. Yet, if we have learned anything about composition studies from the previous generations of educators such as Janice Lauer, it is that the study of writing is rich and complex, engaging and difficult, and, most importantly, united in topic but multimodal in inquiry.

Rhetoric and Composition Studies: A Multimodal Discipline (1993)

Janice M. Lauer

This chapter proposes composition studies as a new rhetoric devoted to the multimodal study of written discourse and its facilitation. Through the use of at least three modes of inquiry—rhetorical, historical, and empirical—composition studies direct the rhetorical tradition to the problems of literacy at all levels. In the 1960s, composition studies claimed this new domain hitherto unstudied by any academic area, using multiple modes to investigate the construction of discourse, writing dysfunction, processes and arts of inquiry and critique and, in the 1980s, the political and social contexts of writing.

At the outset, this new rhetoric differentiated itself from rhetorical work in classics and speech communication in at least two broad ways. First, it studied new subjects and issues including written discourse, writing pedagogy, broader discursive conceptions than persuasion, developmental problems, and writing processes. It was not interested in rehashing and filling in the interstices of traditional readings of historical texts but in reinterpreting these texts in the light of problems in understanding and teaching writing. It did not follow the lead of speech communication into research on oral discourse of the media, interpersonal communication, or organizational oral discourse but created new theories to explain writing of all kinds—expressive, expository, persuasive, and literary.

Second, this new rhetoric used multiple modes of inquiry, doing revisionary histories of traditional rhetorical texts, creating new theories of discourse, informed by other fields such as psychology, linguistics, anthropology, and recently by literary theory and cultural studies, and conducting a range of empirical studies on problems of literacy. The nature, costs, and benefits of this multimodality, however, require fuller investigation, a task this chapter undertakes.

This essay first appeared in *Defining the New Rhetorics.* Ed. Theresa Enos and Stuart C. Brown. Sage Series in Written Communication. Newbury Park, CA: Sage, 1993. 44–54. Copyright © 1993 by Sage Publications. Reprinted by permission of Sage Publications, Inc.

Multimodality

Bakhtin's concept of heteroglossia is useful in thinking about multimodality—which I take to be the employment of several modes of inquiry such as historical, rhetorical, and empirical to study problems of literacy and its facilitation. Multimodality represents, if we're using Bakhtin's terms, a dynamic diversity of modes grounded in different points of view on the world, in diverse forms for conceptualizing the world, each characterized by its own objects, meanings, and values. In rhetoric and composition, these modes mutually supplement each other and are interrelated dialogically. Just as languages interanimate each other, so do modes of inquiry within a field. Each mode intersects with the others in convergences and divergences in the social space of study (291–92).

This multimodality in rhetoric and composition did not develop in a vacuum. It began in particular historical circumstances—as a response to problems of written discourse that were being ignored in the 1950s and early 1960s. No field was devoting serious study to writing dysfunction, nonliterary discourse, construction of texts, or the political and social contexts of writing. To begin investigation in these areas, the early researchers chose whatever modes were at their disposal to examine problems they deemed important. Because they began working outside the framework of a recognized discipline, their use of historical, rhetorical, and empirical modes was not an act of imperialism or colonizing—that is, bringing a foreign mode under a reigning method of inquiry. In fact, the modes they used were not owned by classical studies or speech communication. Empirical inquiry was not the exclusive tool of either psychology or sociology. Theory building was not in the corner of philosophy. Because these modes were free to migrate, they were brought without tariffs to issues of literacy.

Consider the ways in which three of the first composition problems were studied in the 1960s and 1970s—the period preceding the first doctoral programs in rhetoric and composition. Writing dysfunction was investigated by Mina Shaughnessy, who drew on linguistics, sociology, and psychology and who analyzed hundreds of students' texts. Writing processes were researched empirically by Emig, Flower, Perl, and Sommers and *rhetorically* by Young, D'Angelo, and those building new theories of invention. Classifications of discourse such as the entrenched modes were critiqued by Britton and colleagues, who conducted empirical studies, by Moffett and Kinneavy, who did theory building, and later by Connors and Berlin, who used historical research. This triangulation of perspectives began to create networks of understanding in these areas.

By the time the first rhetoric and composition doctoral programs began in the late 1970s and early 1980s, a body of multimodal scholarship already existed. A community of researchers using differing kinds of designs had already formed. Journals like *College Composition and Communication* and the *Rhetoric Society Quarterly* were publishing studies in different modes, a direction followed later by *Written Communication, Rhetoric Review,* and even *Research in the Teaching of English.* It was in this context of modal heteroglossia that graduate programs in rhetoric and composition situated themselves to help students enter the dialogue already in progress. These programs became environments in which professor and graduate students could become increasingly literate in these diverse kinds of inquiry, that is, could learn to *read* diverse studies critically and to *write* or conduct them (or at least learn what doing so entails). The centripetal force of these modes was the domain—written discourse, its development, contexts, and facilitation.

In English departments where rhetorical and composition programs have been initiated, this multimodal core has become contextualized by different fields—literature, literary theory, linguistics, cognitive studies, and so on. For example, students in the program at Carnegie Mellon integrate rhetorical work with cognitive studies of problem solving. The program at the University of Southern California entails an interaction among rhetoric, linguistics, and literary theory. Our program at Purdue requires a second specialization in a literary period, in linguistics, or in literary theory. Students in these programs cope, then, not only with multimodality within rhetoric and composition but also with other disciplinary modes.

Empirical Research: Reliability and Validity

Empirical research remains, however, the least understood mode of inquiry for both new rhetoric students and members of English departments. This chapter will not elaborate on the nature of empirical research with its range of designs from case study to meta-analysis (which Asher and I have explained elsewhere) but instead will discuss the two governing criteria of empirical research—reliability and validity—suggesting that as social constructions they are not alien positivist notions but are shared by the other types of scholarship in rhetoric and composition.

As the core signifying practices in empirical research, reliability and validity are criteria that have been developed by the empirical community over the last century to guide its interpretive acts and thereby to shape researchers' consciousness of the community's concrete economic, social, and political conditions. Reliability and validity have been constructed as ground rules for discriminating the quality, value, and credibility of studies and results. The two concepts are not foundational, self-evident features inherent in the nature of empirical research but are rules of evidence and inference agreed upon and continually modified and refined over the decades by the natural and social sciences, each in somewhat different ways.

These criteria are imbricated in the history of empirical research as an interpretive enterprise, as a creation of systematic probable knowledge based on observation. The goal of empirical researchers is to create patterns and constructs to explain behavior, conditions, or interactions they observe in experience. Examples of such constructs in composition research are revision, planning, and writing anxiety. Construct formation is a rhetorical act, an act of naming a behavior and elaborating its distinctive features and its typical conditions or networks.

This interpretive activity, as well as that in critical or historical investigation, is never disinterested but always driven by many cultural factors. Bourdieu characterizes qualitative empirical research, for example, as *subjectivist:* the ethnomethodologist has "presuppositions inherent in the position as outside observer, who in his preoccupation with *interpreting* practices, is inclined to introduce into the object the principles of his relation to the object" (2). He describes all empirical research as partial representations or perspectives that are adequations but never equal to primary experience.

Reliability is a hedge against this interested or subjectivist character of empirical research because it authorizes the possibility of constructing systematic knowledge about experience in the face of randomness, an impossibility if a researcher works alone. Reliability is an argument used by the research community to discriminate levels of probability or adequation in claims. It requires multiple observers, observations, or measures in the analysis. No results are credible if they represent a solitary effort. Thus reliability counters idiosyncratic interpretations made on the basis of isolated observation.

It promotes collaboration in other ways. In the conduct of research, investigators are guided by socially established empirical designs and means of data collection and by expectations such as for triangulation of observations, for multivariate analyses, for meta-analytic calculations. To meet these expectations, researchers provide fine-grained, richly specified accounts of the patterns or constructs they are advancing in order to enable others to cocreate them. They use statistical probability as the *lingua franca* for demonstrating levels of interrelationships. Rigorous, meticulous, grounded, and complexly elaborated accounts allow others to participate in the interpretation rather than marveling at its unique and inscrutable nature. In other scholarship such as historical or hermeneutical studies, reliability implicitly urges that interpretations be bolstered by intertextuality and argued extensively so that the community can understand, assess, and possibly adopt them as preferable ways of symbolizing the historical events or textual patterns under scrutiny.

In empirical studies, reliability checks can be made both during the process of analysis and in the publication of results. Researchers test for agreement early in a study as a heuristic to determine whether others have trouble creating the same patterns and constructs they have begun to develop. If so, investigators either adjust or abandon their explanations or increase the specificity of their definitions or descriptions. In the later published reports, acceptable or high levels of reliability become arguments for the strength of the interpretation.

Validity, the other major empirical criterion, is also shared by the other modes of inquiry. When researchers establish validity, they argue for consensus not about observations as in reliability but about governing theories. Validity signifies that a piece of research and its claims are compatible with the community's theoretical structures, assumptions, and paradigms. Such arguments for theoretical coherence are based on several assumptions. The research community expects studies to address those it deems appropriate and worth investigating. If inquirers want to study other problems, that is, to resist, their new problems are still community related because they are provoked by anomalies festering in its intertext.

In addition, a community expects researchers to use its design practices—from ethnography to meta-analysis—which are shaped by prevailing conceptions of the relationship among discourse, knowledge, and experience. These practices are situated in particular economic and political contexts in the academy and the larger culture. The knowledge that is created through research is thus mediated by many factors—prevailing theories of writing and language and knowledge, current discursive practices in the research community, the economic and political status of scholars, the perceived value of the research for creating cultural capital for users, and so forth. If investigators can demonstrate that both their problems and their results are compatible with acceptable theory, design, and assumptions, this argument strengthens the interpretation. If, on the other hand, researchers work outside these conceptual boundaries, they must first establish new governing theories and then argue for their specific results. Either way, validity strongly influences the community's acceptance of the results as reasonable and valuable explanations of the experience studied.

Validity is a collaborative criterion in several ways. Most empirical researchers create knowledge incrementally, one study building on the findings of another, qualifying, testing, exploring new aspects. Empirical constructs are developed gradually by repeated and varied studies (see Lauer and Asher for an example of planning as a developing construct). Researchers also invoke validity by showing that the subjects in their studies demonstrate the individual differences expected by the community on that construct, such as social classes, maturation, or education. If a construct does not violate these expectations, a researcher has a validity argument to bolster the interpretation. Accounts of validity therefore betray a field's ideology or conflicting ideologies. Understanding how reliability and validity function as arguments forms a part of the enterprise of multimodality.

Costs

But graduate programs that foster such multiple modes are costly, a fact that I have come to appreciate after a decade of working with such a program. Let me now explore some of these expenses. As journals and books increase, reading the composition scholarship produced by multiple modes has become formidable for newcomers. It takes time to read primary texts in each mode rather than only learning about them from secondary accounts such as North's or Lindemann's, which summarize or distill theorists' work. Doctoral programs in rhetoric and composition do not transfer their students' interpretive authority to these overviewers nor to works such as Murphy's *Synoptic History of Classical Rhetoric* or Kennedy's or Barilli's histories of rhetoric in place of reading Aristotle, Quintilian, Campbell, or Genung.

It also takes time to study different forms of inquiry—the issues in historiography, the procedures and constraints of qualitative and quantitative research, and the requisites of theory building. One response has been for certain graduate programs in rhetoric and composition to ignore or marginalize a mode or two. For example, some programs within English education departments pay little attention to historical and rhetorical modes, while some programs in English departments ignore empirical research and sometimes rhetorical theory—concentrating instead on composition theory and pedagogy.

Another ongoing challenge is the necessity of comprehending and following the changes in terms and theories that are brought to composition from other fields—not to restrict their suggestive potential but to sharpen their explanatory power. For example, in the 1960s, the notion of heuristics was introduced to explain an inventional type of discursive thinking that was neither mechanical nor entirely random. This concept has followed a circuitous course in our field as it has in the disciplines in which it was first studied, where it has never been unproblematic or static. Another example is James Moffett's theory of the universe of discourse, which was based on Piagetian notions of cognitive development, a concept that was later quali-fied and enriched by the work of Vygotsky, Perry, and Kohlberg. Keeping abreast of these changes requires persistence.

A final cost I'll mention occurs during the process of promotion and tenure. Composition specialists often face a double task—to produce first-rate scholarship and to explain its nature and value. This cost is decreas-ing, in my judgment, as an understanding of multimodality increases in pluralistic departments, which have been leavened by postmoderism. The costs of multimodality, then, are not minimal. But are there compensating benefits? I believe so.

Benefits

In speaking of benefits, I do so as someone who together with my colleagues and students is continually learning what multimodality entails, as one who struggles to read and write in different modes. From this perspective, I have watched some developments. First, I have noticed that, in this kind of grad-uate program, students acquire a sense of modal conventionality. They come to view modes as social constructions, as culturally initiated and shaped, con-stantly changing, and boundaried. They value modes as alternative points of view, interdependent, partial, and in need of negotiation. They come to understand the differences in designs, intertextual records, epistemologi-cal assumptions, and warrants of each mode more readily by contrast with other modes. Students who read in different modes see, for example, the finiteness of experiments, the pitfalls of thick description and data overload, and the disappearance of the subject in deconstructive theorizing. For them, the notion of terministic screens becomes palpable as they experience how modes both enable and blind researchers. Students recognize the losses and gains in establishing correlations and causalities on the one hand and ar-ticulating discontinuities and gaps on the other.

They also begin to realize some identifications among modes—that each entails interpretation and argument—even in empirical studies where data do not speak for or justify themselves. They conclude that all modes are problem driven and meanings need to be negotiated in all communities that authorize validity and reliability.

The graduate students in rhetoric and composition, then, develop a lit-eracy and flexibility in multimodal reading. But does such multimodality carry over into their own research? To try to answer this question, I will ex-amine the work of seven former graduate students as they wrote their dis-sertations. I'll look at the kinds of problems they investigated and at the methods they employed. The first two, Bernard Miller and Michael Carter, became intrigued by dissonant views of the initiation of discourse that they encountered in four literatures: classical views of *kairos* and *stasis,* cognitive research on problem formulation, contemporary conceptions of the composing process, and arguments in rhetorical and literary theory over the relationship between knowledge and discourse. These dissonances were heightened by their frustration in helping students to begin to write artfully.

Two others, Mark Simpson and Jennie Dautermann, decided to study the ill-defined concept of audience because of inconclusive and conflicting treatments of it by both empirical researchers and composition theorists, who were debating the relative merits of audience addressed, audience invoked, universal audience, and discourse communities. They were also dissatisfied with the conceptions of audience found in classroom research, in communication studies that did not account for readers of texts, and in scholarship that did not explain audiences in the workplace.

Lee Campbell was motivated to develop a new theory of argument by a dissatisfaction with narrow and divergent conceptions of it in composition theory and pedagogy, communication studies, linguistics, and philosophy of language. Janet Atwill became aware of the occlusion of productive knowledge through her study of rhetorical history and her work with composition theory and pedagogy. Finally, Myrna Harrienger has been provoked to examine the literacy of elderly ill women, after conducting an ethnographic study that revealed a gap in composition research and shortcomings in constructivist critiques of biomedical discourse. While her empirical research opened up the problem, her study of rhetorical and literary theory enabled her to frame the problem as a discursive one rooted in the modern Cartesian episteme. It was in this intertextual context that these seven problems became compelling.

As they carried out their research, these former graduate students actually used multimodal methods, arguments, and citations. Bernard Miller wrote a revisionary history of *Gorgias's* concept of *kairos,* problematizing historical studies of *Gorgias's* through Heidegger. Michael Carter constructed a rhetorical theory of the genesis of discourse, interweaving historical studies of *stasis* and *kairos,* composition theory on inquiry, and cognitive work on problem formulation.

Although Mark Simpson and Jennie Dautermann used ethnography as their basic mode of inquiry, they incorporated work form other modes in their analysis. In Mark's profile of multiple audiences for software documentation and in Jennie Dautermann's account of the formation of a discourse community of nurses, both used notions of audience from composition theory, rhetorical history, discourse analysis, and work in technical communication.

Lee Campbell's theory of argument built on the concept of relevance from pragmatics, on studies in phenomenology and argumentation, and on classical rhetoric. After establishing his constituents of relevant argument—strategic, rational, and life worldly—through a linguistic mode of argument, he used his conception to critique composition theory and pedagogy. Janet Atwill reconstructed the concept of productive knowledge, writing a revisionary history of the notion of *techne,* particularly in Aristotle, deploying poststructural theories such as Bourdieu's to challenge the theory/practice binary, which she argued has been enshrined in the humanist paradigm. Myrna Harrienger is constructing a discursive theory of healing through a poststructuralist critique of biomedical discourse, drawing on feminist criticism and composition theory. Each of these projects has made its new garment of understanding out of multimodal fabrics, raising new kinds of questions and investigating them in more complex ways than one mode allows.

This research inevitably needs to be communicated to a variety of audiences. Cheryl Geisler, a graduate of Carnegie Mellon's rhetoric program, spoke of this aspect of her work at the CCCC's research network workshop in 1990. She explained that her study of essayist literacy was sociocognitive, combing empirical methods of data collection and analysis with an examination of the cultural and social frames of reference for issues of cognition in literacy. Because this work was of importance to several fields, she reported it in five forums: the National Council of Teachers of English, the CCCC, the American Education Research Association, the National Reading Conference, and the Society for the Social Studies of Science. Learning to make such adaptations for multiple discourse communities is, then, another aspect of multimodality, both a cost and a benefit.

As different as all these projects are, the researchers nevertheless appear to share a common attitude toward inquiry—an emphasis on problems rather than on methods. Instead of striving to become ethnographers, cultural critics, or revisionary historians talking to other ethnographers, critics or historians, they seek to master modes as ways into pressing issues. Their respect for diverse modes makes room for blurred genres and coherencies among studies that elaborate and qualify each other rather than cancel each other out. They view multimodality as a means of deflating any one mode's claims to certainty or imperialism. In short, they do not want to be trapped in the pretensions of a single mode but empowered by several modes to study how, in Bakhtin's words, individuals and culture interanimate each other through language, how diverse literacies can be facilitated. They value heteroglossia, because it enables them better to investigate the complexity and consequences of written discourse with its academic, social, and political contexts.

Works Cited

Atwill, Janet. "Refiguring Rhetoric as Art: Aristotle's Concept of Techne and the Humanist Paradigm." Diss. Purdue U, 1990.

Atwill, Janet, and Janice Lauer. "Refiguring Rhetoric as an Art: Aristotle's Concept of Techne." *Discourse Studies in Honor of James L. Kinneavy.* Ed. Rosalind Gabin. Washington, DC: Scripta P, [1989].

Bakhtin, M. M. *The Dialogic Imagination.* Ed. Michael Holquist. Trans. Caryl Emerson and Michael Holquist. Austin: U of Texas P, 1981.

Bourdieu, Pierre. *Outline of a Theory of Practice.* Trans. Richard Nice. Cambridge UP, 1977.

Campbell, Lee. "The Relevant Communication of Rhetorical Arguments." Diss. Purdue U, 1990.

Carter, Michael. "Genesis of Written Discourse: Features of the Art." Diss. Purdue U, 1986.

Dautermann, Jennie. "Writing at Good Hope Hospital: A Study of Negotiated Discourse in the Workplace." Diss. Purdue U, 1991.

Geisler, Cheryl. "Toward a Sociocognitive Perspective: An Account." Paper delivered for the Research Network of the CCCC. Chicago, March, 1990.

Harrienger, Myrna. "Discursivity, Subjectivity, and Empowerment: Elderly Ill Women." Diss. Purdue U, 1991.

Lauer, Janice, and William Asher. *Composition Research: Empirical Designs.* New York: Oxford UP, 1988.

Miller, Bernard, "Heidegger and Gorgian Kairos." Diss. Purdue U, 1987.

Simpson, Mark. "Shaping Computer Documentation for Multiple Audiences: An Ethnographic Study." Diss. Purdue U, 1989.

8

Introduction to "Two Views on the Use of Literature in Composition"

Wendy Bishop

A good debate provides a snapshot, a freeze-frame of an issue. In the presence of two well-matched, intelligent individuals who hold divergent views, we pause and consider a specific concern from several angles then return to the larger, interconnected questions that shape our teaching lives. Each time I read Erika Lindemann and Gary Tate sharing their opinions about the place of literature in first-year composition classes, I find myself rethinking my beliefs and rechecking my positions. Over time, I have shuttled from agreeing with one part of one essay to agreeing with another part of the other essay and back again. As I mature and change as a writer, writing teacher, writing center director, writing program director, and dissertation director in a graduate program in composition, my own positions evolve and the arguments presented here have new relevance.

For many of us, these essays function as professional Rorschach tests. Friends and colleagues, Erika and Gary agreed to disagree in public on the question "should literature be taught in the freshman composition class," sharing their papers at the 1992 convention of the Conference on College Composition and Communication. Published in the March 1993 issue of *College English,* the essayists ask readers to consider a number of other, related questions: What is literature? Who should read and write it? What is first-year composition? Should it be required, and if so, of whom? And most importantly, how should such a course be taught? Upon what principles, with what content, in service of what goals?

The Lindemann and Tate debate maps out a focused portion of what Marjorie Roemer, Lucille M. Schultz, and Russel Durst call "the Great Debate," whether or not first-year college students should be required to enroll in a writing course. Roemer and her colleagues suggest this discussion began in the late 1880s, continued through the twentieth century, and came into prominence with Sharon Crowley's call for the abolition of the required course in 1991. Crowley and historian Robert Connors continued to explore abolition in notable 1995 essays. Compositionists, of course, have regularly examined the nature of these courses, including James Berlin in his 1982 essay "Contemporary Composition: The Major Pedagogical Theories" and Lester Faigley in his 1986 essay "Competing Theories of Process." Both of these essays function as backdrops for Erika Lindemann and Gary Tate's debate. As committed writing teachers and educators of teachers, Lindemann and Tate take on the "If yes, then how" question (readers here will want to continue to investigate the "If no, then what" question on their own).

Briefly, Lindemann believes our courses should teach students to appreciate "the varieties and excellences of academic discourse." She deplores dichotomous thinking current in field discussions of the time and insists we must consider the purpose of the course if we "are going to drag every first-year student through the requirement." She is against courses that focus on a single genre or on great ideas; that substitute contemporary social issues or skills-based instruction for process oriented instruction; that highlight literature and thereby focus on consuming rather than producing texts. She finds her best models in second-generation Writing Across the Curriculum courses. Students should connect reading to writing, writing to disciplinary knowledge, writing to rhetorical training, and process to product. She believes a literature focus allows teachers to talk more and students to write less, feeling such courses "rarely connect literature with life." Lindemann explains that close analysis of literary style does not translate into students developing their own stylistic fluency and that learning literary criticism emphasizes "only one way of knowing, a process of knowledge-making peculiar to the humanities." Overall, she feels the inclusion of literary texts in first-year courses benefits the literature profession and not the student writer who is entering a broader, multidisciplinary academic environment. Urging us to reconsider our instruction, she explains:

> If we will take the time to appreciate the writing that shapes other disciplines, we can become comfortable, even confident about, constructing student-centered classrooms, where the acts of language we are most concerned about are those of first-year students eager to participate successfully in the rigorous work college demands of them.

Carefully and passionately reasoned, Erika Lindemann's essay drew an equally passionate response from Gary Tate, who argues, "We have denied students who are seeking to improve their writing the benefits of reading an entire body of excellent writing" in the pursuit of the very goals Lindemann outlines. He agrees that literature has often been poorly taught in writing classrooms (particularly the "talk too much, write too little" problem Lindemann alludes to), but Tate is deeply concerned with the substitutes that have been offered up instead by what he provocatively terms "the Rhetoric Police." Readers will need to decide for themselves who falls into this category, but I suspect such individuals are, in general, any of us involved in the professionalization of the field. Aristotle, invention-oriented individuals, cognitivists, and socialists are named, but these labels point to groups of pedagogists who do not necessarily cohabit happily. And that is perhaps Tate's point. Instead of teachers of writing who choose to use or not use literature in required first-year writing courses, we have become composition and rhetoric professionals who advocate positions and pedagogies. It is certainly true that currently we have as many subfields and areas of specialty as our English studies colleagues (look to the CCCC convention proposal categories or job ads to begin to name these), perhaps because we have grown up within the shadow of the field-coverage model that still guides English departments throughout the United States.

In "A Place for Literature in Freshman Composition," Gary Tate explains that "we have lost some valuable words, some valuable concepts." He feels policed. As if he should substitute the term *inventive procedures* for his preferred term *imagination* or teach academic discourse rather than "the entire world of imaginative texts: the canonical texts, of course, but also the imaginative texts of students, young children, and amateurs. Why do we deny our students the pleasure and profit of reading this literature?" Tate questions our abilities to help students attain the discourse fluency Lindemann would have us focus on and wonders at our complicity in "shaping and fitting students to perform their appointed tasks as good little workers in the various artificial—and some would say oppressive—academic/administrative divisions that constitute the modern American university."

Tate's essay is quite different than Lindemann's in tone and vocabulary. He sounds like this: Rhetoric Police, value, enjoy, freedom, boring, love, survive, students' lives. And she sounds more like this: critical awareness, audience, purposes, text, relevance, training writing teachers, students joining the conversation. It would be tempting but impractical to attach labels here to prose styles and pedagogical approaches, since any terms I might choose would be challenged. Still, I find it impressive that in many ways, both writers practice what they preach, enacting the type of discourse they advocate in service of an argument for a curriculum that would teach the same. Each writer does so with energy, urgency, and good will. In the following email, Erika Lindemann captures the spirit of the enterprise these colleagues undertook:

> Gary had called me to ask, "Do you teach literature in freshman English?" I said, "No." (Maybe I said, "hell no, Gary.") "Would you like to explain why?" he responded, so we agreed to take sides in a debate he and I both thought was worth having. Gary felt that literature had been drummed out of composition courses without a fair hearing; I felt that it was still too much of a presence—also without much thought. We agreed in the phone call to define literature as poetry, fiction, and drama. Several responses to the two essays appeared in the October 1993 *College English;* neither Gary nor I responded to the responses because we had both wanted to begin a conversation, which I think we were successful in doing. Eventually, though, I used the "debate" to elaborate and complicate what I thought might be going on as teachers framed their composition courses. (Lindemann, personal communication)

And a debate it was.

Follow-up letters in the October 1993 issue of *College English* revealed that three out of four commentators were concerned with Erika Lindemann's arguments. She overviews their responses and provides a sketch-history of the debate in her essay "Three Views of English 101" published two years later in the March 1995 issue of *College English* as part of a symposium of four articles and a response on the same topic (including a second essay by Gary Tate). In further situating her argument with an exploration of contemporary approaches to composition instruction (writing as product, writing as process, writing as system), Lindemann builds on the sort of work done by Berlin and Faigley in their essays, mentioned above. Lindemann knows and believes that each of the three systems of instruction she outlines can exist simultaneously but asks us to consider what sort of course each perspective promotes and which we are promoting as teachers ("Three" 299).

Gary Tate, in his second essay, asks us to question why the question of teaching literature in composition classes has disappeared (beyond the edges of the debate then being held): "even though literature is apparently still a part of some composition courses, why have discussions of its use in these courses almost ceased?" ("Notes" 304). His questioning of the question is interesting given the proportion of favorable to unfavorable responses Tate received on his initial essay, given the interest *College English* had in printing its follow up symposium, and given the precedent the initial Lindemann and Tate debate created for a second major 1990s debate between David Bartholomae and Peter Elbow at the 1994 CCCC convention (subsequently published in the 1995 issue of *College Composition and Communication*).

The remaining three participants in the 1995 *College English* "Symposium on Literature in the Composition Classroom" provide additional views. Erwin Steinberg feels that there has been more discussion of the issue than Tate acknowledges and Steinberg deconstructs some of the terms of the argument (*the* composition classroom, literature, and so on); Michael Gamer explores the ways imaginative texts can enrich the classroom; and Jane Peterson argues against what she finds to be a disturbingly text-based discussion being conducted in these essays.

By reviewing all the texts cited here, in the order of their composition, one enters a discussion thread that is archived not on a web board but within our journals, attesting to the central importance of these questions. And nowhere are they laid out with more skill, enthusiasm, and cogency than in the two essays you have before you. Reading Erika Lindemann and Gary Tate will encourage you to join this conversation. And that, after all, is why they wrote.

Works Cited

Bartholomae, David. "Writing with Teachers: A Conversation with Peter Elbow." *College Composition and Communication* 46.1 (1995): 62–71.

Berlin, James. A. "Contemporary Composition: The Major Pedagogical Theories." *College English* 44.8 (1982): 765–77.

Connors, Robert J. "The New Abolitionism: Toward a Historical Background." *Reconceiving Writing, Rethinking Writing Instruction.* Ed. Joseph Petraglia. Mahwah, NJ: Erlbaum, 1995: 3–26.

Crowley, Sharon. "Composition's Ethic of Service, the Universal Requirement, and the Discourse of Student Need." *Journal of Advanced Composition* 15.2 (1995): 227–39.

Elbow, Peter. "Being a Writer vs. Being an Academic: A Conflict in Goals." *College Composition and Communication* 46.1 (1995): 72–83.

Faigley, Lester. "Competing Theories of Process." *College English* 48 (1986): 527–42.

Gamer, Michael. "Fictionalizing the Disciplines: Literature and the Boundaries of Knowledge." Symposium: Literature in the Composition Classroom. *College English* 57.3 (1995): 281–86.

Gregory S. Jay, Elizabeth Latosi-Sawin, Leon Knight, Jeanie C. Crain. "Four Comments on 'Two Views on the Uses of Literature in Composition.'" *College English* 55.6 (1993): 673–79.

Lindemann, Erika. Personal communication. 20 Aug. 2001.

———. "Three Views of English 101." Symposium: Literature in the Composition Classroom. *College English* 57.3 (1995): 287–302.

Peterson, Jane. "Through the Looking-Glass: A Response." Symposium: Literature in the Composition Classroom. *College English* 57.3 (1995): 310–18.

Roemer, Marjorie, Lucille M. Schultz and Russel K. Durst. "Reframing the Great Debate on First-Year Writing. *College Composition and Communication* 50.3 (1999): 377–92.

Steinberg, Erwin. "Imaginative Literature in Composition Classrooms?" Symposium: Literature in the Composition Classroom. *College English* 57.3 (1995): 266–80.

Tate, Gary. "Notes on the Dying of a Conversation." Symposium: Literature in the Composition Classroom. *College English* 57.3 (1995): 303–9.

Freshman Composition: No Place for Literature (1993)

Erika Lindemann

Recent discussions at professional meetings and in the pages of our journals have raised persistent questions about the role of literature in a first-year writing course. Some teachers regret that freshman English has become such an unholy "service course," stripped of the imaginative literature we love to teach. They argue that poetry, fiction, and drama offer essential training in the processes of reading. Although literature may have been taught poorly in the past, we should now reassert its importance in writing courses by adopting the insights of recent developments in critical theory. Other teachers find these arguments naively arrogant. When freshmen read and write about imaginative literature alone, they remain poorly prepared for the writing required of them in courses outside the English department. Instead of disparaging "the stuff" written in other disciplines, we ought instead to appreciate the varieties and excellences of academic discourse. Such an appreciation would discourage us from drawing false dichotomies between "them" and "us," between academic and personal writing, between writing inside and outside the academy.

Although imaginative literature disappeared from many first-semester composition classes years ago, it still survives in curricula that require a course in writing about literature, a course that some would argue belongs not to the writing program but rather to the literature program. Such courses, wherever they may appear in the curriculum, are being contested in ways that have not been apparent before. It is as if we have already played out our enthusiasm for writing as process and rejected those opportunities offered by the Writing Across the Curriculum movement to learn more about discourse in other disciplines. As we look about us, waiting for the paradigm to shift, we rediscover literature. For some, the discovery represents a welcome resurgence of interest in reading-as-process; for others, an antidote to writing courses that lack "content."

This essay first appeared in *College Composition and Communication* 55 (1993): 311–316. Copyright © 1993 by the National Council of Teachers of English. Reprinted with permission.

What disturbs me about these discussions is that we have failed to ask a prior question. We cannot usefully discuss the role of imaginative literature (however defined) in freshman English without first asking what the purpose of a first-year writing course is. The debate centers on more important questions than whether or not to include a poem, play, or novel in a freshman composition syllabus. At issue are the goals of a first-year writing course, the training we give the teachers of that course, and the values people ascribe to the course in the college curriculum.

Most writing teachers reject the assumption that first-year writing courses serve primarily as a remedy for poor training in high school. To see freshman composition as remedial is to undervalue its importance as the only required course remaining in most college curricula. Freshman English does what no high school writing course can do: provide opportunities to master the genres, styles, audiences, and purposes of college writing. Freshman English offers guided practice in reading and writing the discourses of the academy and the professions. That is what our colleagues across the campus want it to do; that is what it should do if we are going to drag every first-year student through the requirement.

By defining the course in this way, I am excluding courses preoccupied with grammar, or the essay, or great ideas. As we have known for decades, focusing on grammar instruction reduces the amount of writing practice students are likely to get. Focusing exclusively on the essay—including the critical essay on a work of literature—amounts to collapsing the discourses of the academy into one genre, limiting students' abilities to practice other forms, experience other perspectives, negotiate the expectations of other readers. Focusing the course on great ideas also limits students' attention to writing, primarily because "ideas" courses devote too much time to lecture and discussion and too little time to planning, drafting, and revising. For this reason, I am also unhappy with WAC courses that substitute "global warming" or contemporary social issues for the great ideas listed in the thematic tables of contents of more traditional essay readers. The emphasis is still on the essay; the pedagogy, in practice, still involves too much teacher talk and too little writing.

Second-generation WAC courses come closer to the ideal I am describing. A freshman writing course linked to a freshman history course, for example, gives students practice reading and writing history. So does a first-year writing course that asks students to read and write a variety of texts found in the humanities, sciences, and social sciences. Such courses should have an immediate connection to the assignments students confront in college. They are not mere skills courses or training for the professions students may enter five years later; they raise questions of audience, purpose, and form that rhetorical training has always prepared students to address.

Such courses have as their subject matter the *processes* whereby writers and readers enter the conversation of the academy and begin to contribute to the making of knowledge. They focus not on nouns but on verbs: planning, drafting, revising, using data, evaluating sources, reading critically, interpreting evidence, solving problems in writing, understanding and applying the rhetorical and formal conventions of texts, becoming good collaborators. Such courses demand a persistent, rigorous agenda of reading and writing in the discipline. They are difficult to teach. They look and sound more like writing workshops than literature courses, students always at work on some writing project, the teacher serving as an experienced writer, not a lecturer, guiding students in those uses of language that enable them to become historians, biologists, and mathematicians. To be this kind of teacher requires knowing how writers interpret and create texts in many disciplines.

The sort of writing course I have described neither requires nor finds particularly relevant a significant role for literature. That said, I would offer five additional reasons why using literature in freshman English is inappropriate.

First, literature-based courses, even more essay-based courses, focus on consuming texts, not producing them. The teacher talks 75 to 80 percent of the time. Students do very little writing, and what they write has little relation to the intellectual demands on assignments in a political science or chemistry class. A pedagogy derived from teaching literature looks and sounds different from one that encourages students to produce texts. Literature teachers are conscious of the difference. Not only do they sometimes express misgivings about the writing teacher's use of group work and peer evaluation, but they also report clear preferences for teaching by lecture and discussion. A 1989–1990 survey of upper-division literature courses supports this preference: "almost all respondents devote some time to [lectures and discussions], while relatively few devote time to [small-group activities and writing]. Further, even respondents using small-group activities and writing exercises generally devote only a small percentage of class time to them" (Bettina J. Huber, "Today's Literature Classroom: Findings from the MLA's 1990 Survey of Upper-Division Courses," *ADE Bulletin 101* [Spring 1992]: 50).

But why not teach just one novel or poem, something that will restore the humanistic content to the curriculum? Because the curriculum already has humanistic content. Because college students must take humanities, arts, and literature courses, literature need not necessarily be transported into a writing course for the sake of "humanism." Moreover, many literature courses are not humanistic. They present the teacher's or the critic's truths about the poetry, fiction, and drama being studied. They rarely connect literature with life. If students get to write a paper or two, they must assume the disembodied voice of some abstruse journal as they analyze the ingrown toenail motif in *Beowulf*. Such assignments silence students' voices in the conversation literature is intended to promote. In other words, literature teaching offers the writing teacher no model worth emulating.

But doesn't studying literature help teach style? I don't think so. Examining literary language has limited usefulness in a writing course because our students do not *write* literature; they write about it or respond to it. If our students were writing poems, or short stories, or even dialogues, literary models might suggest stylistic options worth practicing. Most of the time, however, style is taught, not as language to emulate, but as language to appreciate, to respect all the more perhaps because we cannot manage our linguistic resources as well as Shakespeare or Frost did. When teachers ask students to write *about* literature, style becomes a subject matter, an object for analysis. It no longer represents a range of linguistic opinions for treating any subject. A better way to teach style is by asking students to examine the texts they encounter in the academy, texts that define a much larger repertoire of rhetorical options than literary language customarily allows. Simply recognizing or appreciating these conventions is not enough; students must also make them work in their own writing, by creating texts like those they read, by talking back to the models.

Some people believe that recent work in critical theory offers new reasons to teach literature in freshman English classes. Presumably we now have a better understanding of how readers engage texts, how those texts are socially constructed, and how the processes of reading and writing create bridges between the individual and the larger linguistic community. Although critical theory may offer new ways of interpreting texts, we do not have to study literature to apply these new insights. A theory of reading or of texts that depends on literature, that moves aside the texts our students read and write, is no help to a writing teacher. Reader-response criticism, social constructionism, and feminist approaches *can* inform the teaching of writing, not because they need literature to make the point, but because they also apply to nonliterary texts. Critical theory has value only insofar as it gives our students a more self-conscious awareness of their behavior as readers, engaged in significant acts of language in every class they take, not just in a literature class.

Interpreting texts also represents only one way of knowing, a process of knowledge-making peculiar to the humanities. Other disciplines value different methods of making meaning: closely observing natural phenomena, refusing to generalize beyond the data, removing the personal element for the sake of neutrality. Although literary critics value the personal interpretations readers construct from texts, social scientists value the ability to replicate interpretations of data, and most scientists would define "data" in such a way as to exclude texts altogether. Each discipline advances its own understanding of what claims are worth asserting, what constitutes evidence, what sorts of proof may be offered, what aims and audiences are legitimate to address, what genres are appropriate. It is simply not the case that interpreting texts will help students gain confidence in interpreting the results of a chemistry experiment, a field experience in a psychology class, or a sculpture. These contexts all assume different kinds of interpretation.

The final argument for teaching literature in freshman English is perhaps the most insidious: it would enrich our training programs for graduate students. They could learn to teach literature as well as writing, becoming the confident, professional pedagogues we hope to send into the job market, happier until then if we let them teach a poem or a novel once in a while. Happier maybe, but not better teachers. The truth is that few faculty members in English department really care about teacher training. They care about keeping graduate students employed; they want other departments to know that freshmen are learning something; but they do not teach freshman English often enough to know what is going on in that part of the curriculum or what kinds of training writing teachers would find most valuable. Although literature teachers need training too, asking colleagues who rarely examine what they do in a literature class is not the best place to start. Departments can easily erode a good program for training writing teachers by sliding in a few workshops on teaching literature. A few workshops, however, will not do the job; a course, a practicum, or a substantial mentoring program promises better training. Writing teachers have over a decade of experience developing support systems for inexperienced teachers, but we may need to fight hard to assert their importance and unique goals. Those programs also need revising from time to time so that teachers can learn more about workshop teaching, for example, or the uses of writing outside English departments, or methods of peer, holistic, and portfolio evaluation.

As I have suggested, we cannot discuss the role of literature in the first-year writing course without first defining the purpose of the course. Although we are unlikely to reach consensus on either topic, the issues I have raised may usefully complicate their continued discussion. Beyond that, we also may want to ask why the discussion is taking place. What does it mean that this topic merits point/counterpoint debate in the pages of *College English*? In faculty lounges and committee meetings, where colleagues engage in animated arguments about whether or not to use literature in a first-year writing course?

One strength of our profession is our persistent effort to examine what writing courses should be and how to teach them well. Lately, these discussions have taken a more assertive turn, often depending on false dichotomies to support claims about either/or propositions. Are humanists, for example, really so different from scientists? Is the academy necessarily divorced from "real life"? Do we oversimplify matters by asserting that personal writing differs from academic discourse? I believe we do.

We simply do not have a unified theory to guide our work. In such times of disjunction and divergent views, it is tempting to cling to what makes us comfortable—literature. We like literature, we know what to say about it, and we have a lot to say. But that is the problem, not the solution: we are saying too much; our students are writing too little. If we will take the time to appreciate the writing that shapes other disciplines, we can become comfortable with, even confident about, constructing student-centered classrooms, where the acts of language we are most concerned about are those of first-year students eager to participate successfully in the rigorous work college demands of them. We need to join students in exploring these sites of composing found in the academy. Instead of asking our students to write *about* what it means to be educated, let us assist them to join the conversations an education enables.

A Place for Literature in Freshman Composition (1993)

Gary Tate

The presence of literature—fiction, poetry, drama—in freshman composition courses in 1992 is minimal. The last time I talked with Richard Larson about his national survey of freshman writing programs, he estimated that only about one in five programs contains any literature, and the ones that have a literary component are likely to be devoting a semester to "introducing" literature rather than "using" literature to help teach writing. A survey of textbooks or a glance through CCCC convention programs would support the same conclusion. We have denied students who are seeking to improve their writing the benefits of reading an entire body of excellent writing. It is not unlike telling music students that they should not listen to Bach or Mahler. Why have we taken such a seemingly illogical stance? Three reasons seem to me important: the pedagogical sins of teachers in the past, the revival of rhetoric, and changing attitudes about the purposes and goals of freshman composition.

Those of us who can remember how literature was often treated in writing classes are not surprised that it did not survive as a major pedagogical force. Its virtual disappearance, however, was not, I think, the result of all those theoretical reasons given in some recent articles on the topic. In large part, literature disappeared from the composition classes in this country because it was badly misused by teachers desperate to teach literature, teachers who really should not be blamed for trying to teach the one subject they knew. However, a teaching approach will not disappear merely because it is misguided or downright wrong. It will disappear only when there is something to replace it. Remember Thomas Kuhn's argument that a paradigm will not just disappear. It will vanish—or whatever paradigms do—only when it is replaced by another paradigm. So it is with teaching. If there had not been something to replace literature in the writing class, it would never have disappeared.

This essay first appeared in *College Composition and Communication* 55 (1993): 317–321. Copyright © 1993 by the National Council of Teachers of English. Reprinted with permission.

What was waiting to replace literature was rhetoric, supported since the 1960s by the Rhetoric Police, that hardy band of zealots who not many years hence were to become the dreaded enforcement arm of the Conference on College Composition and Communication. Pity the innocent young (or old) teacher in those days who tried to read a CCCC convention paper that did not contain a reference to Aristotle or the word "invention." (A current analogy might be a person today who does not in her paper refer to, at least, collaboration, hegemony, and community.) Of course, the Rhetoric Police are still with us, but much like the KGB, their power and influence have been considerably weakened.

One of the fascinating features of this episode—and one that has gone generally unremarked by historians—is how rhetoric replaced literature in the freshman composition course with no sustained debate. It was not a matter of our deciding after careful and prolonged discussion that a change was needed. The Rhetoric Police merely moved in and we all surrendered. Here and there a sonnet or short story might have been hurled at the invaders, but such weapons were ineffective against the whole array of Aristotelian devices wielded by the RP. The situation changed so quickly and so completely that in 1969, when Ed Corbett and I tried to find current articles on composition and literature to include in our *Teaching High School Composition,* so few were available that Ed finally had to write one to fill out that section of the book.

Today, therefore, I can't *reopen* the debate about composition and literature because no debate occurred in the first place. What I can do is try to start a conversation by asking the question, "Did we give up too much when, without a fight, we allowed the Rhetoric Police to drive literature out of our writing courses?"

Certainly we gave up some words that I regret losing. "Imagination," for example, sounds as antique today as another word we lost: "Style." Instead of imagination, we now have "inventive procedures" such as cubing, looping, and brainstorming. Instead of style, a piece of writing now has "surface features"—always uttered with lips curled in disdain. Cubing and looping and brainstorming are sometimes useful pedagogical devices, but to assume, as many seem to do, that inventive procedures or the plotting or cognitive strategies do more than scratch the surface of the human mind thinking and imagining is to trivialize the creative act of composing. And to ignore the study of style as just another of the many misguided concerns of current-traditionalists (lips curled, again), is to deprive our students of the linguistic possibilities that just might elevate their prose above mediocrity, to use another unpopular word.

So we have lost some valuable words, some valuable concepts. But far more important, we have lost most of the texts that body forth that imagination and that style whose passing I mourn. And I speak here not just of those texts that constitute the traditional canon of literary works, no matter how that term is defined. I am thinking of the entire world of imaginative texts: the canonical texts, of course, but also the imaginative texts of students, young children, and amateurs. Why do we deny our students the pleasure and profit of reading this literature? Some of us don't, of course, but for many years now, we have had to use it furtively, on the sly, with cautious glances over our shoulders. "Pssst. Hey, kid. Want to read a good poem?"

I am not prepared to argue that imaginative literature should be the only kind of reading required of our composition students, nor should it be the only kind of writing they are asked to do. All I am suggesting is that we need to think seriously about why we are neglecting literature. One major reason for this neglect is that many teachers now believe—or, more accurately, have been led to believe—that the freshman composition course is a place to teach students to write academic discourse so that they might "succeed as writers in the academy" or in order that they might "join the conversations that education enables," to use Erika Lindemann's elegant characterization. I have problems with both of these goals. And, inevitably, it is goals we must consider when we are deciding about what to teach, how to teach it, and such matters as what texts to use.

I am increasingly bothered—at least on Mondays, Wednesdays, and Fridays—by the current focus on academic discourse. (I say MWF in order to indicate the degree of my uncertainty about this matter.) I sometimes think that we are very close to turning freshman composition into the ultimate "service course" for all the other disciplines in the academy. I reject—at least on MWF—that vision of the course. Does the vast apparatus of our discipline—all the journals, books, conferences, graduate programs—exist in the cause of nothing more than better sociology and biology papers? I hope not, because such a view is not only intellectually suspect, but impractical as well. Can we, in a semester or two, really help students function effectively in all the different communities they will be entering as they move from course to course, from discipline to discipline, throughout their four years of college? A recent text would have me help my students become writers in the health sciences. Even if I knew that some of my freshmen would be entering the "health sciences," should I force the entire class to learn to write in this particular discipline? And please don't tell me to design a different course for each student. (The freshman class I am currently teaching contains students who plan to study Finance, Journalism, French,

Fashion Design, Advertising, Psychology, and a wide range of other subjects.) Even if I were to focus on the kinds of writing required in the so-called core courses they will all be required to take, those courses exhibit such a wide range of disciplines that the task is hopeless.

The alternative, of course, would be to attempt to deal with academic discourse generally, as if there were some features of all such discourse that could be abstracted and taught. If taken seriously, however, this abstraction would have to take place at a very high level, a level that would not only be too complex for freshmen but a level that would, in the end, prove impractical if we are seriously trying to help students deal with the day-to-day demands of their academic work.

The recent interest in academic discourse and the various communities of writers that exist within the college and university is a small part of what I see as the increasing professionalization of undergraduate education in this country. It is as if all those students who come to college only in order to get a better job have convinced us that a college education is primarily job training and that the task of the freshman writing course is to help make that training more effective. We seem to have accepted this student belief along with a number of others—for example, that a "C" is a failing grade. Whatever our motives, I fear that more and more we are primarily interested in shaping and fitting students to perform their appointed tasks as good little workers in the various artificial—and some would say oppressive—academic/administrative divisions that constitute the modern American university. The analogy between shaping them into good, obedient workers in the academy and shaping them to be good, obedient workers in the world beyond the academy is obvious.

What do I offer in place of academic discourse as a focus for the freshman composition course? Very tentatively, let me suggest that there is another "community" that we should be preparing our students to join. Because I do not want to impose my beliefs on my readers—not that I could even if I wished to—I will speak only about myself. I have no interest in spending my few remaining teaching years helping students learn to write better papers in biology or better examinations in the health sciences. The "conversations" I want to help my students join are not the conversations going on in the academy. These are too often restricted, artificial, irrelevant, and—let's be frank—boring. I refuse to look at my students as primarily history majors, accounting majors, nursing majors. I much prefer to think of them and treat them as people whose most important conversations will take place *outside the academy,* as they struggle to figure out how to live their lives—that is, how to vote and love and survive, how to respond to change and diversity and death and oppression and freedom. I find it ironic, for example, that the unprecedented freedom that many young people seem to enjoy today is largely an illusion. It seems that every time I am allowed to look beneath the surface affluence of the undergraduates in my classes, I discover young people bruised by alcohol or other drugs or by parents. I find young people whose "respectable" families harbor the most destructive physical, emotional, and psychological violence. I do not believe that my writing courses should be therapy classes for battered and confused students, but neither do I believe that I should ignore my students' problems, my students' lives, pretending all along that the smiling surfaces we present to each other are accurate indicators of the lives we are living.

All I am suggesting here is that I am far more interested in my students as individual human beings who will have private and maybe public lives that transcend whatever disciplines they associate themselves with while in college. It is the "conversations" of these private and public lives that interest me far more than the "conversations" of the various academic disciplines. A well-known rhetorician, upon hearing me utter some such words recently, scoffed, "Oh, that old humanist thing!" Probably so. And I know quite well that many writing teachers have quite different interests. Legitimate interests. But their interests are not mine. Maybe it is because I have never given myself wholly to the world of the academy, always holding back some part of me, some part of my life. Maybe it is because my background has often made me feel uncomfortable in the university—always the outsider, at least in my mind. I'm not certain. But I am convinced that true education, as opposed to training, is concerned with much more than what we find in the various academic disciplines.

What literature in the freshman writing class has to do with my concerns seems obvious to me. If I want my students to think and talk and write about human lives outside the academy—"Writing Beyond the Disciplines"— then I certainly do not want to deny them the resources found in literary works, just as I do not want to deny them the resources found elsewhere. I do not advocate having students read only literary works. But they should not be denied that privilege altogether. They should be denied no resource that can help them.

The discipline of composition studies, controlled as it was during its early years by the Rhetoric Police, has erred seriously, I believe, by elevating nonfiction prose and the discourses of the various disciplines to sacred heights, in the meantime ignoring an enormously rich body of literature because that literature was at one time misused by writing teachers and because many members of the Rhetoric Police had themselves been abused in various ways by their colleagues who professed literature. My own guilt in these matters is profound. In the past, at three different colleges, I have argued to keep literature out of writing programs. And even today, the old attitudes die hard. For instance, I am a great fan of the personal essay and find myself gravitating to it in almost every class I teach. But I am wrong in doing so because my fascination with the personal essay leads me to ignore other forms of literature that might benefit my students. What I am suggesting here is simply that it is time for us to adopt a far more generous vision of our discipline and its scope, a vision that excludes *no* texts. Only by doing this can we end the self-imposed censorship that for more than two decades has denied us the use of literature in our writing classes.

PART TWO

Horizons: New Essays in Composition Pedagogy

9

The Slave of Pedagogy: Composition Studies and the Art of Teaching

Nancy Myers

A colleague tells a story of a professor who, deep in study or engaged in intense discussion, would suddenly check his watch, grab up his textbooks, and rush down the hall toward a class, muttering "Slavery, slavery." Occasionally, there have been days when I felt trapped by the teaching schedule, the syllabus, or the student conferences and paperload, days when I felt bound by departmental and university decisions on curriculum, pedagogy, and technology, days when I thought teaching composition was slavery. I would bet that because of circumstances and environment, many of us have thought or made similar comments. But these comments were and are usually laughed off by others and ourselves as exclamations of the moment—glib remarks to relieve stress. This professor, however, trained in Greek and Latin probably knew the import of his words, for pedagogy—in its most literal sense meaning the art of teaching—comes to us via Old French from the Greek *paedagogus,* a slave who escorted the male children to and from school each day. So my momentary emotional reaction of confinement and restriction invokes pedagogy on two levels, through its etymological connections to slavery and through its echo across generations of others who believed how we teach is as important as what we teach. The metaphor of slavery as an institution coupled with the metaphor of slave as a state of being are potent given the institutional history of first-year composition in American universities—its mandate for all students at Harvard in 1885, its history as a service course to colleges and universities, its revenue-generating capabilities, its marginalization of instructors through low wages and lack of rights (See Connors; Crowley; Schell).

In fact, Sharon Crowley employs the term "rhetoric slaves" in her argument that "English departments have colonized composition" and cites a 1971 article by Ray Kytle, "Slaves, Serfs, or Colleagues—Who Shall Teach College Composition?" to illustrate entrenched institutional attitudes about teachers of first-year composition ("Terms" 130–31). For Crowley, these practices and attitudes have held composition studies and its specialists from equal status in the academy. Since 1991, she has regularly argued for a shift away from the institutional requirement of first-year composition and for a change of label from "composition" to "writing." The requirement and the label embody a tradition and history for first-year composition beleaguered by what Robert Connors calls alternating periods of "reformism and abolitionism" ("Abolition" 47). This chronic need to either fix or get rid of first-year composition has added to its low status in postsecondary education. Moreover, this history has directly affected composition teachers, bringing about a pattern in the twentieth century where faculty have been "increasingly marginalized, overworked and ill-paid" ("Licensure" 171). With this history, the association of first-year composition with slavery seems accurate, given that slavery operates as an institution in which, through subjection and oppression, one group constitutes the major work force, usually composed of physical or menial labor.

The slave and slavery metaphors function within the institutional history of composition, but what appears to correspond on one level may also be a mismatch on another. Since "slave" and "slavery" are metaphors, pushing or straining their associations breaks them open while adding to their potency for making meaning. In "Enigma Variations: Reading and Writing Through Metaphor," Louise Smith argues that in the gaps and places where metaphor does not fit, enigmas appear that ask us to create meaning both cognitively and imaginatively, a process which allows us a "taking in and 'owning' [of] an idea" (164). These enigmas, locations of ambiguity, provide us with new ways to see. With our own pressing history of slavery in the United States, we often recoil at such metaphors and respond with loathing at the collapsing of all human suffering as if equal or similar. But the slave metaphor haunts the first-year composition requirement both through its previous references to the status of the course in American postsecondary education and through its etymological relationship to pedagogy. I want to understand the implications of these relationships as they directly deal with the work I do in the classroom, in the institution, and in the discipline. I want to understand how these metaphors fit cleanly and snugly and where my pushing stresses the seams beyond their limits. For it is beyond these limits that the metaphor will offer us new insights and new knowledge. To see these gaps, we must first examine the parallels, the comparisons that match. The slave and slavery metaphors for first-year composition requirements fit all too well for two sites of comparison—the history of the *paedagogus* and the concept of the "good life" for Greek male citizens.

Within the first site of comparison, the familial responsibilities and role of the *paedagogus* parallel both the negative institutional attitudes toward first-year composition and the student-teacher relationships within the university setting. According to Joseph Vogt in *Ancient Slavery and the Ideal of Man,* the *paedagogus* of ancient Greece and Rome served the instructive purpose of character development, for character was believed to develop through associations with others, not through the knowledge of formal schooling. As the constant companion to the young boy, the older slave acted as supervisor, mentor, guide, and guardian, passing on cultural and community values and expectations. This important role in developing a child's character was often assigned to the older slaves partly because of their loyalty but mostly because of their inability to do strenuous physical labor (109–14). Being a *paedagogus* meant that the slave was too feeble to do anything else, which made him and the position easy targets for scorn and ridicule. Cited as an example about societal attitudes toward slavery and the *paedagogus* is Pericles' supposed response to seeing a slave with a broken leg: "He has just been made into a tutor" (Vogt 110; Wiedemann 125). Literary examples often reflected the low status of the tutor-slaves in references to their speech and actions. For example, Plato's *Lysis* ends abruptly and incompletely with the two *paedagogi* interrupting the teacher Socrates by repeatedly calling in broken Greek for Menexenus and Lysis to return home with them (223a). Both the interruption and the nonstandard Greek jar the philosophical discussion. The literary references tend to degrade and joke about the *paedagogi* as a position or group, but as individuals in the private sphere, the *paedagogi* often had close lifelong relationships with their charges, establishing bonds that neither parents nor siblings had. This simultaneously marginalized and centralized status in the family infused a "natural vitality into an over-sophisticated society" (Vogt 114). Vogt explains this "natural vitality" as a combination of foreignness, adherence to standards, and lack of education, all of which created this lifelong bond of obligation in the young boy. Since slaves were either prisoners of war or their offspring, they retained at some level their own cultures and languages. The continual contact with a *paedagogus* provided the young male Greek an interesting mix of Greek language and culture filtered through the lens of "otherness."

Moreover, they were not educated through Greek channels, so *paedagogi* represented a site of power negotiations between older unschooled slave and young educated master. For both, this relationship was a constant dialogic learning process contingent on issues of authority that dealt with family, age, and familiarity, not education or experiences as a citizen of the *polis*.

Because a slave was considered property, thus not a part of the citizenry, the *paedagogus's* role as guardian provided a unique location inside the family but outside of public society. This service role subversively and ironically added a constructive element to Greek society. The history of first-year composition courses and the continuing low institutional status of its teachers correspond to this insider-outsider location of the *paedagogi*. With classifications such as "children, serfs, prisoners, slaves," Crowley recounts the demeaning and deintellectualizing depictions of composition teachers through the metaphors employed across twentieth-century discussions of first-year composition ("Terms" 127–31). In "Composition's Ethic of Service, the Universal Requirement, and the Discourse of Student Need," she argues that postsecondary education has continued to return to the fundamental purpose of the first-year composition requirement as one promoting an "instrumental ethic," a course that meets the needs of the students, the university, and the community through its promotion of "error-free expository prose" (227). According to Crowley, this prevailing belief not only limits the perceptions about those who teach composition but also stigmatizes the discipline.

As this outsider or marginalized status continues, the teachers of this requirement, like the *paedagogi,* simultaneously maintain an insider role within the institution. With first-year composition's lower enrollment caps in comparison to the first-year lecture classes of other disciplines and with its focus on writing instead of machine scored exams, its teachers are one of the first personal contacts many students remember about their undergraduate experience. We know their names, their words, their writing practices—we learn about their character and they learn about ours. Moreover, we have investigated and learned from our pedagogical practices, thus providing some "natural vitality" to the communities' expectations and values, Crowley's "instrumental ethic." In "Reframing the Great Debate on First-Year Writing," Marjorie Roemer, Lucille Schultz, and Russel Durst argue to maintain the first-year composition course requirement because it "was our beginning [and] has maintained its position at the center of our enterprise" (377). Even Crowley reminds us that the derogatory side of this metaphor may represent an attitude about service and may reflect the institutional labor problems that come with it, but this denigration has little to do with the implemented pedagogy or quality of instruction in these courses ("Terms" 118, 130–31). Like the *paedagogi* as a group or position, composition studies, first-year composition, and its teachers and specialists are stigmatized, but also like the *paedagogi,* we bring a "new vitality" to the academy and to its students through our years of pedagogical research and practice.

A second site of comparison for the slave metaphor of pedagogy lies in postsecondary education's privileging of research and new knowledge since World War II and its parallel to the Greek male citizens' pursuit and discussions of the "good life." According to Guiseppe Cambiano in "Aristotle and the Anonymous Opponents of Slavery," slaves performed all of the tasks of free men except for political and military responsibilities thus providing the services needed for domestic survival (29, 34). Slavery as an institution freed citizens for their work in politics and philosophy. Likewise, in an argument that Greek politics and democracy resulted from slavery, Tracey Rihll states:

> The presence of slaves made the freeman aware of possible constraints which might be imposed on him, and he was physically able to resist his reduction to slave-like status—to a position where he would have to take orders from someone else. . . . The free Greek did not wish to be constrained by other freemen, for that made him like a slave. (109–10)

The institution of slavery operated as a means to develop and continue a democracy complete with the responsibilities of its male citizens. Since the Greek citizens were required by duty to be actively involved in the politics of the *polis,* the discussions on the "good life" focused on a life devoted to philosophy or one devoted to politics. The citizens had to be wealthy enough to have the physical and intellectual freedom to pursue their political duty, although not all had the means to. Aristotle's *Politics* promotes slavery as a method to take care of everyday living and the business of the estate. Moreover, his knowledge taxonomy develops out of these ways of existence tied to leisure, a life free from the work needed to procure the necessities of survival. Aristotle's knowledge distinctions of theory, practice, and production, then, are not related to the contemporary oppositional notion of theory as abstract ideas and practice as human action; rather, they implicate active approaches to lives of freedom and choice. According to Nicholas Lobkowicz in *Theory and Practice,* theoretical knowledge equates to today's modes of scientific inquiry and is an end in itself (8, 36). Like the English progressive tense showing habitual action, practical knowledge functions as a chosen and ongoing mode of conduct with each act operating as a syn-ecdoche. Productive knowledge focuses on the end result; a series of acts leads to the creation or development of an artifact, but each act is value-less without the finished product (9–15). These three realms of knowledge were derived from concepts of the "good life" for an elite group of men, the Greek citizens, which excluded the artisans, craftsmen, merchants, women, slaves, and any foreigners who were paying taxes to work within the city-state (18–24).

Again first-year composition parallels the history of Greek slavery, this time in the status designated to types of knowledge and in the attitudes about work. Particularly since World War II, postsecondary education has become embroiled in a teaching-research debate with research and publi-cation winning even in many colleges where teaching is the primary mis-sion (Boyer xi–xiii). The research with the most prestige is the contempo-rary version of Aristotle's theoretical knowledge, knowledge as new or unknown or as discounting or correcting other earlier knowledge. Applied knowledge in the forms of teaching, service, and cross- or interdisciplinary investigations is only beginning to be consistently valued. First-year com-position, its pedagogy, and its composing practices and theories often are seen as working within applied knowledge, the lesser form. This imbalance between the types of knowledge is seen across the history of English de-partments. Citing Albert Kitzhaber, Crowley shows how English faculty by 1900 were trying to avoid teaching composition in order to focus on liter-ary research. This move was not only to generate more time for research, as teaching composition takes time, but also to be regarded by other fac-ulty as a researcher rather than a teacher ("Terms" 122). Research was used in the teaching of upper-division and graduate courses, for those students who were specializing in English, not for the student masses. Connors's his-tories add to this picture by explaining that literary specialists believed that teaching composition was a misuse of expertise and time and that first-year composition was "never meant as a permanent English offering but was instead a temporary stopgap until the secondary schools could improve" ("Abolition" 48–49). So research as a purer form of knowledge became privi-leged within English and postsecondary education, and first-year compo-sition became the location of the lesser, applied knowledge, the home of nonintellectual masses and the kingdom of junior faculty, adjuncts, and graduate teaching assistants. Like the two-tiered system of Greek slavery, the work of composition was performed by the less educated to free up the senior faculty for research, and like the Greek system, the status afforded to work was in direct proportion to those who were performing it.

The Greek slave and slavery metaphors fit snugly for first-year composition. The insider-outsider status of the *paedagogi* parallels the composition teacher teaching a service course by reinforcing the marginalized location while simultaneously promoting habits of mind and character through systematic pedagogy. The two-tiered Greek system with its types of work and its taxonomy for valuing knowledge corresponds to postsecondary education's continued promotion of research and publishing over teaching and service. By understanding the slave and slavery metaphors as specific locations that affect educators in direct ways, distinctions are also made between attitudes, practices, and institutional policies and regulations. The demeaning attitudes and practices of first-year composition and the lowly status of its teachers evolved from more national postsecondary institutional issues as education reacted to societal change. The devaluing of teaching for all general education requirements is still part of the teaching-research debate. This entails more than just a history of first-year composition or its relationship to English. It entails seeing composition within the context of all general education requirements and within the institutional privileging of specific types of research, theory, and practice. So when Crowley argues for abolishing the first-year composition requirement, she is not breaking through these slavery metaphors but only shifting the location of the composition course from required to elective, offering the freedom to choose general education. The result of this type of change may shift attitudes about a first-year composition course as academic service, but it does little to work against the intellectual attitudes that privilege research and theory over applied knowledge or the firmly entrenched two-tiered system of institutional elitism.

By recognizing the exact matches of the slave and slavery metaphors with first-year composition, I can explore the gaps, cracks, and fissures within them, the spaces where new meanings emerge. As Robert Frost explains about the life of a metaphor,

> All metaphor breaks down somewhere. That is the *beauty* [emphasis Smith's] of it. It is touch and go with the metaphor, and until you have lived with it long enough you don't know when it is going. You don't know how much you can get out of it and when it will cease to yield. (qtd. in Smith 164)

Although we may add a "natural vitality" to the institution's required service course and although we may be providing the "good life" for some faculty by freeing them from teaching first-year composition, the slave and slavery metaphors crumble for me in three ways: in pedagogy's affiliation with our discipline, in the definition of service for postsecondary education, and in my individual choice to teach composition. The gaps in the slave and slavery metaphors provide openings for new ways of seeing, what Smith calls in her discussion of metaphor "the beauty of a new wisdom" (165).

These cracks not only begin to undercut the two-tiered system and privileging of research and publishing, but they also allow me a site for understanding my commitment to teaching composition within postsecondary education. First, teaching, unlike the role of the *paedagogi,* is not diminished or dismissed in our discipline; moreover, it is accounted for and valued by our discipline and by the history of American postsecondary education. Second, unlike the two-tiered system of Greek slavery, service is a part of the *polis,* a part of being an active citizen inside and outside of academic institutions, so the insider-outsider role of the slave shifts to a role of citizenry participation in both the community and the institution. Third, as a composition teacher, my work may sometimes be restricted, but I am not enslaved. I have the potential to create change in the classroom, in my institution, in my discipline, and in my community. So I break through the metaphor in my choice to privilege the teaching of composition and use that location as the locus for my service and research. First-year composition as a required course in most American colleges and universities is a vital component of composition studies, and it continually shapes who we are as teachers and what we are as a discipline, but neither our teaching nor our discipline ends there. These fissures that cut into the slave and slavery metaphors offer a broader understanding of my role as a faculty member, a member of an institution that needs to change in its perceptions and actions toward what I do as a composition teacher.

The first gap in the metaphors appears both in composition studies' valuing of teaching and in the historical relationship between teaching and higher education. Our discipline in its theories, its research methodologies, its organizations, and its practices either embraces pedagogy or rejects its value, but either way it is addressed. Moreover, pedagogy as the "art of teaching" composition continues to be one of the founding tenets of the discipline. Roemer, Schultz, and Durst begin and conclude their arguments for maintaining a first-year composition requirement with the contention that "we have shaped our field in relation to pedagogy" (391). According to Connors, one of the main reform trends in contemporary composition since the 1960s has focused on not "what students were taught" but "how they were taught" (*Composition-Rhetoric* 16). This continued emphasis on teaching and first-year composition by specialists in the discipline may appear in opposition to gaining equal status for composition studies, but it echoes a longer tradition across the history of American education in its peda-gogical commitment and in its valuing of knowledge for all.

The two-tiered slavery structure, made up of those who provide service and those who provide knowledge and governance, breaks down when I look at composition studies in relation to the history of my faculty roles of teaching, service, and research in American education. Originally, the central mission of an American college was teaching. Samuel Eliot Morison explains in his history of Harvard University, founded in 1636, that English Puritanism's lasting influence on New England and the United States centered on "educational ideals: a learned clergy, and a lettered people" (45). For approximately two hundred years, teaching was the objective. During the nineteenth century, teaching the student was matched with a responsibility of service to the community. This additional responsibility is illustrated through the founding of Rensselaer Polytechnic Institute in 1824, which trained builders and engineers, producing educated men to build commerce and communication across the nation (Glassick, Huber, and Maeroff 6–7). The Morrill Act of 1862 established land-grant colleges to aid in agricultural and technological growth. Before the twentieth century, teaching and service were challenged by the incorporation of the German model of specialized research, as manifested in doctoral studies and programs beginning with Johns Hopkins University and closely followed by Harvard and Yale. Quickly all three—teaching, service, and research—were considered faculty responsibilities. As Crowley and Connors have shown, first-year composition was formulated and evolved within these institutional and epistemological paradigm shifts.

Never balanced or stable, these three faculty responsibilities went through another transformation during the mid-twentieth century. Ernest Boyer explains in *Scholarship Reconsidered* that because of the exchange between scientists and the American government during World War II, the expectations for a scholar to add new knowledge to the field were paramount after the war. This emphasis on research and publishing in higher education during the 1940s and 1950s promoted research over service and teaching. The attitude was and is still held by some that new and original knowledge evolves out of research and is separate from teaching—teaching often being the location for the transmission of distilled knowledge but not the place for disseminating or forming new knowledge (10–13). Being a part of the conversation through publishing and adding to new knowledge continues to be an expectation of higher education. However, not all new knowledge is judged equally. Specific academic genres were and still are privileged; those texts that speak to the elite fellow scholars and keep the not-as-educated out of the discussion are deemed more original, more valuable. Although this trend is changing and varies depending on the size and mission of the institution, in departments such as English, theoretical articles and books usually garner more prestige than textbooks intended for undergraduates, and texts that cover new territory or integrate concepts often fare better than those that focus on application or teaching. Moreover, service or applications of specialization outside of the university have evolved almost to a conflict-of-interest status, when faculty in many universities are to account yearly for added income due to consulting or master teaching in the community.

This gap of historical awareness shows how teaching, service, and research became faculty responsibilities, how teaching originally was the sole aim for faculty, and how research became privileged. It shows that even though the adage "It's not your teaching but your publishing that gets you tenure" represents the conflicting goals of many academic institutions, the pedagogical work of composition studies has a value and history beyond the teaching of composition. This current imbalance across faculty responsibilities helps to explain why disparaging attitudes continue toward composition studies—our discipline and growth have focused in many ways on teaching and service and research methods related to those two. For example, ethnography is a research methodology that we employ for our own disciplinary knowledge. But we also teach it to our first-year composition students as a way to further their understanding of language, action, and environment. Thus, the practice of our research methods and the modes of writing we value are not exclusive to the "experts" in our field. Through our own disciplinary pedagogy, we have collapsed the two-tiered slavery structure; we have broken open the metaphors.

The second crack in the slave and slavery metaphors opens because of the relationship of first-year composition to the term "service." Service has a much richer heritage and relationship with American postsecondary education than our current discussions of service as focused on institutional need might suggest. Originally, service in higher education meant a faculty member's employing his or her expertise to help solve the direct and pressing problems of society at the local level. Thus, service is not a marginalized location but acts as a bridge among institutions, communities, and individuals. Since the 1970s, composition studies has reevaluated and redefined the relations of student to academy to community. Disciplinary journals in recent years have included more articles of curricular reform, a type of service, as a respected component of composition studies. In "Remapping the Geography of Service in English," Daniel Mahala and Jody Swilky examine the role of first-year composition in light of other general education requirements through the lenses of research, teaching, and service. They outline the value of expertise, critique the dominant vision of service, demonstrate that English studies is an accretion of specialisms without integration, and call for a critical discourse about service by offering the example of curriculum reform at Drake, noting its limitations. This article, like the one on Temple's curriculum reform by Francis Sullivan, Arabella Lyon, Dennis Lebofsky, Susan Wells, and Eli Goldblatt, provides needed testimonies about universities and their faculties making change toward a rebalancing of pedagogy and service with research. But the authors do not go far enough, as they focus only on issues of service at the disciplinary, department, and university levels—all inside academe.

When service became a faculty responsibility in the nineteenth century, it meant "meeting the intellectual challenge of using the most advanced knowledge to address complex social and technical problems" (Glassick, Huber, and Maeroff ix). Service activities required the direct use of faculty expertise and knowledge to solve problems, create vision, and enact change in the public spheres of city, state, and nation. But with research and publication as the goal, service was reformulated into campus committee work, positions in professional associations, and community volunteer work. Composition studies has grown and developed through both the original and the more common definitions of service. Writing centers, writing across the curriculum programs, and computer-aided composition courses have had a profound impact on pedagogy and service across academic institutions. In the communities, the university-school projects (such as the National Writing Project, the New Hampshire Writing Project, and college composition in the high schools programs), the university-community literacy programs, and now service-learning projects continue to share with the community the expertise needed to change education and literacy. By returning to the original meanings of service and showing how our discipline enacts them, we break through the slave metaphor of merely "instrumental ethic" by reestablishing and rebalancing the responsibilities of faculty.

The third break in the slave and slavery metaphors resides within me, a composition teacher. I may work for and within postsecondary institutions that continue to fit the slavery metaphor, but I am not a slave, nor is composition studies, the discipline I am trained in. The divergence from slavery evolves from my choice to teach composition and to recognize and act on the responsibilities that are inherent in that decision. Since one of my responsibilities is, like that of the *paedagogus,* guiding students between school and community, I must understand what implications lie within my role and how they influence the students within and against the various power systems of education and the community. Pedagogy suggests to me an ethical philosophy of teaching that accounts for the complex matrix of people, knowledge, and practice within the immediacy of each class period, each assignment, each conference, each grade. For me that is pedagogy—the *art* of teaching—the regular, connected, and articulated choices made from within a realm of possibilities and then acted on. Historically, it accounts for the goals of the institution and to some extent society; it manifests the goals of the individual teacher, which may include an agenda to help students learn to critique both the institution and society; and it makes room for the goals of the individual students. I see my role and authority as teacher as a push-pull endeavor on two levels—me as the representative of an educational institution within and against society and me as a representative of society within and against the educational institution I work for.

Over the years of teaching first-year composition as a graduate student, an adjunct instructor, and now junior faculty member, I have witnessed and experienced many of the problems and attitudes that continue to challenge first-year composition courses, composition and writing programs, and those who teach and administrate them. I have learned and continue to learn about the intersections among pedagogy, curriculum, and epistemology in first-year and other composition courses. These examinations of my location in composition courses have taught me that if I want change, I must work within the social structures and constraints to make it happen. Michel Foucault describes power as a web-matrix with people as "vehicles of power, not its [power's] points of application" because "they are always in the position of simultaneously undergoing and exercising this power" (98). This continual reinscribing of the status quo while slightly reshaping it at every turn takes on an ethical dimension for me that M. M. Bakhtin addresses as "answerability." Even though he is not talking about teaching, answerability is the condition of my everyday teaching experience, how I answer to myself and to others for my unique, unrepeatable location in time and space and how I respond to the dialogic relationships between me and the environment as they operate through the immediate, specific and ongoing situations of existence: "That which can be done by me can never be done by anyone else" (*Toward a Philosophy* 40). As Bakhtin writes of the poet, so I think of my responsibility to the art of teaching: "Art and life are not one, but they must become united in myself—in the unity of my answerability" ("Art" 2). It is all in how I shape the paradigm, how I envision the future and the institutions I work within. If I do not see beyond the slave and slavery metaphors, neither will my colleagues, for teaching goes beyond the classroom.

For me, first-year composition is the locus for the arts of composition studies. From it, research and theories intermingle, collide, or expand through practice, and the push and pull of our writing programs reverberate through the institution and the community. Whether in the name of teaching, research, or service, it is the location from which we start and return. Like Bakhtin's explanation of the forces of language, the composition classroom is the location where the three realms of faculty simultaneously operate as centrifugal and centripetal forces, the competing forces of disruption and order. Because we understand the distinction between the quality of instruction and the institutional location of first-year composition, we must push our understanding of the term "service" as well as its various meanings to the university and community. By articulating the relationships among these various types of service and our teaching, we can more clearly illustrate the importance of our work in the classroom—the ripple that begins there but continues across the campus and community. Because of our work in the classroom, we have been expanding the institution, just subversively and quietly—one institution at a time. The numerous organizational listservs and the multiple journals support and communicate the local and one-to-one, so our art of localization and immediacy can be critiqued, modified, and appropriated for another situation at another campus.

These three fissures in the slave and slavery metaphors for first-year composition are made wider by our disciplinary practices. Composition studies has integrated the acts of teaching, service, and research. We value new or corrective knowledge but we also value applied knowledge. We are already practicing the model that Boyer designed and argued for in *Scholarship Reconsidered*. In 1990 he called for universities, colleges, their faculties, and their administrations to move beyond the research-teaching debate in higher education by redefining "scholarship." For Boyer, scholarship entails discovery, teaching, integration, and application—all inextricably tied to each other (25). His definition and argument work to bring together and integrate faculty responsibilities rather than to separate and isolate them. The scholarship of discovery includes the investigative, research, and creative work of faculty and promotes the "free rein to fair and honest inquiry, wherever it may lead" (Glassick, Huber, and Maeroff 9). The scholarship of integration works toward synthesis and looks for relationships across and within disciplines by "altering the contexts in which people view knowledge" (9). The scholarship of application focuses on the immediate, the current problems and issues, providing a location where "theory and practice interact . . . and improve each other" (9). The scholarship of teaching transmits, transforms, and extends knowledge to enable students to "participate more fully in the larger culture" (9). For Boyer, all four aspects of scholarship are valuable to higher education, and all four should be assessed equally. In this model, theoretical knowledge spreads across both discovery and integration, while service is incorporated in application, and teaching reflects a mission of preparing students for their roles and lives beyond higher education.

While composition studies has quietly been working in all of these directions since the 1970s, higher education and national organizations have started only recently to act on this 1990 report from the Carnegie Foundation for the Advancement of Teaching. The follow-up report, *Scholarship Assessed,* shows that Boyer's report has had influence. Including evidence such as a study by the American Association of University Professors in 1994, the doubling of participants in the annual American Association of Higher Education Forum on Faculty Roles and Rewards, and their own survey of universities and colleges, Charles Glassick, Mary Taylor Huber, and Gene Maeroff conclude that Boyer's model has not only spurred a debate on the role of faculty but also acted as a catalyst for institutional change. At my own institution in the last four years, new tenure requirements have been adopted, a new general education plan for undergraduate students has been instituted, and a new mission statement has been added to the catalog. Just because the words are in print does not mean that the actions will be in accordance, but the words are a start, and all of the documents reflect faculty responsibility toward research, teaching, and service. If this trend continues, the slave and slavery metaphors for first-year composition may have the opportunity to break down not only through composition studies' continued practices and words but also through the renewed commitment by institutions for a more balanced valuing of the diverse responsibilities, goals, and practices in postsecondary education.

As the institutions' missions evolve and expand—as they are now doing—we as composition specialists with our cross-disciplinary work, writing across the curriculum programs, writing centers, technology-supported instruction, school-university projects, student-centered approaches, teacher-training, and various theory-practice frameworks offer a model for these future institutional shifts, a model that is open to change but is also ready to critique and question itself. We have taken our art of teaching out of the classroom and into the institution. Even with its stigmatizations and institutional problems, composition studies has been altering and continues to transform the face of higher education. I agree with Crowley that we still need "to improve the status and working conditions of its practitioners" ("Composition's

Ethic" 230). But through our continued focus on teaching and service, we have already started to address these and other issues. In the name of good pedagogy, we have so discreetly, but with incredibly hard work, laid a foundation from the inside of individual institutions. We can use this as a political means to continue to influence in more direct ways the vision, motives, and attitudes of higher education as a whole. This is not a call to action but a desire for us to recognize what we are already doing and how we can use that in more influential ways. This breaking open of the slave and slavery metaphors, as well as other deprecating or dismissive metaphors heaped on first-year composition and its teachers, can provide ways of reseeing and reconfiguring our arguments for ourselves and for others. While we continue to search for, debate, and experiment with answers to the low status and pay of marginalized composition teachers, we also need to examine equity issues for teaching assistants and adjuncts across the university. We need not become complacent when program changes are made in the catalog but keep the discussions alive through continual examination and reflection. As we regularly fight for the needed funding to keep our WAC, computer, and school-university programs and writing centers functioning and growing, we need to use them as the nexus for larger discussions of research, teaching, and service across the university and community.

Works Cited

Aristotle. *Politics*. Trans. H. Rackham. Loeb Classical Library 264. 1932. Cambridge: Harvard UP, 1990.

Bakhtin, M. M. "Art and Answerability." *Art and Answerability: Early Philosophical Essays by M. M. Bakhtin*. Trans. and notes Vadim Liapunov. Ed. Michael Holquist and Vadim Liapunov. Austin: U of Texas P, 1990. 1–3.

———. *Toward a Philosophy of the Act*. Trans. and notes Vadim Liapunov. Ed. Vadim Liapunov and Michael Holquist. Austin: U of Texas P, 1993.

Boyer, Ernest L. *Scholarship Reconsidered: Priorities of the Professoriate*. Princeton: The Carnegie Foundation for the Advancement of Teaching, 1990.

Cambiano, Guiseppe. "Aristotle and the Anonymous Opponents of Slavery." Trans. Mario di Gregorio. *Classical Slavery*. Ed. M. I. Finley. London: Frank Cass, 1987. 22–41.

Connors, Robert J. "The Abolition Debate in Composition: A Short History." *Composition in the Twenty-First Century: Crisis and Change*. Ed. Lynn Z. Bloom, Donald A. Daiker, and Edward M. White. Carbondale: Southern Illinois UP, 1996. 47–63.

———. *Composition-Rhetoric: Backgrounds, Theory, and Pedagogy*. Pittsburgh: U of Pittsburgh P, 1997.

———. "Licensure, Disciplinary Identity, and Workload in Composition-Rhetoric." *Composition-Rhetoric: Backgrounds, Theory, and Pedagogy*. Pittsburgh: U of Pittsburgh P, 1997. 171–209.

Crowley, Sharon. *Composition in the University: Historical and Polemical Essays*. Pittsburgh: U of Pittsburgh P, 1998.

———. "Composition's Ethic of Service, the Universal Requirement, and the Discourse of Student Need." *Journal of Advanced Composition* 15.2 (1995): 227–39.

———. "Terms of Employment: Rhetoric Slaves and Lesser Men." *Composition in the University: Historical and Polemical Essays.* Pittsburgh: U of Pittsburgh P, 1998. 118–31.

Foucault, Michel. *Power/Knowledge: Selected Interviews and Other Writings, 1972–1977.* Trans. Colin Gordon, Leo Marshall, John Mepham, and Kate Soper. Ed. Colin Gordon. New York: Pantheon, 1980.

Glassick, Charles E., Mary Taylor Huber, and Gene I. Maeroff. *Scholarship Assessed: Evaluation of the Professoriate.* The Carnegie Foundation for the Advancement of Teaching. San Francisco: Jossey-Bass, 1997.

Lobkowicz, Nicholas. *Theory and Practice: History of a Concept from Aristotle to Marx.* Notre Dame: U of Notre Dame P, 1967.

Mahala, Daniel, and Jody Swilky. "Remapping the Geography of Service in English." *College English* 59.6 (1997): 625–46.

Morison, Samuel Eliot. *The Founding of Harvard College.* Cambridge: Harvard UP, 1935.

Plato. *Lysis. Plato III: Lysis, Symposium, Gorgias.* Trans. W. R. M. Lamb. Loeb Classical Library 166. 1925. Cambridge: Harvard UP, 1991. 1–71.

Rihll, Tracey. "The Origin and Establishment of Ancient Greek Slavery." *Serfdom and Slavery: Studies in Legal Bondage.* Ed. M. L. Bush. London: Longman, 1996. 89–111.

Roemer, Marjorie, Lucille M. Schultz, and Russel K. Durst. "Reframing the Great Debate on First-Year Writing." *College Composition and Communication* 50.3 (1999): 377–92.

Schell, Eileen E. *Gypsy Academics and Mother-Teachers: Gender, Contingent Labor, and Writing Instruction.* CrossCurrents. Portsmouth, NH: Boynton, 1998.

Smith, Louise Z. "Enigma Variations: Reading and Writing Through Metaphor." *Only Connect: Uniting Reading and Writing.* Ed. Thomas Newkirk. Upper Montclair, NJ: Boynton, 1986. 158–73.

Sullivan, Francis J., Arabella Lyon, Dennis Lebofsky, Susan Wells, and Eli Goldblatt. "Student Needs and Strong Composition: The Dialects of Writing Program Reform." *College Composition and Communication* 48.3 (1997): 372–91.

Vogt, Joseph. *Ancient Slavery and the Ideal of Man.* Trans. Thomas Wiedemann. Cambridge: Harvard UP, 1975.

Wiedemann, Thomas. *Greek and Roman Slavery.* Baltimore: Johns Hopkins UP, 1981.

10

Imagining Our Teaching Selves

Christina Russell McDonald

In a roundtable discussion at the 1999 Conference on College Composition and Communication meeting, panelists considered the conditions under which teachers might decide to "do the Full Monty" in front of their students by making their differences, whether racial, cultural, or sexual, public knowledge and a subject of discussion in the composition classroom. They offered poignant "coming out" stories in which their disclosures of working-class roots or homosexual identity had resulted not only in richer discussions of literature and student writing but also in a greater degree of comfort for themselves as teachers in the classroom. Gary Tate, a panelist and a distinguished teacher of composition and, more recently, of working-class literature, wisely advised that in order to avoid using class meetings as therapy sessions, we should choose to disclose such information only once we are comfortable with that aspect of our identity and when it is clearly relevant to students' learning or their understanding of our teaching.

As the audience debated just how and when teachers might make this important choice, I became increasingly uncomfortable with the notion that we could simply pick a moment to make ourselves "visible" (to use the term that defined the convention's theme that year, "Visible Students, Visible Teachers"). At the time, I was eight months pregnant with our first child and consequently feeling more visible than ever, especially as I walked into the classroom each day. This, I thought to myself, was not an aspect of my identity I could choose to share or not. And yet it was a new identity I had been struggling to incorporate into my understanding of myself not only as a woman but also as a professional—as a young female administrator, as an untenured assistant professor, and, most importantly, as a teacher of writing.

An extremely private person, I have always defined my relationships with students more professionally than personally. While our interactions are comfortable, energetic, and often even playful, I seldom allow myself or the circumstances of my life to enter into our conversations. My teaching persona—the person I become when I walk into the classroom or greet a student in my office—is that of a friendly but ultimately formal individual. Since my pregnancy was still readily concealed when I met my classes for the first time that spring semester, I was faced with the daunting prospect of deciding exactly how and when to make the announcement to my students. Should I wait until they can see that I'm expecting, I wondered? What if I wait too long and they begin to talk among themselves as the weeks pass by, trying to guess whether I'm pregnant or just getting fat? The thought of their conversations haunted me because, for the first time, I realized that my carefully constructed teaching persona was about to be shattered: my changing physical appearance, over which I had no control, would alter how students perceived me. Whether I liked it or not, the personal and the professional were destined for a head-on collision.

Despite my worries, students received the news warmly and respectfully and, to no one's surprise but my own, continued to be responsive to me as a teacher. The experience compelled me to forge a more comfortable relationship between my personal identity and my identity as a teacher. In the classroom, my role as teacher is still clearly defined but, from my perspective at least, my demeanor seems somehow easier, softer. Now, I am able to see that my discomfort with the roundtable discussion stemmed from what I understood to be an implicit suggestion that we are at liberty to pick and choose the aspects of our identities we show to students. My pregnancy prompted me to consider all the ways that we are, in fact, present in the classroom—physically, spiritually, culturally, politically—whether or not we choose to make these aspects of our identity subjects of discussion.[1] Students see even what we think we have masterfully concealed. We need only recollect the comments they make in class and course evaluations for evidence of the way they piece together available bits of information about us to formulate their impressions (some accurate, some not): "He wears really nice socks!" she writes in a course evaluation; or "Why do you drink that expensive water?" he asks, staring at the Evian bottle on the desk. In short, students know more about us than we think. Sometimes more than makes us comfortable.

In his essay "The Primary Site of Contention in Teaching Composition,"

Tate urges us to acknowledge the ways in which our theoretical and pedagogical choices are shaped by "how we construct students in our minds": as "semiliterate," as "unthinking repositories of largely conservative beliefs," as "college students who need to be successful in their majors" (2). Similarly, I believe we must also consider how students construct us as teachers in their minds: as self-assured, fair-handed professor; liberal-minded radical; experienced, sympathetic fellow writer; powerless adjunct instructor; young, naive TA? They draw from the versions of ourselves we present in course materials (syllabi, assignments, and evaluation criteria), our classroom manner, and our informal interactions with students as we visit with them in our offices and as we move around campus. In all these ways, many that are obvious and more that are not, we are most assuredly visible to our students. But the identity we project is neither as consistent nor as authentic as we might like to believe.[2]

Many instructors are unsettled by the suggestion that they aren't themselves in the classroom. As Jay Parini points out in a 1997 essay in the *Chronicle of Higher Education,* we all have "teaching personas," whether or not we acknowledge them:

> Teachers, like writers, need to invent and cultivate a voice that serves their personal needs, their students, and the material at hand. It's not easy to find this voice, in teaching or in writing, and it helps to have models in mind. Teachers who are unaware of their teaching personas might get lucky; that is, they might unconsciously adopt and adapt something that actually works in the classroom. But most successful teachers whom I've known are deeply aware that self-presentation involves the donning of a mask.

We don't autonomously create the masks we wear, however. As I suggested earlier, students play an active part in determining who we are (and need to be) as teachers. Each time we greet a new class, we also confront new questions of self-presentation. My own life as a teacher has been an ongoing lesson in both learning to cultivate a comfortable teaching persona and trying hard to understand the implications it has on my ability to be effective in the classroom. In my work with other teachers of writing during the past six years, I've discovered that those who have not examined the complex combination of ingredients that make up their teaching personas are often frustrated—unable to find the key to explaining why a class goes wrong or why students don't respond in desired ways, no matter what adjustments they try to make. Despite our discipline's commitment to reflective pedagogy, I think, we often don't examine closely enough the role(s) our

identity has to play in the classroom dynamic.[3] If we can begin to understand the teaching persona as a natural and necessary act of negotiation in
our lives as teachers, then we might be better equipped to deal with some
of the difficulties we experience in the classroom. Let me offer three scenarios that will help to illustrate what I mean.

Patricia

During my first couple of years directing the composition program for the
English department at my former university, I worked with an adjunct instructor whom I'll call Patricia. Patricia was a serious, self-assured, friendly
woman in her mid-forties who held a Ph.D. with a specialty in early American literature and who had been teaching first-year composition courses and
an occasional 200-level literature survey course long before I joined the department. One of the few adjunct faculty members who participated fully
in nearly all the activities of the composition program, she responded
promptly to a questionnaire I distributed to instructors soliciting their reactions to the new textbooks we adopted that year. (It was the first time in
the history of the department that standard textbooks had been required
in the two-course freshman composition sequence). Patricia's comments
focused on the new rhetoric/reader for EN 102, Barnet and Bedeau's *Current Issues and Enduring Questions: A Guide to Critical Thinking and Argument.* Her response was thoughtful, lengthy, and angry. She began by identifying what she believed to be the primary weakness of the text: the "liberal
bias of the editors," which, she explained, "had the effect of pitting me
against my conservative students, the most vocal of whom were white and
male. . . . Now, like every other woman I know in teaching," she wrote, "I
have enough trouble with white male resentment—I don't need any exac-
erbation from the text."

   Patricia knew she was not alone. Her experience mirrors the experience
of countless other female instructors with whom I have worked, not to
mention my own on more than one occasion. The common thread that runs
throughout, I think, is the conflict between the precarious place that these
teachers (especially part-time and graduate student instructors) occupy on
the margins of our profession and the teaching personas they construct in
an effort to compensate for their relative powerlessness—a part of their
professional identity that they consciously or unconsciously fear students
can see.[4]

   As I read the following extended passage from Patricia's response in which
she describes the way the required textbook inhibited her effectiveness as a
teacher, I sensed how "visible" she felt :

> I was more dissatisfied with my own performance this semester, as well
> as the performance of my students, than I have been in a long time.
> I believe that the primary reason for our collective shortcomings has
> been the textbook. . . . When we analyzed the relative strengths and
> weaknesses of the essays, they [students] would attack me for "favor-
> ing" the liberal essays, and some students alleged that I could not be
> fair to them because they disagreed with my politics. Whenever I
> pointed out that we were looking at *the essays* and that *my politics* were
> private, it was clear from their reactions that they believed because I
> was a liberal college professor, nothing I said could be trusted.

She was troubled not by the textbook, I suspect, but by the way it appeared
to call into question the relationship between her teaching persona and her
self. She seemed most comfortable with a persona of "the objective teacher,"
one who facilitates rather than influences the direction of students' learning by helping them learn to analyze arguments rhetorically. The textbook
moved her into a more vulnerable position because it introduced students
to argumentative writing by inviting them to engage difficult questions
about controversial matters, including sexual harassment, HIV and AIDS,
and multiculturalism, among others. Students' discussions of the readings,
their wrangling with their own beliefs, and perhaps even the text's emphasis on argumentation, demanded that she play a different role—one in
which, as Cheryl Johnson writes, "race and gender conspire in the construction of [her] role as teacher" (410).

When students lodged what she felt were personal attacks, trying to
confirm their perceptions of her "liberal" bent (which were likely pretty
accurate) and intruding into the "private" realm of her political beliefs
(which probably *were* contrary to those of her conservative male students),
her teaching persona was rendered useless; she discovered that "they believed
. . . nothing I said could be trusted." Patricia was forced to confront the
fact that students were able to see past the teaching persona that she had
so carefully designed for them. "The social construction of the students'
gaze" (Johnson 410) revealed both her private and professional identities—
as a woman, a Democrat, a feminist, a cancer survivor, a part-time instructor, an evaluator of students' writing about controversial topics, and more.
In all of these terms, she was quite visible.

Patricia's teaching persona as the "objective facilitator," then, both sub-
verted the traditional hierarchy of power in the classroom (shifting the focus from the teacher's to students' knowledge-making activity) and compensated for her own secret feelings of powerlessness (as a female part-time

instructor using a required text to teach a first-year composition course). Her stance was designed to protect her against the tide of "white male resentment" that she felt she faced from some of her students for being, ironically, a woman in a position of authority. And while it may have helped her to feel safe, it didn't reassure her students, who were being asked to put their own opinions and beliefs on the line without knowing where she stood.

Her dissatisfaction with her teaching that semester and her relentless indictment of the textbook suggests that Patricia was largely unaware of the role her teaching persona played in fostering the conflict she experienced in the classroom and how altering her stance may have altered students' reactions as well as her own feelings toward the class.

William

When I arrived to observe William's first-year composition class, the last of twenty students were filtering in to take seats in the large circle of desks that had been arranged for them. I offered William a supportive smile and nod as I made my way to the back of the room to find an inconspicuous place to sit. He began the meeting by distributing a handout of excerpts from students' drafts along with examples of effective peer responses. The purpose of the class appeared clear and well conceived: to continue their training as critical readers who could respond productively to one another's writing-in-progress. He called on the students to read their work aloud, and as each finished, he stepped in immediately to explain, at great length, the strengths of each peer response.

As I looked around the circle, the students sat motionless. A few even began to doze, sitting upright, while William continued talking about their writing but without inviting the students themselves to participate in any substantial way. Once or twice he lobbed what seemed like an obligatory nonquestion to a student after describing and extolling the virtues of her response: "So, is that what you intended, Laura?" To which Laura wisely but vaguely and unthinkingly replied, "Right." William's observations were insightful and sensitive, but it didn't take me very long to perceive that the well-planned "lesson" was being lost on students who had become thoroughly disengaged by what sounded increasingly like a lecture—ironically, a lecture on peer response. What's more, the class didn't seem nearly as surprised as I was by the instructor's approach. In fact, even though they sat facing one another in a circle, their posture suggested that they were perfectly prepared for a lecture on this, as on previous, occasions.

In my office afterward, William and I met to discuss our impressions of what had transpired. In characteristically reluctant fashion, he said he thought it had gone pretty much as planned, though he was frustrated that students' answers to his questions in some instances seemed superficial, lacking in depth. A few, he worried, hadn't "gotten it." Delicately at first, I described the dynamic I had seen in the classroom. I talked about the rich possibilities for this kind of class, given a different pedagogical approach— one that took advantage of the circle-seating to get students talking to one another, about their own texts, and the role he might played in facilitating that discussion, contributing his insights throughout the conversation rather than as a monologue. Visibly surprised by my comments, he was eager to assure me that he usually used a more "student-centered" approach but that he had structured this class differently for the purposes of the observation. He wanted to be sure that I could see him "teaching," he explained. Satisfied that at least his intentions were good, I didn't think much more about our conversation until the end of the semester when I reviewed the course evaluations from William's students.

The overwhelming majority of students confirmed the impression of William's teaching that I had taken away from the class observation. They resented his tendency to "talk too much" and, with an amazing consistency, simply asserted that both the instructor and the class were "boring." Most disturbing, however, were the *many* students who appeared eager for the opportunity to call attention to the "disrespect" they felt he routinely showed them, reporting that classmates who disagreed with the teacher's ideas weren't treated very well. In great detail they described occasions when he had laughed openly at a question or a point raised for discussion, belittling their ideas in front of the class. These, of course, were serious claims—ones that William, in a subsequent meeting with me, seemed unwilling to accept, much less address in ways that would have led to productive change.

At first, I was perplexed by the apparent contradiction between the teacher I had seen in the classroom that day (and that the students described in their evaluations) and the colleague I had come to know. William was quiet and often remote individual, but he didn't appear rude, and he had a quick but dry sense of humor that most people around him seemed to enjoy. In his professional life, he identified himself as a teacher above all else and devoted himself to those concerns, so it was difficult to understand his seemingly dismissive attitude toward students' evaluations. The longer I worked with this instructor, however, the more I came to realize that his teaching persona—that of "the one who knows," who requires absolute autonomy in the classroom—was, in fact, self-protective. I suspect that the pattern of students' negative responses gradually resulted in his defensive posture in the classroom and his low opinion of students' capacity to understand what he thought he had to teach them. Unable to reconcile his intellectual understanding of effective writing pedagogy and his increasingly bad feelings about their reactions to his teaching, he dismissed their comments and became even more steadfast in his belief that his approach was the right one: if some students didn't "get it," that was just too bad. In William's case, his persona in the classroom protected him from students' attacks but concealed the best parts of his personality, perpetuating his miscommunication and conflict with those he was charged with teaching. In many ways, he had actually become *in*visible.

Suzanne

At the beginning of her second semester as a graduate teaching assistant, Suzanne had come by my office to discuss a particularly negative set of course evaluations from the previous semester. They contained stinging, often personal criticisms, and they had understandably hit her hard. She needed help sorting through her reactions to students' comments, which she knew had already begun to affect her teaching.

Suzanne was a young woman in her early twenties who was smart, kind, conscientious-to-a-fault, eager to please others, and unquestionably attractive—long dark hair, soft brown eyes, and a slender figure. While she outperformed her colleagues in the graduate course I taught to prepare prospective teaching assistants for first-year composition courses, I had worried about her ability to cultivate authority given her soft-spoken demeanor and obvious youth. When I observed an early class meeting, her presence in the classroom was tentative and almost painfully polite. Her sometimes halting speech revealed her nervousness and betrayed the comfort that the outfit she was wearing, a pullover sweater and jeans, tried to suggest. Despite these early impressions, bimonthly meetings with her faculty mentor indicated that the semester had gone reasonably well. But the course evaluations told a different story, one that surprised even Suzanne. "She couldn't speak a single declarative sentence!" exclaimed a student in large capital letters. "It was chaos. We all knew she never had control of the class," proclaimed another. "This instructor isn't worth the money I'm paying for this course," someone else insisted. What had prompted such attacks, I wondered. In presenting herself as teacher, what had Suzanne done that had gone so wrong?

Suzanne's presence in the classroom was similar to that of most other graduate teaching assistants with whom I've worked. When asked how they will present themselves to students, they typically summon up memories of a favorite professor's comfortable authority and familiar rapport with students to use as their model. Suzanne had cast herself as an approachable young instructor whose credibility was tied to her proximity in age to her students and her still firsthand knowledge of what it felt like to submit writing for a grade. At first, students seemed willing to accept her as "one of them." But that was only until they began to sense her uncertainty as they inevitably came to need, and expect, more from her.

Although Suzanne was painstaking in her preparations for class, in her responses to students' drafts, and in her grading, students were unable to see virtually any aspect of her teaching as deliberate and informed. Instead of being able to appreciate the student-centered writing workshop she had tried to create, for instance, their comments indicated that they saw only a teacher without a plan, one who did not know how to maintain control of a classroom. Instead of reading the facilitative commentary she offered on their drafts as a way of enhancing their ability to make fruitful choices as writers during revision, they saw her comments as lacking in explicit direction—i.e., a teacher who doesn't know what she wants. Instead of accepting the grades she assigned to their essays as the teacher's informed, authoritative judgments, they compared their grades and confronted her with apparent inconsistencies. And so on. How did students perceive the person she had presented to them as "teacher"? As an attractive, friendly young woman—cute but not overly smart—who might make a nice friend but who was, as a teacher, unqualified.

For Suzanne and other young new teachers like her (in my experience, more often women than men), when it comes to the matter of self-presentation, the stakes are high and the choices narrow. Unlike their mentors in the profession, these instructors have to be prepared for the difficulties that often arise when their identity in the classroom is tied too closely to their lives outside of class. Their lack of experience in dealing with students' expectations and concerns prevents them from being able to cultivate teaching personas that mirror older, more experienced faculty. When young teachers invite that level of familiarity—when they *don't* cultivate a teaching persona that complements and augments their identity—they are often *too* visible to students. Students see exactly who stands in the front of the room: an earnest, bright, well-intentioned but nevertheless naive and inexperienced new teacher who is vulnerable under the best circumstances and an easy target under the worst.

In recollecting and compiling these scenarios, I realized that the question of self-presentation has been a recurring theme in the conversations of my professional life since the moment I stepped into the classroom as a teaching assistant myself. It's a topic I've been pondering seriously, in fact, since a casual conversation with the graduate director one afternoon led me to make a presentation at the spring departmental workshop on the problem of the "teaching persona." In the notes I recently uncovered from that presentation, I wrote about how "I felt like a fraud during my first semester teaching composition"; how I worked from "a syllabus that was essentially a hodgepodge of three other instructors' syllabi and three separate textbooks, each grounded in a different philosophy of composition"; and how I "shifted from one instructor's rhetoric to another, moving in and out of voices, none of which were my own—teaching their truths, until I could gather some of my own." Around the same time, I had discovered an essay by Marian Yee called "Are You the Teacher?" that helped me to assign meaning to my early experiences in working with students. In the following passage, Yee articulates the problem of identity as she describes her experience during every first class meeting of a required freshman composition course:

> From our respective positions we feel out our parts: English teacher and college students. As always, I wonder, as I go over the attendance and shuffle my official handouts, whether I will get The Question. Sometimes it comes; sometimes it doesn't. Sometimes it hovers, unasked, over the desks; sometimes a wise-mouthed student, or just an unwitting one, will snap it out like a sudden, sharp burst of gum: "Are you the teacher?" (24)

For Yee, the problem of self-presentation arises from the apparent conflict between her two identities as "a Chinese woman and an English teacher" (26). When she walks into the classroom, her race, her youth, even her small stature all play a role in the way students construct her as teacher. Of course, sometimes our identities are externally visible: our race, gender, age and other obvious facets of our physical appearances. Other times, however, as in the situations I've described here, they convey themselves in more subtle terms: our politics, our powerlessness, our defensiveness, our inexperience—even, as recent conversations in the discipline have revealed, our social class. And because these less obvious aspects of our identities are often so tied to our private selves, our lives in the world outside the classroom, too often we're inclined to conceal them rather than to confront and ponder the degrees to which they might actually contribute to an effective teaching persona.

As a means of understanding and assessing the effectiveness of our teaching personas, occasionally we need to ask ourselves some difficult questions—to discover the connections and the gaps between who we "really" are and who our students perceive and need us to be. Let me suggest a way of beginning this kind of inquiry by framing some questions that writing teachers might ask themselves (in private or public forums):

- *Consider: "Who is this 'you' that [your students] are looking at?"* (Yee 24). I frequently begin workshops for instructors with a short two-part writing assignment that grows out of this very question. First, imagine that you are a student in your class. Write a description of who you see when the instructor walks into the room on the first day of class, taking note of everything that leads you to form this impression. (I might also ask them to write another description of the instructor after mid-term or near the end of the semester.) Second, write a description of yourself outside the classroom. What are the most significant differences between the two identities?

- *In what ways do you convey your identity as teacher to students—and how consistent are your messages?* Is your teaching persona expressed in your classroom manner, the tone and content of your syllabus and other course materials, and your written and oral responses to students' essays, or are there points on which these representations of your teaching persona contradict one another? (The scare-them-away-from-my-section syllabus delivered with a smile and an I'm-going-to-be-your-best-pal posture is the best example of the multiple and competing personalities we sometimes exhibit to students.)

- *How might your persona as teacher facilitate or inhibit students' learning?* While I may not be the kind of person who regards deadlines as important, for instance, I might need to be a teacher who values them (and imposes penalties when they are missed) so that I can help a student who is failing, not because she isn't capable but because her academic life is out of control.

The answers to these questions change, certainly, as we encounter new students and as we grow as teachers. We need not retreat for a weekend of intense self-analysis from which we should expect to emerge with a full-blown, flawless, and eternal teaching persona. As I hope my own experience suggests, a teaching persona is a work-in-progress—a multi-faceted identity to which we make both slight and significant adjustments to help meet students' changing needs. Nor should we try to be all things to all students. However, I do think that we need to recognize the role students play in constructing our identities in the classroom—the way they force us to negotiate, and renegotiate, a relationship between our identities at home and at work. We need to listen to their confusion or resistance or disrespect for what it might have to tell us not only about the viability of a particular theoretical or pedagogical choice but also about ourselves. Occasionally, what we hear may be disconcerting; some of it may be so transparent as to render it unworthy of serious consideration. Still, I think we must listen. And as we do, we must also be willing to look inward—to do the Full Monty *before* we walk into the classroom.

Notes

1. Having done my doctoral work in the late 1980s and early 1990s, I grew into the profession with the awareness that teaching writing is a political act, having read such works as Maxine Hairston's "Diversity, Ideology, and Teaching Writing" and Richard Bullock and John Trimbur's *The Politics of Writing Instruction: Postsecondary.* My realization on this occasion was different. If I recognized that my politics were present in the classroom, then how could I continue to ignore the many other dimensions of my self that also were there?

2. Students uncover the contradictions in our teaching rather quickly. For instance, they learn that our encouragement to "find their own voices" and to "discover the appropriate form for communicating their ideas" isn't necessarily good advice when they get their essays back covered in directive commentary and carrying a low grade for not adhering either to our "ideal text" or to the more obvious conventions of academic discourse. We need to do a better job of communicating consistent messages to students, especially our expectations for performance.

3. For two recent and opposing points of view on reflective pedagogy, see Wendy Bishop, "Places to Stand: The Reflective Writer-Teacher-Writer in Composition," and Robert P. Yagelski, "The Ambivalence of Reflection: Critical Pedagogies, Identity, and the Writing Teacher."

4. Eileen Schell's historical study of the status of women in the discipline, *Gypsy Academics and Mother-Teachers,* provides an important and much needed context for understanding this instructor's experience. See also *Feminine Principles and Women's Experience in American Composition and Rhetoric,* edited by Louise Wetherbee Phelps and Janet Emig.

Works Cited

Bishop, Wendy. "Places to Stand: The Reflective Writer-Teacher-Writer in Composition." *College Composition and Communication* 51.1 (Sept. 1999): 9–31.

Bullock, Richard, and John Trimbur, eds. *The Politics of Writing Instruction: Postsecondary.* Portsmouth, NH: Boynton, 1991.

Eichhorn, Jill; Sara Farris; Karen Hayes; Adriana Hernandez; Susan C. Jarratt; Karen Powers-Strubbs; Marian M. Sciachitano. "A Symposium on Feminist Experiences in the Composition Classroom." *College Composition and Communication* 43.3 (Oct. 1992): 297–322.

Hairston, Maxine. "Diversity, Ideology, and Teaching Writing." *College Composition and Communication* 43.2 (May 1992): 179–95.

Johnson, Cheryl. "The Teacher as Racial/Gendered Subject." *College English* 56.4 (Apr. 1994): 409–19.

Parini, Jay. "Cultivating a Teaching Persona." *Chronicle of Higher Education* 44 (Sept. 5, 1997): A92.

Phelps, Louise Wetherbee, and Janet Emig, eds. *Feminine Principles and Women's Experience in American Composition and Rhetoric.* Pittsburgh: U of Pittsburgh Press, 1995.

Schell, Eileen E. *Gypsy Academics and Mother-Teachers: Gender, Contingent Labor, and Writing Instruction.* Portsmouth, NH: Boynton, 1998.

Tate, Gary. "The 'Full Monty' in the Classroom?" In "Bungee Jumping from the Ivory Tower to the Construction Site: How Much Should We Make Visible in the Classroom?" Session at the meeting of the Conference on College Composition and Communication, Atlanta, Mar. 27, 1999.

———. "The Primary Site of Contention in Teaching Composition." *Teaching Composition in the 90s: Sites of Contention.* Ed. Christina G. Russell and Robert L. McDonald. New York: HarperCollins, 1994. 1–7.

Yagelski, Robert P. "The Ambivalence of Reflection: Critical Pedagogies, Identity, and the Writing Teacher." *College Composition and Communication* 51.1 (Sept. 1999): 32–50.

Yee, Marian. "Are You the Teacher?" *Composition and Resistance.* Ed. C. Mark Hurlbert and Michael Blitz. Portsmouth, NH: Boynton, 1991. 24–31.

II

Imaginative Literature: Creating Opportunities for Multicultural Conversations in the Composition Classroom

Linda Woodson

> If people want to believe that literature must have no traffic with rhetoric, if they want to believe that rhetoric is always and only "a tradition of instruction in persuasive public discourse," I'll be sorry, but I'll not be bound by them. Unlike that of many scientists, our work is cumulative, and we rightly keep, prize, and study all earlier texts. We do not, however, have to be stuck in any one of them.
> —Jim W. Corder, "Studying Rhetoric and Literature"

Whether or not imaginative literature has a place in the composition classroom, a debate long familiar in English department hallways, was once again addressed in two essays in the March 1993 issue of *College English*—Gary Tate's "A Place for Literature in Freshman Composition" and Erika Lindemann's "Freshman Composition: No Place for Literature." Recreating Lindemann and Tate's public exchange on the topic in a special session at the 1992 CCCC meeting, the publication of these two essays indicates a major journal editor's belief that the profession might be prompted into new ways of looking at an old argument in the discipline. In his article, Tate refers to the fact that at "three different colleges" he had "argued to keep literature out of writing programs" (321). At the time I read the article, I was surprised by his stance because during the height of the process movement, I had been a graduate student in one of Tate's courses on teaching composition where he had made such an argument, urging those in the class to realize that too many frustrated literature instructors, forced to teach freshman composition to survive, were teaching literary criticism and requiring of their students far too little writing. Impressed, I had made the same argument at three other universities, and because I was then directing the writing program at my university, I had had the opportunity repeatedly to keep literature out of our program. Nevertheless, at the time that I read the Tate article, my own thoughts about the issue had begun to change. While I still wasn't ready to argue that literature had a definite place in freshman composition, I was certain that the alternative we were providing to our students, introduction to literature classes with two hundred students each, was certainly not the way to introduce literature. Based on the Tate-Lindemann exchange, I assumed that the position of literature in the writing class would become a topic of interest again in journals and at conferences focused on composition. That didn't seem to have happened for me or for the profession.

Intensely engaged in my own struggles to catch up with postmodern and postcolonial theories of rhetoric and to stay abreast with the literature on how to incorporate the newly acquired access to the Web into our composition classes, my colleagues and I had all we could do to stay afloat. I certainly didn't have time to address an issue that had been around since I had entered the composition teaching profession and well before. I assume that that's what happened in general. Our attention was engaged with what seemed to be more pressing matters. In fact, in a search of the issues of *College Composition and Communication* since 1993, I found only seven articles about literature and writing, and four of those actually concerned the relationship of reading and to writing and only partially addressed imaginative literature.

Nevertheless, the relationship of imaginative literature to composition seems to appear with some slight regularity in our professional conversations every few years. In one recent article, "What I Learned in Grad School, or Literary Training and the Theorizing of Composition," Patrick Bizzaro investigates the literary backgrounds of some major composition theorists—David Bartholomae, Peter Elbow, Lisa Ede, and Erika Lindemann, among others—revealing that they had written literary dissertations that, for the most part, were connected by worldview or direction to the work they had later done in composition research. Bizzaro concludes that, in most of their cases, their "theorizing in composition inevitably carries, continues to carry, the indelible imprint of literary analysis" (725). To avoid the chicken-and-egg inevitability of addressing whether or not the composition researchers found their interests in literature because of their attitudes and worldview, or whether those attitudes and worldviews had been initiated and transformed by their literary research, let me simply make the point that Bizzaro stops short of the argument that his research suggests readily to me. While he states that "certain habits of mind follow these seven theorists from literary studies into composition" (738), he does not make the argument that these same literary studies could benefit composition students as well. He does assert that "we must employ methods of analysis learned from our study of 'the literary and critical values of our discipline'" (739), but his focus is on the researchers in composition, not on its students. As I have thought about the issue, I have come to believe, with Tate, that we cannot answer the question about the use of literature in composition unless we look critically at its use for our students, its potential effects on their lives.

Because at my university over half the students are minority , I have developed an intense personal awareness of a compelling reason for incorporating imaginative literature into the composition classroom—a reason informed by research into writing in multicultural settings that has begun to illuminate the rhetorics of other cultures and the ways in which these rhetorics encourage or frustrate communication and understanding. In the remainder of this essay, I should like to look at support for this direction and then to suggest some ways of incorporating imaginative literature into the composition classroom that may be productive in fostering rich interactivity—a foundational, humanistic relationship—between literature and composition studies.

In his essay "Rhetoric 2001," Richard M. Coe calls for revamping the modes of analysis that we teach:

> One rule of ordinary Western thought asserts that a whole is equal to the sum of its parts. (People who read and teach poems have always doubted this one.) A methodological corollary has been that one takes apart what one would understand, analyzes each of the parts (or variables) separately, and then arranges the analyzed parts in a logical series. This procedure is an example of mechanical thinking; it is very effective if you want to understand how a gasoline engine produces power. It does not work as well when you are trying to understand a person or a poem. (9)

I am interested in Coe's statement because it suggests that the logical analysis that is often taught in academic settings is inadequate to understand a person or groups of persons fully. In *Comparative Rhetoric,* George A. Kennedy offers support for the concept of language connected to emotion or, as he calls it, "rhetorical energy." Citing as precedents Aristotle's concept of *energeia* and eighteenth-century British rhetoricians' interest in the concept of vivacity, Kennedy defines rhetoric as a "form of energy that drives and is imparted to communication," a form of mental and emotional energy (215). He asserts that this energy may be most clearly illustrated by the natural human (that is, animal) response when we are confronted with a threat or other opportunity provoking an utterance. The emotions that rise in response—anger, lust, hunger, pity, and so on—emerge from the instinct for self-preservation. However, communication rather than physical force presents itself as more conserving of energy and, thus, more desirable (3–4).

The concept of rhetorical energy asserts the need for college writing programs to join an emphasis on technological advancement and critical thinking skills with an emphasis on the emotional development of students within that program. Certainly in the writing class, the diversity of that classroom can often lend itself to this emotional development through students' sharing the many experiences that they bring from a variety of backgrounds, narratives, and histories. But through imaginative literature, these emotional experiences are extended in innumerable ways. Imaginative literature allows us, in a somewhat privileged way, to exist for a time in the mind of another, to share that other's thoughts, emotions, and feelings and to be moved by them. Whether we find ourselves elated, horrified, discouraged, or confused by existing in another mind for a time, our potential for emotional response is nonetheless expanded. I am not suggesting that emotional responses are not fostered by other forms of literature—autobiography, memoir, narratives about intellectual discoveries, academic essays—and that these should not be included as well. I am simply suggesting that, as Corder asserts in my epigraph, there is no compelling reason to exclude imaginative literature because of its powerful ability to place us in a world outside our own.

This expansion of our potential for emotional response links to increasing advances in our understandings regarding writing in multicultural settings and the rhetorics of other cultures. In explaining how his concept of *identification* functions to assist in persuasion, Kenneth Burke names many facets of necessary identification: "You persuade a man only insofar as you can talk his language by speech, gesture, tonality, order, image, attitude, idea, *identifying* your ways with his" (55). As if in response to these elements, the various rhetorics, their traditions, and their origins are being well documented in many available sources. For example, for those in composition studies, Gary A. Olson and Lynn Worsham's *Race, Rhetoric, and the Postcolonial,* Gary Olson and Sidney I. Dobrin's *Composition Theory for the Postmodern Classroom,* and Carol Severino, Juan C. Guerra, and Johnnella

E. Butler's *Writing in Multicultural Settings* are invaluable resources. But also works such as the earlier cited *Comparative Rhetoric* by George Kennedy, *Borderlands* by Gloria Anzaldúa, and *American Indian Literature and the Southwest* by Eric Gary Anderson are extremely helpful in understanding other rhetorical traditions. With this diversity in mind, with our words being posted electronically, it becomes more and more difficult to define the universal audience in any kind of simplistic way in the composition class. There, outworn designations of "majority/minority" and "traditional/ non-traditional" have lost their meanings.

Many students in the composition classes I teach work in the community to pay for or supplement the cost of their education, some at two jobs. Many are older; many have children. Many come from underfunded, underenriched high schools. The returning Latina, reflecting in her journal the estrangement she feels when knowledge separates her from the traditional values of her immigrant parents and husband, sits alongside the returning Anglo man, divorced, children grown, studying geology as a replacement for the other life he's lived as a mechanic. These sit beside the younger Latino, and down the aisle is the African American woman, daughter of a mother who works as a domestic, a young mother herself. The young woman who is the daughter of a rancher concerned with conservation practices sits beside an animal rights activist who believes that all ranchers are engaged in immoral practices. There too is the biology major who is finding contradictions with her family's religious beliefs in the instruction given by her biology professors.

In one such classroom recently, we were reading "For My Indian Daughter" by Lewis P. Johnson, which is anthologized in our reader. Together we were discussing how the Native American father must have felt having to protect his young daughter from the insensitive "war whoops" of the Anglo man. A student who had not spoken before raised his hand well into the discussion: "I am Native American, and my father is a tribal elder. You will never be able to understand how that father feels." Most of us probably felt instinctively that he was right. But the African American woman described above spoke up: "I know something about how he feels. When my son goes out in our neighborhood, I can't let him wear his baseball cap backwards because if he does, the cops automatically assume he's a gang member and hassle him."

Insights into other experiences and their attending emotions, like the one just described, are often present in the writing class, but they can be made more directly through the use of imaginative literature that powerfully describes those experiences. As Hephzibah Roskelly says, "telling a story is the best, sometimes the only, way to explain things that are vexed or complicated" (199). In a recent informal survey of faculty who teach writing in my own department, as if understanding Roskelly's point implicitly, instructors responded that they used literature in a variety of ways that aided invention and understanding of audience. For example, one instructor reported that she used excerpts from *The Joy Luck Club* by Amy Tan to stimulate students' own memories of events and to explore various relationships between children and mothers. Another described using an excerpt from *Burning Daylight,* the best-selling novel by Jack London from 1908, in which the protagonist analyzes his feelings for his secretary and decides that to act upon those feelings would be harassing her. The instructor uses the excerpt to illustrate that even that far back sexual harassment was discussed. To continue this process of invention, she also includes some of the Wife of Bath's *Prologue* to emphasize the importance of context and develop a long view of discussion of topics.

In my own classes I have found a productive approach to including imaginative literature for the purpose of understanding the diversity of audience in a multicultural setting or environment. In a recent writing class as a major project for the semester, I combined several types of writing into one assignment that allowed students to write in several genres and at the same time become aware of the rhetoric of a culture other than their own. For the purposes of the class we defined *culture* broadly, using Stuart Hall's words to enlarge our understandings:

> Fewer and fewer cultures are originary; fewer and fewer cultures can identify any lines of stable continuity between their origins and the present. The more we know about all these cultures, including the ones that do their best to preserve their internal homogeneity, the more we understand how diverse their sources are, how much they've been influenced by others, how much they've borrowed across the borderlines. The borders have all been porous. So, our condition, the condition of all of us—even people who haven't moved an inch—is to discover our increasingly diverse cultural composition. (qtd. in Olson and Worsham 212)

Students were first asked to identify a culture that they were not part of but in which they had an interest. They were encouraged to explore a range of possibilities for defining *culture.* For example, a Chicana chose to focus on Chicana lesbians. Others chose other races and ethnicities: African American, Latina/Latino, Native American, Vietnamese, and so on. One, interestingly, chose Latina/Latino children and their representation, or lack thereof, in literature. The study produced two separate kinds of writing considered one project: the first was an analysis of the language of the culture, using outside resources, as well as their own observations and experiences; the second was an analysis of a short piece of literature from the culture: a poem, a short story, an excerpt from a novel, or a literary essay. In the meantime, in their journals, they created dialectical responses to some literary works that I gave to the class, and we read and discussed essays that characterized the language of other cultures. In addition to the project, the students compiled a portfolio that consisted of the dialectical journal, two annotated bibliographical entries each week concerning the language and characteristics of the culture they were studying, and a scrapbook filled with articles, newspaper clippings, pictures, Web material, anything that seemed useful to them in understanding the culture. Once the students began their searches into the characteristics of other cultures' languages, they were able to enlighten our class discussions about writing in multicultural settings and assessing audience in a technological community. As one student so aptly wrote in his journal in response to a poem by Sandra María Esteves:

> Stuart Hall cautions us to refrain from speaking for each other (*Race* 206). I agree. But, while we avoid talking for each other, I think we need to be careful to still speak to each other. It is important to remember that Sandra Esteves has a different experience from me; I can never speak with the voice of authority and experience about racial discrimination or living in the barrio. But I do know what it is like to speak an alien tongue—to be alive and oppressed.

While I could cite many moments in the analyses of literature in which I believe students expressed broadened understanding of the cultures they were studying and in which they seemed to share the emotions of the literature in a deep way that allowed identification, I have chosen two to illustrate. In her paper "Being and Writing as a Lesbian Chicana," one student analyzed Cherríc Moraga's "Loving in the War Years." She begins her paper:

> There are no homosexuals in the Chicano culture. At least this is what I thought for a long time growing up on the west side of San Antonio. Not because my family preached a hatred towards homosexuals, but more because the subject was never discussed, and so I never gave the issue much thought.

Then later she writes: "For the author, love is war when it is the forbidden love between two women." And further,

Moraga examines the basic human desire for love and affection; the human need to connect with another human being. This is an example of how Moraga sets out to change the reader's perceptions regarding the attraction felt between two gay women. The author's depiction of two people coming together is universal; there is nothing strictly homosexual about the scene described in the second stanza. Moraga is crossing all borders by showing how two women can need one another like a man and a woman.

In yet another example, a student who analyzed the Native American culture through Leslie Marmon Silko's *Storyteller* writes:

Silko weaves Native American songs, religious rituals, histories, and myths of the Laguna Pueblo Indians of New Mexico into the fabric of *Storyteller;* she includes both Pueblo Indian folklore and poetry, and woven into the spiderweb-like structure is a narrative which takes a kind of free-verse poetic form even though it is not actually poetry. Silko also includes short stories, anecdotes, family history, autobiographical notes, portions of letters, and photographs. *Storyteller* is, in fact, centered much more around family and Pueblo history than around personal narrative, bearing out Krupat's conclusion regarding the absence of a sense of self in Native American writing. One of the clear examples of this concept, indeed, is the inclusion of "Uncle Tony's Goat," which is "a story Simon [Ortiz] told me when he called one morning about 4 A.M. and we had a long discussion about goats" (170). Probably few writers have a sense of community that is strong enough to prompt them to include another author's writing within their own.

As both of these examples illustrate, the writers have reached out to another culture with understanding. The path they have taken to that understanding is not the only possible path, but the examples do demonstrate the identification that can be achieved. The result seems to be a more accomplished ability to assess audience in a multicultural setting, a postmodern world.

At the conclusion of his *College English* essay, Gary Tate suggests that the profession "adopt a far more generous vision of our discipline and its scope, a vision that excludes *no* texts. Only by doing this can we end the self-imposed censorship that for more than two decades has denied us the use of literature in our writing classes" (321). I agree with him. Through reading such literature, through tapping into and attempting to comprehend what Richard Lanham once called "literature's mythic energy" (21), students are encouraged to conversation, to an articulation of their stories of experience.

And through these experiences students enlarge their capacity to speak in a way that embraces many others; they add to their own base of direct experiences the emotional experiencing of others' worlds. This essay was begun with the words of Jim Corder, and his words provide a fitting conclusion, as well: "Perhaps, one day, we'll learn that we do not have to be either this or that, but can, with a little luck and a little work, be both this and that" (352).

Works Cited

Anderson, Eric Gary. *American Indian Literature and the Southwest.* Austin: U of Texas P, 1999.

Anzaldúa, Gloria. *Borderlands/La Frontera.* San Francisco: Aunt Lute, 1987.

Bizarro, Patrick. "What I Learned in Grad School, or Literary Training and the Theorizing of Composition." *College Composition and Communication* 50.4 (1999): 722–42.

Burke, Kenneth. *A Rhetoric of Motives.* Berkeley: U of California P, 1962.

Coe, Richard M. "Rhetoric 2001." *Freshman English News* 3.1 (1974): 1–13.

Corder, Jim W. "Studying Rhetoric and Literature." *Teaching Composition: Twelve Bibliographical Essays.* Ed. Gary Tate. Fort Worth: Texas Christian UP, 1987. 331–52.

Johnson, Lewis P. "For My Indian Daughter." *Developing Connections.* Ed. Judith Stanford. Mountain View, CA: Mayfield, 1995.

Kennedy, George A. *Comparative Rhetoric.* New York: Oxford UP, 1998.

Lanham, Richard A. "One, Two, Three." *Composition and Literature: Bridging the Gap.* Ed. Winifred Bryan Horner. Chicago: U of Chicago P, 1983. 14–29.

Lindemann, Erika. "Freshman Composition: No Place for Literature." *College English* 55.3 (1993): 311–16.

London, Jack. *Burning Daylight.* Murrieta, CA: Classic Books, 1998.

Moraga, Cherríe. "Loving in the War Years." *Loving in the War Years.* Cambridge: South End Press, 2000. 23–24.

Olson, Gary A., and Sidney I. Dobrin, eds. *Composition Theory for the Postmodern Classroom.* Albany: State U of New York P, 1999.

Olson, Gary A., and Lynn Worsham, eds. *Race, Rhetoric, and the Postcolonial.* Albany: State U of New York P, 1999.

Roskelly, Hephzibah. "Rising and Converging: Race and Class in the South." *Coming to Class: Pedagogy and the Social Class of Teachers.* Ed. Alan Shepard, John McMillan, and Gary Tate. Portsmouth: Boynton, 1998. 198–208.

Severino, Carol, Juan C. Guerra, and Johnnella E. Butler, eds. *Writing in Multicultural Settings.* New York: MLA, 1997.

Silko, Leslie Marmon. *Storyteller.* New York: Arcade, 1981.

Tan, Amy. *The Joy Luck Club.* New York: Putnam, 1989.

Tate, Gary. "A Place for Literature in Freshman Composition." *College English* 55.3 (1993): 317–21.

12

Irrigation: The Political Economy of Personal Experience

Carol Reeves and Alan W. France

As teachers of writing, we have inevitably formed our professional identities around a central ethic—that composition is neither a stepchild nor a bastard of the traditional arts curriculum. It bears instead an honorable lineage, intimately related to the highest goals of the liberal education. The writing classroom as a crucial curricular space where students might make sense of their lives, where they may use writing to articulate a self out of the undifferentiated flux of remembered experience. Composition is always more than writing, always more than a way to "get ahead" in school and work, always more than an institutional requirement. Composing is an intentional act.

Yet the traditional repertoire of liberal arts virtues and the critical practices fostering the goals of a humane education have come up against the world our students will inhabit: the brave new illiberal—or neoliberal—world of intense global winner-take-all economic competition. More difficult, as well, because the very media of communication in which we might conduct traditional, reflective humanistic inquiry have been subsumed and commodified. The modernist discourse of the self, in other words, has suffered a hostile takeover. Who a person "really is"—and of course what it means to write a personal experience narrative—can no longer be considered self-evident. We are all now, in Haraway's sense, cyborgs: amalgams of electronic media and personal histories. And only the most disciplined of critical practices stand any chance of isolating the substance of the self from these complex compounds.

To do the educative work of self-articulation entailed by the precept "know thyself," our students need to learn certain critical practices that are not part of the traditional repertoire of liberal arts virtues. And so, although our teaching returns for nurture to the faith that self-knowledge is liberating, it is not an easy or placid faith. In the essay that follows, we will try to map out one path this faith has taken: an assignment that works with the narrative representation of the self by attempting a disciplined and critical interrogation of selfhood's social origins.

In our essay on this pedagogical work—its origins, its development, its relationship to critical theories of discourse—we will be distinguishing three authorial modes (or "voices" as we usually say): Carol's, Al's, and our collaborative persona. We will use explicit textual directions to help our readers know who is at the authorial helm. In the two sections that follow, first Carol, then Al will write about Carol's "Irrigation: An Essay," the originating point of our collaboration on this essay. Carol will reflect on the essay's composition and on the larger implications for the writing process itself. Then, in the next section, Al will recount his reading and appropriation of the essay.

Carol: Writing as Irrigation

Water flows out to the parched crop rows from ditches or pipes running from a pump, electric nowadays, but in the old days, diesel. Big GMC or Oldsmobile engines without bodies, without mufflers, raging into the night, pull water up through hundreds of feet of bedrock and loamy topsoil. The water is cold when it comes out of the ground and foamy with minerals—calcite, sodium, selenium, magnesium. It flows eagerly to its destination, picking up an occasional rat or water moccasin, moving down a slope so subtle that only a careful surveying will find it. The flatness is real, of course, but nothing is ever entirely flat. There are always gradations, slight depressions and calm slopes. Much of the water evaporates in air so dry it is electric, charged with positive emptiness (you know exactly what will happen if you walk in the dust and touch the side of your pickup truck). After you set the tubes and stand on the far bank of the irrigation ditch, you can watch the water moving down the straight rows of wheat or cotton or soybeans or sorghum—doing its work—and you have this feeling. You watch the water stumble over the sod, wiggle like a tiny finger through the jungle of leaves, and you look up at the dusky sky, slightly brown with dust, and you know plenitude. It is a fleeting knowledge in this country.

Seamus Heaney has a poem, "Digging," in which he pays tribute to his father's farming life while setting up a metaphor between "digging" the earth and "digging" in one's consciousness for the material for art. Annie Dillard relates writing to chiseling rock (3). We must all find ways to explain to ourselves why we have chosen not to live as our fathers lived, why we write, why it is so hard, and why we keep turning back to what we thought we had left behind for those explanatory metaphors.

In his approach to teaching writing, Al has reminded me to connect my own needs as a writer with those of my students. Aren't we all searching for metaphors? Aren't we all forever finding a name for that experience or place that we wanted to leave but that continues to haunt us? If I can't stop wondering why my ancestors would have wanted to settle in such a drab, harsh landscape, and if I can't forget the sound of an irrigation pump, and if I continue to hold a clear vision of water flowing down a crop row, then surely, they have their pasts to irrigate imaginatively as well.

In my own teaching, I have too easily fallen into the pragmatic as an end in itself. They need to know how to write a solid thesis, how to defend it solidly, how to use solid evidence, how to document sources. Yes, yes, yes. But we need to nudge them toward the water, no matter how murky, of their lives.

As I was writing the irrigation essay, I was also writing a scholarly essay on the language of AIDS. As I was writing the irrigation essay, I was also drafting guidelines for our college professional standards committee for tenure and promotion proceedings. As I was writing the irrigation essay, I was teaching Aristotle in a befuddling way to befuddled students. And each time I sat down to work on the irrigation essay, I had this feeling. As I watched the words flow so easily from the bedrock of me, my fingers feeling the territory of a blank screen, I knew plenitude. And that is a fleeting knowledge in this country.

Al: Reading "Irrigation"

When I first read "Irrigation: An Essay" (shortly after publication during a Thanksgiving visit at Carol's), I didn't think about pedagogical applications. I thought: in the twenty minutes it took me to read this essay, I've come to *know* someone—already a friend—better. This first, *personal,* reaction is probably closest to authorial intention. The essay allowed Carol and, over her shoulder, her readers to make sense of how a person came to be who she now is. I liked the essay most immediately because I know Carol and know therefore how finely the essay worked. But because of what I do, it's impossible merely to enjoy a good story. Its "effectivity" must be identified.

"Irrigation" worked so well, it seemed to me, because it "rationalized" a bundle of characteristics and idiosyncrasies that I knew as Carol Reeves—

knew well enough already to say to mutual friends things like "That sounds like something Carol would say!" "Irrigation" explained how a selfhood had emerged out of "material culture" by placing "personal experience" in its historical context. It did not just "express" that experience; it *accounted* for it by supplying what Michael Bernard-Donals has called "structures of experience" (259). As an aggregate, these experiences are called by discourse theorists "subjectivity"; but of course as an aggregate, experiences are useless to someone writing—or reading—an essay. However, by supplying both the experience and its structuring context—the dancer and the dance—the essay allowed me to say with conviction that I could *understand* Carol (better) as a person. And composition is in the understanding business. So my assignment sequence began with a close reading, in class, of "Irrigation."

To the teacher of writing, most anything we read has potential for "pedagogical application," and it didn't take me long to see that "Irrigation" did exactly what I wanted my students to do when I assign them to write a personal essay. So I quickly appropriated Carol's essay as a model for an assignment in an advanced composition course. More recently, I've begun to use it in my introductory courses as well.

"Irrigation" has, for me, two great virtues. First, it contains a dense—to some perhaps overly so—concentration of rhetorical and literary techniques: note, for example, how descriptive detail is marshaled in the opening four sentences to produce a powerful, unified, and multiply-allusive theme—a motif, actually. Second, and most important to me, "Irrigation" shows how to historicize experience. It illustrates a process by which a person writing reflectively in the present can discover—recover, actually—the social and economic determinants of identity, which is to say culture's transparent sculpting of the self.

Now, it is time for you, our readers, to read Carol's essay yourselves. In the following section, then, we reproduce the text of "Irrigation: An Essay" as it was originally published in *The Flying Island,* a little literary magazine, in 1994.

IRRIGATION: AN ESSAY

For years, the irony was preserved: a sea of tall, dry, yellow grass sitting atop an underground sea enclosed in bedrock. Above, bleached bones, prickly pear, dry creek beds with red sand, weathered, dry-land wheat farmers with hard scrabble psyches to match the land they farmed. Below, a swelling surge of cool water with nowhere to go.

Nowhere to go, that is, but up, once farmers discovered they could drill wells and water their crops and plow up more dry grassland and pump more water and change the texture of that country and their lives forever. Back before the settlers, tall grasses—blue stem, switch grass, and Indian grass—covered the flat plain, and you could look out across the West Texas plains in the early fall and see the silver tips of grass folding and dipping in the wind. You'd have to look away or become dizzy. Old timers say that the grass was high enough to tickle their horses' bellies. There was always danger of grass fires that made the sky black for days.

By the time I was born in the fifties, and especially by the time I was old enough to help out on the farm, our pastures contained no more tall grasses, only short grasses—Blue Grama, Side Oats Grama, and wild rye—because cows can graze them down bare as a table-top, and they'll come back with a good rain. The remaining land was in long furrows of rich brown loam extending on the flat plane of the land toward infinity. You'd get dizzy if you gazed down them too long and hard. Bordering the fields were irrigation ditches, about two feet deep and four feet across, from which water ribboned smoothly through the milo and corn and cotton. Huge muffler-less diesel engines, with their ear-pounding roar, pumped the water from the ground. Where I grew up, fives miles west of the Caprock, thirteen miles south of Silverton, twenty miles north of Floydada, thirty-five miles east of Plainview, a good seventy miles northeast of Lubbock, the land was so flat that in the evening when the clouds rolled in, I'd pretend they were mountains. I'd look out over a flat field of young cotton and pretend I was a giant treading through an ancient forest. Those irrigation ditches were oceans. Blowing sand was really blowing snow, clean and pure. So much imaginative freedom can be oppressive.

In the summers, there was nothing like slipping into the icy water of the ditch and allowing the currents to push you from one end of a field to the other. Ditch surfing, we called it. We'd be hoeing a cotton field, the air so dry and hot that you couldn't sweat, the sun broiling the back of our necks. At the end of a complete row, we'd jump in, settle our bodies into the neat V, and let the murky water move through our clothes. Anyone coming upon us would find five mud-smeared, sunburned heads lined up down the middle of the ditch like mud puppies keeping their bottoms in the water, their tops to the sun. Naturally, we weren't supposed to be swimming in the ditches because there was always the danger of hitting a tube and causing it to lose suction, or worse, breaking holes in the dams. Changes in the flow of water running down one field row would change the water level through the rest of the field; water running into the road next to the field caused a real mess. Dad always got angry when he discovered we'd broken a dam, not necessarily because water was being wasted, for we all thought the Ogalala was everlasting, but because of the time and trouble involved in repairing broken dams.

Irrigation farming in the sixties was incredibly labor intensive. You had to check the well pumps because they were always running out of diesel, always needing minor adjustments and repairs. You had to check the flow of the water every four hours to make sure that some sudden change in the water level had not broken the suction.

They needed special adjustments, and sometimes the water pressure would just increase suddenly, causing water to spill over the tops of the dams. The tubes, three-inch aluminum pipes that fed water from the ditches into the crop rows, had to be reset often because they'd lose their suction with the movement of the water or the bump of an occasional rat or ground squirrel. Dad would tromp out in waders just before 9:00 PM to set tubes, sometimes leaving again at 3:00 AM, then again at 6:00. To set a tube, you had to stand with one mud boot in the crop row, the other just close enough to the dam to get leverage, and bend low, filling the tube with water. They you'd hold one hand over one end of the tube and while the other end was still in the water, you'd swish the tube back and forth. The trick was to swish back and forth and then, in one swift move, take your hand from the end of the tube and place it down in the row. If you did it right, water would flow from the tube. I was never very good at it, so Dad always followed behind me, patiently resetting every tube.

No one ever gave a thought to the amount of water that was lost to evaporation. It didn't matter because there was plenty of water down under the surface, a huge water-bearing formation, 300 feet deep in some places, that stretched up to Nebraska, a geologist once explained to my father. That explained and somehow justified our barren lives on the surface: never mind, we lived over an ocean. An endless ocean that had made our lives golden.

Before irrigation, back when my dad was a boy, every crop was dry land, which meant that you planted your seeds in hard scrabble and hoped for the best. You planted wheat because if you got enough moisture, you could graze your cattle on it during the winter. You were a gambler to plant cotton or soybeans or corn. They all required too much attention, chemicals, water, cultivation. And even if you did have grasshoppers or careless weeds, you didn't spend money on chemicals, because what would be the point in spending money for chemicals if you didn't get rain? In the good years, you knew exactly what to do with abundance: you dried it, stocked it, canned it, ground it, stored it, sold it, cherished it because you expected not to have the same kind of year next time. And in the bad years, you lived off what you'd stored from the good years; you sold off most of the livestock, you managed. There was no such thing as bumper crops that couldn't be used. Life was hard and honest and predictable, not golden.

And then came all that glorious water. Suddenly there were no longer any quiet drives down the country roads because every half mile you heard the blaring roar of those engines. Suddenly, all the sons of the old hard scrabble farmers were driving new Ford and Chevy pickups and building new ranch-style brick homes and filling them with new furniture from the showrooms in Amarillo and Lubbock. Our new home was Readi-built, the latest in construction technology, according to the pamphlet. On the day they brought it out to us, all put together, a house on wheels, a sandstorm blew in. We waited out by the mailbox anyway. Mother's new dress getting sandblasted and grandmother standing slightly behind us, clutching a new patent leather purse, as if she half expected that Dad would need a loan. She never carried more than eleven dollars at one time. Then we saw it come floating down the newly paved country road in all its pink-shingled glory, sliding helter-skelter on its trailer like a pink whale resigning itself to the force of the ocean. In my new bedroom several nights later, I imagined we were moving still, traveling to some place with trees and mountains.

That water changed our habits of mind, our vision of ourselves. We became hopeful. What we imagined might actually be possible. My great grandmother's collection of Harvard Classics wouldn't have to sit rotting on the shelf because one of us from the "irrigated" generation might read them for college, and we wouldn't necessarily study agriculture. I thought I might move out to live with my cousin Jerry who lived in Los Angeles and who had been on American Bandstand.

With the first irrigation well he dug in 1953 and the first Cummins engine he used to pump the water to his new crops, my father became an agri-businessman. He experimented with new crops: sunflowers, kocia weed, highly specialized seed crops, the latest hybrids. Every year, he bought a new pickup, always posing next to it while Mother took his picture. Every few years, he'd move up to a more powerful tractor, from the little blue Ford to the revolutionary John Deere 4010 in

1962 to the 4020 to the 4430—all with radios in the cabs—to bigger plows, from two-row to four-row to eight-row, to the latest in chemical treatments. That operation was the epitome of modern farming technology and productivity. Between 1965 to 1970, land prices in the area jumped from $1150 per acre to $1500 per acre.

My mother became the wife of an agri-businessman, which meant that she didn't keep chickens or a cow, didn't spend long, sweaty hours at the cannery stocking up the summer's produce. We always had a garden, of course, but Mother didn't can much, preferring to freeze, which was faster and easier. She didn't need to sew our clothes, and she certainly didn't work in the fields or drive the trucks filled with wheat to the local co-op. But while Dad was challenged to keep up with the latest agricultural developments, Mother became restless, suddenly free to reinvent a totally different farmwife identity but with no models to imitate. The only woman in our family who had divorced her husband and left the farm was Aunt Ike, and there were rumors that she had become loose in Lubbock. For a while, Mother sold Wonder Bras to every woman in our church, all of whom sat in their pews with their new wonderful secret under their jersey dresses. She took ceramics and needlepoint and flower-arranging classes, and when those activities didn't satisfy her cravings, my mother began to dream of becoming a single-mother-working-in-the-exciting-city-with-an-exciting-career. So she left Dad, and we moved to Amarillo where she worked as a convenience store clerk because that was all she could get, a person with no job experience and little formal education. And no credit. Irrigation couldn't change every landscape. My dad suddenly had to live alone in the newly remodeled Readi-built with wall-to-wall shag carpet that he allowed to get clogged up with dirt and cowdog fur.

You just think the water will keep coming on up, year after year. It's the one thing you count on. Even when you have to dig your wells a little deeper every year, even after these occasional moments when water pressure slows to a dribble, you don't allow yourself to think the unthinkable: the ocean is drying up. That's impossible; it's an ocean after all. All the young farmers were taking courses in irrigation technology at Texas Tech; surely this meant something. Plus, my dad and the other farmers in the county had educated themselves about water conservation, replaced the old ditches with pipeline irrigation, which took care of the evaporation problem, and used more efficient engines that ran as quietly as dishwashers.

Still the water level dropped. There is an underlying formation below the Ogalala called the Red Bed which geologists had claimed also held water, and several farmers decided to try pumping it up. Mr. Ferguson was the first to try, bringing a sample of the salty water to the Gin Office where everyone had to taste it for themselves. G. W. Lee decided to pump it up anyway and blend it with Ogalala water to dilute the salt, but everyone else just decided to continue pumping from the Ogalala until their water ran out; then, they'd go back to farming the old way.

The water started running out on my dad's place in the mid-seventies, and the wells have gone bone dry on all but one half-section of land. Now there are no more ditches or even pipelines; those who still have some water under their land have gone to drip-irrigation. Now, instead of planting corn and milo, Dad plants wheat and a hybrid of the old tall grass, Blue Stem, that turns bluish red in the summer and silvery in October and will tickle your horse's belly if you've a mind to ride out across it. Dad is no longer really an agri-businessman, and his land is now worth $200 an acre. He says things like, "If we don't get rain in the next few weeks, we're going to lose our hay crop," and "Even if it rains this week, it's too late to save our hay crop," and "Every day that goes by is a day closer to rain—it may be next year though."

Now, in mid-October, if you wait until just before sundown or sunup, drive down the road that borders two of my dad's pastures, get out of your car, stand in the middle of the road, and look out across that sea of silver-tipped Blue Stem, folding and dipping in the wind, you can get dizzy. But there won't be any sea beneath your feet.

Al: Teaching "Irrigation" as a Model

As indicated earlier, I selected "Irrigation: An Essay" as a model of the writing process that I wanted to teach to my students in undergraduate composition courses for two basic reasons: its rhetorical and literary accomplishment and its success in understanding one person's experience in its social and historical context. But two other advantages to this project suggested themselves as well. First, I knew the author and knew that I could prevail on her to speak—actually, to write—directly to my students. Teaching "Irrigation" allowed me to reanimate the author function, so to say, and to let students see a real person, using the medium of writing and the genre of the personal essay, doing for herself exactly what I wanted them to do for themselves. When I first used Carol's essay as a model, three years ago in a basic writing class (without any of the elaborate incremental steps I've since added), I just mailed copies of student essays to her. A week later, a long email turned up with personal comments for each of the students in my class. They were transformed. While we were reading "Irrigation," students had complained that it was "long and drawn out." She could have said all this stuff about the water and the divorce in one page, they said. Suddenly, though, this abstraction, the author, had become a presence, explaining to them by name exactly why they needed to "draw out" some vacant generality or some cryptic allusion. Writing had, in short, become a living, dialogical process. They responded to Carol's comments—her encouragements to elaborate—much more positively than ever they had to my teacherly marginalia. Carol was more than a teacher; she was an author(ity).

A second advantage to using "Irrigation" as a model for a personal essay had to do with the essay's topicality. On one hand, the historical and geographical setting of Carol's essay is, for my metro-Philadelphia students, unfamiliar, not to say exotic. The attention "Irrigation" pays to reproducing the ambient detail of agricultural life on the West Texas prairie requires students to look much more closely at—to de-familiarize, really—their own backyards and front stoops, at least if they are going to reconfigure their experience as the assignment asks them to do. And it's not just detail for detail's sake. The central insight of "Irrigation," I think, is that part of who we are is encrypted in the detail of our historical setting and that detail itself offers one referent—the literal—of a metaphor that can "recover" that figurative essence of self by which one's culture reproduces itself. The invention of the irrigation metaphor enabled Carol to "emplot" (in the sense Hayden White uses the term) her autobiography as a story with a real—that is, historical—referent. Because the social context of Carol's childhood was so foreign to them, they could see more clearly the power of "irrigation" to explain essential features of her biography. And my hope was, therefore, that they themselves might find such a metaphor to understand their own biographies.

In teaching "Irrigation," then, it is necessary to focus on the trope of *antithesis,* which actually organizes the essay into sets of binaries: dry and wet, past and present, "hard scrabble" and "agri-business," privation and abundance, the provincial and the metropolitan, tradition and modernity, necessity and—perhaps, whatever it might mean—freedom. The central metaphor of "irrigation" serves as a kind of semantic trunk-line, shunting and transforming meaning between domains, from one pole of a binary to the other. In the course under consideration here, we spent four hours reading "Irrigation," one on the first two paragraphs alone. An experienced reader will easily see why: not only is the opening image crucial to estab-lishing the antitheses; its language actually *performs* it. For instance, con-sider the fricatives ("bleached bones, prickly pear") of the sea above are placed in opposition to the sibilants ("a swelling surge") of the sea below. And notice how the text dissolves that "irony . . . preserved" by the bed-rock. In the transition from the first to the second paragraph, water with nowhere to go becomes water with "Nowhere to go, that is, but up, once farmers discovered they could drill wells. . . ." The crescendo "Nowhere to go, that is, but up" actually produces the effect of the water rising through the pierced bedrock. Throughout, "Irrigation" requires—and repays—this kind of close reading to give up its underlying tropological unity and to make its techniques available to less experienced student writers.

We now reprint the assignment sequence that Al used with his class. It at-tempted to help students conceive and write a personal essay like Carol's "Irrigation" by breaking the invention or prewriting process down into a series of ascending incremental steps, which could be synthesized finally into an extended exploration into the "political economy of personal experience," as we had begun to call this project.

The Assignment Sequence

The following weekly assignments and the instructions for the major es-say, "Writing Project #1: Environment and Identity," were handed out to-gether with a photocopy of Carol's essay with the syllabus at the beginning of the 1991 fall semester.

Assignment #1: Write a short interpretation of Carol Reeves's "Irriga-tion: An Essay." This means that you should explain what you see as her central point—her *purpose*—or what she seems most interested in telling us. Use some short quotations to illustrate your interpretation.

Assignment #2: Make a picture in your mind of a place that had a strong positive or negative meaning for you when you were growing up. Look at it carefully in your imagination, take notes on it, and then write a description of it (about two pages), using some of the tech-niques Reeves uses in her essay, "Irrigation."

Assignment #3: Create a metaphor for your essay (comparable to Reeves's "irrigation"). Your metaphor should be a word or phrase that describes both your physical environment—as in last week's assign-ment—and the effects or influences of that environment on your personality: the person you have come to be. Explain how the meta-phor expresses your personal history and how you feel about it.

Assignment #4: Email a personal letter to Carol in which you (1) ex-plain your interpretation of her essay, and (2) using your metaphor, explain how your environment—your past experience—has influ-enced or shaped the person you are now.

Writing Project #1: Environment and Identity: Carol Reeves's "Irriga-tion: An Essay" is a model for the kind of explorative personal essay this assignment sequence is asking you to write. Essentially, you are examining the relationship between the social and material world and the person you have come to be. I call this process "explorative" be-cause each person has a different environment, and none of us can really know how that environment—the landscape, the architecture, the religious and moral traditions, the racial and ethnic composition, the social class, the family interrelationships among many other fac-tors make it impossible ever to really allow us to follow Socrates' dic-tum to "know thyself." Nevertheless, the goal of a liberal arts educa-tion is for each of us to work toward the deepest and most honest knowledge of ourselves possible. For Reeves, *"irrigation"* is a meta-phor—a concept that expresses *not only* the hydraulic technology of watering fields *but also* the changing social relationships that have shaped—in a way *"irrigated"*—her imagination, her view of herself and of the world she has come to inhabit. The same kinds of forces that shaped Carol Reeves's life have also shaped yours (and mine). And the purpose of this writing assignment is to help you do for your own life what Carol Reeves has done for hers: come to understand it bet-ter by explaining it in the form of a written text, an *essay.* Having worked through the four preparatory weekly assignments, it is now time to use them in writing an extended essay (5–6 pages). Your meta-phor (Assignment #3) should give your essay a central, unifying point (a "theme"), and you can use it for your title, as Carol has done.

Al: The "Irrigation" Assignment Sequence

Students' attempts at the first two incremental assignments—interpreting and describing—were naturally impressionistic and fragmented. At least they were compared to the objectives of the "Environment and Identity" project. Their interpretations of "Irrigation" tended to focus on the essay as cautionary tale. Some read it as a warning of environmental catastrophe: "taking resources for granted will lead to us having nothing," as Melissa put it; others, like Karen, as a moral warning against "materialism [that] eats away at our sense of family." There was little evidence that students were making causal connections between the two domains of Carol's controlling metaphor, her "turn" from literal irrigation—the ditches, pipes, and water—to the nourishment of imagination and intellect entailed figuratively by references to the "irrigated generation." Nor was there much appreciation of the inherent contradiction in Carol's ambivalence toward the new irrigated order, exhilarating but disorienting ("dizzying," as she puts it several times).

With few exceptions, the students involved in this writing project were long removed from the rural—perhaps even preindustrial—agricultural past that Carol re-calls to life in "Irrigation." For my students, all that remained of the traditional social organization of "hard scrabble" family farming were bromides and pieties from the likes of *Little House on the Prairie.* Their lives and mine were lived in the greater Philadelphia metropolitan area, our work around the place likely limited to mowing the lawn or walking a pet.

For all of us, though, the threat or experience of family breakdown that seemed to be set in motion with the advent of irrigation was real. In their letters to her, a number of students asked Carol for more details about the divorce: "How did [the move to Amarillo] really affect you?" or "Did your mother ever think she made a mistake to leave your Dad?" But the student interpretations of the essay that made the divorce the climax of the narrative (roughly half) did not link it to the socioeconomic changes Carol describes. The culprit was "materialism," as Wendy pointed out: "irrigation" could be understood figuratively as a "washing away" of family bonds and boundaries, a concomitant effect of abundance that caused people to "forget their commitments to each other," thus confounding as well as awakening the irrigated generation.

In the majority of students' descriptions (Assignment #2), the larger social and economic contexts of experience were absent, no matter how obvious or inevitable they had seemed to me. The "inner city," the suburbs, or the rural "ex-urbs" were, for the students, strictly extrinsic elements of setting for their memories. The differences between Karen's "woods behind my house" and Mike's "EA" (the Eire Avenue section of North Philadelphia) were entirely accidental. One was clean and quiet, the other dirty and noisy; one supported tree forts, the other street gangs.

Only when students began to search for metaphors in Assignment #3 did the causal relationships start to appear. Some students struck gold early in the process. Adrianna began with a literal grapevine that knit together the backyards of the neighborhood where her extended Italian American family lived in door-to-door row houses. The grapevine, of course, stands figuratively for family intimacy and solidarity and as well, Adrianna suggests, for overly assiduous business-minding. In any case, the call of upward mobility—a suburban home with multiple bathrooms and its own half-acre lot—proved too much of a strain. Her parents' move out of the old neighborhood created family dissension, although Adrianna suggests that the figurative grapevine still lives in the close relationships among those of her own generation. Steve also hit upon a fruitful metaphor: the basement of his grandparents' house as "a place with strong positive or negative associations." The child of what he calls a "dual-income lifestyle," Steve uses his metaphor to link the material objects of family history, the faded photographs and toy soldiers, with his sense of alienation from a living past and with his deep desire to reconnect with it.

In the rest of this section I would like to recount in more detail the process by which two students, Wendy and Malik, worked through the assignments and formulated insights that they themselves believe they could never have done without considering the real-world contexts of their lives. These exemplary "case studies" of students working their way through the "Irrigation" assignment sequence represent, in my judgment, strong arguments for the pedagogy Carol and I are proposing here: teaching a more "comprehensive" (in the sense of complete and of self-reflective) approach to writing the personal essay by including the historical and material agents of private experience.

In her interpretation (Assignment #1) of "Irrigation," Wendy was the only student to focus on the causal link between economics (broadly construed) and the familial tensions Carol relates in the final third of her essay. Wendy, who grew up in rural Missouri, read Carol's central metaphor of irrigation as a washing away of traditional knowledge, as if the water coursing up from the Ogalala were instead from the River Lethe, dulling the soul's memories for the afterlife. As Wendy put it, "the discovery of the water had 'irrigated' the minds of past knowledge, and almost made people ignorant." The result, she wrote in her letter to Carol (Assignment #4), was

> an eye opener for everyone, including the reader. Realizing how little things can come between people, and tear families apart. Usually the culprit is money, but not always. I also came to the realization that it is the small things that count in life, not the big things. I guess I am trying to say we live in a materialistic world, and people have to [lose] things before they realize how important they really are. . . . The

misuses of the land, your mother's reaction with your father's obsession with farming, and how you became stuck in the middle of everything. It really was quite sad.

The personal history underlying Wendy's interpretation of "Irrigation" became clearer in Assignment #2 as she worked to describe a significant place or "scene" from her memory. Her paper, "Radio Waves," focused not on a traditional locus of habitation—what I guess we expect when we assign descriptions of the familiar—but on a *network,* a system of interstices between places. For Wendy, it was the interstices, not points they connected, that were most memorable.

> I chose radio waves for my title [she explained to Carol], and focused my essay around my parents being divorced since I was about six years old. I call it "Radio Waves" because the trips made in my dad's Volkswagen Beetles were memorable times from my childhood, and the music I heard along the way still remains clear in my mind. As a matter of fact, they are some of the few memories I have of my childhood. I discussed the feelings I felt in the Beetle, and the transmission of the music and myself from point A to point B. The hour and a half transmission was that made between my parents' houses on Interstate 29 in Missouri. The Beetle hosted a place for my father, brother, and I to make a relationship that would be made and broken throughout my childhood, and now into my adulthood.

As it is for many of us and for many more of our students, experience becomes increasing "ungrounded." There is a greater and growing sense of participation in networks like the interstate, the Internet, and the media of popular entertainment. It is, in a word, postmodern. For Wendy, as for many of us, the networks (the radio waves) represent *both* connectedness or togetherness *and* separation, isolation, loss. As a reader of Wendy's emerging essay, I learned how much—and how little—culture studies and postmodern theories of discourse explain one person's experience. And it is perhaps not too much to claim that Wendy learned a lot about herself by "theorizing" (contextualizing) her experience.

A more traditional response to the "Irrigation" assignments—one with a distinctly urban flavor—was Malik's. While Wendy distrusted "materialism," as she called it, as corrosive of family and community, Malik's interpretation of Carol's essay stressed the positive side of "irrigation"—especially the opportunities that abundance offered to *escape* social dysfunction and disorientation—which he called "moving up the ladder of success." What had been the decisive event in Wendy's interpretation, the divorce,

Malik ignored as a kind of "opportunity cost." For him, Carol's narrative had a happy ending.

Also different from Wendy's interpretation was Malik's specificity of place. He drew a map of the exact "crossroads" (the precise geographical intersection in West Philadelphia) from which he drew the vehicle or literal referent of his metaphor. Until he was eight, Malik's family lived on Whitby Avenue, north of Cobb's Creek Parkway,

> a run-down part of the city. The streets were filthy, the walls written on, and there were dealers and hustlers everywhere.
>
> The southern part of Whitby Avenue was the suburb. Once you cross Cobb's Creek Parkway, you travel through a small set of woods and you would be in paradise. This was the same street I lived on . . . about a ten minute drive down the road. . . . The houses were nice, the streets were clean, and everyone had a lawn and a swimming pool.

The tenor of Malik's metaphor, the figurative "Crossroads" of his title, was a reversal in fortune between his cousin's family and his own. His cousin's family, who had lived in the relative paradise of Cobb's Creek Parkway, foundered on the urban perils of drugs and prison. They had "to move into a cheap apartment complex for low-income families . . . in the neighborhood that I was accustomed to." Meanwhile, his father's promotion allowed Malik's family to move up—to cross the intersection—into the suburban "paradise" that his cousin's family had just had to abandon.

Malik did not hesitate to call his "Crossroads" essay a "'rags to riches' story" and compare to it to Carol's "escape" from the rural nowhere of the West Texas prairie. His narrative valued, much more than Wendy's, Carol's achievement if not of riches, then of professional success. Malik's life on Whitby Avenue north of Cobb's Creek Parkway was all there was "for a lot of people I knew," he wrote, "but I always wanted more." His essay realizes his personal commitments to upward mobility, achievement, and the material indicators of social status as a measure of escape from the lower rungs of the ladder of success. While Malik's "success ethic" is probably as much a postmodern cultural formation as Wendy's "Radio Waves," I would speculate that the residual bonds of African American culture—admittedly and obviously strained as "Crossroads" attests—offer some protection from the more disorienting ("dizzying") effects of social disruption and anomie that afflict many of us from the dominant white "mainstream."

Malik's and Wendy's essays are the two pieces of support I intend to offer for my claim that historicizing personal experience can help our students uncover the social dimension of their perceived selves (see my "Dialectics of the Self" for an extended argument that this is an important objective of a liberal education). It remains now for Carol to explain what we both perceive (I only after extended conversation with her) as an inherent problem with the "Irrigation" assignment: it imagines, quite naively, that, as Gary Tate once put it in jest, "students might write their way out of ignorance."

Carol: Evaluating the "Environment and Identity" Essays

When I replied to Al's students' letters (describing their own evolving attempts to follow the model of "Irrigation"), I told them that my essay had not resulted from any assignment, that it had come instead from my own sense of guilt and wonder at my present incarnation as a college professor. I was raised to be a farmwife: I learned to cook for the hungry, to can peaches so that they retain their fresh color, to grow tomatoes and corn and okra, and to keep myself busy at all times. But by age eighteen, I considered the farm life to be about as fulfilling as a career at the county dump. I ran from the dust, the hailstorms, the literal and physical flatness, sought a life with trees, maybe even mountains, and longed for a time when a rain just meant a rain and not the make or break point in the year's profits.

But once I got what I wanted, I looked around me and saw that I was very different from my colleagues who had grown up in cities, among educated people, and whose speech and mannerisms fit their professional status perfectly. I have a thick, West Texas accent, a "howdy, ya'll" friendliness that doesn't quite suit the intellectual persona. I was even advised by someone interviewing me for a position that I ought to consult a speech therapist. Pretty soon, the dissonance I felt made me uneasy, like I was balancing on the top rail of a fence, with the farm and the farmwife on one side and the university and the professor on the other. The person sitting on that fence had become a stranger. So I began to write, with no intention of crafting any controlling metaphor, or as Al says in his assignment, "a concept that expresses not only the hydraulic technology of watering fields but also the changing social relationships that have shaped—in a way 'irrigated' her imagination, her view of herself and of the world she has come to inhabit." He's right about what eventually grew out of this fence-sitting, but the call to write was simply a raw despondency. And it was a call, not an assignment.

So, unlike me, Al's students were nudged toward that fence by something extrinsic to their life experience. Some of them, like Josh, have no fence to sit on. They are quite prepared to tackle such an assignment as an intellectual exercise; they are already polished intellectuals who seem to suffer from no conflict between their home culture and the university. Josh, whose father is a doctor, grew up in a lovely valley "between two farms adjacent to the Brandywine river in the township of East Fallowfield." His childhood was "void of the pressure and insecurities we develop later in life." Josh offers me a sophisticated interpretation of my essay:

> Your metaphor, irrigation, led me to believe that your essay was not only about your childhood, but was also about reliance and change. Reliance on irrigation provided a material and imaginative existence. Change was simply the realization that irrigation shaped the landscape and the people on the land from one existence to another, and because of change we have impermanence.

But Josh is not sitting on the fence. So while he can intellectualize and interpret, even appropriating Al's own language—"material existence"—his own "material existence" has led quite naturally to the place where he is now.

On the other hand, there is Amy. I recognize Amy as coming from a background that may eventually collide with—if it hasn't already—the demands of academia. She reveals, in her interpretation of my essay and in her description of her own essay, a dissonance of which she is probably unconscious. In her interpretation, she struggles with the academy, wrestling with its language, its critical terminology. She tries to discuss the essay using analysis and critical terminology, the way she thinks a good student should:

> In the story you wrote, I do not believe it was foreshadowed or dealt with by the mother or father real well. There was drama in that implement that you added . . . . What I did appreciate was the lengthy descriptions of the whole process of how the family operated. The comparison of how intense the work was, and how it became fruitful, in addition, was also the time frame which was made reference to. . . . The use of colors . . . and technological terms was a real plus to this piece.

But when she tells me about her essay, she clings defiantly to the values and habits of home, including its speech patterns. She reveals an interpretation of my essay that differs from what she provided in her (assigned) academic voice. Here, she says that my essay explains "that the family did the best they could do no matter what happened." And she "talks" to me in the language of her home:

> In your essay you explain the photo that was taken every year of the brand new truck. I finally got my "brand new" car. We had those times too. When my brother got his first car, he took pictures. And Lord,

we knew the art of labor. We were always taking pride in some aspect of our home. Whether it was washing the car, mowing the lawn, planting flowers, digging post holes, cleaning windows . . . , we worked. And we worked together.

Here, she equates family, hard work, and the reward of material possessions. But she doesn't seem to understand the irony in my essay—that material gain can somehow become a personal loss. But there is a hint that she is beginning to climb the fence when she uses the past tense in the last sentence: "And we worked together."

Al wanted his students to find a metaphor that would, like mine, explain the tensions between their past and their present, would illustrate "the social and economic determinants of identity." But many of the students, both those whose college career was a natural progression from an upper-class, suburban childhood and those who entered college as aliens because of their working-class or urban-poor family lives, were unable to do what Al wanted them to do because of that very identity that he hoped they would explore. On the other hand, students with better academic preparation who can conceptualize permanence and change, as did Josh, can be agents of their academic experience. But without the tension of two competing worlds, they aren't experiencing the agony of competing selves. While self-expression can be liberating for these students, their own selfhood has not yet been challenged by a culture that tells them they don't really fit in. Other students, who know very well that they don't fit in, and who struggle to do so, have either run for their lives from a suffocating home culture, never looking back, so they resist looking now. Or they try to play the game of being a good student, as does Amy, while remaining rooted in a worldview that does not prepare them to be Al's good student who can critique material conditions as he contributes to identity. A few students—like Wendy and Malik—managed to do what Al wanted, but many of them, despite his careful teaching and his careful assignment, were just not ready to critique their current self-assured identity or to explore the roots of the conflicts between home and the demands of college life. They either had no fence to sit on because their experience lacked dissonance, or they had a fence and had not yet climbed up. We try to use our assignments to nudge them toward these discoveries, because, after all, that is what we have—assignments. We look through their papers for those nuggets, those sentences thrown off like old clothes that say more than the writer intended. We look for movement, if only the slightest ripple, on the calm surface of their attempts at academic writing. In the end, our faith is in them, in their ability to discover, and in writing as a route to those discoveries.

Carol and Al: Irrigation and the Cultivation of the Self

Paul Kameen's recent review essay, "Re-covering Self in Composition," notes in the four books it considers a "general unease with the extent to which those keystone terms of expressivist approaches to teaching writing *[self, voice, experience, the personal]* have been exiled from our disciplinary discussions for too long" in favor of social-constructionist, "audience-based conceptions of composing . . . and postructuralist critical theory" (101). While we are in sympathy with most of these "neoexpressivists" (Donna Qualley and Kathleen Blake Yancey, in particular), we don't believe it desirable—or possible, for that matter—to return to the golden age of yesteryear, to a prelapsarian innocence before there was "theory." We have tried here to make a persuasive case for the advantages of assimilating cultural/ critical theory, appropriating it for our pedagogy, thus making its insights available to our students in a form they can use to accomplish the traditional self-reflective, self-revelatory purposes of a liberal arts education. We have applied a theory of human consciousness that generally asks us to question the very idea of "knowing thyself" as a consciousness separate from the prescriptions of class, gender, and race consciousness. We have applied a general theoretical perspective that questions the idea of the intending subject, and we have done so in order to engage our students in conscious acts of self-revelation and intentionality.

But what was the outcome of that engagement? Some students could consciously employ a metaphor to explain their past life as it contributed to their identity. Some students unconsciously revealed a cultural identity that problematizes self-revelation in an academic setting. Some students' attempts at what they think is dutiful writing for an English teacher reveal a cultural dissonance they were not yet prepared to acknowledge or explore. Some students exhibit an uncanny ability to think in just the way we hoped, who came to us already prepared to fulfill the demands of any assignment given by an English professor. Did all three groups of students recognize the cultural dimensions of their identity as Al had hoped? Perhaps. Did any of these students come to see composing as an intentional act, as a way to "articulate a self out of the undifferentiated flux of remembered experience," as we put it at the beginning of this essay? Perhaps. Perhaps not.

Still, teaching writing is an act of faith. Our writing assignments, though emerging from our own intentions, are the rituals through which we hope to engage students as agents in the academy and in their lives. Our assignments stand in for the impulse to explore the roots of identity and self, but in standing in for organic impulse, assignments may lead students—we hope—to the impulse, to the need to write.

[Alan France died September 19, 2001. Al's colleagues are indebted to him for his careful yet passionate scholarship on the politics of writing and teaching and on the centrality of composition in the liberal arts, his students for his tireless efforts to teach them to write and thus to become agents rather than subjects in the grand battle with culture for personal identity. We will all miss his warmth, generosity, humor, and loyalty, and we are all better people for having known him. —C. R.]

Works Cited

Bernard-Donals, Michael. "What Is Writing About?" *College Literature* 25 (1998): 249–60.

Dillard, Annie. *The Writing Life.* New York: Harper, 1989.

France, Alan W. "Dialectics of the Self: Structure and Agency as the Subject of English." *College English* 63 (2000): 145–65.

Haraway, Donna. "A Manifesto for Cyborgs: Science, Technology, and Socialist Feminism in the 1980s." *Socialist Review* 80 (1985): 65–107.

Heaney, Seamus. "Digging." *Death of a Naturalist.* London: Faber, 1966. 13.

Kameen, Paul. "Re-covering Self in Composition." *College English* 62 (1999): 100–111.

Qualley, Donna. *Turns of Thought: Teaching Composition as Reflexive Inquiry.* Portsmouth: Boynton, 1997.

Reeves, Carol. "Irrigation: An Essay." *The Flying Island* 3.1 (1994): 1–2.

Tate, Gary. "Halfway Back Home." *Coming to Class: Pedagogy and the Social Class of Teachers.* Ed. Alan Shepard, John McMillan, and Gary Tate. Portsmouth: Boynton, 1998. 252–61.

White, Hayden. *The Tropics of Discourse.* Baltimore: Johns Hopkins UP, 1978.

Yancey, Kathleen Blake. *Reflection in the Writing Classroom.* Logan: Utah State UP, 1998.

13

What Are Styles and Why Are We Saying Such Terrific Things about Them?

Rebecca Moore Howard, Heidi Beierle, Patricia Tallakson, Amy Rupiper Taggart, Dan Fredrick, Mark Noe, Artist Thornton, Kurt Schick, and Melanie Peterson

Our title parodies that of Stanley Fish's 1973 "What Is Stylistics and Why Are They Saying Such Terrible Things about It?" Up through the 1960s, stylistics had been a unified textual discipline in which scholars pursued objective, true descriptions of the ways in which texts expressed the individual genius of their authors. In this stylistics, the text was a stable, reliable object, and through it one could read the author and judge the level of his genius. And the way one accomplished this reading was through objective, even scientific means. Fish meets these assumptions with deep skepticism:

> It is not my intention flatly to deny any relationship between structure and sense, but to argue that if there is one, it is not to be explained by attributing an independent meaning to the linguistic facts, which will, in any case, mean differently in different circumstances. (99)

Although he criticizes textualist stylistics, it is not Fish's intention to dismantle the discipline of textualist stylistics but instead to offer a different direction for it. Fish suggests an application of reader response theory: Stylistics can be salvaged by turning "information about language" into "information about response" (109). "In the kind of stylistics I propose, *interpretive acts are what is being described;* they, rather than verbal patterns arranging themselves in space, are the content of the analysis" (110).

In his entry on "Stylistics" in *The Johns Hopkins Guide to Literary Theory & Criticism,* James V. Catano observes, "By 1980 it was impossible to argue for any stylistic model without addressing [the] trends" in which Stanley Fish was a major figure. Yet in one realm of stylistic study—the realm of composition studies—only one part of Fish's 1973 critique resonates in subsequent scholarship. In composition studies, the study of style did not turn to interpretive acts; rather, the study of style was abandoned almost entirely. What survives is a remnant pedagogy of style—style as clarity. That remnant represents only a fragment of the rhetorical approach to style that had prevailed for centuries.

In this essay, we offer an overview of the reasons for abandoning style in composition pedagogy and explain the losses incurred by this abandonment. Then we suggest a variety of ways in which style might be incorporated into a variety of contemporary composition classes. Our hope is that readers will find in these suggestions ideas that can be adopted or adapted in their own syllabi and that these suggestions will generate many more techniques for valid contemporary pedagogies that embrace the teaching of style. Our ambition is to contribute to the revitalization of rhetorical pedagogy and scholarship on style.

Abandoning Style

While making a case for teaching style in the advanced composition class, Mary Fuller illustrates one reason that the scholarly and even pedagogical attention to style has subsided to a whisper in composition studies: "Most of us agree, I expect, that we can anticipate stilted, passionless prose from first-year writers if workshops in finding ideas and developing fluency fall victim to endless lessons in style" (120). One paradigm—the process paradigm—here competes with and rejects the earlier paradigm of textualism.

Style still matters to composition scholars, but for the most part they do not study it. To study style is to mark oneself as a conservative. Alan Wright limns this position:

> The orderly procession of thesis, evidence, and conclusion, the imperial advance of instrumental reason, breaks down when it charts the alien territory recently claimed in the name of postcolonial theory. Against the steps of a demonstrative and expository logic, whose primary goal is justification and explanation, postcolonial studies suggests an itinerant method, alive to the uncertainties of reference and representation, the vagaries and ambiguities of thought and feeling, which upset the canonical principles of literary criticism. (91)

Scholarship and pedagogy of style, in other words, are outdated; their principles are denied by postcolonial theory. Wright concludes, "The assured prescriptions of a Strunk and White seem woefully inadequate when placed in the context of the provisional and contingent formulations of postcolonial criticism" (102–3).

Style still matters to composition teachers—many base some of their grading on it—but as Fuller's statement indicates, they may nevertheless abstain from teaching it. Kathryn T. Flannery explains that to teach style is to mark oneself as an elitist. Prose style, she says, is "cultural capital, a commodity differentially legitimated, controlled, and distributed among members of a given society" (3). Flannery explains the message that may be conveyed in textbooks that treat style: "Linguistic health is . . . not natural . . . but a contested cultural form requiring frequent reiteration of standards and norms to maintain" (23).

In writers' handbooks, these standards and norms may be rendered in checklists of the sort that are offered in Aaron's *Little, Brown Handbook* (69); Anson and Schwegler's *Longman Handbook* (402); Hacker's *Bedford Handbook* (268); and Hairston, Ruszkiewicz, and Friend's *Scott, Foresman Handbook* (83). If such checklists are included in required texts for composition classes and alluded to in teachers' injunctions and paper responses yet are not being taught in the composition class, they become a means of mystifying the act of writing—and affirming the student writer's place at the bottom of a culturally-supported hierarchy of writing. Yet if the items on style checklists *are* taught in composition classes, those classes become current-traditionalist purveyors of context-free standards for writing.

Composition studies is a young discipline; in the few decades of its existence, it can hardly have covered all the ground of writing; nor can it have addressed all the pressing issues. Nevertheless, the collective pedagogical and scholarly silence on issues of style constitutes an acute absence, given the value that Western culture places on prose style—as attested by its multichapter inclusion in every writer's handbook. Marshall Brown explains the importance and the difficulty of style: "style is the most minute, the least ideal, the most concrete universal with which our writing confronts us" (807).

Bringing Style to the Classroom

In a doctoral seminar on stylistics at Texas Christian University, nine scholars—the authors of this essay—pondered the situation and began to generate ideas for a valid, vibrant pedagogy of style. We took as our agenda a provocative statement made by Catano in his encyclopedia entry:

At the turn of the twentieth century, allegiance to linguistic procedures was the primary defining element of stylistics as a discipline, and it remains so in the last quarter of the century. The major question facing stylistics is whether movement away from that defining characteristic, no matter how slight, will result not only in a loss of self-definition but also in a shifting back of the entire field into the related disciplines of literary criticism, linguistics, or more probably Rhetoric, which is enjoying a strong rebirth.

We began work in the spirit of the "forgotten" part of Fish's critique, the part that was concerned not so much with criticizing the status quo as with forging new directions. Fish's alternative to textualist stylistics was a reader response approach. Our alternative to a remnant pedagogy of style is to offer a rich range of possibilities, all of which place style at the center of a writer's activities. In the remainder of this essay, we present the outcomes of that seminar: contemporary approaches to a pedagogy of style in which style is neither singular nor prescriptive. We offer these possibilities as a conversation starter; none of our proposals constitutes the end of scholarly inquiry but rather a beginning.

Style and Formality

One of the reasons for the decline of style pedagogy may be its association with top-down, deductive, current-traditionalist instruction. Even today, when style is taught in composition classes, the methods often center around a little guidebook that offers "lessons" or "principles" of style. Learning style in this pedagogy amounts to comprehension of and adherence to received principles.

Extracting style from such current-traditionalist quandaries can open up whole new vistas for pedagogy. Instead of encountering, comprehending, and adhering to received stylistic principles, composition students can, individually or collaboratively, approach issues of style as issues of discovering how a text works upon readers. Peer-response prompts can ask fairly straightforward questions of formality, for example,

> Where do you notice a formal style in this text? Where does the style seem informal? What features of the text lead you to these judgments? How appropriate is the range of formality and informality? Given the assignment, audience, and purpose of this text, should the writer revise for more formality or informality?

But a pedagogy of style can go even further. In place of—or in addition to— the preceding questions, which alone might inspire conformity rather than creativity on the part of student writers, one might ask peer responders to take a rhetorical turn that focuses not on what conscious decisions the writer should now make but on what unconscious gaps or quandaries might be made explicit:

> Mark the places in the text where you see a shift in level of formality. What might have caused these shifts? Sometimes shifts in formality occur when writers are working with difficult material or with ideas that aren't yet fully developed. Do you see such possibilities in this text—do you see places where style shifts suggest that the writer might work further with or talk more about the ideas under consideration?

Style and Invention

Published in 1987, Karen Burke LeFevre's *Invention as a Social Act* challenges compositionists to think of invention in broader terms than those that she believes have already received "more than a fair share" of disciplinary attention (51). The notion of invention that she resists is that of expressivism (which she labels "Platonic"):

> Based on Plato's myth of the soul's journey to the realm of ideal forms, this perspective concerns invention as a private, asocial activity engaged in by an individual who possesses innate knowledge to be recollected and expressed, or innate cognitive structures to be projected onto the world. (49–50)

Scholarship since LeFevre's book has, indeed, worked for a more expansive repertoire of approaches to invention, and much of this scholarship has accepted LeFevre's assertion that invention is social rather than individual.

Expanding on LeFevre's work, we suggest yet another approach to invention: a stylistic approach. Though invention and style are described in the classical tradition as two separate canons of rhetoric (the first and third, respectively—with arrangement as the intervening canon), overlapping the two can prove fruitful. In this intersection, style is not simply the application of ornament to an already-invented, already-arranged text; instead, it provides a means of accessing and developing ideas and meaning. In one invention strategy, writers might choose a metaphor, an analogy, or some other trope that seems related to their topic and then spin out some prewriting about that figure, in a seemingly random pursuit of connections and associations. Then the writers can explore the possible implications and applications of the figure as well as the potential assertions buried within it. This tactic can be employed in collaborative invention: Because the stylistic associations can be made somewhat randomly in pursuit of more information and development of ideas, groups can begin with a word or figure and make associations until they have developed several possible trails to be followed.

Even if one attends to style only after text has been generated, writers can continue the process of invention by challenging their own stylistic choices. In this activity, writers discover what they already know but have not yet articulated; what they did not know before; what might logically lead from where they were at the beginning; and what creative possibilities can arise from their topics. Style's inventive possibilities lie primarily in word choice, and the use of tropes yet might conceivably be extended to whatever contributes to tone—even punctuation. In this context, though, issues of punctuation would not be issues of correctness and convention but instead issues of choice and variation.

Style and Ethos

The ancient Greeks viewed style as a means of establishing a proper ethical image. A rhetor's style could convey his ethical beliefs, enabling the audience to make personal judgments about the rhetor. Those judgments determined the rhetor's credibility, his ethos. The importance of ethos in ancient rhetoric should not be underestimated; Sharon Crowley remarks that the rhetor's character "was almost the most impressive mode of persuasion he possessed" (3). Contiguous approaches to style resonate in succeeding eras. Ralph Waldo Emerson counts style as an index of the rhetor's attunement with God:

> wise men pierce . . . rotten diction and fasten words again to visible things; so that picturesque language is at once a commanding certificate that he who employs it is a man in alliance with truth and God. . . . A man conversing in earnest, if he watch his intellectual processes, will find that a material image more or less luminous arises in his mind, contemporaneous with every thought, which furnishes the vestment of the thought. (2)

And of course the modern textualist stylistics against which Stanley Fish rails is a stylistics that strives to discover the genius of the author in his prose style. Louis T. Milic (one of Fish's chief targets amongst the textualist stylisticians) begins his 1996 *Encyclopedia of Rhetoric* entry, "Stylistics," with a revealing definition of *style:* "the manner of setting forth linguistic expression that distinguishes one person or group from another" (703).

In contemporary letters, however, such approaches to style are met with deep suspicion. How can a text provide a stable environment for analyzing the character of an author? Indeed, how can any author be regarded as a stable, unified subject? With indeterminacy attributed both to text and to subject/author, any ethical analysis of style must be turned toward the reader and the moment, not the writer and the text. In the composition classroom, an ethical approach to style centered not on text and author but on reader and context can be of great value to readers and writers. Consider, for example, the potential of the following prompts in a peer group response:

> *To the reader:* Ask the following questions about your partner's text. These questions ask for your *impressions;* you're not judging the text but describing your reactions to it.
>
> 1. Listen to the voice that is speaking in the narrative. What kind of a mood is conveyed? Is this writer elated? Nervous? Sad? Angry? Etc. In what passages do you detect mood?
> 2. Listen to how this voice is approaching the reader. What kind of a relationship is being established? Is the writer superior to the reader? Contemptuous? Subservient? Chummy? Confident? Etc. In what passages do you detect the writer's relationship to the reader?
> 3. Listen to the attitude toward its own material that this voice conveys. How much does it sound as if the writer cares about what he's saying? Where does the intensity of the writer's commitment to the material seem to peak, and where does it seem to lag?
>
> *To the writer:* Now that you have a reader's opinion on these three issues, what changes do you want to make in your text? Is it producing the effects that you desire? If not, you'll want to revise. And even if it is producing the desired effects, you may want to do some additional crafting of the voice in your text.

Style and Community

For an extended illustration of how a pluralistic, nonprescriptive approach to style might be taught, we turn to the pedagogy that is variously labeled *community service, civic/community engagement,* or *civic/community literacy*—pedagogy that endeavors to teach students how to use writing responsibly, ethically, and influentially. Absent from socially engaged composition pedagogy has been any sustained, foregrounded engagement with prose style. Instead, community-oriented pedagogies have explicitly tended to focus on entering into the real-world experience of writing; learning new genres to fit writing in context; learning about social issues; engaging in those social issues and contexts to improve situations through writing; solving problems; making decisions; communicating; thinking critically; planning; considering audience; and participating in collaborative groups.

Style has been omitted from this pedagogy in part because most of the energy of twentieth-century literary stylistics was dedicated to discovering the individual, autonomous, originary author in his (the pronoun is deliberate) canonical text. In composition, the teaching of style lapsed into the teaching of usage, with clarity (of, presumably, a message whose creation predates the composing of the text) the measure of a good prose style. Literary studies has busily celebrated ambiguity as an identifying feature of literary texts, while composition studies has busily endeavored to remove ambiguity from students' writing.

Not surprisingly, such constrained representations of style could not indefinitely sustain a high level of scholarly activity. Hence attention to style has fallen by the scholarly wayside. Contemporary literary theory challenges notions of authorial individuality, autonomy, and originality, and contemporary composition scholarship endeavors to provide students not with a restricting set of usage rules but with an expansive sense of authorial possibilities. In the face of these countercurrents, stylistics—in both literary studies and composition studies—has subsided.

For the purposes of teaching socially engaged reading and writing to college students, we wish to advocate a pedagogy of style—not in its outdated, constricted forms, but in expansive terms oriented toward community. We wish to recognize style in its social roles, and we wish to use the study of style as a means of rupturing the closed classroom. If the composition classroom is a closed community, the exploration of style is limited because the immediate experience of community is limited. But when the composition classroom is open to other communities (cither those within which the classroom already lies, such as the university, or those that are brought into the classroom in the person of a student), the exploration of style becomes dynamic. We advocate teaching style in both reading and writing, with the focus on cultural meaning making.

In many communities (including those in the academy) in which students write, they may well find that their conversational contributions come from a relatively powerless subject position. Sensitivity to the available stylistic options within a community—as well as the implications of those options for individual roles in the community—may, however, enable students to claim subject positions of increased power and thereby to make more effective contributions to the community conversations of which writing is a part. Once students have read the literature of the community and studied its stylistic options, they may begin to formulate situationally appropriate styles of their own.

A sample assignment sequence demonstrates the contributions that a situated stylistics can make to students' understanding of themselves, their community, and their work:

1. The teacher—or better yet, the class—collects a variety of texts from the community in which the class is involved. *Text* may be taken broadly, not in a print-exclusive manner but in the wider scope suggested by social science theories. Clifford Geertz, for example, differentiates "writing as discourse" from "action as discourse" and counts both as text:

   > The great virtue of the extension of the notion of text beyond things written on paper or carved into stone is that it trains attention on precisely this phenomenon: on how the inscription of action is brought about, what its vehicles are and how they work, and on what the fixation of meaning from the flow of events—history from what happened, thought from thinking, culture from behavior—implies for sociological interpretation. To see social institutions, social customs, social changes as in some sense "readable" is to alter our whole sense of what such interpretation is and shift it toward modes of thought rather more familiar to the translator, the exegete, or the iconographer than to the test giver, the factor analyst, or the pollster. (30–31)

2. Students draft their own preliminary texts for the community. These can be position statements, policy proposals, memoranda, reports, interviews—whatever is appropriate to the community in which the class is involved and to the task(s) that the class intends to accomplish. The instructor keeps these drafts.

3. The class engages in prose style analysis of the texts collected in step one. The term "prose style analysis" is similar to other types of analyses that break down artifacts into their constituent parts in order to understand things as a whole. But what exactly does one break down in a prose style analysis? If we say "prose," we are, of course, referring to words. A prose style analysis attends specifically to which words are chosen and how they are arranged. These two categories—word choice and arrangement (primarily at the sentence level)—are the bases of prose style analysis. As they compare and contrast the stylistic features of the community texts, students should concentrate on interpreting what those features suggest about cultural beliefs, subject positions, backgrounds, and biases. Is

deviation from stylistic convention an error, or a political move? The following questions may prove helpful:

a. What does style reveal about the constructed identity of the author?
b. What does style reveal about the culture and/or community of the author? The community the author is writing to?
c. Does the style reveal anything that the author might not have wanted the audience to know about his or her prejudices, beliefs, perspectives?
d. Are you part of the author's community? In what role?
e. Does the author's community interact with yours? Positively or negatively?
f. To what extent are your interpretations derived from your own community allegiances?

Additional analytic categories can be built upon word choice and arrangement. For example, how are words visually presented: are they in bold type, calligraphy, misspelled? And how often do they appear? How does synonymy operate? For example, how often is the title "commander in chief" used instead of "president"? What can such choices tell the reader about the community in which the text appears, its expectations, the writer's sense of position in that community? Just one valuable insight to share with the class is Gunther Kress's assertion, "Participants who have greater power are able to force other participants into greater efforts of interpretation" (14). What levels of authorial power are suggested by the extent to which the text strives for clarity or demands that readers work in order to comprehend? On that principle, how does the class interpret the visual presentation of words—does that presentation lend itself to, ignore, or detract from reader comprehension? To what extent does the class see Kress's principle at work in this community? What other principles might explain writers' efforts to aid readers' comprehension and interpretation?

In the community service writing class, prose style analyses will be concerned with learning more about community relations. Malcolm X's famous example of examining word choice serves as a ready example. While copying words from a dictionary in order to increase his vocabulary, Malcolm noticed that word choices for the definition of *black* were marked by cultural bias. *Black* was defined as sinister and dirty. Illustrating the white bias that Malcolm found in the dictionary is the 1950s children's book, *Harry the Dirty Dog*. Harry, a big white mutt, gets lost in a city. The more trouble the dog gets into, the dirtier his fur becomes;

that is, the blacker he becomes. When he arrives home, the family bathes the unwilling dog in order to make him clean again.

Harry the Dirty Dog illustrates how word arrangement, seen in traditional composition pedagogy of style as a simple tool of clarity, can have wider implications for the meaning of a text. An analysis of word arrangement that is expanded beyond the sentence level becomes an analysis of form, of narrative, of organization, and in the case of *Harry the Dirty Dog*, of causality. It is the placement of words in a certain order, the syntagmatic relationship of words, that creates connections between "dog," "dirty," and "black" and between "family," "clean," and "white"—which creates symbolic, paradigmatic meanings in the story. A stylistic analysis of *Harry the Dirty Dog* would conclude that this story teaches that troublemaking misbehavior is linked to being black. In addition, one might conclude that although (in the view of white bias) blacks may be as harmless as pets, it takes the love of the white community to control, care for, and baptize those pets clean.

Attention to word choice inevitably involves an attention to metaphor. One can study the associations created by metaphor. The class should attend, too, to the words associated with or used by certain groups.

4. Now the class returns to the preliminary drafts they generated in step two. Because they have conducted the analyses of step three, they are better prepared to analyze their own writing to understand their own cultural assumptions. Now they apply the step three analytic methods to their own work. After seeing what their style says about them and their own community allegiances, they revise their texts for style, consciously considering the identity they wish to construct, the stylistic conventions of their target community, and the interaction of the two.

5. The assignment sequence continues with reflection. Some questions that might come at this time are:

   a. What community has your writing style placed you in? Some students may find themselves writing within the community of the classroom, the community of the university, the community with which the class is engaged, or some other larger or exterior community.

   b. What is your identity within that community? How have you constructed that identity in your writing?

   c. To what extent have you revised your style and/or your identity in relationship to the community within which you are writing? If you were to change communities, how would your style change?

  d. To what extent have you become engaged with the community within which you are writing? With the issues?

  e. Are there other actions to which this involvement might lead you?

6. Now it's time for students to put style into practice, demonstrating discourse adaptability in a practical, real-world situation. This application stage will depend upon the target community and task(s) of participation that guide the overall course design. Whatever that community and whatever those tasks, though, students' awareness of the mutual construction of style, community, and individual will contribute to their literacy in the community.

Revitalizing the Scholarship on Style

We offer the preceding classroom strategies as a suggestion for how style might be engaged for a pedagogy in which students are authors, not error makers. Min-Zhan Lu has offered still more alternatives in her article "Professing Multiculturalism: The Politics of Style in the Contact Zone." But considerable work remains to be done. The section on "Styles" in *The Writing Teacher's Sourcebook* (see the third edition—Tate, Corbett, and Myers; and the fourth edition—Corbett, Myers, and Tate) demonstrates in two ways how pressing is this need. First, *The Writing Teacher's Sourcebook,* in both its third and fourth editions, does in fact include a section on style*s,* notwithstanding how little scholarly activity is being conducted on the topic. The editors of this much-used text have exerted enormous influence on the discipline of composition studies and especially on its practices and representations of pedagogy. Both of them distinguished scholars, Tate and Corbett obviously know the real needs and concerns of writing teachers and not just the concerns and fads of scholarship. *The Writing Teacher's Sourcebook* is aimed at the former—at writing teachers' real needs and concerns; hence it includes a section on style*s,* even though scholarship on style is on the wane in composition and rhetoric.

  But the successive editions of *The Writing Teacher's Sourcebook* demonstrate in a second way the need for fresh scholarship on the topic. In the third edition (1994), the four selections on style were notable not only for their wisdom but also for their antiquity: the Rankin selection dates from 1985; Connors, from 1983; Ohmann, from 1979; and Weathers, from 1970. In other words, while the editors recognize teachers' concern for and interest in style, they also recognize the paucity of fresh scholarship. That observation becomes even more acute in the fourth edition of *The Writing Teacher's Sourcebook* (1999), which reproduces those same four essays.

Karen Burke LeFevre's 1987 book raised an alarm about invention, one of the five canons of rhetoric. LeFevre described the near-extinction of that first canon and suggested how it could be revived in a socially grounded pedagogy. Here we raise a similar alarm about the third canon, style: it is an endangered species in current composition scholarship. We offer the present essay as an argument that style, contextualized in avant-garde theory, is still a worthy topic of instruction and scholarship. It is true that outdated textualist approaches to style fit poorly into contemporary pedagogy, but instead of discarding the canon of style along with outdated theories of it, our discipline and our students will benefit from fresh approaches. Let us simply say that a fifth edition of *The Writing Teacher's Sourcebook,* we hope, will be able to select its style readings from a wide range of new scholarship.

Works Cited

Aaron, Jane. *The Little, Brown Handbook.* 7th ed. New York: Longman, 1998.

Anson, Chris M., and Robert A. Schwegler. *The Longman Handbook for Writers and Readers.* 2nd ed. New York: Longman, 2000.

Brown, Marshall. *"Le Style est l'Homme Même:* The Action of Literature." *College English* 59.7 (Nov. 1997): 801–9.

Catano, James V. "Stylistics." *The Johns Hopkins Guide to Literary Theory and Criticism.* Ed. Michael Groden and Martin Kreiswirth. Available <http://www.press.jhu.edu/books/guide>. First published Baltimore: Johns Hopkins UP, 1997.

Connors, Robert J. "Static Abstractions and Composition." *Freshman English News* 12 (Spring 1983): 1–4, 9–12. Rpt. in *The Writing Teacher's Sourcebook.* Ed. Gary Tate, Edward P. J. Corbett, and Nancy Myers. 3rd ed. New York: Oxford UP, 1994. 279–93.

Corbett, Edward P. J., Nancy Myers, and Gary Tate, eds. *The Writing Teacher's Sourcebook.* 4th ed. New York: Oxford UP, 1999.

Crowley, Sharon. *The Methodical Memory: Invention in Current-Traditional Rhetoric.* Carbondale: Southern Illinois UP, 1990.

Emerson, Ralph Waldo. *Nature. Selected Writings of Emerson.* Ed. Brooks Atkinson. Vol. 4. New York: Modern Library, 1950. 3–44.

Fish, Stanley E. "What Is Stylistics and Why Are They Saying Such Terrible Things about It?" *Approaches to Poetics.* Ed. Seymour Chatman. Columbia UP, 1973. Rpt. in *The Stylistics Reader: From Roman Jakobson to the Present.* Ed. Jean Jacques Weber. New York: St. Martin's, 1996. 94–116.

Flannery, Kathryn T. *The Emperor's New Clothes: Literature, Literacy, and the Ideology of Style.* Pittsburgh: U of Pittsburgh P, 1994.

Fuller, Mary. "Teaching Style in Advanced Composition Classes." *Teaching Advanced Composition.* Ed. Katherine H. Adams and John L. Adams. Portsmouth, NH: Boynton, 1991. 119–32.

Geertz, Clifford. *Local Knowledge.* New York: Basic, 1983.

Hacker, Diana. *The Bedford Handbook.* 5th ed. Boston: Bedford, 1998.

Hairston, Maxine, John Ruszkiewicz, and Christy Friend. *The Scott, Foresman Handbook for Writers.* 5th ed. New York: Longman, 1999.

Klein, Julie Thompson. "Text/Context: The Rhetoric of the Social Sciences." *Writing the Social Text: Poetics and Politics in Social Science Discourse.* Ed. Richard Harvey Brown. New York: Aldine de Gruyter, 1992. 9–30.

Kress, Gunther. *Before Writing: Rethinking the Paths to Literacy.* New York: Routledge, 1997.

LeFevre, Karen Burke. *Invention as a Social Act.* Carbondale: Southern Illinois UP, 1987.

Lu, Min-Zhan. "Professing Multiculturalism: The Politics of Style in the Contact Zone." *College Composition and Communication* 45.4 (Dec. 1994): 442–58.

Malcolm X. *The Autobiography of Malcolm X.* African American Images, 1989.

Milic, Louis T. "Stylistics." *Encyclopedia of Rhetoric and Composition: Communication from Ancient Times to the Information Age.* Ed. Theresa Enos. New York: Garland, 1996. 703–9.

Miller, Keith D. *Voice of Deliverance: The Language of Martin Luther King, Jr. and Its Sources.* 1992. Athens: U Georgia P, 1998.

Ohmann, Richard. "Use Definite, Specific, Concrete Language." *College English* 41 (1979): 390–97 Rpt. in *The Writing Teacher's Sourcebook.* Ed. Gary Tate, Edward P. J. Corbett, and Nancy Myers. 3rd ed. New York: Oxford UP, 1994. 310–18.

Pappas, Theodore. "Truth or Consequences: Redefining Plagiarism." *Chronicles* (Sept. 1993): 41–42.

Rankin, Elizabeth D. "Revitalizing Style: Toward a New Theory and Pedagogy." *Freshman English News* 14 (Spring 1985): 8–13. Rpt. in *The Writing Teacher's Sourcebook.* Ed. Gary Tate, Edward P. J. Corbett, and Nancy Myers. 3rd ed. New York: Oxford UP, 1994. 300–309.

Tate, Gary, Edward P. J. Corbett, and Nancy Myers, eds. *The Writing Teacher's Sourcebook.* 3rd ed. New York: Oxford UP, 1994.

Weathers, Winston. "Teaching Style: A Possible Anatomy." *College Composition and Communication* 21 (1970): 114–49. Rpt. in *The Writing Teacher's Sourcebook.* Ed. Gary Tate, Edward P. J. Corbett, and Nancy Myers. 3rd ed. New York: Oxford UP, 1994. 294–99.

Wright, Alan. "Sentence Fragments: Elements of Style, Postcolonial Edition." *JAC: A Journal of Composition Theory* 18.1 (1998): 91–104.

Zion, Gene. *Harry the Dirty Dog.* New York: Harper and Row, 1956.

14

Valuating Academic Writing

Kurt Schick

My earliest experiences in composition studies taught me the value of seeking good reasons for what and how we profess. Why should we teach this text and not that one? Why should we prefer one style or convention of writing over another? At my first conference as a graduate student, Andrea Lunsford asked participants to confess their bêtes noires as writing teachers. Not yet having taught composition myself, I didn't feel qualified to respond. But I heard a lot about *its* and *it's, their* and *there* (I still make that mistake myself), clichés, and so forth. In their presentations, both Lunsford and Robert Schwegler argued that "error" mostly has to do with taste, with preference. Indeed, they argued that our most common dislikes represent and reinforce educated middle-class taste. Research conducted by Lunsford and Robert Connors suggests that what constitutes good taste changes with trends in common usage, and that the most frequently marked errors on students' papers don't significantly affect meaning (though they do make for easier grading). Therefore, argued Lunsford and Schwegler, we should preach the practice of "correctness" as social etiquette—a necessary though perhaps ideologically unsavory price of seeming educated.

Ever meekly, I raised my hand (though I had to write it all down first) and asked:

IF we assume that (1) formal rules of grammar are frequently arbitrary, capricious, and meaningless, (2) social conventions can be ideologically unsound (partisan, undemocratic), (3) conventions change over time, (4) it is we who write and teach the handbooks that help drive the evolution of convention, THEN should we not exert our power and influence to subvert Oppressive Correctness in our classrooms and published textbooks? In other words, as grammar cops, we created a Frankenstein monster—society's overemphasis on "surface errors"—in the first place; isn't it time we took some responsibility to remedy this unnatural disaster?

I can no longer recall an exact response, but I was left unsatisfied. Perhaps, as is often the case, my question was too long and complicated.

Later that year, I proposed the following presentation to the Conference on College Composition and Communication:

We are perennially caught between our conservative and progressive roles as educators: Should we privilege our position as guardians of culture and knowledge, or embrace our capacity to be leaders of change? Recent discussions have highlighted an ethical imperative to recognize and accommodate multiple literacies in the academy. Error is central to these discussions. We have determined that what we consider to be "correct" is mostly arbitrary, sometimes capricious, and continuously evolving. We must reexamine the relationships between how we view and teach literacy, style, and correctness. Should we liberate our students from the oppression of "error" or acclimate them?

While I recognize my responsibility to provide students with adequate education in the conventions of standard written English, I also respect my students as writers with diverse literacies. I also accept my inevitable authority as a composition teacher to shape the attitudes of readers—both in and outside the academy—toward stylistic integrity and correctness. The question is not whether we have a right to assume the power to enact change, but how we can ethically employ our already existing influence. In my presentation I will propose a model for conceiving correctness under the rubric of style, which will enfranchise students alongside teachers in an ethical negotiation of discourse conventions.

This time, my long and complicated question was answered with a polite letter of rejection.

There is, I think, no point in the philosophy of progressive education which is sounder than its emphasis upon the importance of the participation of the learner in the formation of the purposes which direct his activities in the learning process, just as there is no defect in traditional education greater than its failure to secure the active co-

operation of the pupil in the construction of the purposes involved
in his studying.

—John Dewey, *Experience and Education* (1938)

Defining "good" academic writing is difficult for us in part *because* we have
tried so hard to democratize traditional introductory composition. Reform-
ers who define democracy primarily in terms of equality, individuality, ac-
cessibility, and inclusiveness have sought to "open" academic rhetoric
through such strategies as reviving the canon of invention, celebrating individual expressiveness, and guaranteeing students' rights to their own language. Defining good writing seems to contradict these attempts at openness. The act of definition is itself a kind of closure, since it focuses and
formalizes meaning. Definition that involves judgment of what is good
versus undesirable indicates a preference that potentially excludes and de-
values alternatives. Such bias troubles pluralistic culture.

Rejecting the strict textualism of current-traditional rhetoric, a variety
of postformal pedagogies have deemphasized both formalism (the written
product as opposed to the writing process) and formality (compulsory com-
pliance with conventions). Postformal compositionists have argued successfully that traditional pedagogy's overemphasis on standards and correctness
was antidemocratic, effectively creating a mechanism for exclusion, discrimination, or "gatekeeping" through forced conformity to a dominant discourse. In particular, postformalists have targeted evaluation as a principal
weapon for enforcing the "closed" rhetoric of traditional academic discourse.

My own arguments continue those begun by my reform predecessors.
I, too, seek to democratize academic discourse by enabling students to participate in reforming the means and purposes for composition instruction.
However, I believe that neither defining conventions of good writing nor
a teacher's constructive intervention in student learning necessarily constitute a violation of student freedom. Indeed, as Dewey explains, "Since freedom resides in the operations of intelligent observation and judgment by
which a purpose is developed, guidance given by the teacher to the exercise of pupils' intelligence is an aid to freedom, not a restriction upon it"
(*Experience and Education* 71). How, then, might we enhance student cooperation in defining meaningful and authoritative discourse standards?
How can we avoid traditional composition's coercive, arbitrary imposition
of discourse preferences? How can our pedagogy enact democracy, defined
in terms of cooperative self-governance?

This chapter proposes that we reconceive evaluation in democratic terms,
as a participatory rhetorical practice of "valuation." Valuation, which involves both the practice and judgment of discourse conventions, enables a

solution that (1) is theoretically sound; (2) provides standards for judgment that are describable, explainable, and justifiable without being arbitrary, capricious, static, or overly prescriptive; and (3) works simultaneously toward achieving and perfecting the purposes we envision for teaching composition. As an application of performative, epideictic rhetoric, valuation leads toward considering academic discourse as a style, which ultimately provides more practical terminology for explaining to ourselves and our students what constitutes good academic writing.

Evaluation as Valuation

> The problem is to extract the desirable traits of forms of community life which actually exist, and employ them to criticize undesirable features and suggest improvement.
> —John Dewey, *Democracy and Education* (1916)

Valuation approximates our current best understanding of rhetoric, defined as the reconstructive "art of discovering warrantable beliefs and improving those beliefs though shared discourse" (Booth xiii). Unlike traditional evaluation, which effectively grants uncontroversial, fixed Truth status to discourse conventions, the process of valuation is adaptive, purposeful, and participatory—a means of practicing cooperative self-governance in the composition classroom.

As currently conceived, traditional evaluation seems to be anything *but* a means of cooperative self-governance. Traditional evaluation is undemocratic because it limits freedom by precluding student participation in determining what counts as good writing. Traditional evaluation presumes the sufficiency of preexisting, externally imposed authority instead of the need to justify within the classroom the value of the standards used for judgment. In this sense, traditional evaluation functions arhetorically in that it fails to take into account the particulars of the situation, namely, what students already consider to be good writing and more specifically, the value of student texts before evaluation intervenes in their writing. Denying their participation in defining standards leaves students disengaged from the learning process. No wonder so many of our discourse conventions have become meaningless formalities except as symbols of academic tyranny.

In contrast to traditional evaluation's rhetorically closed approach, valuation is an experimental, experiential process involving observation, judgment, and reflection. Literally, valuation ascribes, versus extracts, value to writing. John Dewey defines valuation as a process of judgment designed to improve not only what we judge but also the procedures and criteria we employ. Instead of basing judgment exclusively on static, preexisting criteria, Dewey defines valuation as a type of imaginative or "creative" judgment that is "concerned with estimating values not in existence and with bringing them into existence" ("Valuation" 275). Valuation is simultaneously pragmatic and idealistic—a rhetorical process that compares *what is* with *what ought to be,* thus allowing us to continuously adapt our criteria to changing situational constraints. Valuation, thus conceived, becomes a tool for discovering, improving, and advocating community values. Valuation enhances not just individual performance but also the conventions and knowledge of the community we represent as teachers.

As a closed process, judgment based solely upon preset standards can too easily become dogmatic or meaningless habit. The openness of valuation enables adaptability by rendering our criteria plastic enough to evolve. As in Peter Elbow's "believing game," valuation suspends terminal judgment until observation or invention can occur. Indeed, Elbow argues that valuative belief can be a powerful mechanism for measuring relative value: "Where the doubting game tests an idea by helping us to see its weaknesses and shortcomings, the believing game tests an idea by helping us see the strengths of competing ideas" (*Writing Without Teachers* xxiii). Because the critical gaze of traditional evaluation is based upon a priori criteria, evaluative doubt cannot recognize strengths or weaknesses outside its own "mental frame of reference." Believing enables us to see beyond our existing perspective by provisionally accepting "very different ideas—ideas which at first may appear odd or threatening" (xxiii). Elbow seeks a dialectic between belief and doubt, a method of testing ideas that uses existing criteria but is also open to constructively experiencing student writing to discover new standards and ideas inherent in the texts being evaluated.

Valuation is an experimental and creative estimate of an evolving ideal. Put another way: we cannot know exactly what we will like until we see it. Valuation is imperfect because it is anchored to the past; it is contingent because it is tied to present situations; it is idealizing because it requires imagination and faith. For example, in making an assignment, we have some idea what type of written product to expect, along with some idea, based in previous experience, how students will respond to the rhetorical situation we are trying to devise. However, we are often surprised by what students write. Regardless of what clear-cut, well-defined standards and criteria we have planned beforehand, the results never absolutely match our expectations. This is good for two reasons. First, it means that standards are adaptable. Recognizing the metamorphic nature of our criteria might help us better understand, expect, and even nurture the evolution and improvement of what we value. Valuation perfects values. Second, flexibility allows us to be pleasantly surprised by student writing—that we can actually appreciate students' authorial power and agency.

Pedagogically, traditional evaluation and valuation share a common purpose: for students to internalize discourse standards and become their own best judges. Traditional evaluation attempts this internalization without respect for the student as an individual or even for students as a group. Evaluation is pedagogically less effective than valuation because evaluation is a one-directional process; because students do not participate in defining standards, they do not understand them as well as if they learned them more experientially. Valuation is fundamentally participatory and cooperative in that the rhetorical acts of reading and writing are both reciprocal and transactional. Writers are never alone because they always imagine an audience. Indeed, educating this imagination makes writers more deliberate and adaptable rhetorical agents.

As a rhetorical means for discovering and improving what our discourse community believes, valuation serves to enhance cooperation as well as self-governance. Valuation criteria remain legitimate only so long as they enact the ideals of our academic community. As symbolic action, a valuative approach can restore ethical justification to evaluation practices and provide guidance for better understanding and explaining the criteria we use to interpret student writing. In more familiar rhetorical terms, the performance and valuation of academic writing can be seen as epideictic activities that can simultaneously constitute and authorize academic culture in accordance with democratic ideals. Conceived as epideictic rhetoric, valuation functions not as individual critical acts but as reconstructive social action.

Valuation as Epideictic Rhetoric

Education is rhetorical in that we attempt to enhance students' knowledge, skills, and attitudes through discourse. Since literacy is acquired experientially (by practicing discourse modes within the contexts that give them meaning), our role as teachers is to lend expertise, to facilitate learning experiences, and to motivate or persuade students to learn. In rhetorical terms, then, teaching is a two-fold rhetorical act involving both communication of knowledge and persuasion to belief. Specifically, evaluation is intended to establish standards and motivate learning through a process of "praising" successful performance and placing "blame" where students fall short in meeting the desired standards. The rhetoric traditionally associated with praise and blame, rhetorical performance, and education is of course epideictic. In classical epideictic rhetoric, the audience functions not to reach a decision that ends in action but as critics who judge the rhetorical performance itself—namely, the skilled enactment of formal qualities (specifically, style) by the speaker. The similarities between epideictic and academic discourse of students are obvious: academic composition is the performance of apparently nonpragmatic discourse by student writers; as the audience, professors evaluate students' success in employing the desired forms of our discourse community; evaluative response resembles the characteristic epideictic form of praise and blame.

Historical criticism of epideictic rhetoric parallels our current misgivings about traditional academic writing and evaluation practices. Theorists since Plato have questioned the validity of performative rhetoric, especially when it seems to lack any real exigence. Traditional evaluation and its associated product, grading, often seem to serve no real purposes except those that many of us would rather forget about: elitist gatekeeping, ranking students for prospective employers, or the equation of a GPA with a college education. In contrast, as a form of epideictic or symbolic rhetoric, valuation is a precondition to pragmatic discourse because it reinforces rhetorical (that is, socially contingent, community-authorized) foundations. Chaim Perelman and Lucy Olbrechts-Tyteca explain that epideictic rhetoric directs this process by: (1) formulating the beliefs already inherent in a community; (2) identifying, among sometimes competing preferences, which values are or should be salient; (3) building and reinforcing a community based on common belief; and (4) strengthening our "disposition toward action" by building a foundation of common values upon which to base practical decisions (50–52). Epideictic valuation has the power not only to form but also to re-form community. As Cynthia Sheard explains:

> To see the motives behind epideictic discourse in general and pedagogical discourse in particular as similar is to acknowledge the capacities in both not only for induction and indoctrination into communities but also for critical reflection upon the day-to-day operations of those communities and others, as well as the short- and long-term consequences of those operations. (786)

By dealing in abstraction—apparently transcendent and universal qualities—epideictic "idealization" allows us to appeal to values that are beyond our present reality. Treating the ideal as contingently real helps us envision and call forth a more ideal reality.[1]

Still, in teaching composition we must remember that epideictic's imaginative potency should not materialize as blind, uncritical allegiance to discourse standards. Discourse should not be predicated, as was successfully argued by critics of current-traditional rhetoric, on the misconception that whatever values undergird a community are fixed, universal, uncontroversial, or unquestionable. For too long, we have treated academic writing as either noncontroversial or too controversial. Valuation highlights the reformative function of teaching, evaluating, and also practicing (through scholarship such as this) academic discourse. Seen this way, academic-as-epideictic discourse "can help us to scrutinize our own privately and publicly held beliefs and prejudices, to evaluate them, and to decide whether to reaffirm or reform them" (Sheard 777). Ultimately, examining the epideictic functions of discourse conventions should enable us to better understand, teach, and improve the knowledge of our academic community.

Academic conventions are not sacred, nor should they be mystical. They may not be easily definable, but in order to use them, we should at least be able to describe, explain, and justify them. Walter Beale suggests classifying epideictic discourse as a genre, a "rhetorical performative" that unites function and form in a recurrent rhetorical situation. Epideictic genre does not merely communicate but also "constitutes (in some special way defined by the conventions or customs of a community) a significant social action in itself" (224). Similarly, Carolyn Miller's "Genre as Social Action" defines genre as "typified rhetorical action" encompassing substance (situation and motive) and form (152). Genre provides a medium through which individuals identify with a community by "mediating private intentions with social exigence" (164). Beale's and Miller's work contributes to what I propose as a tentative description of academic discourse, in which:

a. Conventions are typical, not universal. Since conventions themselves are an abstraction, every member of the community is not always a full practitioner and not every text enacts the conventions completely. Thus, any attempt to define or describe conventions will be incomplete.
b. Conventions are socially mediated and thus imperfect, multivocal, culturally and historically contingent. Therefore, while there may be more or less "appropriate" or "convincing" discourse, there are no standards of absolute "right" or "wrong."
c. Conventions reveal and enact the beliefs of the discourse community.

While conventions tend to be conservative, they are not unchanging. Indeed, the viability of a discourse community depends on its adaptation through continual interrogation of the social, rhetorical functions of its conventions. Conventions should serve the community, not the other way around. Like laws, they are meant to enact and embody our will, our motives, our values. We should not, as Pat Belanoff argues, allow ourselves to believe the myth that there is a such thing as a "Platonic standard of writing which we can apply uniformly" to all academic discourse (55). However, as Belanoff also advises, we should continually engage in conversation about what we think "good writing" is since this process fuels the evolution of our discourse standards. Valuation enables and encourages these kinds of discussions among ourselves and with our students.

We might be tempted to teach our conglomerated conventions as an "academic genre." However, having been trained in literature, most of us associate genre with particular, monolithic forms; academic writing appears in various formats. Likewise, "academic literacy" seems too restrictive if we want to acknowledge the myriad voices of academic disciplines. The slipperiness of academic discourse has led some compositionists to give up trying to define or describe (or sometimes even teach) it; Peter Elbow, for example, claims as "fact" that "we can't teach academic discourse because there's no such thing to teach" ("Reflections" 138). Given that "discourse conventions," "genre," and "literacy" are inaccurate or inadequate terms to describe academic writing, we need an alternate approach to begin explaining discourse conventions to our students.

Academic Discourse as a Style

[A] speaker persuades his audience by the use of stylistic identifications. . . .
—Kenneth Burke, *A Rhetoric of Motives* (1950)

Again, epideictic rhetoric can provide a starting point for reframing our discussions of discourse conventions in the classroom. As mentioned previously, what epideictic audiences traditionally judge is the performance of style. Not coincidentally, in his explanation of "symbolic" rhetoric, Burke identifies style as the formal link between persuasion and identification; style, for Burke, is the principal vehicle of consubstantiation. Yet, as Elizabeth Rankin explains, close attention to text and in particular to style no longer seems to occupy much of our professional scholarship or classroom pedagogy; "style," she laments, "is out of style" (8). Rankin attributes style's disfavor to an overcompensating departure from current-traditional rhetoric, a shift that placed style (product) and invention (process) in opposition. Because traditional evaluation conflated style with usage, error, and grammar, when we rejected formalist pedagogy we also quit teaching and evaluating style. Therefore, it is no coincidence that teaching process-not-product produced disdain for both stylistics and evaluation, for they are the same thing. Evaluation is a type of stylistic analysis or criticism: *judgment of the performance of discourse conventions according to community standards.*

Obviously, I'm using the term style here in an unconventional way but a way for which I hope to offer sound reasons. Our scholarly canon does not offer a unified theory of style. Not only is there no single, standard definition of style; there is no reliable description of what formal elements are to be considered "stylistic." Traditional uses of "style" in rhetoric, literature, and composition are too restrictive, defining style in terms of form and limiting its features to the sentence level (e.g., diction, syntax, voice, use of tropes). My broader definition begins with descriptions of style as "the manner of setting forth linguistic expression that distinguishes one person or group from another" (Milic 703) and "the sum total of the variations a speaker makes on standard linguistic schemes" (Hart 163). I want to reconceive style as not merely words on a page but the meanings we give them, as readers and writers, according to discourse conventions, which serve as a contextual constraint. As John Gage explains, "Meaning results from conventional agreement within a rhetorical community" (620). Style is thus an effect of rhetorical transaction—a type of meaning generated through the intercourse of author, text, audience, and context. The reason we have been unable to pinpoint precisely what formal features constitute academic style is because style is not form but meaning—a synthesis of ways that a text conforms to or deviates from conventions in a meaningful way. Style is a type of synthetic meaning generated at the nexus of symbolic action and social convention. We misconceive style if we valuate it as *either* product *or* process. Style is not *either* textual (formal) *or* contextual (conventional); it is both. Thus, style encompasses not only linguistic or sentence-level features such as clarity and correctness but also more global abstractions such as coherence, unity, and purpose.

In our classrooms, "style" is particularly useful for discussing discourse conventions because it expresses a complex, multifaceted rhetorical concept in terms already meaningful to students. Students come equipped with rich connotations of style, which these commonplace *American Heritage Dictionary* definitions demonstrate:

> 1. The way in which something is said, done, expressed, or performed; *a style of speech and writing.* 2. The combination of distinctive features of literary or artistic expression, execution, or performance characterizing a particular person, group, school, or era. 3. Sort, type; *a style of furniture.* 4. A quality of imagination and individuality expressed in actions and tastes; *does things with style.* . . . 7. A customary manner of presenting printed material, including usage, punctuation, spelling, typography, and arrangement. (1785)

In plain language, these definitions can lead our students and us toward a more sophisticated understanding of academic style: as sometimes distinction, sometimes convention; as creative or customary; as a mark of individual or communal identity. I want to retain the connotation of style as an interplay between individual and social expression, but I want to expand the features included in traditional stylistics to include, in the case of academic style, conventions that function to achieve the communicative, cognitive, and social goals we envision for composition instruction.

Academic discourse's potential for improving citizens' cognitive and social faculties is implicit in Aristotle's definition of rhetoric, not as persuasion per se but as a capacity for imagining the available means of persuasion in various situations. Argumentation—as outlined in such works as Aristotle's "theory of civic discourse," Chaim Perelman's "theory of practical reasoning," or James Crosswhite's "rhetoric of reason"—provides the structure of what I'll call "civic-academic style." Based on the fundamental practices of claiming and substantiating, deliberative argumentation promotes democracy by simultaneously teaching habits of cooperation and developing capacities for deliberation.

A claim is really an interpretation: a proposed conclusion based on "data" or reasons such as evidence, explanation, or examples. In contrast, unsubstantiated assertions treat subjective knowledge as if it were objective truth. According to Perelman and Olbrechts-Tyteca's definitions, "everybody agrees" that facts are facts, whereas beliefs are matters of preference . The act of claiming helps to distinguish facts from opinions. By claiming and substantiating, rhetors take responsibility for the contingent, "interested" nature of their propositions: "a claim is an assertion which contains an implicit plan of its own criticism" (Crosswhite 59). Merely asserting a conclusion without substantiation denies both audience and rhetor the opportunity or right to evaluate data for themselves. Argumentation based on claiming and substantiating thus incurs moral responsibility. Indeed, Perelman explains that the moral "strength" of an argument may be evidenced by its "fullness": "to give reasons in favor of a thesis is to imply that the thesis is not self evident and does not compel everyone" (*Realm of Rhetoric* 139). Most successful arguments "prove" claims with reasons that are already accepted by the audience. Arguing effectively in public (in a democracy or in a classroom) therefore requires an ability to discover proof that will convince the intended audience. Similarly, Aristotle's enthymeme teaches rhetors to employ preexisting agreement to resolve conflict; thus, "rhetoric seems to be able to observe the persuasive about 'the given,' so to speak" (37). Perelman adds to Aristotle's rhetoric a more explicit social and moral dimension when he explains that argumentation "presupposes a meeting of minds: the will on the part of the orator to persuade and not to compel or command, and a disposition on the part of the audience to listen" ("The New Rhetoric" 154). Argument, as Perelman defines it, is based on voluntary adherence, not compulsion. Similarly, Kenneth Burke explains, "Persuasion involves choice, will; it is directed to a man only insofar as he is *free*" (50). Argument is ethical within a democracy when based on freedom of choice (self-governance) versus coercion or manipulation.

From Rhetoric to Composition

Notwithstanding his copious criticism of academic writing, Peter Elbow describes the "intellectual practices" of academic discourse as similar to those outlined above: "the giving of reasons and evidence rather than just opinions, feelings, experiences; being clear about claims and assertions rather than just implying or insinuating"—"yet doing so in a way that acknowledges an interested position and tries to acknowledge and understand the positions of others" ("Reflections" 140, 148). Still, Elbow's postformal orientation precludes a more meaningful and explicit discussion of what argument "looks like" in terms of particular discourse conventions. More specifically, Mina Shaughnessy suggests that the cognitive and social conventions of academic writing emerge as "the skills of elucidation and validation and sequencing" that are enabled by literacy itself ("Some Needed Research" 318).

As a "technology," literacy enables writers to organize, develop, and connect ideas in ways that memory and speech alone may not allow.[2] Frequently, "basic" or inexperienced academic writing exhibits characteristics similar to oral discourse: "additive rather than subordinative," "aggregate rather than analytic," "redundant or 'copious,'" clichéd, paratactic, recursive, narrative, and inductive (Ong 36–41). Indeed, what Walter Ong calls "oral residue" counters much of what we value in academic style. "Alphabetic literacy," according to Patricia Bizzell,

> gives rise to the following characteristics of *style and thinking:* hypotaxis, the subordination of one idea to another in logical hierarchies; generalizations that appeal to reason and text-assisted memory for validation; and a dialectical relation to authority, encouraging the ongoing, disinterested criticism of ideas. (241, emphasis added)

Clearly, as Bizzell adds, we would be myopic to presume that academic style is the only type of literacy or that there are no special advantages to orality, as well. The crucial point is that the formal features of academic style are more than ornamental. Indeed, as Shaughnessy claims, it is our failure to explain the cognitive and social functions of academic style that frequently leads so many inexperienced academic writers—who ultimately constitute the general public—to equate composition instruction and evaluation with "error" and "correctness" (*Errors and Expectations* 273).

We are partly to blame for our public image as grammar police because we so often unwittingly proliferate unquestioned biases about what constitutes "good writing." Rarely do we ask, as does Dawn Skorczewski, "What are the unstated 'rules' of my pedagogy, and how do they influence my ability to recognize what my students are trying to say?" (234). As I have suggested, valuation provides a method for overcoming what Kenneth Burke would call the "trained incapacities" of our own "terministic screens." Valuation can help us recognize what amounts to stylistic discrimination, or *stylism.* Stylism simultaneously embodies and obscures our own prejudices, blinding us to the fact that many of our students' miscommunications and "errors" are in fact stylistic faux pas—that is, "errors" bound to the idiosyncratic preferences of a particular discourse community.

For example, teachers trained in literary studies regularly impose upon student writing their bias against clichés. A composition student or teacher who consulted St. Martin's *1998 Daily Writer's Advice Calendar* for January 16 found the following, typically prescriptive entry:

> *Clichés* are trite expressions that have lost all meaning because they have been so overused. Familiar sayings like "fun-filled days," "care-free moments," and "roaring campfire," for example, are now virtually meaningless. Take the time to think of original, fresh expressions.

I've often wondered why composition teachers so frequently badger their students about avoiding clichés. The St. Martin's advice leaves a thorn in my side for two reasons. First, I suppose that the opposite of a cliché is an "original" idiom or trope. While this may be a worthwhile literary outcome, the stated goal of most introductory composition courses is to familiarize students with conventions, not to inspire poetic license. Why, then, should our literary tastes dictate how we teach academic writing? Second, it's ridiculous to assert that clichés are "meaningless." They may be aesthetically bland, but they are in some ways more meaningful than "original, fresh expressions." Through their "overuse," clichés have gained nearly universal and unambiguous denotative meaning. If our intent is to teach our students to compose clear, understandable prose, then clichés are perhaps indispensable tools, like the *koinoi topoi,* or commonplaces, of classical rhetoric.

Taking a more valuative approach to our convention of unconventionality, we might discover value not in our distaste for clichés but in our enthusiasm for original expression. Dewey identifies Ralph Waldo Emerson as our premier "philosopher of democracy" because like Plato, Emerson believes in each individual's capacity to realize a unique relation to knowledge ("Emerson"). In "The American Scholar," Emerson argues that creative expression potentially activates *"Man-Thinking,"* whereas "in the degenerate state, when the victim of society, he tends to become a mere thinker, or, still worse, the parrot of other men's thinking" (54). By questioning the received wisdom of Old World dogma, Emerson's new American Scholar develops intellectual freedom: agency, "intelligence," or what Northrop Frye terms "the educated imagination." Although we might question Romantic notions of authorship today (especially for our students),[3] we should continue to value a tradition of exceptional eloquence in academic style. As I explain to my students, eloquence and imagination constitute the "wow factor" that for many professors distinguishes an "A" paper. However oppressive it may seem to "force" students to conform to any particular stylistic convention, we hope that what we sometimes call "grace" potentially teaches students *"not* to make common sense" and to "complicate received ideas" (Skorczewski 221, 234). In academic style, we interpret inventive language to reveal active learning, whereas the "banking" of clichés may reflect passive thinking. Similarly, the development of an argumentative thesis signals purposeful, deliberate inquiry.

Deliberateness

If we define "grace" as the elegance and creativity of an "original" thesis or inventive language, yet conceive "clarity" as transparent, unambiguous readability, then Joseph Williams's pairing of "clarity and grace" might seem somewhat oxymoronic to our students. While clarity embraces the lucidity of clichés, grace excludes them as prosaic. Such apparent inconsistencies in academic style frequently contribute to student "error," which violates *deliberateness*—the most universally accepted quality of "good" writing within or beyond the university. Audiences gauge writers' stylistic integrity by their apparent control, or self-governance, over their use of language. Good writing therefore corresponds to Dewey's "work of intelligence," which "involves foresight of consequences" and the effective "formation of purposes and the organization of means to execute them" (*Experience and Education* 67). A primary "consequence" or effect of writing is style: meaning created by conforming to or deviating from conventions. Good writing intentionally conforms to or deviates from conventions. In contrast, Shaughnessy defines "errors" as "accidental," "unintentional and unprofitable intrusions upon the consciousness of the reader" (*Errors* 12).

Traditional formalist composition rigorously prescribed "correctness" as the universal panacea for "error." However, being deliberate does not necessarily require being correct, if "correctness" means strict adherence to Standard Written American English. To begin with, like academic style, SWAE is an abstraction—as difficult to define adequately as it is to practice perfectly. More importantly, traditional composition's conflation of academic discourse with correctness and SWAE violates the democratic ideals of inclusiveness and tolerance. Civic-academic style should not exclude the deliberate practice of student vernacular. Civic literacy is by definition inclusive; as a shared secondary discourse, civic-academic style need not replace students' primary language for them to participate in the civic-academic discourse community. Valuation's plasticity should enable us to embrace diversity while simultaneously recognizing that common conventions are what literally constitute the discourse community. Standardized grammar, spelling, and usage function appropriately as tools for avoiding distortion, disruption, and disconnection between a writer and reader. "Clarity" is not so much correctness, then, as it is *intentional* readability—evidence of writers' commitment to elucidate their ideas for their audience. Clarity also implies an ethical obligation to strive for understandability; as Shaughnessy explains:

> Central to [a student writer's] task is an understanding of the expectations and needs of the academic or professional audience, for we see many evidences in [basic writers'] papers of the egocentricity of the apprentice writer, an orientation that is reflected in the assumption that the reader understands what is going on in the writer's mind and needs therefore no introductions or transitions or explanations. (*Errors* 240)

Thus, elucidation also incorporates the abstraction of "coherence," commonly defined as "a logical, orderly, and aesthetically consistent relationship of parts" (*American Heritage Dictionary* 369). Coherence reveals and potentially enhances a writer's ability to create connections among ideas. Experienced academic writers transform their prose from writer-centered to reader-centered by developing sophisticated hypotactic forms to guide their readers. As Linda Flower explains, "effective writers do not simply express thought but transform it in certain complex ways for the needs of a reader"; "reader-based prose" is "both a *style* of writing and a *style* of thought" (19, emphasis added). Careful subordination and coordination not only guide the reader; they also prompt writers to think through the logic of sequencing or cause and effect. Interestingly, Shaughnessy compares "coherence" as an academic convention with Dewey's notion of "continuity"—the synthesis of various ideas in ways that build new understanding (*Errors* 240). Coherence is not mere deference to readability but also functions as a technology for enabling reason.

Coherence reveals the strength of the relationship between claims and substantiation. This connection is reason itself; therefore, coherence signals reason. By "reason" I do not mean mechanical logic or scientific positivism. Like Aristotle's rhetoric, traditional academic discourse has often been criticized as formulaically logocentric. Yet, Aristotle's rhetoric clearly integrates *ethos* and *pathos* because rhetoric is most powerful when it appeals to the whole person (Grimaldi). Similarly, civic-academic style should not exclude the other human faculties or arbitrarily deny the personal voice of the student writer. As evidenced by the preceding discussion of academic stylism, our imperfect conventions are a mix of seemingly illogical preferences. As Shaughnessy explains, we are as subject as any discourse community to "field dependent" strategies of persuasion:

> The [experienced academic] writer, often with great cunning, strives to present his or her intent in a way that will be seductive to an academic audience, which, while it aspires among other things to high standards of verification and sound reason, is nonetheless subject to other kinds of persuasion as well—to the deft manipulation of audience expectations and biases, to shrewd assessments of what constitutes "adequate proof" or enough examples in specific situations, to the stances of fairness, objectivity, and formal courtesy that smooth the surface of academic disputation. ("Some Needed Research" 319)

Civic-academic style invokes many of these "expectations and biases"—standards of verification, adequate proof, fairness, and objectivity—because they support reason and the ideals of democracy.

For example, we employ fallacies as a tool for measuring the force of argumentative reason: the strength of continuity between proofs and claims they substantiate. Fallacies do not arbitrarily restrict reasoning to logic; they reflect a preference for seeking the widest possible agreement as to what is reasonable. Similarly, civic-academic style valuates the abstraction of "development" as evidence of an argument's "fullness," of writers' deliberate efforts to provide their audience with full access to the reasons, assumptions, and even biases that support their claims. Undeveloped claims resemble partial truths, treating audiences as unequal participants in rhetorical inquiry, denying their right to participate in reasoning.

Citation provides the clearest means of enabling the discourse community's participation in a writer's argument and of allowing writers to participate in the ongoing arguments of the discourse community. Our seemingly irrational obsession with plagiarism and the formalities of documentation demonstrates our commitment to high standards of elucidation and validation, but also serves as a community-sanctioned means for intertextual collaboration. Although citation practices may lag behind recent developments in authorship theory (see (In)Citers, "Citation Functions"), scholarly documentation also allows students access to authorial agency by appropriating the *ethos* of source texts. Citation practices not only enfranchise student writers to converse in our disciplinary discussions; the emphasis that civic-academic style puts on research may teach students to become more objective participants in public deliberation.

Like most other stylistic abstractions, objectivity is an ideal. Postmodernism tells us that we cannot completely escape our own subjectivity, that our positions are always-already "interested." However, this does not mean that our own interests must overshadow all others. Although academic writing prompts students to develop strong claims as evidence of intellectual autonomy and deliberate textual agency, theses are ideally not monological. Too often, our overemphasis on the argumentative thesis has led to an individualistic "stance of arrogance and narrow-mindedness," which tempts scholars to shortchange counterargument in order to bury their opposition (Tannen). By emphasizing elucidation over persuasion, we can guide students toward more cooperative, less competitive discourse. To this end, civic-academic style employs research to expand students' ability to overcome involuntary servitude to arrogance, ignorance, and dogma. Our preferred rhetorical stance of disinterestedness means "neutrality" only in the sense of fairness, tolerance, and open-mindedness. Writers should clearly express their interests, but they should also demonstrate an ability and willingness to see beyond the inherent limitations of their own perspective. Disinterest is not the opposite of interest; disinterest is inclusive interest. The earnest inclusion of alternate arguments in civic-academic style requires the willful suspension of disbelief, thereby teaching that responsible argumentation is itself a valuative process.

Valuation holds us more responsible for academic conventions. As leaders of the academic community, we have a special obligation to explicate our operating rules. Teaching gives us greater authority than our students—authority represented in our academic and institutional credentials, authority granted and sanctioned by society and the community whose values we represent as teachers. Representative authority comes with commensurate responsibility, since, as writing teachers, we proliferate the public's sensitivity to conventions via our pedagogy and through the textbooks we publish. A valuative approach teaches that we and our students should be less obsessed with formal minutiae. Considering conventions as a style—as an intersection of individual and community identity—also reminds us to be more tolerant of approximated, even caricatured, performance.

Ultimately, valuation also teaches students responsibility for the standards of the community in which they are participants. When that community is a reasoned democratic society, the inculcation of rhetorical values is a highly ethical endeavor. Evaluating academic style does not need to be an exercise in oppression. The difference between advocacy or argument on the one hand and brain washing or propaganda on the other is the provision of good reasons. As Shaughnessy explains, while many teachers view evaluation as "an intolerable kind of academic colonizing, discouraging the student from developing his 'native' talent," we might remember that a student writer

> did not choose his style but was confined to it by his unfamiliarity with the conventions that govern academic or discursive writing, conventions that would require him, for example, to address directly the questions posed to him . . . and to defend those parts of his answer that would be open to argument. (*Errors* 239)

Civic discourse should protect personal freedom while serving the public good. Citizenship within a democratic community implies a social responsibility to maintain and improve through criticism the wisdom of that community—especially the wisdom that enables and promotes free inquiry. By making our pedagogy less opaque, by giving good reasons for what we preach, we are practicing the very modes of discourse that we conceive as ideal.[4]

Notes

1. A popular example of epideictic rhetoric's idealizing power is Martin Luther King Jr.'s "I Have a Dream" speech, which appealed to an ideal notion of justice (equality) to criticize unjust social reality (racism). Invoking a common, foundational American ideal enabled King to call forth a more perfect reality. Celeste Condit claims that such rhetorical strategies were crucial to the success of abolitionist and Civil Rights rhetoric.

2. Claims for the cognitive advantages of literacy have an extensive and impassioned history. Based initially on the scholarship of Eric Havelock and Walter Ong, Thomas Farrell and Mina Shaughnessy *(Errors)* claim special advantages for academic literacy in particular. Mike Rose criticizes these arguments as overly reductive and deterministic, in that they imply that less "literate" writers are less capable of abstract thought and reason. Literacy-orality debates turned explicitly political and ideological as race and students' rights to their own language became more serious issues for the discipline (see also Patricia Bizzell; Donald

Lazare; and especially Geneva Smitherman). Farrell, for example, has been criticized for implicating the intellectual inferiority of black English vernacular.

I want to be very clear that I am not associating orality with cognitive deficiency. What I do claim is that inexperienced academic writers' prose contains heavy oral residue. Shaughnessy supports Rose's position that we should not equate thinking with writing because we do not yet know enough about cognitive processes to make this claim. Following Shaughnessy, I do not claim that inexperienced writers lack a capacity for intelligence but that academic discourse can serve as a tool for developing intelligence as a capacity. This I take to be a primary function of rhetoric since Aristotle, who defined rhetoric not as persuasion itself but as a *dynamis*—a cognitive "ability" or "capacity"—to imagine what can be potentially persuasive in particular situations.

3. Rebecca Moore Howard argues that as evaluative conventions, citation and plagiarism practices effectively constrain student agency by denying student-writers status as "real" authors.

4. I credit the development of my ideas on valuation to my mentor, Gary Tate, whose primary "mode of operation," Robert McDonald describes, "is to encourage speculation, rather than quick conclusion" (37). Tate taught me that teaching requires hope, which is also the best tonic against the onset of grumpy old age. I am also greatly indebted for the contributions of my colleagues Ann George, Jeanette Harris, and Joseph Petraglia, along with the other contributors to this volume.

Works Cited

The American Heritage Dictionary of the English Language. 3rd ed. Boston: Houghton, 1996.

Aristotle. *On Rhetoric: A Theory of Civic Discourse.* Trans. George A. Kennedy. New York: Oxford UP, 1991.

Beale, Walter H. "Rhetorical Performative Discourse: A New Theory of Epideictic." *Philosophy and Rhetoric* 11.4 (Fall 1978): 221–46.

Belanoff, Pat. "The Myths of Assessment." *Journal of Basic Writing* 10.1 (1991): 54–66.

Bizzell, Patricia. *Academic Discourse and Critical Consciousness.* Pittsburgh: U of Pittsburgh P, 1992.

Booth, Wayne C., *Modern Dogma and the Rhetoric of Assent.* Chicago: U of Chicago P, 1974.

Burke, Kenneth. *A Rhetoric of Motives.* 1950. Berkeley: U of California P, 1969.

Condit, Celeste Michelle. "Crafting Virtue: The Rhetorical Construction of Public Morality." *Quarterly Journal of Speech* 73 (Feb. 1987): 79–97.

Connors, Robert J., and Andrea Lunsford. "Frequency of Formal Errors in Current College Writing, Or Ma and Pa Kettle Do Research." *College Composition and Communication* (Dec. 1988): 395–409.

Crosswhite, James. *The Rhetoric of Reason: Argument and the Attractions of Writing.* Madison: U of Wisconsin P, 1996.

Dewey, John. *Democracy and Education: An Introduction to the Philosophy of Education.* 1916. New York: Free, 1966.

———. "Emerson—The Philosopher of Democracy." *International Journal of Ethics* 13 (1903): 405–13.

———. *Experience and Education.* 1938. New York: Collier, 1963.

———. "Valuation and Experimental Knowledge." *Philosophical Review.* 31 (1922): 325–51. Rpt. in *Ethics, Logic, Psychology.* Vol. 2 of *The Essential Dewey.* Ed. Larry A. Hickman and Thomas M. Alexander. Bloomington: Indiana UP, 1998. 272–86.

Elbow, Peter. "Reflections on Academic Discourse: How It Relates to Freshmen and Colleagues." *College English* 53.2 (Feb. 1991): 135–55.

———. *Writing Without Teachers.* New York: Oxford UP, 1973.

Emerson, Ralph Waldo. "The American Scholar." Oration delivered to the Phi Beta Kappa Society at Cambridge, 1837. *Essays and Lectures.* New York: Library of America, 1983. 53–71.

Farrell, Thomas J. "Developing Literacy: Walter J. Ong and Basic Writing." *Journal of Basic Writing* 2.1 (1978): 30–51.

Flower, Linda. "Writer-Based Prose: A Cognitive Basis for Problems in Writing." *College English* 41 (Sept. 1979): 19–37.

Frye, Northrop. *The Educated Imagination.* Bloomington: Indiana UP, 1964.

Gage, John T. "Philosophies of Style and Their Implications for Composition." *College English* 41.6 (Feb. 1980): 615–22.

Grimaldi, William M. A. "Studies in the Philosophy of Aristotle's Rhetoric." *Hermes* 25. Wiesbaden: Franz Steiner, 1972. 1–151. Rpt. in *Landmark Essays on Aristotelian Rhetoric.* Ed. Richard Leo Enos and Lois Peters Agnew. Mahwah, NJ: Erlbaum, 1998. 15–159.

Hart, Roderick. *Modern Rhetorical Criticism.* Boston: Allyn, 1997.

Havelock, Eric A. *Preface to Plato.* Cambridge: Harvard UP, 1963.

Howard, Rebecca Moore. *Standing in the Shadow of Giants: Plagiarists, Authors, Collaborators.* Stamford, CT: Ablex, 1999.

(In)Citers, The [Collaborative moniker for Paul Amore, Rebecca Moore Howard, Mary R. Lamb, Thomas Reedy, Amy Rupiper, Kurt Schick, and Patricia Tallakson]. "The Citation Functions: Literary Production and Reception." *Kairos* 3.1 (Spring 1997). Online. <http://english.ttu.edu/kairos/3.1/coverweb/ipc/authorship.htm>.

Lazare, Donald. "Orality, Literacy, and Standard English." *Journal of Basic Writing* 10.2 (1991): 87–98.

Lunsford, Andrea. "Putting Error in its Place(s)." Fourth Spilman Symposium on Issues in Teaching Writing. Virginia Military Institute, Lexington. Nov. 1997.

McDonald, Robert L. "Interview with Gary Tate." *Composition Studies* 20.2 (1992): 36–50.

Milic, Louis T. "Stylistics." *Encyclopedia of Rhetoric and Composition: Communication from Ancient Times to the Information Age.* Ed. Theresa Enos. New York: Garland, 1996. 703–9.

Miller, Carolyn. "Genre as Social Action." *Quarterly Journal of Speech* 70.2 (1984): 151–67.

Ong, Walter. *Orality and Literacy: The Technologizing of the Word.* London: Routledge, 1982.

Perelman, Chaim. "The New Rhetoric: A Theory of Practical Reasoning." *Great Ideas Today.* Encyclopaedia Britannica, 1970. Rpt. in Theresa Enos and Stuart Brown, eds. *Professing the New Rhetorics: A Sourcebook.* Englewood Cliffs, NJ: Prentice, 1994. 145–77.

———. *The Realm of Rhetoric.* 1977. Trans. William Kluback. Notre Dame: U Notre Dame P, 1982.

Perelman, Chaim, and Lucy Olbrechts-Tyteca. *The New Rhetoric: A Treatise on Argumentation.* Trans. John Wilkinson and Purcell Weaver. Notre Dame: U Notre Dame P, 1969.

Rankin, Elizabeth D. "Revitalizing Style: Toward a New Theory and Pedagogy." *Freshman English News* 14 (Spring 1985). 8–13.

Rose, Mike. "Narrowing the Mind and Page: Remedial Writers and Cognitive Reductionism." *College Composition and Communication* 39.3 (Oct. 1988): 267–98.

Schwegler, Robert A. "Errors, Exclusions, and Aspirations." Fourth Spilman Symposium on Issues in Teaching Writing. Virginia Military Institute, Lexington. Nov. 1997.

Shaughnessy, Mina. *Errors and Expectations: A Guide for the Teacher of Basic Writing.* New York: Oxford UP, 1977.

———. "Some Needed Research on Writing." *College Composition and Communication* 28 (Dec. 1977): 317–20.

Sheard, Cynthia Miecznikowski. "The Public Value of Epideictic Rhetoric." *College English* 58.7 (Nov. 1996): 765–94.

Skorczewski, Dawn. "'Everybody Has Their Own Ideas': Responding to Cliché in Student Writing." *College Composition and Communication* 52.2 (Dec. 2000): 220–39.

Smitherman, Geneva. "Conference on College Composition and Communication's Role in the Struggle for Language Rights. *College Composition and Communication* 50.3 (Feb. 1999): 349–76.

"Students' Rights to Their Own Language." *College Composition and Communication* 25 (Fall 1974): 1–32.

Tannen, Deborah. "Agonism in the Academy: Surviving Higher Learning's Argument Culture." *Chronicle of Higher Education* Mar. 31, 2000. <http://chronicle.com/weekly/v46/i30/30b00701.htm>.

Williams, Joseph M. *Style: Ten Lessons in Clarity and Grace.* 5th ed. New York: Longman, 1996.

15

Brave New (Cyber)World: From Reader to Navigator

David W. Chapman

This year, for the first time, my students purchased a textbook with a CD-ROM attached to it. The CD-ROM is considered a supplement to the text, and it will not affect my teaching of the course in any significant way. Yet, one wonders if it is a harbinger of some portentous change—the first cloud on the horizon that signals the coming storm. Living at the end of the twentieth century, we know just how quickly technology can transform our daily lives. One minute you are stirring your soup on the stove; the next you are "nuking" it in a microwave oven. And even such small changes in technology can have momentous effects on the way we order our lives. Like many of my colleagues, I find I can save time in my day if I bring a dish from home to microwave for lunch. It is a far cry from a leisured meal at the faculty club where people from across campus can meet to discuss books and ideas, people and politics.

With an awareness, then, of what changes may be wrought by seemingly innocent technologies, what should I think of this silver disk that has fastened itself, leechlike, on the back of my textbook? At first glance, the contents of the disk seem redundant. Much of it consists of chapters of the textbook in electronic form. But for the true cyberphile, the question may be posed the other way around: Hasn't the CD-ROM made the textbook redundant? This debate has profound consequences for both academe and society at large. Some have compared the impact of the new digital culture to the role that Gutenberg's press played in the Renaissance. Let us imagine, then, two academics engaged in a dialectic, concerning the benefits of the digital revolution that is underway. Our defender of the traditional print culture shall be known as Augustus Textus, and Beta will be his rival for supremacy in this new world order.

Beta: Augustus, I have often passed by your office and seen your shelves covered with books and journals of every kind, and I know you have a sentimental attachment to these dusty old tomes, but I didn't see any papyrus scrolls or wooden tablets. I think even you must recognize that antiquated means of storing and preserving knowledge must give way to more advanced forms. A CD-ROM is capable of holding 650 megabytes—enough to store several hundred books. The DVD, the next generation of storage media, can hold 17 gigabytes of information—thousands of books could be stored on a single disk. Applying the simplest measure of "bytes per buck," these new ways of storing textual information are superior to the venerable old mode of the codex book.

Augustus: Not so fast, my cybernetic friend. I can read my books without any assistance from an electronic device. The CD requires a considerable investment—well over $1000 for a laptop computer—to make it usable. Nor is this a one-time expense. I have walked by your office as well, and I saw a dizzying array of digital paraphernalia: floppy disk drives, external hard drives, Zip drives, Jazz drives—some of which are sitting in a pile in the corner—and today you are touting the new DVD drive. In fact, while you have been busy installing new drives and converting files, I have been . . . reading.

Beta: Yes, I'll admit that the current rate of technological change is sometimes confusing and frustrating, but progress comes at a cost. I am sure if your way of thinking were the norm, we would still be huddling around fires in our caves. What you don't seem to realize is that the change that is underway is not about simply moving from one kind of "book" to another. Multimedia publication provides a richer experience than traditional books. Why should students be limited to reading *Hamlet* silently, when they could also hear a great Shakespearean actor delivering the famous soliloquy? Why shouldn't a student in biology see a 3-D representation of the human body instead of the two-dimensional pictures in most textbooks? Why shouldn't a student interested in aviation be able to see a dynamic representation of the airflow as it passes over a wing and creates lift? The CD-ROM that you so despise has made it possible to greatly enhance the visual and aural elements of instruction.

Augustus: Excuse me, Beta, but I thought we were talking about new technologies. I think the idea of a moving picture is from the nineteenth
   century. All of the examples you present have been available for years
   in film and video. Are students of this generation better educated
   because they have had access to such materials? I think you know the
   answer. The truth is that such media have produced an appetite for
   entertainment, not knowledge. Look at the faces of a high school class
   when the teacher shows a video on *Hamlet* or human physiology or,
   perish the thought, the physics of flight. Most of them are bored beyond words. The medium does not create more intellectual interest;
   it creates an insatiable need to be teased, titillated, and tranquilized.
   Placing video on CD-ROM is just another way for students to escape
   from the discipline necessary to read a text.
Beta: Certainly, film and video can result in passivity in their viewers,
   but a multimedia CD-ROM is an interactive tool. Students choose
   what they will read and watch. They explore new ideas, make connections with related subjects, and apply the knowledge they have obtained. You may say that we are pandering to students by offering them
   more entertaining ways to pursue knowledge, but where's the harm
   in that? Why settle for tuna fish when you can have caviar? The multimedia environment is a wonderful way to learn, and our students
   should have the benefit of the best that technology has to offer.
Augustus: My dear duped friend, you sound like a commercial for a software manufacturer. One of the things I learned in those old books
   you so despise is that calling someone "old-fashioned" won't substitute for an argument. The question is not about what we are doing
   with the technology but what the technology is doing to us. I understand you prefer to talk not about readers but about "navigators" of
   the "hypertext." Well, I think your students are more "voyeur" than
   "voyageur." Have you ever observed them in the computer lab, moving constantly from one image to the next, never stopping for more
   than a minute to read and analyze what they have read. The linear
   text is not a limitation imposed by a primitive technology; it is an
   enduring landmark of a civilized society. It makes, out of all the chaotic elements of life, a coherent vision. It asks that the reader think
   through a logical series of ideas and come to a reasonable conclusion.
   Certainly, there are catalogs and indexes that are more conveniently
   stored and searched in electronic form, but the real book is another
   matter altogether. It is meant to be read from cover to cover. No one
   needs to teach my students how to jump from one trivial bit of in-

---

formation to the next, which is the way I interpret your high-sounding description of the electronic navigator. What they do need is the ability to engage in sustained, concentrated reflection on a subject of importance. The book is not, as you suggest, simply pages bound together; it is an intellectual construct of the highest order.

The reader will forgive me if I let dear old Augustus have the last word. He is, after all, a dying breed and represents no real threat to the digital juggernaut. I do think the implications of digital media have grave importance for the future of those teaching composition and rhetoric. And because these implications are so fundamental, they deserve a closer look.

Reading in a Digital Age

Most scholars agree that the research on reading hypertext documents (or even traditional documents that are being read online) is limited and inconclusive. Advocates for hypertext stress the value of the reader actively choosing a pathway through various links in hypertext documents, that is, "navigating" the text. Based on his experience in California schools, L. M. Dryden asserts that hypertext "energizes individual learners and gives them greater control over their literate thinking and behavior" (294).

However, most research on hypertext has led to the opposite conclusion. Navigating a hypertext often produces disorientation and cognitive overload for a reader who must determine what to read and what order to read it in. Davida Charney summarizes the difficulties confronting the reader of a hypertext:

> The strategies for structuring texts . . . are the product of centuries of experimentation by writers striving to make their texts more comprehensible to readers. These strategies, however, place the burden of selecting and arranging information, and providing signals to the arrangement, primarily on the writer. Hypertexts, by shifting a large portion of the readers' choices about what portions of a text to read and in what order, compound the difficulties of producing a coherent mental representation. (245)

Part of the euphoria about hypertext has been based on the patterns of behavior observed in Internet use. Many users of the Internet do report being "energized" by the access to information available in this form. They sometimes lose themselves in a virtual world, surfing from one Website to the next, hardly aware of where they are or what time it is. But it is important not to confuse this kind of engagement with retention—much less comprehension—of information. Even in controlled experiments with a finite set of pages and links, readers do not recall more information from a hypertext than a traditional print text. A study by Sallie Gordon and others found that college students remembered less from a hypertext document than a traditional linear text. Furthermore, the students expressed a preference for the traditional texts because they required less effort to read (qtd. in Charney).

Another argument advanced in favor of hypertext is its ability to free students from the authority imposed upon them by traditional print texts. Ruth Garner and Mark G. Gillingham, for instance, deride textbooks for conveying "legitimate school knowledge" and for their failure to present "multiple interpretations of events and phenomena" (228). Dryden ridicules the "doggedly Gutenberg text-based scholars" (284) and commends hypertext for "redistributing power and authority within classrooms" (294). Randy Bass has extended this argument from the effect on individual classrooms to the transformative power of hypertext for the entire field of English studies. He suggests that hypertexts will not only make texts more accessible but also make us less dependent on "print and linear argument as the sole vehicle for the theoretical apparatus of our culture-texts" (665).

Of course, not everyone agrees that hypertext will prove to be such a transformative event. David N. Dobrin argues that there is a great deal of "hype" in hypertext:

> Hypertext is not a new text form. It is not an evolutionary advance. It forces no reconsiderations. It has no potential for fundamental change in how we write or read. Hypertext is simply one text structure among many, made unique by the text conventions it has, conventions that guide the reader's attention and allow him or her to navigate through the text. The conventions are interesting, and a proper understanding of them enables us to answer the questions I have about hypertext. But these conventions are not different in kind from other text conventions. Thus, teaching hypertext is very much like teaching encyclopedias or comic books; you have to teach how the conventions work, and, once you do, you've taught people to be literate in hypertext. (308)

Even if you accept the premise that hypertext does substantially alter the reading experience, it is not clear that the change is for the better. The liberation rhetoric about more democratic classrooms presupposes that current teachers and textbooks are inherently oppressive. Surely on some subjects (the periodic table? the Pythagorean theorem?) knowledge should be stable and predictable. And even in the more interpretive disciplines, does the presence of a linear text of, say, *The Scarlet Letter* or the Declaration of Independence mean that neither the text nor the teacher will admit multiple interpretations? Conversely, a hypertext can be created that will reinforce the biases of the multimedia designer. In some cases, we may be merely trading one "authority" for another. There is no convincing evidence that reading a hypertext is more beneficial to learning than traditional print documents.

Composing in a Digital Age

As well as considering the effect of multimedia documents and hypertextual organization on reading, we must also consider the impact such forms will have on student writing. One of the supposed advantages of electronic documents is that they can easily be appropriated into the students' own discourse. Jay David Bolter celebrates the way that electronic texts change the relationship between author and reader:

> Hypertext and electronic communication in general tend to erode the authority of the text and the author (Bolter, 1991; Landow, 1992). The relationship between author and reader is more egalitarian. The reader can more easily intervene in electronic texts and even become an author. (6)

However, Bolter is quick to acknowledge that such intervention is actually limited to word processing documents and electronic mail exchanges. The more typical means of accessing a hypertext document—CD-ROMs and Web pages—are not generally conducive to the reader's intervention.

In fact, such hypertextual documents tend to prevent not only intervention but also imitation. Composition scholars have long argued for the importance of including student-written compositions in the anthologies used in first-year composition courses. Essays written by professional writers often discourage students because they seem beyond their ability to imitate. How much more this must be true of a hypertext document that has enlisted the aid of a technology specialist, a graphic designer, and other experts in order to produce the finished product.

And yet, some voices in the digital avant-garde are calling for precisely this kind of expertise in order for students to complete their rhetorical education. Kathleen Tyner, for instance, suggests that schools are being left behind through their insistence on traditional print literacy:

> The literacy of schooling, based on a hierarchical access to print literacy, is increasingly at odds with the kinds of constructivist practices necessary to accommodate the more diverse, interactive, and less lin-

ear media forms made available by digital technologies. In the absences
of strong theory, literacy practices are splitting into the kind of literacy practiced in school and the kind practiced in the *real* world of
home and community. (8–9)

Tyner advocates placing all the new technologies into the forefront of public
education, including both video production and multimedia design.

Tyner is certainly not alone in her call to prepare students for these new
technological frontiers. J. L. Lemke believes that "multimedia authoring
skills, multimedia critical analysis, cyberspace exploration strategies, and
cyberspace navigation skills" should be the required literacies for the coming generation of students (287). Bolter is enthusiastic about the possibility that "high school teachers may soon be assigning Web projects in lieu
of traditional essays" in order to encourage the integration of visual and
textual elements. He places the responsibility on teachers to help students
"create and deploy . . . images (as well as animation and digital video)" (11).

But are such practices truly literacies, or are they merely technical skills
that will soon be replaced by another generation of tools? In order to re-
ceive a high school teaching certificate, I was once required to take a course
in the use of audiovisual equipment. Among the valuable skills I learned
in this class was the procedure for threading 16mm film onto a film pro-
jector. No one at the time could anticipate the way that VCRs would make
this entire operation unnecessary. Already, software for Web page design has
made a knowledge of HTML redundant. Any course design that emphasizes the development of technical skill is doomed to obsolescence. The
current rate of technological change has only accelerated the rate at which
such skills will be rendered useless.

This is not to say that an understanding of visual elements does not have
an important role to play in contemporary documents. In some ways the
debate over the inclusion of these technological skills parallels the great
grammar debate that polarized the discipline during the 1960s and 1970s.
No one disputed that linguistic instruction, including traditional English
grammar, had intrinsic value. But study after study indicated that such study
was ineffectual in improving student writing. As Braddock, Lloyd-Jones,
and Schoer bluntly stated: "The teaching of grammar has a negligible or,
because it usually displaces some instruction and practice in composition,
even a harmful effect on improvement in writing" (37–38). One could easily substitute "the teaching of HTML" or "the teaching of Web page design" for "the teaching of grammar" in this sentence. Indeed, no studies to
date have proven that any composition instruction assisted by the use of
computers has improved student writing (Wahlstrom and Selfe 42).

This is the reason that the real debate about the value of teaching new media in the classroom ultimately leads to a discussion of the nature of literacy itself. The greatest proponents of hypertext and other electronic documents generally must mount an assault on print literacy itself.

Digital Texts and Literacy

In a rush to legitimize their own interests, many different specialists have appropriated the use of the term *literacy*. Thus, we hear talk of "visual literacy," "information literacy," "multimedia literacy," and so on. The reference to a "literacy" not only suggests the symbolic nature of the interaction but also the essential value of its study. The "ability to access information on a database," for instance, has much less cachet than "information literacy."

What was once *the* literacy but is now "print literacy" has been relegated to just one in a panoply of literacies that must be mastered by all students. But the widespread use of "literacy" for all kinds of competencies has greatly debased the meaning of the word. Although, as Walter Ong has observed, literacy requires the support of some form of technology—whether a stylus, a printing press, or a computer—the importance of literacy goes beyond the communicative act: "Technologies are not mere exterior aids, but also interior transformations of consciousness, and never more than when they affect the word. Such transformations can be uplifting. Writing heightens consciousness" (82). We may express this "transformation of consciousness" in various ways—as objectivity, as intentionality, as critical thinking, as contextualization—but however it is expressed, the significance of literacy extends beyond the ability to capture speech in written form.

Myron Tuman has explored at length the profound implications of this confusion between "functional literacy," or transcription skills, and the more advanced literacy that is the goal of most English classes beyond the elementary level.

> As long as we can provide enough technicians so that information flows freely and steadily between data banks . . . we should be able to claim continued high levels of "literacy." Levels of literacy, therefore, if we understand the term to mean certain mechanical aspects of verbal transmission, could well appear to be increasing at the very moment when we as a people are becoming less literate. Meanwhile, fewer and fewer people may be interested in whether "literate" technicians, or any of the rest of us, can do more than store and retrieve information. (5)

The call for multimedia literacy strikes me as one more move toward producing technicians and away from the more significant and enduring goal of teaching students to use logical patterns of organization and to write clear and coherent prose. It is not surprising that the critics of print literacy are antagonistic toward logocentric discourse. Bolter, for instance, suggests that the persuasive essay may be a "dying form" which will give way to hyper-textual discourse:

> Many, perhaps most, educators still teach expository writing as the art of establishing a consistent point of view and delivering a coher-ent conclusion. Reading nonfiction is taught as the art of discover-ing the point of view, identifying the conclusion, and then adopting one's own point of view in agreement or dissent. Hypertext challenges those goals. . . ." (7)

Ultimately, the debate about the merits of any digital text are not about technology—about storage capacity or transferability of files or network-ing. It may be true, as Paul Levinson writes, that "books as a medium of convenient reading . . . have a deep vulnerability in their competition with digital media" (184). However, it is possible to embrace the ease and con-venience of new forms of communication and to simultaneously cling to the venerable goals of producing a literate citizenry—one capable of read-ing extended discourse on matters of importance and writing in patterns that are clear, logical, and persuasive. The linearity of the traditional codex book is not, as the detractors of print literacy have supposed, an artificial limitation of an outmoded technology but as old Augustus has it, "an in-tellectual construct of the highest order." So even if my textbook should disappear into a CD-ROM or dissolve into hyperspace, it will still be the symbolic representation of an ordered mind in a world of chaotic experi-ence. There may, indeed, be many "literacies," but for most first-year com-position teachers, it will be enough to help students develop *the* literacy that transcends the various media in which it is expressed.

Works Cited

Bass, Randy. "Story and Archive in the Twenty-First Century." *College English* 61 (1999): 659–70.

Bolter, Jay David. "Hypertext and the Question of Visual Literacy." Reinking et al. 3–13.

Braddock, Richard, Richard Lloyd-Jones, and Lowell Schoer. *Research in Written Compo-sition.* Urbana, IL: NCTE, 1963.

Charney, Davida. "The Effect of Hypertext on the Processes of Reading and Writing." Selfe and Hilligoss 238–63.

Dobrin, David. "Hype and Hypertext." Selfe and Hilligoss 305–15.

Dryden, L. M. "Literature, Student-Centered Classrooms, and Hypermedia Environ-ments." Selfe and Hilligoss 282–304.

Garner, Ruth, and Mark G. Gillingham. "The Internet in the Classroom: Is It the End of Transmission-Oriented Pedagogy?" Reinking et al. 221–31.

Lemke, J. L. "Metamedia Literacy: Transforming Meanings and Media." Reinking et al. 283–301.

Levinson, Paul. *The Soft Edge: A Natural History and Future of the Information Revolution.* London: Routledge, 1997.

Ong, Walter J. *Orality and Literacy: The Technologizing of the World.* London: Methuen, 1982.

Reinking, David, et al. *Handbook of Literacy and Technology: Transformations in a Post-Typographic World.* Mahwah, NJ: Erlbaum, 1998.

Selfe, Cynthia L., and Susan Hilligoss, eds. *Literacy and Computers: The Complications of Teaching and Learning with Technology.* New York: MLA, 1994.

Tuman, Myron C. *A Preface to Literacy: An Inquiry into Pedagogy, Practice, and Progress.* Tuscaloosa: U of Alabama P, 1987.

Tyner, Kathleen. *Literacy in a Digital World: Teaching and Learning in the Age of Information.* Mahwah, NJ: Erlbaum, 1998.

Wahlstrom, Billie J., and Cynthia L. Selfe. "A View from the Bridge: English Departments Piloting among the Shoals of Computer Use." *ADE Bulletin* 109 (1994): 35–45.

16

Learning to Walk the Walk: Mentors, Theory, and Practice in Composition Pedagogy

Paul Heilker

When I was a baby, I learned to walk, and then I learned to talk. Learning to walk came easily, naturally, when the time was right, but I needed lots of help learning to talk. As an adult, on the other hand, I have learned to talk the talk and *then* I have learned to walk the walk. Talking the talk comes easily, but I need lots of help walking the walk.

For instance, in my mid-twenties, I joined a prayer group in an effort to stave off what seemed to be an endless series of crises in my life. At first, all I could do was listen. I studied and picked up the discourse. I learned to talk about honesty, acceptance, tolerance, fear, change, pain, balance, peace, growth, love, faith, and the like. Learning to *talk* about these things didn't mean that I had learned how to *do* them, however. Talking the talk didn't mean I could walk the walk. But by watching other people in the group walk through the crises in their lives, I learned how to do it, too. "Oh, so *that's* what honesty looks like! *That's* how you do acceptance! *That's* how you walk through pain! *That's* how you do faith!" I was lucky: I had good mentors; they offered me repeated concrete demonstrations of how to connect talk and walk; they demystified and illuminated that hazy gulf between theory and practice. They *embodied* theory and made it *real*.

While it is hardly an earth-shaking thesis, I submit that the same is true

---

A version of this essay first appeared as "Pedagogical Heresy, Uncommon Sense" in *The Writing Instructor.* <http://www.writinginstructor.com>. 2002. Copyright © 2002 by *The Writing Instructor.*

for composition professionals: if we are lucky, we have good mentors who *embody* theory and make it *real,* who teach us how to walk the walk by offering us explicit, living demonstrations of how to connect theory and practice as writers and teachers. I have been fortunate enough to have a number of strong mentors in my career as a writing specialist (including Elizabeth Barton at Wantagh Junior High School, Donald Frye and Charles Huffman at SUNY Stony Brook, Bill McBride and Kate Kiefer at Colorado State, Win Horner at Texas Christian, Peter Vandenberg at DePaul, and Eileen Schell at Virginia Tech), and they taught me remarkable things: "Oh, so *that's* what revision looks like! *That's* how you do collaboration! *That's* what political commitment in the classroom looks like!" These things may seem mundane, I suppose, but at the time, for me, they were practically epiphanic.

What I'll offer here, then, is an extended example of how a series of living, explicit, concrete demonstrations by one mentor taught me a specific way of connecting theory and practice in my composition pedagogy, a particular path upon which to walk the walk as a writing teacher, one I still find especially difficult to navigate yet crucial to whatever success I have as a thinker and writer and teacher. Gary Tate taught me about *resistance,* which we can define as an active movement against the dominant culture and movement toward emancipation, as an ideological, liberatory refusal of the dominant knowledge, language, and social practices legitimized by a discourse community (Chase). My universe as a student and teacher of writing has repeatedly lurched off its axis as a result of Tate's resistance, his pedagogical heresy, his uncommon sense.

Perhaps the most important thing I have learned from Tate is that, at some point, even the most well intentioned movements in writing pedagogy gain a snowballing momentum of their own and begin to hurtle along until what otherwise might be seen as hyperbolic or even foolish perspectives become construed as "common knowledge" or "conventional wisdom." The various pedagogical movements in our field serve as galvanizing agents for our communal sense of who we are and what we are about as a profession. But as our devotion to them grows, they eventually acquire an almost religious status and, like the Baltimore Catechism, supply ready answers for so many questions and concerns that our allegiance to them becomes more automatic than mindful. Our pedagogical movements become, in fact, more important in what they do for us as we continue to attempt to validate our field as a worthy academic discipline, more important in how they help us conduct our business of publishing scholarship and textbooks, than in what they do to help our students become better writers. Hence, we are loath to criticize them much, and they frequently develop, unchecked, until they spiral into strained, ethereal constructions. What Tate has repeatedly demonstrated is how important it is for writing teachers to have the courage and conviction to do the unpopular thing, to speak the unspeakable, to point out that the emperor has no clothes, to spear the sacred cow: to recognize when the momentum of a pedagogical movement that has gained wide acceptance is allowing excessive (sometimes even silly) ideas to be passed off as axiomatic truths and is thus hampering rather than helping us in our efforts to help students become more effective writers.

The pedagogical movement that had gained the widest acceptance when I began my doctoral study at Texas Christian in the fall of 1989 was, of course, the new paradigm for teaching writing. The salient feature of the new paradigm, as Maxine Hairston put it, was that it focused on the writing process. During my training as a GTA in my M.A. program a couple of years earlier, I had been thoroughly immersed in writing process pedagogy. We pored over Donald Murray's *A Writer Teaches Writing,* with its seemingly endless menus of activities for each stage of the writing process; we had our students practice brainstorming, freewriting, looping, talk-write, clustering, branching, cubing, the W questions, Aristotle's *topoi,* Jacqueline Berke's twenty questions, tagmemic grids, and Burke's pentad; we traded hundreds of ideas for students' daybook and journal entries; we quoted sections of Nancy Sommers's "Revision Strategies of Student Writers and Experienced Adult Writers" and "Responding to Student Writing" verbatim; we collected first drafts and responded in ways that encouraged students toward holistic, global, fundamental revision of their papers, toward "re-vision," toward literally "re-seeing" their papers on a basic level to find the gems of meaning buried within even the most ragged texts; we even required students to revise one of their ostensibly finished papers as the final assignment of the semester.

It was within this context that I began auditing Tate's class on the personal essay, which, by all appearances, was the quintessential writing workshop that process pedagogy valorized. We met once a week, desks in a circle, and read our essays aloud, and our classmates offered supportive comments as to which sections seemed to have a strong voice, arresting details, and the like, all with an eye toward revising our essays toward possible submission for evaluation. My experience as a student writer in the class cemented in my mind the value of student-centered, process-centered teaching: I felt good—good about my writing and good about myself as a writer.

But then the universe pitched, rolled, and yawed. One day in class, after I had finished reading my "Pre-Mortem on the Mighty Nova," an admittedly mawkish and sophomoric paean to my old Chevy, Tate allowed the typical feedback to come from my classmates for a while, but then he interrupted. "You know," he said, "it simply is not true that all drafts should be revised or that all drafts will be improved by revision. Sometimes there just isn't enough of value there to work with. Sometimes it would take far too much effort to try to salvage what little good is there. Sometimes revision even makes a draft worse. Sometimes we would be wise to just leave a draft alone, to abandon it."

I was dumbfounded. Everything I had learned in my indoctrination about effective teaching, everything I had learned about the faith of—and our faith in—writing process, about our unflagging optimism and confidence, that, given enough drafts, effective prose would simply have to emerge, had been rent asunder. But Tate's blasphemy was so right on target, so painfully apt. That essay was dreck. It was unworthy of revision, unworthy of the time I might squander on it, time that would be much better spent on a different draft that had at least some potential. No amount of work was going to salvage that wreck. It was then that I realized the depths of my process worship and proselytizing, my uncritical complicity in promulgating some foolish excesses of process pedagogy, and my misleading and mystifying of my students as a result. It's a pretty, self-serving fiction that revision will always improve a draft, but it's a lie, nonetheless, one that Tate taught me to resist. So now, just as I refuse to dupe myself anymore, I refuse to dupe my students. I am unhappy, of course, when I have to say it—almost as unhappy as they are when they hear it—but I do tell students when I think their drafts are dead in the water and they should abandon ship. If I want my students to make clear-eyed and strategic yet ethical and humane decisions as writers and collaborators and citizens, it seems only fitting to try to model that behavior.

Much like our naive and overweening faith in revision as the universal balm, other features of the new paradigm also warped into bad teaching. An equally troubling development amounted to a classic case of throwing out the baby with the bath water, as the new paradigm juggernaut eventually moved from emphasizing writing process over written product to teaching writing process to the exclusion of written product. The current-traditional paradigm, we knew, was bad; and the most prominent features of that paradigm were that it focused on the written product, conventional usage, style, and editing. So we cut back and cut back on teaching those things until we practically didn't teach them at all. "Grammar" moved from being one of the most heavily weighted components of evaluation rubrics to one of the least. When we graded papers as GTAs in my M.A. program in the mid-1980s, for instance, we used a program-wide list of grammatical and mechanical errors, a list that was divided into "Errors That Count" and "Errors That Don't Count." The number of items in the latter category was at least double that in the former, as I remember.

During my doctoral study, however, my relationship to written products experienced a disorienting quantum leap. In my second semester at Texas Christian, I took a course in literary criticism from Tate called "Reading Texts." We got our first small assignment, to write a two-page response to some critical text we had been reading, as I recall. I went to work, and using all of my training in writing process, I completed (well, almost completed, as it turns out) a strong response. But when I got it back, I was rather surprised to see that I had earned a "B." Me?! A "B"?! There must be some mistake, I thought. I scoured the paper for an explanation. But he liked the focus I had chosen, it seemed, and he appreciated the quality of my analysis, and he praised the evidence I had brought to bear. Then why the "B"? And then I saw it: there, in the first paragraph (I can still see it now!), where I had written that the author's suggested teaching practice "would be a horrific thing to do to students," the word *horrific* was circled in red ink. But there was no marginal comment to go with that circle. Confused, I went to see Tate during his office hours.

"Dr. Tate," I ventured, "I was wondering why I got a 'B' on the last assignment."

"Let me see," he said, taking the paper from my hands. "Oh, that! You misused the word *horrific*. You didn't mean *horrific*."

"Yes I did."

"No," he said, "you didn't."

And I realized, with a sinking feeling that began at my larynx and moved swiftly downward, that he was right, that I had used the wrong word, that I had, rather mindlessly, plugged in almost the right word as I was working through my writing process but not the right word. I had gotten it down, in a good process over product economy, but I had never gone back and gotten it right. The heresy—the uncommon sense—here is that process is not an end in itself but rather the means to an improved product. What I learned from the universe's reeling that day was to resist our collective demonizing of current-traditional rhetoric; I learned that we need to teach students that editing and proofreading are writing processes too, ones as crucial as invention and revision and as essential to one's effectiveness as a writer. I learned that while writing may never be finished, it is, nonetheless, inevitably *due* at some point. And I learned that our excessive emphasis on process over product runs a real risk of never giving students the opportunity to move past imprecise language and sloppy thinking.

.

While the new paradigm was already fully, deeply entrenched by the late 1980s, social construction theory was fast on its way to becoming so. At that time, about three years after the publication of Kenneth Bruffee's "Social Construction, Language, and the Authority of Knowledge," social construction theory had not only established itself within the mainstream of our disciplinary thought but had, in fact, in its own way become, oddly, ironically, *foundational.* I found myself citing with absolute certainty, without qualm or question, Bruffee's assertions, such as:

> A social constructionist position in any discipline assumes that entities we normally call reality, knowledge, thought, facts, texts, selves, and so on are constructs generated by communities of like-minded peers. Social construction understands reality, knowledge, thought, facts, texts, selves, and so on as community-generated and community-maintained linguistic entities. (774)

What a powerful and empowering perspective for writing instructors to adopt. The work we help students do with words is creative in a biblical sense: it constitutes reality, constitutes the world(s) in which we live. I am sure this is why I found—and still find—social construction theory so attractive.

But being sucked along in the wake of this movement, I could not see how and to what the wave I was riding was blinding me. But Tate could, perhaps because he has been here since the beginnings of the field, has seen other movements rise and fall, come and go, in their time, and has thus had lots of practice in resisting our ever-changing theoretical tides. In any event, the day soon came when my universe as a writing teacher and my relationship to my composition students careened jarringly, again, when—much like Dr. Johnson, who kicked a stone to refute Bishop Berkeley—Tate came into our composition theory class, placed a chair upon the table and announced, "This is not a socially constructed linguistic entity." At that moment, I realized merely that my mentor had gleefully located a gaping hole in my favorite theory. But soon after, as the image of the chair resonated and the significance of his point expanded in my mind, the tremendous influence of material reality on a student's ability to learn to write came crashing down on me. I had never considered how much students' access to things, how much their access to things like chairs, desks, books, paper, pens, let alone computers—hell, how much their access to things like food, shelter, medicine, and clothing, for that matter—fundamentally affected their ability to learn to write. My ignorance had been appalling, and I was ashamed of it. While, on the whole, brute, material realities in our class-divided society still remain practically unacknowledged in the theorizing of our field, we can nonetheless address them in our teaching: we can order old editions of the textbooks we use rather than forcing students to shell out the ludicrously high prices they pay for new ones; we can place a full set of class texts on reserve at the library rather than insist that students buy every book; we can make hard copies of our teaching materials available and allow for alternative ways students may submit their work rather than insisting that they somehow find Internet access; and we can negotiate due dates around students' work and childcare schedules, to name just a few.

Closely related to the rise of social construction theory was the rise of teaching academic discourse as a programmatic goal in the late 1980s and early 1990s. Driven by arguments such as David Bartholomae's "The Study of Error" and "Inventing the University," our new curricula sought to help students assimilate academic discourse conventions and so enter their chosen disciplinary discourse communities. Writing across the curriculum programs were formed to help advanced undergraduates garner the discipline-specific writing skills they would need for their professions. We worried much about carryover, and we worked hard to convince ourselves that the skills we taught in freshman English courses would, in fact, prepare our students well for the writing they had to do in their majors. In English 101, we told students, "You'll need this when you get into English 102." In English 102, we told students, "You'll need this when you get into your major." In the writing across the curriculum courses in their majors, we told students, "You'll need this when you get into the working world." But our emphasis on how their current efforts would somehow pay off for them later in school or work became excessive and silly, became a perpetually deferred orientation to some vague and misty future. The insistence that working hard in a writing class now would have some kind of amazing, almost mystical reward somewhere down the line became an article of faith for us. The notion that composition courses were places where students were prepared for their academic and professional futures, prepared for some other time and place when they might actually need to know and apply what we were teaching them, went unquestioned and unchallenged until it became practically our sole *raison d'etre*.

In 1992, as I was nearing the end of my time at Texas Christian, as I was picking a dissertation topic and preparing to put myself on the job market, Tate shared with me another pair of universe-altering heresies, which fundamentally changed how I construe myself as a professional and go about my job as a writing teacher. The first bit of resistance and uncommon sense is simply that composition courses should be worth taking in the present. They should be of immediate—not deferred—value to the students who are required to take them. Our students should experience the payoff for their hard work right now, not somewhere down the line. Our courses need to be valuable in their own right, for their own sake. The second, related bit of resistance and wisdom will be familiar to anyone who has read Tate's debate with Erika Lindemann on the place of literature in the writing class: since the vast majority of students will spend only four, maybe six, years in college, teaching students to produce academic writing is an extremely short-sighted objective. I'll go further: it's more than just short-sighted, it's self-important, self-aggrandizing. While our students will spend about five years within academics, they will spend decades upon decades outside of academics, "writing beyond the disciplines," as Tate put it, living real, whole lives and encountering real, whole problems, rather than working through highly controlled simulations within neatly, scholastically categorized slices of experience. In the long run, our students' ability to compose personally meaningful writing *beyond* the curriculum is far more important than their ability to compose academic writing *across* the curriculum. Offering our students experience and practice in using writing as a way of exploring their personal, affective responses to pressing social issues and the vexing, end-lessly mutating difficulties of everyday living, as a means of learning about and negotiating the complexities and conflicts of their personal relation-ships, as a means of discovering themselves, what they think, what they feel, what they value, and why—these should be both the immediate payoff and the long-term legacy of our writing courses. We should, in short, not sim-ply be unapologetic about teaching expressive, personal writing, we should be aggressive about it. What more worthwhile goal can we pursue? What more valuable process can we teach our students than how to invent and revise and compose themselves?

In conclusion, then, while I readily admit that I may be exceptionally gullible or exceptionally susceptible to groupthink or exceptionally enthu-siastic in my embracing of the movement *du jour,* and while it would be foolish and arrogant of me to assume that my idiosyncratic relationship to our field is somehow normative, I would, nonetheless, hope that my expe-riences serve as a cautionary tale. As Sharon Crowley has argued, "fresh-man English" began with an absence, a void, with students' inability to write, and we have been trying to fill that void with everything—anything—we can lay our hands on ever since. Of late, in addition to writing process and academic discourse, we have also tried to fill that void with cultural studies, for example, and the familiar pattern has exerted itself here as well. As the movement has become ensconced in our pedagogical mainstream, some foolish excesses have begun to go unchecked. In recent years, my students have rendered fascinating semiotic interpretations of the ideology of household appliances and the Pillsbury Doughboy's homoeroticism, for instance, but still I am left wondering, "Has their writing really improved at all?" So I end here with the hope and the plea that we might watch ourselves and watch each other more closely so that our currently rising pedagogical movements in writing instruction—like service-learning, civic discourse, and the new expressivism, for example—don't meet a similar fate and turn from being helpful to hindering, from mindful to silly. And should these new movements turn the corner anyway, despite our efforts, let us lovingly call each other on our foolishness. Let my mentor be our mentor. Let us follow Tate's example, walk the walk of resistance, and speak the uncommon sense of pedagogical heresy.

Works Cited

Bartholomae, David. "Inventing the University." *When a Writer Can't Write: Studies in Writer's Block and Other Composing-Process Problems.* Ed. Mike Rose. New York: Guilford, 1985. 134–65.

———. "The Study of Error." *College Composition and Communication* 31 (1980): 253–69.

Bruffee, Kenneth A. "Social Construction, Language, and the Authority of Knowledge: A Bibliographical Essay." *College English* 48 (1986): 773–90.

Chase, Geoffrey. "Accommodation, Resistance, and the Politics of Student Writing." *College Composition and Communication* 39 (1988): 13–22.

Crowley, Sharon. "The Perilous Life and Times of Freshman English." *Freshman English News* 14 (1986): 11–16.

Hairston, Maxine. "The Winds of Change: Thomas Kuhn and the Revolution in the Teaching of Writing." *College Composition and Communication* 33 (1986): 76–88.

Murray, Donald M. *A Writer Teaches Writing.* 2nd ed. New York: Houghton, 1984.

Sommers, Nancy. "Responding to Student Writing." *College Composition and Communication* 32 (1982): 148–56.

———. "Revision Strategies of Student Writers and Experienced Adult Writers." *College Composition and Communication* 31 (1980): 378–88.

Tate, Gary. "A Place for Literature in Freshman Composition." *College English* 55 (1993): 317–21.

Postscript: The One Who Attends

Steve North

> We need to hear not only researchers talking in personal ways about
> their research, but teachers talking about their teaching, students talk-
> ing about their writing, theorists talking about their theorizing, etc.
> One great danger as a discipline grows is that it loses its human face.
> Such a loss is unfortunate for any discipline. For composition stud-
> ies, it would be tragic.
>
> —Gary Tate, Review of *Methods and Methodology*

I think I can assert, without provoking too much controversy, that the scene
of scholarship in the United States has long been dominated by a figure we
might call The Speaker or The Writer or, to frame it in a way that includes
both these modes of performance, The One Who Holds Forth. That is, in
the disciplinary mythology by means of which nearly all fields constitute
themselves as collective scholarly enterprises, the lion's share of influence
and prestige goes to those who are, one way or another, monologists—de-
scendants, as it were, of those idealized nineteenth-century German professors whose image exercised such a powerful formative influence over this
country's knowledge-making practices. These are the scholars who are invited to give the keynote addresses, who deliver their learned papers to
packed conference rooms, who author the journal articles and book chapters and monographs—those who, to echo standard usage, establish themselves as "major players," "big names," "voices to be reckoned with."

Nor has composition studies been exempt from this pattern. As the field
has sought to gain institutional legitimacy—or, to put it in a more concretely
agentive form, as its members have sought to gain something approaching
full-fledged academic standing—this figure has become the centerpiece of
our scene of scholarship, as well. Indeed, it is difficult to see how it could
have been otherwise: this is the figure nearly everyone involved in award-

ing such legitimacy—department chairs, tenure and promotion committees, even the staff in the accounting office where travel expenses are ap-
proved—is systemically constrained to look for. Legitimacy of this kind is
a function of (self-declared) expertise, which is, in its turn, understood to
be embodied in properly anointed experts: major players, big names, voices
to be reckoned with. The Ones Who Hold Forth.

At the same time, however, many of us who identify with composition
studies like to believe—and not entirely without reason—that our disciplinary enterprise has done as much as any, and rather more than most, to
improve on this inheritance. In particular, insofar as this inherited pattern's
most serious shortcoming is its tendency toward *ex*clusivity—and it isn't
hard to demonstrate, of course, that in most U.S. academic disciplines for
most of this century, only a relatively small number of people have func-
tioned as One Who Holds Forth and that nearly all of them have been of
a certain gender, race, class, academic background, and so on—composition studies has made uncommon progress toward being more inclusive:
has sought to distribute the opportunities for holding forth, along with the
prestige and influence that pertain thereto, much more widely.

You can see this impulse at work in any number of venues: in the prolif-
eration of journals, newsletters, listservs, and Websites; in the establishment
of the edited collection as the field's favored form of book-length publication; in the striking number of national, regional, state, and local conferences organized around the field's various subdivisions. Perhaps the most
visible of these manifestations, though—and maybe, too, the most emblematic—comes in the way we organize the field's major annual conference,
the meeting of the Conference on College Composition and Communication. As the meeting has grown from its very modest 1949 beginnings to
a four-day affair that can attract as many as thirty-five hundred registrants,
program chairs—reflecting the wishes of the membership—have worked
hard to keep the event multi- or polyvocal, as it were: to retain what is often referred to as the meeting's "democratic" feel. Thus, while the conference has come to include "featured speakers"—a select few who are marked
as first-rank Holders-Forth by having their photos and biographical sketches
included in the program—all sorts of other devices have evolved to expand
the number of speaking slots. These include the obvious measures, of
course—increasing the number of concurrent sessions and supplementing
these with an extensive slate of pre- and postconvention activities—but also
the rather less likely strategy of replacing a number of the standard three-
and four-presenter "panels" with other formats, thereby distributing in quite
a different way the available time for holding forth: "roundtable" sessions

and "classroom samplers," each comprising at least four and often five or six presenters; and "forums," each of which lists as many as a dozen presenters. The 1995 meeting in Washington, D.C., where the forum sessions were first deployed on a large scale, stands as the most striking instance to date of efforts along these lines. A rough count suggests that, on average, something like 160 presenters were listed for each of thirteen concurrent seventy-five-minute time slots of about thirty-three sessions each. At a conference where about thirty-two hundred people registered, this meant that well over two thousand were listed as presenters in concurrent sessions alone—not including, that is, pre- and postconvention workshops, where the designation "presenter" is also frequently used; nor including the other official roles ("chair," "moderator," "respondent"), which provide attendees a formal opportunity to speak. The net effect, in short, was to create a conference at which a remarkably high percentage of those in attendance— almost everyone, in fact—was given a chance, however brief, to be One Who Holds Forth.

As justly proud as composition studies can be of these redistribution efforts, however, there is still something troubling about—or, at any rate, I am still troubled by—the centrality of The One Who Holds Forth in our disciplinary mythology. That is, despite the figure's distinguished genealogy—and, more to the point here, because of the way composition studies has sought to redistribute its attendant authority—I have found myself concerned more and more about the other half of the disciplinary interaction this whole mode of scholarship implies: how it is, in other words, that we "figure" any sort of attendant or attending counterpart.

So far as I can tell, the broader disciplinary mythology makes no provision whatever for such a creature: has never accorded anything like equal significance to a figure that might be called The Listener or The Reader or, to again meld the two activities, The One Who Attends. To some extent, of course, Holders-Forth are understood to have "attended" in this sense to at least some other Holders-Forth—hence the custom, for example, of lists of works cited—but such efforts have no official standing apart from their validation in a monologue. (No one gets to publish a list of works attended.) In fact, there is a fairly clear hierarchy among The Ones Who Hold Forth in this regard. At the very top are those who cite—attend to— their contemporaries least: those who are presumed to be too "original" or "cutting edge" to be bogged down by the more pedestrian claims of their erstwhile peers or the more pedantic demands of scholarly custom. At the bottom, meanwhile, are those who, having attended closely to a range of their fellows—other Holders-Forth, yes, but maybe also those who are never officially heard from—and having learned thereby that such fellows are not particularly clear concerning some One Who Holds Forth (French philosophers and historians being the most recent obvious examples of those in need of clarification), devote themselves to the project of explication: making that work accessible. For these efforts—for situating themselves, in essence, so visibly as ones who have paid close attention to their colleagues—these writers are usually only considered to be marginally Holders-Forth at all and labor under the unmistakably pejorative title of Popularizer.

The situation in composition studies, although certainly different in other respects, hardly seems any better in this regard—and may, indeed, be a bit worse—than other disciplines. That is, while we may have succeeded in distributing the power and the privilege of holding forth to a greater percentage of our members, we have—in the process—further validated that activity's knowledge-making centrality, provided it with a broader base of popular support, and quite possibly rendered even less likely any attendant counterpart's emergence. Think about it: with more and more members pursuing the increasingly realistic ambition to be One Who Holds Forth, who is likely to be doing the attending, how, and why? In principle, of course, presenters at a meeting like that of the CCCC will, once their turn is over, listen to a full slate of other speakers. A similar principle might be invoked for the universe of publications: once my own piece of writing is on its way into print, I can turn my full attention to absorbing the writings of others.

Except it doesn't work that way, does it? This is partly a matter of channel limitations: of physiology, psychology, and logistics. Take, for example, the forum sessions at CCCC meetings, with maybe a dozen speakers all addressing a more or less common topic, to be followed—or such is the plan—by an audience-encompassing discussion . . . all in the space of seventy-five minutes! It's difficult enough to remember what each of a series of twelve speakers says, even if that's all you have to concentrate on. It's practically impossible to do so if—as one of the presenters—you are also trying to concentrate on delivering your own prepared remarks. Similar kinds of constraints affect the conference process as a whole; taken together, they can be formulated as a kind of dictum: it is far easier to increase the number of occasions for attendees to hold forth than it is to increase their collective capacity to attend—to be there, to really listen, or both—at such occasions. And of course much the same holds true for what appears in print, as any number of commentators on the Information Age have long since pointed out: it has proven much simpler to increase the volume of material published than to alter in any significant way our ability to process it.

However, as I have been suggesting right along, there are also discipline-based limits placed on our abilities to attend. That is, given the absolute primacy holding forth has enjoyed in our disciplinary mythology, there is neither significant systemic incentive to make attending a serious priority nor—and the relationship here is very much chicken-and-egg—much available by way of models for doing so. To put it in slightly less abstracted terms: there is no place on the standard c.v. to list all the talks one has heard, articles one has read, conversations one has engaged, etc., no matter how important those interactions might have been. All that matters is what talks you gave, what articles you published. And in the absence of systemic incentive, of course, we can point to very few careers that have been deemed "successful," not *despite* having let such activities figure as a scholarly priority but *because* these activities figured as such. We have few mortal prototypes, in short, from whom we might develop a mythological One Who Attends.

In this essay, therefore, I want to make a first pass at addressing this prototype shortage by focusing on a scholar who might well serve as one, Gary Tate. I might easily have focused on other scholars, to be sure: Richard Larson comes to mind, for example; or, from a different generation and with a very different sort of career profile, Cynthia Selfe. And there are others. But this essay grew out of a meditation on Tate's career and out of a very strong sense of my professional indebtedness to the man and his work. For those reasons, then, and because I also think it is tactically sound, I will be arguing that over the course of some forty-five years, Tate's work as a scholar—in English studies generally and in composition studies in particular—featured Attending, capital *A,* as the central activity of a successful career.

This is, I realize, somewhat dangerous territory. I can already imagine people asking: "North, you cynic, does nothing matter if it doesn't show up on the c.v.? Don't you think that elevating the efforts of any single scholar to the status of professional and disciplinary icon in this regard threatens to discount the myriad acts of attending—lowercase *a*—that all members of the field engage in at least some of the time?" And I understand, honest. As teachers and colleagues, all of us—even the most single-minded Holders Forth—necessarily attend to our students and to one another, however rarely or grudgingly. Moreover, I know enough about Tate's career to be certain that his willingness and ability to attend in this lowercase, more quotidian sense made an enormous difference in the disciplinary and professional lives of his students and colleagues.

My point here, however, is that in the field's scholarly economy, such work—this broad set of attending activities we deem so valuable elsewhere—is already discounted: not only rendered invisible because of the way we enshrine The One Who Holds Forth but also, and in fact therefore, actually discouraged. What makes Tate's career useful as an exemplar in this context, then, is the way he was able to overcome that discounting pattern and carry on a campaign of Attending remarkable in its range, intensity, and duration. Sure, lots of us have done some of the things Tate has done by way of Attending, but no one I know of has done more of them so well for so long. For the purposes of learning how to transform elements of a valued private practice into a sustained and equally valuable public performance, then—or, to put in another way, for the purposes of constructing a scene of scholarship in which The One Who Attends plays more than a default role—I will argue that Tate's is a career from which there are lessons to be learned about how it is done.

Lesson 1: Gather What They Need

It is an ironic and disturbing fact that English teachers are seldom trained to teach composition effectively. The education of the typical English teacher is predominantly a literary education, and few colleges require the future teacher to take a single composition or rhetoric course beyond the freshman level. Prospective teachers seldom complain during their college years about this situation because most of them have been drawn to English studies in the first place because of their interest in literature. Yet when they become teachers of English, they soon discover that they are judged, to a large extent, not by the literary sophistication their students achieve but by the writing ability their students acquire. That this discrepancy between what their college education prepared them for and what they are expected to accomplish in their own classrooms is eventually disturbing to most English teachers can be verified by merely questioning any group of experienced teachers. The majority of them will say that it is for the teaching of composition that they feel most poorly prepared and, consequently, frustrated.

—Gary Tate and Edward P. J. Corbett,
Teaching High School Composition (1970)

It is symptomatic of Attending's (non)standing in our field that the only word we have to cover much of what Gary Tate has done in this regard is the beleaguered, not to say bedraggled, "editor." In a good chunk of the English studies world, if you prepare archival material for publication; assemble an anthology or reader of previously published material; launch and publish a newsletter or journal; work with authors on manuscripts; commission a collection of previously unpublished material; conceive and produce a book series; prepare for publication the proceedings of a conference—if you engage in any of these Attending-heavy, academically essential, and obviously very different sorts of activities (and there may be others), you are not only likely to be dubbed an "editor," but at many post-secondary institutions, you might have such work categorized not as scholarship but as service—work roughly comparable, as I have been known to say in particularly bitter moments, to running the departmental 50-50 drawing.

I am not going to offer any new terminology here—Attending is neologistic load enough—but I want to differentiate at least some of these kinds of Attending that Tate has done. And among his earliest ventures, carried on rather famously, I think it fair to say, with Edward P. J. Corbett, are the kind of compilations represented by *Teaching Freshman Composition* and *Teaching High School Composition.* I've chosen to open this section by excerpting from the preface to the latter because, while it was published a few years later and is maybe a little outside of what composition studies has come (rather sadly) to regard as its central concern, I love the way the highlighted portion foregrounds attending. It's maybe a little on the stuffy and academic side—"That this discrepancy between what their college education prepared them for and what they are expected to accomplish in their own classrooms is eventually disturbing to most English teachers" and so on—but the message is clear enough: If you want to know what's bothering people, you have to ask . . . and then attend to the answer. That's what these two books, and later the three editions of *The Writing Teacher's Sourcebook,* represent: Tate and Corbett (and, later, Nancy Myers) gathering what they understand teachers to be saying they need.

Under the regime of The One Who Holds Forth, of course, this attending and gathering are usually seen as no big deal: "Anybody," a Holder Forth might say, "can do that." Maybe, but I doubt it. Or let's put it this way: anybody can indeed assemble a reader of previously published scholarship, but not many anybodies have, and certainly not over so long a span—some thirty years—or so successfully. Why? Well, in this as in any other such activity, I have to assume it is some blend of ability, erudition, and commitment: that Tate and Corbett were sufficiently skilled at attending to what teachers said they needed; that they were sufficiently aware of what relevant material was available; that they were sufficiently committed to matching the two up; that the books they assembled genuinely did answer those needs—enough so, on all three counts, that the relationship thus established has proved to be this long and this fruitful.

Lesson 2: Assemble Good Attenders and Get Them to Share What They Have Learned

Some may argue that a book written by one author might have brought a single perspective to bear on the work of composition specialists. We believe, however, that no one person today can speak with authority

> about the variety and richness that characterize work in composition studies. Consequently, we have asked nine knowledgeable people, all of whom have demonstrated their commitment to the field, to address their assigned topics in their own voices. Their unique perspectives reflect one of the current strengths of this new discipline—the vitality and number of voices speaking to important issues about writing and its teaching.
>
> —Erika Lindemann and Gary Tate,
> *An Introduction to Composition Studies* (1991)

This second lesson derives from another of the "editorial" roles Tate played so effectively, this time in producing first two versions of the bibliographical *Teaching Composition*—in a 1976 edition with ten essays, in 1987 with twelve—and then, in 1991, *An Introduction to Composition Studies* (with Erika Lindemann). Despite certain commonalities with the projects listed as lesson 1, these obviously represent a rather different kind of work, a different mode of Attending. For one thing, they construct their audiences quite differently. Thus, the college composition teachers featured as the projected readers of two *Teaching Composition* editions need to be—as Tate suggests in the preface—chastised. Both volumes clearly echo the sermonic tone of Braddock, Lloyd-Jones, and Schoer's *Research on Written Composition* (1963); and the first edition specifically invokes Paul Bryant's essay "A Brand New World Every Morning" by way of contending that what Tate hears us saying about our work suggests not that the training system has somehow failed us but that we have failed the system—and one another—by being insufficiently attentive:

> Too often we behave as if there is no continuity in the teaching of composition, as if the subject has just been invented and every idea for teaching it is new at the moment. We fail to draw on the experience of colleagues. We learn neither from past successes, of which there have been a few, nor from past failures, of which there have been all too many. As a group, we are the living proof of the adage that those who do not know history are condemned to repeat it. (qtd. in Tate, *Teaching Composition* vii)

The rather different audience shift represented by *An Introduction,* meanwhile, is implicit in the title. There is no chastising here. Nor do the editors address that broad and rather miscellaneous range of people in English departments who have traditionally been assigned, interest and credentials notwithstanding, to teach first-year writing. Rather, and in what is arguably a disciplinary first, they focus on prospective composition studies "specialists": those who, while presently "unfamiliar with [the field's] assumptions, history, bibliographical resources, methods of research, and professional activities"; or else somewhat familiar but "uncertain that it deserves the status of a separate discipline"; might nevertheless be persuaded to consider making "the act of writing" the central focus of their professional and disciplinary lives (v).

And Tate (with Lindemann, of course) goes about addressing these two audiences and their needs not by gathering published material—the situation, in both cases, requires something other, something more—but by commissioning new work: assembling some of the best attenders in the business, as it were, and getting them to share what they have learned and, especially in the bibliographical essays, to model how attending is done. I am always somewhat bemused when I read that line from *An Introduction* in the epigraph to this section to the effect that "no one person today can speak with authority about the variety and richness that characterize work in composition studies." I have always had the impression—I think without too much presumption—that this line was directed at least partly at me and the distinctly monological *The Making of Knowledge in Composition* (1987), where I argue the advantages of having one person offer this sort of overview. Nor will I report here, however diplomatic it might be, that Tate and Lindemann have somehow convinced me of their rightness on this issue. Or let me put it this way: if no one person can speak with authority about this "variety and richness," there is no logical reason to believe that nine can (the number they assemble), or eighteen, or twenty-seven.

Still, the gesture this kind of rationale supports seems to me quintessentially Tate-esque, and I would take the occasion of it to call your attention not to the figures it foregrounds—not, that is, to the nine essayists it allows to Hold Forth in *An Introduction,* or to the thirteen featured in the two bibliographical volumes, but to the figure who makes the gesture. Imagine the level of Attentiveness it must have taken to get these twenty-two writers into print: the letters, the phone calls, the lunches and dinners and cups of coffee, the supportive readings, the editorial exchanges, the sheer publishing-project savvy and tenacity it took to get Richard Young, Richard Larson, Mina Shaughnessy, and the like—incredibly busy people all—to compose in what was, for this field, the unprecedented form of the bibliographical essay. Indeed, we get just a glimpse of the challenges involved in the preface to *An Introduction,* which ends with a "special thanks" to its contributors "for having produced such excellent work at a time when most of them were deeply involved with other projects" (vi). We have every reason to value these books for the scholarship their contributors present, and for the disciplinary services they perform; but these books should also serve as a tribute to the scholarly work that brought them into being: that Attentiveness that we know to be most effective precisely when it is so nearly invisible.

Lesson 3: Create Institutional Spaces That Make Regular, Long-Term Attending Possible

I thought it would be interesting to start a *news*letter that gathered and focused on facts about freshman composition programs—what was being taught, how it was being taught, what textbooks were being used, and so forth. . . . So, I published the first issue. I soon discovered, however, that people would not send in the facts and descriptions I had hoped for, but they wanted to submit articles and to *theorize* about what was going on or what should be going on. So, quite soon after the first issue, it became an ordinary journal—although the first of the independent journals.
—Gary Tate, interview with Robert L. McDonald (1992)

One of the most exclusive clubs in composition studies consists of people who have earned the title "founding editor." Exclusivity in this case, however, is a function not so much of snobbery—pretty much everyone has been and presumably still is free to "found" whatever they like. Rather, a relatively small number of scholars opt to take on this work of creating institutional spaces because it is generally the least rewarded of Attending activities in the scholarly realm: in a holding forth–centered economy, as it were, it offers the smallest return on effort invested.

Thus, founding things of this kind nearly always involves a relatively long-term commitment: a considerable trek from conception to initial realization and then, once such enterprises—newsletter, journal, book series, whatever—are up and running and beginning to prosper, the founder's workload generally increases: the manuscripts or proposals pile in; the correspondence multiplies; the funding, production, and distribution issues get more and more complex; and so on. And, while the relevant increment of measurement is not the week or the month but the year, this sort of sustained investment basically gets "counted" only once, and even then— again—often as "service." One year, five years, ten years—no matter how long one carries on, or how deeply one gets involved, the c.v. line stays pretty much the same: "Founding editor, *Name of Enterprise,* 19XX–19XX." (By way of generating some contrastive leverage, suppose that journal editors were officially encouraged to list each issue as a separate publication, just as they would single-authored journal articles—a fairer representation, surely, of the actual work involved. Then imagine how this would alter their standing with regard to at least the quantitative means by which most institutions measure scholarly success.)

As it happens, of course, Tate belongs to that even more exclusive sub-set of this self-selected group: those who (having failed to learn their les-son first time around, I always want to say) have been founding editors more than once. In Tate's case, the two outings were a newsletter-cum-journal, *Freshman English News* (now known as *Composition Studies*); and a book series, the SMU [Southern Methodist University] Studies in Composition and Rhetoric. I believe it fair to say that both enterprises are quite highly regarded in the field. The journal has long since evolved into one of the field's top ten publishing venues, has featured any number of influential articles, and continues to flourish and evolve. And while the series is no longer active—a victim of the tough economic situation facing all univer-sity presses—it, too, includes a number of titles that show up regularly in lists of works cited: Albert *Kitzhaber's Rhetoric in American Colleges, 1850–1900,* Derek Owens's *Resisting Writings (and the Boundaries of Composition),* Richard Haswell's *Gaining Ground in College Writing,* and so on.

In this context, though, I am concerned less with the relative merits of the enterprises themselves than with the nature of Tate's performance—the quality of his Attendance—in bringing them to life. The problematic pro-fessional status of this kind of work notwithstanding, the principal chal-lenge any founding editor faces is negotiating between his or her vision of where the undertaking ought to go and the material he or she has to work with. My own metaphors for the process run to interior design: the founder has a fair amount of initial control over the shape of the institutional space being created, but it can only be furnished—and very often, however gradu-ally, remodeled—in collaboration with the authors who are invited to in-habit it. This is the heart of the heart of the hard work: being clear and passionate but not doctrinaire, flexible but not muddled or indifferent.

Tate has been usefully frank about his struggles on this score in found-ing *FEN.* As he suggests in the passage I quoted at the head of this section, he had in mind "a *news*letter" (38, emphasis in original). In other words, the institutional space he wanted to create was very much what, given what we know now of his track record, one would have expected: an exchange that balanced a modest (as opposed to a more monumental) kind of hold-ing forth with a mode of attending appropriate for the sort of interest—that is, in how to construct a university writing program—that motivated him in the first place. Tate makes it clear he never has actually lost that mo-tivation—"I may be strange," he says in the same interview, "I don't know, but I'm fascinated to know what's going on, actually, on a day-to-day ba-sis, in freshman composition at Ohio State or New Hampshire or TCU or wherever" (38). But he allowed the journal to become what its authors and presumably its audience needed it to become: he Attended and—at whatever cost to his own preferences—acted accordingly.

So far as I can tell, much the same is true of his work on the SMU series. This is, to be sure, a very different kind of undertaking; the submissions are, by definition, along more monumental lines, and any shaping vision will almost certainly have to be more elastic. But Richard Haswell was willing to share this recounting of his interaction with Gary Tate, series editor, and I expect it is representative of the enterprise's informing dynamic:

> My relationship with [Tate] was purely as writer to editor. I sent him an early manuscript version of *Gaining Ground* that had been rejected by two NCTE committees and every other publisher of composition monographs that I could think of. He corresponded with me during the year I rewrote it for his SMU series. He was a very friendly editor and rarely give direct editorial advice—you had to read it at a slant. With the last two-thirds of the book, I don't think he recommended any changes. But his initial response was fairly sharp: "One of the problems I had finishing my reading of the manuscript was that I found I couldn't read very long at a time. Because of the level of attention that you demand in several parts of the work, my mind just plain got tired trying to focus and keep up," and so on.
>
> That bothered me, because I knew the truth in it, but I was too immersed in the rewriting (I essentially rewrote the whole thing) to do anything about it. I figured I would have to go back later for a third rewrite to satisfy him. So his response to the next set of chapters was totally unexpected. Here's what he wrote: "The strangest thing has happened. This morning I re-read the two chapters you sent me, expecting to spend a good deal of time marking sections that bothered me stylistically. To my surprise, I found very few. Whether I'm getting used to the style or whether I was tired and unattentive when I read the material the first time, I don't know. In any case, I'm now even more pleased with the work," etc.
>
> I don't know what this says about my style. But it puts Gary, to my mind, in an elite league, of editors who open themselves up to a new writer and let the work work on them instead of setting out to work, as an editor, on it. That takes deep-down listening.

Lesson 4: When You Do Hold Forth, Model Attending Behaviors

It is self-evident, I assume, that Gary Tate has not spent all of his career handling only the Attending end of scholarly exchanges: so long and distinguished a life in this profession inevitably presented plenty of opportunities for holding forth. Even when Tate has acted on those opportunities, however, it is striking—to me, at least—how often and how thoroughly his performance seems to be permeated by his desire for a genuinely two-sided give-and-take: for opportunities to listen as well as speak, read as well as write. My emblem for the latter sort of occasion is quite old, and in fact I have chosen it not least because it helps to suggest how consistent Tate has been in this regard, how long he has been at it. The text in question is a 1978 review of E. D. Hirsch's 1977 *The Philosophy of Composition* published in the *CEA Critic*. Tate makes it clear that his is far from the first review to appear; one has the clear sense, in fact, that it is to a considerable degree a response not only to the book, but to its reception: to the flurry of reviews—most of them, if memory serves, quite negative—issued by the composition community when Hirsch's book first came out.

This is absolutely not to say that Tate's own review is even remotely positive. On the contrary: while Tate is at some pains to characterize in upbeat ways Hirsch's autobiographical account of how, being "ashamed (his word) of his neglect of composition during his chairmanship" of the English Department at the University of Virginia, he made the mid-career decision to move "into the vineyard [of composition] with his fellow workers (again, his words)" (28); and while he welcomes Hirsch's own characterization of composition as "a field of study 'more complex and challenging than any I have undertaken in literary history or literary theory'" (28), he cannot be so generous about the book itself: "Unfortunately, however," he writes, "we cannot . . . praise Hirsch's entire book with the same enthusiasm that we praise his hard work, his enthusiasm, and his helpful words about the complexities of our field of study" (29). And indeed, Tate goes on to devote all of the next three pages (of his four-page review) to explaining his dismay with such things as the book's positing of the notion of "'relative readability'" as some sort of "'simple first principle'" for the teaching of writing; its conflation of that concept with the equally problematic "'communicative efficiency'" as a property of written texts; its preoccupation with a reductive understanding of assessment; and so on. That Hirsch should have invested so much energy in such a misguided project, Tate suggests, is very sad: "A good mind should not be wasted in such a manner" (29).

What is far more telling for my purposes here, however—the lesson for prospective Attenders—is the way Tate moves to end this otherwise stern review. He has already demonstrated, of course, how carefully he himself has read Hirsch's book, how seriously he has taken it, whatever its possible flaws. As he closes out his account of that reading, however, he shifts his

Attention away from *The Philosophy of Composition* and toward what I confess I picture as the congregation of composition, a large and rather unruly
group—those workers in the vineyard—a few of them rapt at Hirsch's offering, far more muttering darkly in response or simply tuning out. The
significance of Tate's message in terms of what he has to offer this group—
its absolute centrality, that is, to Tate's understanding of what it means to
be a composition scholar—is reflected in the sermonic, not to say incanta-
tory, rhythms in which he delivers it and especially its closing four sentences:

> Although I have spent most of my time disagreeing with Hirsch, I
> would urge the readers of this review to read *The Philosophy of Com-
> position.* Although I am convinced that he is misguided both in the
> topics that he is researching and in his methods of research—a sub-
> ject I have not touched on—Hirsch is clearly a person to be reckoned
> with. His prominence in the field of literary studies alone will con-
> vince many that what he writes about composition is correct. We must
> see that this kind of blind belief occurs as seldom as possible; we must
> also make certain, however, that Hirsch is not dismissed merely be-
> cause he has not always been "one of us." Let us listen to what he says.
> Let us reflect upon what he says. Let us experiment with his ideas.
> Let us, above all else, welcome him. (32)

The other emblem I have chosen—my illustration, that is, of the extent
to which Tate's handling of speaking and listening occasions also offers a
model of Attending behaviors—is much more recent. As with the Hirsch
review, this choice of timeframe is deliberate: evidence from this end of Tate's
career, as it were, of just how faithful to his vision of Attention he has remained. The occasion is a 1997 piece in the *Journal of Basic Writing* that
Tate coauthored with two doctoral students, John McMillan and Elizabeth
Woodworth, called "Class Talk." It is based on a workshop presentation the
three conducted at the 1996 Conference on Basic Writing in Phoenix, Arizona; the three take turns recounting their parts therein. For my purposes
here, though, the really telling portion of this article is Tate's short preface,
in which he seeks to describe how the workshop got underway:

> When I walked into the meeting room at the Hyatt in Phoenix where
> the basic writing workshop was to be held, I saw a room filled with
> round tables and chairs for participants and a microphone and lec-
> ture stand for the speakers. Because it seemed to me inappropriate to
> "lecture from above" on the topic of social class, I suggested that John,
> Elizabeth, and I just sit at one of the tables near the middle of the room
> so that our voices could be heard and so that we would be a part of

the workshop. This worked well. And the presence of several workshop participants at our table as we talked gave me the feeling that a conversation was taking place. (13)

To my way of thinking, anyhow, this is absolutely vintage Tate—maybe, in this instance, doubly so: that is, by reporting on such behavior in the pages of a well-regarded journal, he manages at once to both encourage the behavior itself *and* to sanction the reporting of it. If I had any skill in drawing at all, I would end here with a sketch of this setting Tate describes, one that is so clearly a version of this scene of composition scholarship he has worked so hard and so long to foster: large room, round tables, nobody lecturing "from above," Tate himself lost somewhere in the middle of it all. In keeping with what I know would be his wishes, the sketch would be rendered in such a way that the Tate figure would be indistinguishable from all the other participants—would, in fact, be rendered with his back to the viewer. The only bit of self-indulgence I would allow myself, a kind of "Where's Waldo" gesture, would be to make sure that the Tate figure sported a pair of wonderfully outsized ears—a symbol of how very advanced he has become as One Who Attends.

Attending to Business

At this point, you might reasonably be wondering just how serious I am about this Attending business. My obvious admiration for Tate's individual work notwithstanding, that is, do I really expect that this figure of One Who Attends will come to stand side by side with The One Who Holds Forth in ways that really matter? In job advertisements, for example: "Department seeks scholar in composition studies with primary credentials in Attending to and acting upon the concerns of both students and colleagues"? In hiring decisions: "I don't see that we have any choice: this candidate is the only founding editor in the pool, and the only one whose follow-up letter on her campus visit was devoted to Attending to our various concerns"? In decisions about tenure and promotion: "You seem to be known in your field—and, however puzzlingly, highly regarded—as much for your demonstrable Attention to the work of others as for your own publications. As Provost, and as someone whose own training is in biology, this is a somewhat puzzling paradigm. However, since this Attending work is clearly held in high esteem in composition studies (one measure of which being the word's insistent capitalization), I feel compelled to honor it as well"?

Honestly? No—or not, at least, in anything that might be called the immediate future. Like most large institutions, the educational system of the U.S. is very, very conservative: change happens but ever so slowly, glacially. On the other hand, I have been astonished at how much that system in general has changed in the twenty-five years I've been employed in it and—more specifically—by how much change there has been in the place writing and the teaching of writing occupy within it. Twenty-five years ago, it seems unlikely that a volume like this would have been imaginable, let alone an essay like this—one that tries, that is, to honor by naming a kind of work to which scholars like Tate have given disciplined form. In that sense—and even for someone as skeptical as I generally am—there is reason for optimism.

More to the point, perhaps, it may also be—or at least I feel—that movement in this direction is needed more urgently now than it has ever been. Tate's preface to this volume argues that it deals with two major themes: the troubled relationship between theory and practice, and composition studies' search for a usable past. His analysis of the situation—just what you would expect—is that we have had problems in these two areas because we have not sufficiently attended to one another: the practitioners have engaged in "mutterings" about the theorizers; the theorizers have "expressed in private or indirectly" their reciprocal impatience with the practitioners; and the compositionists of the present have tried to shake off their insecurities by villainizing their counterparts in the past. I could easily enough have concurred with Tate's reading of the situation any time in the past decade or so: these are indeed familiar behaviors, and I have engaged in them myself.

But I am also writing this a week after the September 11, 2001, terrorist attacks on the World Trade Center and the Pentagon, and I find myself thinking that these behaviors might be of a piece with a much larger pattern of non-Attending, hands-over-ears-while-mouths-keep-muttering behavior that eventually puts people in situations where talking—and especially listening—are considered futile and abandoned. I don't really know if it works that way—if, that is, our failure as compositionists to Attend to one another, to properly honor the act of Attending, really contributes to a world-wide pattern in which analogous fears and insecurities give rise to violence. But it might, so why take the chance? Especially when we have alternative models, when a career like Tate's has demonstrated so convincingly that a committed and disciplined Attender can thrive, and in ways that surely help us to do what we do? Hence my fervent hope that while we may always reckon it high praise to call our scholars Holders-Forth— that we might admire them, in essence, because they had our full attention—we will soon reckon it equally high praise to hail them as Those Who Attend—and thus admire them because we know we had theirs.

Works Cited

Haswell, Richard. Personal correspondence, Sept. 1999.

Lindemann, Erika, and Gary Tate, eds. *An Introduction to Composition Studies.* New York: Oxford UP, 1991.

McDonald, Robert L. "Interview with Gary Tate." *Composition Studies* 20.2 (Fall 1992): 36–50.

North, Stephen M. *The Making of Knowledge in Composition: Portrait of an Emerging Field.* Upper Montclair, NJ: Boynton, 1987.

Tate, Gary. "Relative Relevance." Rev. of *The Philosophy of Composition,* by E. D. Hirsch. *CEA Critic* (Nov. 1978): 28–32.

———. Rev. of *Methods and Methodology in Composition Research,* ed. Gesa Kirsch and Patricia A. Sullivan. *Composition Studies* 20.2 (Fall 1992): 98–100.

———, ed. *Teaching Composition: Ten Bibliographical Essays.* Fort Worth: Texas Christian UP, 1976.

Tate, Gary, and Edward P. J. Corbett, eds. *Teaching High School Composition.* New York: Oxford UP, 1970.

Tate, Gary, John McMillan, and Elizabeth Woodworth. "Class Talk." *Journal of Basic Writing* 16.1 (1997): 13–21.

Contributors
Index

Contributors

David Bartholomae is a professor of English and the department chair at the University of Pittsburgh. He is founder and coeditor of the Pittsburgh Series in Composition, Literacy, and Culture. Bartholomae has served as chair of CCCC and has published widely on composition and the cultural and institutional contexts of literacy. With Anthony Petrosky, he is a coauthor and editor of *Facts, Artifacts, and Counterfacts* (1986), *The Teaching of Writing* (1986), and *Ways of Reading* (1999).

Wendy Bishop, Kellog W. Hunt Professor of English at Florida State University, teaches composition, rhetoric, poetry, and essay writing. Her books include *Teaching Lives: Essays and Stories* (1997), *Thirteen Ways of Looking for a Poem: A Guide to Writing Poetry* (1999), and *The Subject Is Research: Processes and Practices* (2001). She lives in Tallahassee and Alligator Point, Florida, with her husband and children.

Lynn Z. Bloom is Board of Trustees Distinguished Professor of English and Aetna Chair of Writing at the University of Connecticut. Her most recent works include *Composition Studies as a Creative Art* (1998); "The Essay Canon" (*College English,* 1999), the subject of a book in progress to be published in 2003; and (with Louise Z. Smith) *The St. Martin's Custom Reader* (2001), a pedagogical application of her essay canon research.

David W. Chapman is the dean of the Howard College of Arts and Sciences and a professor of English at Samford University in Birmingham, Alabama. He is the author of over thirty articles related to the teaching of composition and a coauthor (with Lynn Waller) of *The Power of Writing* (1994).

Richard M. Coe is a professor of English at Simon Fraser University. He founded and chaired the Canadian Council of Teachers of English's Commission on Public Doublespeak, served as a director of British Columbia's Plain Language Institute, and was an active member of the Ministry of Education's Communications Assessment Committee. He has published numerous articles on rhetoric, literacy, composition theory and pedagogy, Kenneth Burke, popular culture, and literary criticism. He is the author of *Towards a Grammar of Passages* (1988) and *Process, Form, and Substance: A Rhetoric for Advanced Writers* (1990).

Robert J. Connors was a professor of English and the director of the Writing Center at the University of New Hampshire. From 1990 until his accidental death in the spring of 2000, he also served as Executive Committee Chair of the National Archives of Composition and Rhetoric. A winner of both the Richard Braddock Award (CCCC, 1982) and the Mina Shaughnessy Award (MLA, 1985), he wrote such books as *Essays on Classical Rhetoric and Modern Discourse* (1984) and, most recently, *Composition-Rhetoric: Backgrounds, Theory, and Pedagogy* (1997).

Lisa Ede is a professor of English at Oregon State University, where she also directs the Center for Writing and Learning. She has coauthored or co-edited several projects with Andrea Abernethy Lunsford, including *Singular Texts/Plural Authors: Perspectives on Collaborative Writing* (1990) and (with Robert Connors) *Essays on Classical Rhetoric and Modern Discourse* (1984). She is the author of *Work in Progress: A Guide for Writing and Revising* (2001) and the editor of *On Writing Research: The Braddock Essays, 1975–1998* (1999).

Peter Elbow, a professor emeritus of English at the University of Massachusetts, Amherst, is the author of *Writing Without Teachers* (1971), a manifesto that helped revolutionize the teaching of writing. This was followed by *Writing with Power* (1981), *Embracing Contraries* (1987), *Portfolios: Process and Product* (1991), *Landmark Essays on Voice and Writing* (1995), and numerous other important articles, such as "Ranking, Evaluating, and Liking: Sorting Out Three Forms of Judgment" (*College English*, 1993).

Janet Emig is a professor emerita of English education at Rutgers University. Emig served as president of the National Council of Teachers of English in 1989. Her scholarly and professional contributions have been recognized with many awards, including the MLA Mina Shaughnessy Award for her 1983 *The Web of Meaning: Essays on Writing, Teaching, Learning, and Thinking* and the CCCC's Exemplar Award. Among her publications are *The Composing Processes of Twelfth Graders* (1971) and *Feminine Principles and Women's Experience in American Composition and Rhetoric* (1995), coedited with Louise Wetherbee Phelps. In 2000, the NCTE established the Janet Emig Award to honor Emig's contributions to research by recognizing an outstanding article published in English education.

Richard Leo Enos is a professor of English and, since 1995, Holder of the Lillian B. Radford Chair of Rhetoric and Composition at Texas Christian University. His research emphasis is in the history of rhetoric with a specialization in classical rhetoric. Much of his work deals with understanding the relationship between thought and expression in antiquity.

Alan W. France was a professor of English at West Chester University of Pennsylvania. His publications include *Composition as a Cultural Practice* (1994) and, with Karen Fitts, *Left Margins: Cultural Studies and Composition Pedagogy* (1995). Most recently, he published "Dialectics of the Self: Structure and Agency as the Subject of English" in *College English* (2000) and "Historicizing the Posthuman" in *Journal of Advanced Composition* (2001).

Paul Heilker teaches courses in rhetoric, writing, and composition pedagogy at Virginia Tech, where he serves as the director of the First-Year Writing Program and as an associate professor of English. He is the author of *The Essay: Theory and Pedagogy for an Active Form* (1996) and the coeditor with Peter Vandenberg of *Keywords in Composition Studies* (1996).

Rebecca Moore Howard is an associate professor of writing and rhetoric at Syracuse University. With Linda K. Shamoon, Sandra Jamieson, and Robert A. Schwegler, she is a coeditor of *Coming of Age: The Advanced Writing Curriculum* (2000), to which she contributed an essay on teaching advanced courses on style. Her coauthors—Heidi Beierle, Patricia Tallakson, Amy Rupiper Taggart, Dan Fredrick, Mark Noe, Artist Thornton, Kurt Schick, and Melanie Peterson—were all students in the Ph.D. program at Texas Christian University when the article was written.

Janice M. Lauer is Reece McGee Distinguished Professor of English at Purdue University, where she founded, directed, and teaches in the graduate program in rhetoric and composition. In 1998, she received the CCCC Exemplar Award. She is a coauthor of *Four Worlds of Writing* (2000) and *Composition Research: Empirical Designs* (1988) and a coeditor of the composition entries in the *Encyclopedia of English Studies and Language Arts* (1995). She has published on invention, persuasive writing, classical rhetoric, and composition studies as a discipline. For thirteen years she directed a national summer rhetoric seminar. She has chaired the College Section of NCTE and has served on the executive committees of CCCC, the MLA Group on the History and Theory of Rhetoric, and the Rhetoric Society of America.

Erika Lindemann is a professor of English and the director of the Writing Program at the University of North Carolina at Chapel Hill, where she teaches writing courses and courses for writing teachers. She is the author of *A Rhetoric for Writing Teachers* (2001) and founding editor of the *CCCC Bibliography of Composition and Rhetoric* (1990–92). With Gary Tate, she coedited *An Introduction to Composition Studies* (1991).

Andrea Abernethy Lunsford is a professor of English at Stanford University. Formerly a director of the Center for the Study and Teaching of Writing at Ohio State University, she has been writing happily with Lisa Ede for almost twenty years. Her books include *Singular Texts/Plural Authors: Perspectives on Collaborative Writing* (1990), *The New St. Martin's Handbook* (1999), *Everything's an Argument* (2001), and *Reclaiming Rhetorica: Women in the Rhetorical Tradition* (1995).

Christina Russell McDonald is Institute Director of Writing and an associate professor of English at Virginia Military Institute. Previously, she founded and directed the Writing Program, an independent academic unit, at James Madison University.

Robert L. McDonald is a professor of English and the associate dean for Academic Affairs at Virginia Military Institute. With Christina Russell McDonald, he coedited *Teaching Composition in the 90s: Sites of Contention* (1994). His other publications include two books on the American writer Erskine Caldwell and, most recently, *Southern Women Playwrights: New Essays in Literary History and Criticism* (2002).

Nancy Myers is an assistant professor of English at the University of North Carolina at Greensboro, where she teaches composition, linguistics, and the history of rhetoric. Along with Gary Tate and Edward P. J. Corbett, she is an editor of the third and fourth editions of *The Writing Teacher's Sourcebook.*

Steve North is a professor of English at the University at Albany, State University of New York. His most recent book is *Refiguring the Ph.D. in English Studies* (2000).

Carol Reeves is an associate professor of English at Butler University. Her scholarship in scientific rhetoric has appeared in such journals as *Quarterly Journal of Speech* and *Written Communication* and in the volume *Landmark Essays on the Rhetoric of Science* (1997), edited by Randy Allen Harris. Her other interests include creative nonfiction and African American rhetorics.

D. Gordon Rohman was a professor of English and the dean of Justin Morrill College at Michigan State University and was, for a time before his retirement in 1994, Special Consultant for Lifelong Learning in the office of Michigan State's president.

Kurt Schick is an assistant professor in the Writing Program at James Madison University. His current research concerns John Dewey, civic literacy, and composition and rhetoric. He is a coeditor, with Gary Tate and Amy Rupiper, of *A Guide to Composition Pedagogies* (2001).

Nancy Sommers is Sosland Director of Expository Writing at Harvard University. She has twice won the CCCC Braddock Award for the best essay appearing annually in *College Composition and Communication.*

Gary Tate is Cecil and Ida Green Distinguished Emeritus Tutor in the English department at Texas Christian University, where he began teaching in 1971. Founding editor of *Freshman English News* (now *Composition Studies*) and Southern Methodist University Press's Studies in Composition and Rhetoric series, his publications include *Teaching Composition: Twelve Bibliographical Essays* (1987), *An Introduction to Composition Studies* (1991), *The Writing Teacher's Sourcebook* (2000), *Coming to Class: Pedagogy and the Social Class of Teachers* (1998), and *A Guide to Composition Pedagogies* (2001).

John Trimbur is a professor of writing and rhetoric and the director of the Technical, Scientific, and Professional Communication Program at

Worcester Polytechnic Institute. *The Politics of Writing Instruction* (1991), a collection he coedited with Richard Bullock and Charles Schuster, won the CCCC Outstanding Book Award. He has published widely on writing theory and cultural studies of literacy. His books include the textbooks *The Call to Write* (2002) and, with Diana George, *Reading Culture* (2000) and the collection *Popular Literacy: Studies in Cultural Practices and Poetics* (2000).

Edward M. White is a professor emeritus of English at California State University, San Bernardino, and an adjunct professor in the Rhetoric, Composition, and Teaching of English Program at the University of Arizona. The best known of the nine books he has written or edited is *Teaching and Assessing Writing* (1994, 1998). He was an editor of *Composition in the Twenty-First Century: Crisis and Change* (1996) and is currently working on a follow-up to that book, scheduled for publication in 2003.

Linda Woodson is a professor of English and the chair of the Department of English, Classics, and Philosophy at the University of Texas at San Antonio, where she was formerly the coordinator of composition for twelve years. Her books include *A Handbook of Modern Rhetorical Terms* (1979), *From Cases to Composition* (1982), *The Writer's World* (1986), and most recently, *Writing in Three Dimensions* (1996), with Margaret Batschelet. She has published numerous articles on rhetoric and composition as well as on literature.

Index

Aaron, Jane, 216

academic discourse (*see also* pedagogy of writing; rhetoric; style): arbitrariness of, 98–101, 107, 228–31, 235–36, 242–45; authority issues in, 100, 109–11, 115, 223; clarity and coherence in, 38, 106–7, 215, 241–43; collaboration in, 127–29, 142; costs of, 129–30; definition of, 95, 98–101, 104, 235; detachment of, 102–3, 107–9, 244; discrimination using, 98, 107–9, 117, 143, 216, 242–45; ethos of, 111, 219–20, 244; evaluation of, 231–36; generic version of, 101–2, 104; history of, 117–18; jargon in, 25–26, 92–94, 107–10, 114; learning and, 97–98, 112–13, 245n. 2; stylistic conventions of, 93, 98–101, 105–11, 114–17, 235–41; teaching of, 95, 112–17, 140, 148–49, 265

"Act of Discovery, The" (Bruner), 9

American Indian Literature and the Southwest (Anderson), 188

"American Scholar, The" (Emerson), 241

analogies, 10, 13–14

Ancient Slavery and the Ideal of Man (Vogt), 157

Anderson, Eric Gary, 188

Anson, Chris, 80, 216

anthropology, 22

Anzaldúa, Gloria, 188

"Are You the Teacher?" (Yee), 180

argumentation. *See* rhetoric

Aristotle: on knowledge, 160; on rhetoric,

186–87, 238, 243; on slavery, 159; on *techne,* 132

"Aristotle and the Anonymous Opponents of Slavery" (Cambiano), 159

Art and Answerability (Bakhtin), 166

attending (*see also* service): assembling peers as, 274–77; definition of, xiv, 270–71, 282; discounting of, 270–73; motivation and, 272–73; publishing as, 273–74, 277–79

Atwill, Janet, 131, 132

Auden, Wystan, 3

Bakhtin, Mikhail M., 98, 110, 125, 132, 166–67

Barnet, Sylvan, 174

Bartholomae, David, 55–58, 101, 138, 265

basic writing (*see also* errors): definition of, 59–60; idiosyncratic styles of, 60–64, 67–68, 71–73; instruction for, 61, 65, 70–72, 75; as learning, 57, 60, 62, 63, 75; as second language, 61, 62, 65–66

Bass, Rand, 253

Bateson, Gregory, 22, 40n. 1

Bay Area Writing Project, 43

Beale, Walter, 235

Becker, Howard, 110

Bedeau, Hugo, 174

Bedford Handbook (Hacker), 216

Belanoff, Pat, xi, 79, 235–36

Bell Laboratories, 84

Berlin, James, 106–9, 112, 125, 135

Bernard-Donals, Michael, 196

SMU Studies in Composition and Rhetoric, 278, 279
social construction theory, 44, 143, 212, 264–65
sociology, 22, 33, 222
"Some Needed Research" (Shaughnessy), 243
Sommers, Nancy, 79–82, 125, 261
Sound and the Fury, The (Faulkner), 50
Southern Methodist University, 278, 279
speech: argumentation as, 239; for error detection, 68–71, 73–75, 77nn. 12, 14; learning and, 245n. 2; writing compared to, 44, 46–48, 51–52, 65–66, 113
Spencer, Herbert, 29
Stafford, William, 111
Standard Written American English (SWAE), 242
Steinberg, Erwin, 138
Steiner, George, 62
Storyteller (Silko), 191
Straub, Richard, 80
"Study of Error, The" (Bartholomae), 55–58, 265
style (*see also* academic discourse): of academic discourse, 93, 98–101, 105–11, 114–17, 235–41; analysis of, 214–15, 217, 220–25; citations and, 111, 243–44, 246n. 3, 270–71; clichés and, 13, 240, 241; creativity and, 8, 12–15, 50; decline of, 147, 215–17, 221, 225–26; definition of, 219, 237–38; errors and, 60–64, 67–68, 71–73, 228–29, 239–40; ethos and, 219–20; invention and, 218–19; peer-based, 220–23; politics of, 217–18, 223; racism and, 223–24; of rhetoric, 105, 121–26, 218, 236–38, 263; textualism and, 57, 214–15, 217–19, 226, 230
"Stylistics" (Catano), 215
summativity, 19, 26–27, 31–32, 35, 186
Swilky, Jody, 164
Synoptic History of Classical Rhetoric (Murphy), 129
syntax, 65–68, 74, 85
systems theory, 27, 32, 33

Tan, Amy, 189

Tannen, Deborah, 244
Tate, Gary: as attender, xiv, 268, 273–79; collegiality of, xiv, 272–73, 279–82; on first-year composition, 19, 277–78; on literature, 134–38, 184–86, 191; on orthodoxy in pedagogy, 260–62, 263, 264, 265–67; on style, 225; on valuation, 246n. 4
teaching (*see also* editing; errors; first-year composition; pedagogy of writing): of academic discourse, 95, 112–17, 140, 148–49, 265; attitudes in, 80, 81, 84, 172–73, 177–79; authority issues and, 100, 110–11, 115, 174–80, 223; commenting styles of, 79–80, 84–88, 90–91; competency in, 178–80; consistency in, 181, 182n. 2; to freshmen, 112–17, 135–38, 148–49, 265; literary criticism in, 135–38, 141, 185, 215; needs for, 89, 90–91, 273–77; persona in, 172–77, 179–81, 229; politics and, 175, 182n. 1; responsibilities of, 163–68, 233, 244–45; status of, 156, 158–59, 160–61, 164, 169; students and, 65–71, 80–81, 83–87, 172–75, 181; thinking and, 33–34, 36, 37, 38; valuation in, 143, 230–36, 240–42, 244–45
Teaching Composition: Ten Bibliographical Essays (Tate), 275
Teaching High School Composition (Corbett and Tate), 147, 273, 274
Teaching the Universe of Discourse (Moffett), 43
technology: hypertext and, 249–52; learning and, 249; literacy and, 251–57; rhetoric and, 252, 253
textualism, 57, 214–15, 217–19, 226, 230
Theory and Practice (Lobkowicz), 159
theory versus practice: criticism and, 260–61; general comments on, vii–ix, xi, 259–60, 283; integration of, 167–68; personal essays and, 261–62; social construction theory and, 264–65; value of writing and, 265–67; writing process and, 262–63
thinking (*see also* cybernetics; rhetoric): cognition and, 5, 15n. 2, 46–47, 114, 130–31; consciousness and, 22–26; errors